Palms of Southern Asia

ANDREW HENDERSON

Palms of Southern Asia

THE NEW YORK BOTANICAL GARDEN

PRINCETON UNIVERSITY PRESS PRINCETON AND OXFORD

Requests for permission to reproduce material from this work should be sent to Permissions, Princeton University Press
Published by Princeton University Press, 41 William Street, Princeton, New Jersey 08540
In the United Kingdom: Princeton University Press, 6 Oxford Street, Woodstock, Oxfordshire OX20 1TW
and The New York Botanical Garden, Bronx River Parkway at Fordham Road, Bronx, New York 10458

Library of Congress Cataloging-in-Publication Data

Henderson, Andrew, 1950–
    Palms of southern Asia / Andrew Henderson.
        p. cm. — (Princeton field guides)
    Includes bibliographical references and index.
    ISBN 978-0-691-13449-9 (hardback : alk. paper)   1. Palms—South Asia—Identification.
I. Title.   II. Series.
    QK495.P17H445 2009
    584'.5095—dc22   2008030892

British Library Cataloging-in-Publication Data is available

This book has been composed in Cheltenham Light and Gill Sans
Printed on acid-free paper. ∞
nathist.princeton.edu
Printed in the United States of America
10 9 8 7 6 5 4 3 2 1

For Flor, Lidia, and Alfred

Contents

Foreword

From the deserts of Afghanistan to the limestone hills of southern China and the rain forests of Peninsular Thailand, the natural vegetation of Southern Asia, the area covered by this exciting new book, includes some of the most interesting and unusual palms. For some fortunate areas within the region, taxonomic accounts that include palms are already in existence, but many of these were published in the last century and are already very out of date as far as taxonomy or nomenclature are concerned. Several suffer from the chauvinism of local botany, where apparently distinctive species were described without looking over the border to the next country to see what had already been described from there.

Andrew Henderson provides an amazing synopsis of the entire palm flora of this vast region. Not only does the book account for all names that have been published for palms for this region (and includes several important corrections to long-accepted nomenclature) but it includes many species that have only recently been described, based on the author's collab-

orative fieldwork with his local counterparts in Asia. Nowhere is this more evident than in Vietnam, where the author has had several trips, uncovering astonishing palm diversity, a diversity hardly imagined a decade ago. The author has reviewed existing literature and has made detailed herbarium studies that have resulted in new synonymy and the uncovering of previously unrecognized species. His lucid account is easily accessible, not just to the experienced botanist.

When Henderson, Galeano, and Bernal's *Field Guide to the Palms of the Americas* was published, it immediately filled a gaping void. Here was a compact book that helped immeasurably in the identification of palms throughout the New World. I have no doubt that Henderson's *Palms of Southern Asia* will be equally used and useful. I emphatically endorse this book—it will prove to be immensely useful in furthering palm diversity studies in the region and to all field naturalists wanting to identify palms in Southern Asia.

John Dransfield
Honorary Research Fellow
Herbarium, Royal Botanic Gardens, Kew

Acknowledgments

Field and herbarium work in India and Sri Lanka was supported by grants from the Central Florida Palm and Cycad Society, the South Florida Palm and Cycad Society, the Palm Beach Palm and Cycad Society, and the Palm Society of Southern California. I thank Dr. M. Sanjappa, Director of the Botanical Survey of India for his support; Dr. Bipin Balodi, Ms. Minya Lollen, and Mr. Abdul Hussain of the Botanical Survey of India, Arunachal Field Station, Itanager for their help in the field; and Dr. C. Renuka of the Kerala Forest Research Institute for her help in Kerala. In Sri Lanka I thank Dr. Siril Wijesundara of the Royal Botanic Gardens, Peradeniya, and Mr. Martin Wijesinghe at Sinharaja.

Field and herbarium work in Myanmar was supported by grants from the Center for Environmental Research and Conservation, Columbia University, and from the National Geographic Society. I thank the Ministry of Forestry, Yangon, for granting permission to collect in Kachin State, the staff of the Wildlife Conservation Society office in Yangon for logistical support, and all the rattan team—Dr. Charles Peters, New York Botanical Garden, U Myint Maung, Hukaung Valley Tiger Reserve, U Saw Lwin, Myanmar Floriculturist Association, U Tin Maung Ohn, University of Yangon, U Kyaw Lwin, Mandalay University, and U Tun Shaung, Wildlife Conservation Society Myanmar Program. In southern Myanmar, I thank U San Hlaing and Kyi Myat Min for their assistance in the field.

Field and herbarium work in China was supported by grants from the Montgomery Botanical Center, the Center for Environmental Research and Conservation, Columbia University, and the International Palm Society. In Yunnan, I thank Dr. Dao Zhiling and Dr. Pei Shengji, Kunming Institute of Botany, and Dr. Cui Jing-Yun, Xishuangbanna Tropical Botanical Garden. I also thank Ms. Liu Yanchun for her help in Kunming and Ms. Long Bo for her help in Kunming and Xishuangbanna. In Guangxi, I thank Dr. Wei Fanan, Ms. Tang Saichun, Ms. Huang Yuqing, and Ms. Qin Xiang of the Guangxi Institute of Botany, Guilin, for their help. In Guangzhou, I thank Ms. Guo Lixiu and Mr. Zhou Lianxuan of the South China Botanical Garden. Ms. Guo Lixiu and Mr. Zhou Lianxuan accompanied me in the field in Hainan, and I thank the Hainan Forestry Bureau for permission to visit forest reserves in Hainan. I also thank Dr. Huang Zhangliang of Dinghushan Biosphere Reserve.

Field and herbarium work in Vietnam was supported by the National Science Foundation and a Fulbright Research Award. I thank the Director, Dr. Le Xuan Canh, and staff of the Institute of Ecology and Biological Resources (IEBR), Hanoi, for hosting me during my time in Vietnam. I thank my counterpart at IEBR, Dr. Ninh Khac Ban, and other staff members—Mr. Bui Van Thanh, Mr. Nguyen The Cuong, Dr. Nguyen Tien Hiep, Dr. Phan Ke Loc, Ms. Tran Thi Phuong Anh, and Dr. Jack Regalado. I am also grateful to Mr. Nguyen Quoc Dung of the Forest Inventory and Planning Institute, Hanoi, for his help and support.

Field and herbarium work in Thailand was supported in part by a grant from the International Palm Society. I thank Mr. Poonsak Vatcharakorn for accompanying me in the field in Peninsular Thailand and for sharing his knowledge of Thai palms.

Computer equipment for this project was funded by a grant from the International Palm Society.

Many friends and colleagues helped with various parts of the work. Dr. Tom Evans kindly supplied his rattan database, reviewed parts of the manuscript, and shared his knowledge of rattans. Dr. Neela de Zoysa provided much information on the palms of Sri Lanka. Mr. Martin Gibbons and Mr. Tobias Spanner shared their knowledge of *Trachycarpus*, Dr. John Dowe his knowledge of *Livistona*, and Mr. Don Hodel his knowledge of Thai palms. Dr. John Dransfield answered my many questions on palms of Southern Asia. In New York, I thank Mr. Nate Smith, Dr. Chuck Peters, Dr. Holly Porter Morgan, and Dr. Berry Brosi for help with technical matters. I thank Drs. Anders Barfod and Henrik Balslev for inviting me as a Visiting Professor to Aarhus University in the summer of 2006. This enabled me to study the rich collections of

Thai palms in the Aarhus Herbarium, and to benefit from Dr. Barfod's knowledge of Asian palms. The final manuscript was reviewed by Drs. John Dransfield and Scott Zona. I thank the staff of The New York Botanical Garden Press, particularly Mr. Nate Smith and Dr. William Buck, and that of Princeton University Press, particularly Dr. Robert Kirk and Mr. Dimitri Karetnikov, for bringing the book through publication.

I thank the curators of the following herbaria for making specimens available for study: Aarhus University Herbarium; Arnold Arboretum, Harvard University; Bailey Hortorium, Cornell University; Bangkok Herbarium, Department of Agriculture; Botanische Staatssammlung, Munich; Botany Department, Natural History Museum, London; Cat Tien National Park Herbarium, Vietnam; Central National Herbarium, Howrah, Calcutta; Cuc Phuong National Park Herbarium, Vietnam; Forest Inventory and Planning Institute, Hanoi; Forest Research Institute, Yezin, Myanmar; Guangxi Institute of Botany, Guilin; Hanoi University Herbarium; Hong Kong Herbarium; Institute of Ecology and Biological Resources, Hanoi; Institute of Tropical Biology, Ho Chi Minh City, Vietnam; Kerala Forest Research Institute, India; Kunming Institute of Botany, Chinese Academy of Sciences; Museo di Storia Naturale dell'Università, Florence; Missouri Botanical Garden; Muséum National d'Histoire Naturelle, Paris; National Botanic Garden of Belgium; National Herbarium, Peradeniya, Sri Lanka; New York Botanical Garden; Pu Huong Nature Reserve Herbarium, Vietnam; Pu Mat National Park Herbarium, Vietnam; Research Institute of Tropical Forestry, Chinese Academy of Forestry, Guangzhou; Royal Botanic Gardens, Kew; Royal Forest Department Herbarium, Bangkok; South China Botanical Garden, Chinese Academy of Sciences, Guangzhou; Vietnam National University Herbarium, Hanoi; V. L. Komarov Botanical Institute, St. Petersburg; Xishuangbanna Tropical Botanical Garden, Chinese Academy of Sciences; Yangon University, Myanmar; Zhongshan University Herbarium, Guangzhou; and the United States National Herbarium.

All images were taken by the author, except those of *Calamus nuichuaensis*, taken by Professor Phan Ke Loc; *Ceratolobus subangulatus* and *Nannorrhops ritchiana*, taken by Dr. John Dransfield; *Clinostigma savoryanum*, taken by Dr. Jean-Christophe Pintaud; *Corypha lecomtei*, taken by Mr. Nguyen Quoc Dung; *Cyrtostachys renda, Eleiodoxa conferta, Iguanura bicornis, Johannesteijsmannia altifrons, Korthalsia flagellaris, Pholidocarpus macrocarpus*, and *Trachycarpus oreophilus* taken by Mr. Poonsak Vatcharakorn; *Guihaia grossifibrosa*, taken by Mr. Bui Van Thanh; *Hyphaene dichotoma* and *Rhopaloblaste augusta*, taken by Dr. Carl Lewis; and *Phoenix roebelinii* and *Trachycarpus geminisectus* taken by Dr. Leonid Averyanov. The illustrations in the Morphology of Palms section were drawn by Ms. Bee Gunn.

Introduction

Following the publication of *A Field Guide to the Palms of the Americas* (Henderson et al. 1995), I had in mind a similar volume for the Old World. There are, however, many more species of palms in the Old World, and the area is much larger, including as it does all of Europe, Africa, Madagascar, the islands of the Indian Ocean, Southern and Southeast Asia, New Guinea, Australia, and the islands of the western Pacific. This is too big an area with too many species for a single field guide. Therefore I decided to work first on the Southern Asian palms—the subject of this book.

The region defined in this book as Southern Asia includes all of Afghanistan, Bangladesh, Bhutan, Cambodia, China, India (including the Andaman and Nicobar islands), Japan (including the Ryukyu and Bonin islands), Laos, Myanmar, Nepal, Pakistan, Sri Lanka, Taiwan, Thailand, and Vietnam. This region is hereafter referred to as "our area" (Fig. 1).

Palm Regions in Southern Asia

The area covered in this book is extremely diverse in terms of topography and climate, and comprises several different biogeographic regions. In this section I discuss these as "palm regions," that is, regions that have similar environmental conditions and a suite of palm species. This is obviously a large-scale division of the area and masks a lot of local variation. However, I think it is useful for understanding the diversity and distribution of Southern Asian palms. Starting from the west, brief descriptions of these regions and their palms are given.

I also give notes here on the best places to see palms in those places with rich palm floras. These notes are based either on my own experiences or are taken from articles that have appeared in the journal *Palms* (formerly *Principes*).

Iranian Plateau

The most westerly area covered by this guide comprises the countries of Afghanistan and Pakistan. The mountainous regions of these countries are part of a larger mountain system known as the Iranian Plateau (Fig. 2). This system includes the mountain regions of southwestern Afghanistan and western Pakistan and continues through Iran. The northeastern part of the plateau is continuous with the Hindu Kush, which provides a link between the Iranian Plateau and the western Himalayas. The western limit of the plateau is the Zagros Mountains of western Iran and Iraq.

The area is mostly arid and includes few palms—except of course for the widely cultivated date palm. However, there is one native species of outstanding interest, *Nannorrhops*

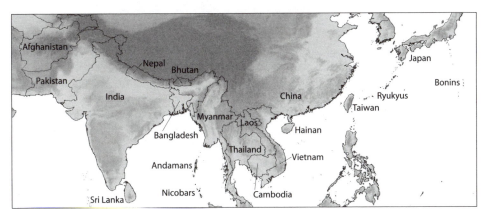

Figure 1. Countries and islands of Southern Asia.

ritchiana, which occurs all along the eastern margins of the Iranian plateau in Afghanistan and Pakistan and continues into southeastern Iran. Gibbons and Spanner (1995a) have given an account of looking for *N. ritchiana* in Pakistan.

Indo-Gangetic Plain

The Indo-Gangetic Plain (Fig. 2) gets its name from two great rivers of the region, the Indus and the Ganges. The plain is a large, low-lying alluvial crescent of land stretching from the Indus Plain in Pakistan through to the Ganges Plain of northern India and Bangladesh, a distance of almost 3000 km. To the west is the Iranian Plateau, to the north are the foothills of the Himalayas, and to the south the Deccan Plateau of India. Between the Indus and Ganges plains are several drier areas of northwestern India; the Great India Desert (also known as the Thar Desert), and a large area of salt marshes known as the Rann of Kutch.

The flat and fertile river plains of the Indus and Ganges are ancient centers of civilization and are densely populated areas. Almost no natural vegetation remains. There is, however, one palm of interest. This, *Hyphaene dichotoma*, is an eastern outlier of an otherwise African and Arabian genus. It occurs in the Indian states of Guyjarat and Maharashtra, in arid, low-lying regions.

Western Ghats

The Western Ghats (Fig. 2) are a mountain range running parallel to India's Arabian Sea coast. They range over a distance of approximately 1600 km, from the boundary of Guyjarat and Maharashtra states in the north to the southern tip of India at Cape Comorin. From the narrow coastal plain (historically known as the Malabar Coast), the mountains rise steeply to an average elevation of about 1000 m. The highest peak, in the southern part of the Ghats, is almost 2700 m. The western slopes of the Western Ghats receive the full force of the annual monsoon, from June to September, and rainfall is high. Because of this rainfall the western slopes have a band of tropical rain forest running along their windward slopes. The region is rich in species and is considered one of the world's biodiversity hotspots.

Most of the palms of the Western Ghats occur in the southern, wetter part, from Goa southwards, and most of them are endemic to the region. About 30 species of palm are present, and more than 23 are endemic, while 7 species also occur in Sri Lanka. Notable among the endemics are *Arenga wightii*, *Bentinckia condapanna*, *Pinanga dicksonii*, and 18 species of *Calamus*.

Eastern Ghats and Deccan Peninsula

Mirroring the Western Ghats along India's Arabian Sea coast, the Eastern Ghats (Fig. 2) run along the coast of the Bay of Bengal (historically known as the Coromandel Coast). The Western and Eastern Ghats form the boundaries of the Deccan Plateau (Fig. 2) of south-

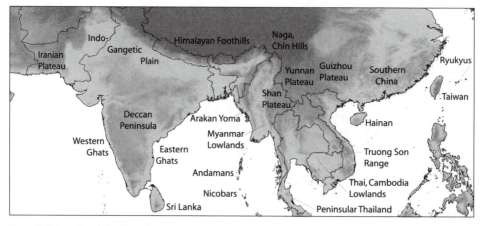

Figure 2. Palm regions in Southern Asia.

central India. The Eastern Ghats extend over a range of approximately 1750 km, from the state of Tamil Nadu in the south through Andra Pradesh to Orissa in the north. Unlike the Western Ghats, the Eastern Ghats are broken into a series of hills, and these seldom reach 1500 m elevation.

The Eastern Ghats and the Deccan Plateau are drier than the Western Ghats and consequently have fewer palms. Only a few species occur there, including *Calamus rotang* and *C. viminalis*. In the northern parts of the Eastern Ghats, where rainfall allows the development of tropical semievergreen forest, a more interesting palm flora occurs. Such species as *Licuala peltata*, *Calamus guruba*, and *C. nambariensis* are found there. There is a possibility that *Caryota maxima* and *Wallichia disticha* also once occurred there.

Sri Lanka

The pear-shaped island of Sri Lanka (Fig. 2), lying just off the southeast coast of India, is about 500 km long and 220 km wide in its widest part. A large upland area, the Central Highlands, occurs in the central-southern part of the country, with elevations reaching 2500 m. The climate of Sri Lanka is tropical, with the southwestern regions, especially the windward slopes of the Central Highlands, receiving the highest rainfall.

The flora of Sri Lanka contains a high number of endemics and also has strong affinities with that of the Western Ghats. The palm flora reflects this. Of the 18 native species of palm found on the island, 10 are endemic including the genus *Loxococcus*, 7 are also found in the Western Ghats, and 4 are widespread.

The best place to see native palms in Sri Lanka is undoubtedly the Sinharaja Forest Reserve, situated in the southwest of the country. Here there are beautiful stands of the endemic *Loxococcus rupicola*, as well as *Oncosperma fasciculatum*, and at least three species of *Calamus*. In nearby areas one can see *Corypha umbraculifera*, *Caryota urens*, *Phoenix pusilla*, as well as the ubiquitous *Borassus flabellifer*, *Areca catechu*, and *Cocos nucifera*.

Himalayan Foothills

The great mountain chain of the Himalayas forms a huge arc in northern India, Nepal, and Bhutan, from the Hindu Kush in the west to the Yunnan Plateau in the east. The mountains rise to great heights, with Everest reaching 8848 m elevation. Along the foothills of the Himalayas (Fig. 2), from just above sea level to almost 2000 m elevation, there is a band of lowland and montane rain forest.

These forests of the Himalayan foothills are rich in palms, especially the genera *Calamus*, *Caryota*, *Phoenix*, *Pinanga*, *Plectocomia*, *Trachycarpus*, and *Wallichia*. Many species in these genera are endemic to the region, for example, *Phoenix rupicola*, *Pinanga gracilis*, *Wallichia oblongifolia*, and several species of *Trachycarpus*. Another species of *Phoenix*, *P. acaulis*, occurs in lower foothills, and Dhar (1998) has described and illustrated a population near Dehra Dun in India.

The Tibetan Plateau occurs north of the Himalayas. From here rise several of the great rivers of Southern Asia—the Ayeyarwaddy, Bramaputra, Ganges, Indus, Mekong, Salween, and Yangtze. Very few species of palm are found on the Tibetan side of the Himalayas, and these occur in deep, moist valleys formed by these rivers and their tributaries. Examples are *Arenga micrantha*, *Pinanga gracilis*, *Wallichia triandra*, and a couple of species of *Calamus*, all of which occur in the valleys of the Bramaputra and its tributaries.

There are more palm species in the eastern part of the Himalayan Foothills than in the western part. In the Indian states of Arunachal Pradesh and Assam there are still large areas of forest, and it is possible to see many palms from roadsides. However, access to several states of the region requires special permission.

Naga Hills, Chin Hills, and the Arakan Yoma

This area includes a long, curving range of mountains, approximately 950 km in length, that stretches from the Himalayan Foothills of Arunachal Pradesh in northeastern India southwards to Myanmar's west coast along the Bay of Bengal. The northern parts of this range are known as the Naga Hills and Chin Hills (Fig. 2), and the southern part as the Arakan Yoma (Fig. 2). The highest point is Mount Victoria in Myanmar, at 3000 m elevation. Also included here are the hills of the Assam Range (Garo,

Khasi, and Jaintia hills), mostly in Meghalaya State in northeastern India. These mountains have large areas of montane rain forest.

Few palms are endemic to these mountains, although *Pinanga griffithii* and *Wallichia nana* are confined to the northern parts of the ranges. However, the mountains provide a high-elevation corridor so that several species from the more northerly ranges of the Himalayan Foothills occur farther to the south along these hills, such as *Caryota maxima* and *Wallichia disticha*. Conversely, some southern species reach northwards along this range, such as *Calamus longisetus*.

Henderson et al. (2005) have described the palms of northern Myanmar, on the eastern slopes of the Naga Hills, and Hodel (2004) has described a visit to see the palms of the Chin Hills and Arakan Yoma, including Mount Victoria. Gibbons and Spanner (1994) gave an account of a visit to see the palms, principally *Trachycarpus martianus*, of the Khasi Hills in India.

Andaman and Nicobar Islands

The Andaman and Nicobar islands (Fig. 2) represent, geologically, a continuation of the Arakan Yoma. They are a volcanic island chain stretching from north to south in the Bay of Bengal for approximately 800 km. The Andamans are about 350 km long, and consist of several hundred small islands. The main islands are the Greater Andamans and Little Andamans. The Nicobars are about 300 km long and consist of fewer islands, the largest of which is Great Nicobar.

The climate of the Andaman and Nicobar islands is tropical, and the islands were mostly covered by lowland rain forest. The most northerly Andamans are less than 200 km from the coast of Myanmar, and their flora is essentially a continuation of Myanmar's. On the other hand, the most southerly of the Nicobars are only about 150 km from Sumatra, and their flora is a continuation of the Sumatran one. This division is reflected by the palms.

Twenty native species of palm occur in the Andaman Islands, and 11 in the Nicobars. Only four or five species are shared by both island groups. Remarkable is the diversity of

Daemonorops—five species in the Andamans—a genus absent from the Nicobars.

Access to the Nicobar Islands is currently restricted, but the palms of the Andamans can be seen around Port Blair. Mathew and Abraham (1994) have described the palms of the Andamans and Nicobars.

Myanmar Central Lowlands

The central lowlands of Myanmar (Fig. 2), running through the central part of the country from north of Mandalay to Yangon, are mostly low-lying areas with a highly seasonal climate, giving rise to deciduous forests. The only higher-elevation area is the Pegu Yoma, a low mountain system running north–south and reaching almost to Yangon (the Shwedagon Pagoda is built on one of the most southerly outliers of the Pegu Yoma).

There are few palms in the central lowlands, except for huge numbers of *Borassus flabellifer*. However, the Pegu Yoma, famous for its teak forests, now highly disturbed, is quite rich in species, including such endemics as *Pinanga hexasticha* and *Wallichia lidiae. Calamus arborescens* is also abundant there.

Shan, Yunnan, and Guizhou Plateaus

This large mountainous area, centered on the Chinese provinces of Yunnan and Guizhou, also includes all Shan State, Myanmar, and parts of northern Thailand, northern Laos, and northwestern Vietnam. The Shan, Yunnan, and Guizhou plateaus (Fig. 2) are actually a highly dissected mountain system, with many of the valleys running in a north–south direction. In Guizhou there are large areas of karst limestone, giving rise to spectacular scenery.

In southwestern China, in the province of Yunnan, there are about 35 palm species. The best place to see these is in the most southerly prefecture of Xishuangbanna. The Xishuangbanna Tropical Botanical Garden is a good base from which to visit various nature reserves in the area, including the Xishuangbanna National Nature Reserve. A few palms of interest occur farther north in Yunnan, especially species of *Trachycarpus*. Gibbons and Spanner (1993) have described a journey in search of *Trachycarpus nanus* in central Yunnan, and another trip (Gibbons & Spanner 1995b) to see *T. princeps* in western Yunnan. Another palm of the Yunnan Plateau is *Phoenix roebelinii*. Although one of the most commonly cultivated ornamental palms, in the wild it has a highly fragmented and local distribution along the banks of the Mekong, Nu Jiang (Salween), and Lancang Jiang rivers.

In Myanmar, the palms of the Shan Plateau remain almost completely unknown. Much of Myanmar is currently restricted for foreigners, and it remains difficult to see the rich and diverse palm flora of this part of the country.

Southern China

This area includes all the Chinese provinces of Guangxi and Guangdong, and adjacent areas of Hunan, Jiangxi, and Fujian (Fig. 2). Also included here is the island province of Hainan. The southwest boundary of this region is the Red River in northern Vietnam, and so the region includes part of northeastern Vietnam.

Several palms occur in Guangxi and Guangzhou, but they tend to be few and far between, although the area is famous for its spectacular limestone scenery. However, there is one notable palm here, *Guihaia*, and both species can be seen in Guangxi. Perhaps the city of Guilin, the namesake of the genus, is the best place to see *G. argyrata*, which grows on limestone outcrops right in the city center (Dransfield et al. 1985).

There are about 26 native species of palm in Hainan, including 10 endemic species. The palm flora of Hainan is closely related to that of northern and central Vietnam, and there are some closely related pairs of species. Examples are *Chuniophoenix humilis* in Hainan and *C. nana* in Vietnam; *Licuala hainanensis* in Hainan and *L. centralis* in Vietnam; and *Licuala fordiana* in Hainan and *L. radula* in Vietnam. There are several major forest reserves in Hainan where palms can be seen, for example, the Bawangling National Nature Reserve, the Diaoluoshan National Forest Park, and the Jianfengling National Forest Park. The palms of Hainan have been described by Henderson and Guo Lixiu (2008).

Taiwan

The island of Taiwan (Fig. 2), lying off the southeast coast of China, is almost 400 km

long and 140 km wide at its widest point. Most of the eastern part of the island is mountainous, with peaks reaching almost 4000 m. Taiwan is dissected almost in half by the Tropic of Cancer, so much of the island is outside of the tropics. This is reflected by the flora—most of the plants from the central and northern parts of the island have affinities with temperate floras, especially with those of China and Japan. The plants of the southern parts, particularly the Hengchun Peninsula and the islands of Lanyu and Lutao, have affinities with the tropical flora of the Philippines.

Just seven species of palm occur in Taiwan, with three of them endemic (*Arenga engleri*, *Calamus beccarii*, and *C. formosanus*). Two species, *Calamus siphonospathus* and *Pinanga tashiroi*, occur only on the island of Lanyu, off the southwest coast of the main island, and represent the northernmost extension of the Philippine flora. Of the other two species, *Livistona chinensis* just makes it to Taiwan, occurring off the west coast on Chishan Island, and *Phoenix loureiroi* is widespread.

Ryukyu Islands

The Ryukyus (Fig. 2) are an island chain running for about 1000 km in a great arc from the northeastern tip of Taiwan to the southwestern tip of Japan, forming the eastern boundary of the East China Sea. They represent the exposed summits of submarine mountains, most of which are volcanic in origin. The largest island is Okinawa. The islands are outside of the tropics and have a subtropical climate with high rainfall.

Four species of palm occur on the Ryukyus, including the endemics *Arenga ryukyuensis* and *Satakentia liukiuensis*. *Livistona chinensis* also occurs there, and just reaches southern Japan, and an isolated population of *Nypa fruticans* occurs on Iriomote, hundreds of kilometers from its nearest neighbors in the Philippines. Pintaud and Setoguchi (1999) have described and illustrated *Satakentia liukiuensis* on Ishigaki, one of the Ryukyu Islands.

Bonin Islands

The Bonin Islands (Fig. 1), also known as the Ogasawara Islands, are a group of about 30 small, remote islands occurring in the western

Pacific. They are about 1000 km south of Tokyo and are administered by Japan.

Two species of palm occur on the Bonin Islands, both endemic, *Livistona boninensis* and *Clinostigma savoryanum*.

Lowlands of Thailand, Laos, Cambodia, and Vietnam

This area includes the low-lying areas of southern and eastern Thailand, southern Laos, almost all of Cambodia, and the southern part of Vietnam (Fig. 2). Also included here are the deltas of two large rivers, the Chao Phraya in Thailand and the Mekong in Vietnam, and the Cardamon and Elephant mountain systems of southern Cambodia. Much of the low-lying area of this region is covered in semievergreen or dry deciduous forest, and consequently has few palms. However, there are exceptions.

There are several nonclimbing rattans in this region. In southern Laos, *Calamus harmandii* is endemic, and its recent rediscovery was described by Evans (2000). The enigmatic *Areca laosensis* occurs in the same area. Also in southern Laos and reaching across into eastern Thailand is *Calamus acanthophyllus*, which occurs in areas subject to burning. Its habitat is described by Evans and Sengdala (2001). In the Mekong Delta, *Calamus salicifolius* occurs along the main river and its tributaries, scrambling in scrub forest along river margins. *Corypha lecomtei* is widespread in this region. Along Cambodia's coast, and just reaching into adjacent Thailand and Vietnam, there is a rich "mangrove" palm flora, including *Calamus erinaceus*, *Licuala paludosa*, *Nypa fruticans*, *Oncosperma tigillarium*, and *Phoenix paludosa*.

This low-lying, relatively dry region of Thailand, Laos, Cambodia, and Vietnam separates two major centers of palm diversity in Southern Asia—central and southern Vietnam, and Penisular Thailand.

Truong Son Range

The Truong Son Range (Fig. 2), often referred to as the Annamites, is a mountain range running for almost 1200 km along central and southern Vietnam's border with Laos and Cambodia. The range varies from 50 to 75 km wide and is generally less than 2000 m in elevation.

The Truong Son Range is not continuous but comprises three separate upland areas. In the north a relatively narrow range runs along the border between Vietnam and Laos, from the Ca River in the north to Khe San in the south. This is made up of mostly low mountains, seldom reaching above 1300 m elevation. Here there are large areas of karst limestone. The central part of the Truong Son Range comprises a broader, higher range, running from Khe San south through the Kon Tum and Play Ku plateaus. In the northern part of this central section a spur of mountains runs from west to east, to the coast just north of Da Nang. This range marks the boundary between the more seasonal northern part of Vietnam and the more tropical southern part. The southern part of the Truong Son comprises three large upland areas—the Da Lat, Di Linh, and Dac Lac plateaus.

The Truong Son Range has a diverse but still poorly known palm flora. The three upland areas each have their own endemic palms. In the northern ranges two species of *Rhapis* are endemic, *R. puhuongensis* and *R. vidalii*. The discovery of the former has been described by Trudgen et al. (forthcoming) and the latter by Averyanov et al. (2006). In the central part of the range, several species of *Licuala*, as well as *Nenga banaensis* and *Caryota sympetala*, are endemic. In the southern parts there are also endemic *Licuala* and *Pinanga* species, as well as several rattans. The central and southern parts of the Truong Son Range represent a previously unsuspected center of palm diversity. Many new species have recently been described from there (Henderson et al. 2008a, 2008b, 2008c), and many remain to be described. With about 75 known species and more to come, this area may eventually rival Peninsular Thailand in its palm diversity.

Probably the best place to see palms in the Truong Son Range, at least in the central part, is Bach Ma National Park near Hue. Here there are about 27 species of palm. In the northern part of the Truong Son Range there are fewer palms, but a good place to see these is Cuc Phuong National Park, with about 17 species. In the southern part of Truong Son Range, Cat Tien National Park is rich in palms, with about 20 species.

Peninsular Thailand and Myanmar

The southern part of Thailand and adjacent Myanmar is essentially a peninsula (Fig. 2), running north–south from just south of Bangkok, and continuing into Peninsular Malaysia. This peninsula, approximately 800 km long, is bounded on the western side by the Andaman Sea and on the eastern side by the Gulf of Thailand. The peninsula has a low mountain backbone, divided into several distinct ranges. The peninsula narrows near the southernmost border of Myanmar, in a region sometimes called the Isthmus of Kra.

This last of our palm regions is also the richest in terms of number of species. Many species from Peninsular Malaysia have their northernmost populations here. Rainfall is high in Peninsular Thailand and adjacent Myanmar, but falls off rapidly around the Isthmus of Kra. The palm flora north of the isthmus is much less diverse than that to the south. As many as 100 species of palm are confined to this peninsular region, almost one-third of all Southern Asian palms.

Although many of the palm species in Peninsular Thailand are Malaysian species that reach their northern limit in southern Thailand, there also appears to be a center of endemism in the central part of Peninsular Thailand and southern Myanmar. Such species as *Calamus platyspathus*, *Caryota kiriwongensis*, *Iguanura tenuis*, *Kerriodoxa elegans*, *Licuala distans*, *L. merguensis*, *Pinanga fractiflexa*, *P. wataniana*, and *Wallichia marianneae* are all restricted to this area, mostly on the western side of the peninsula, possibly associated with limestone soils.

Thailand has a well-developed system of national parks and other protected areas, and these are the best places to see palms in the wild. Unfortunately the most extreme southern part, adjacent to the border with Malaysia, has been politically unstable recently. However, the middle parts of the peninsula are rich in palms. Phuket, an easy flight from Bangkok, is a good place to start, and the Ton Sae Waterfall in Khao Pha Kaeo National Park is home to spectacular stands of *Kerriodoxa elegans* and many other species of palms (Dransfield 1983). Not far from Phuket, also in the central part of the peninsula, is Khao Sok National Park, where at least 26 species of palms may be seen, including a second population of *Kerriodoxa*. Khao Chong National Park near Trang and Raksa Warin near Ranong are also rich in palms.

For Myanmar, by far the richest area for palms is the southern part of the country, in Tanintharyi Division, again much of it off limits to foreigners. The islands of the Myeik Archipelago are very diverse. The best places to see palms are often the areas surrounding holy sites. For example, in the forests surrounding the Golden Rock one can see at least 10 species of palms. Hodel (2004) has described a visit in search of palms of Tanintharyi Division.

Layout of the Book

Forty-three genera are included in this book. This number includes all the naturally occurring genera in our area, as well as the commonly cultivated coconut, *Cocos*. A few other economically important palms are introduced into some places in Southern Asia (e.g., *Elaeis guineensis* and *Metroxylon sagu*), and many other ornamental palms are cultivated in parks and gardens, but these are beyond the scope of this guide.

A key is given to all the naturally occurring genera in our area as well as *Cocos*. Note that the characters used in this key apply only to the species in our area—and so the key may not work for species from outside the area.

Genera are arranged in alphabetical order. Accepted generic names are capitalized and in boldface, and are followed by generic synonyms. Each generic name is followed by its author, using abbreviations given in Govaerts and Dransfield (2005). Generic descriptions are based mostly on Uhl and Dransfield (1987), but emphasize nontechnical characters. Descriptions apply to the whole genus, even if certain features are not found in species in our area. Derivations of generic names are given for all genera, and in many cases are taken from a series of articles by Harold Moore ("What's in a name"), published in the journal *Principes* in the 1960s and 1970s.

Numbers of species in each genus are taken from Govaerts and Dransfield (2005), with some modifications. The number of species recognized in each genus is based on my own interpretation and may not necessarily correspond with the reference works cited. The most recent references to the taxonomy of the genus are given, and these are usually the basis of the species I recognize. A total of 352 species are included in the book.

Keys are given to species in all genera with two or more species. An attempt has been made to use only those characters that are apparent to an observer in the field. Geography is used extensively in the keys, so they may not work for palms in cultivation of unknown origin.

Species within genera are arranged in alphabetical order. Accepted species names are in boldface, followed by their author.

Following the species Latin name, common names are given. These are taken from various sources—monographs, floras, herbarium specimen labels, and from local informants. These are only a selection of the many common names in use in the region, and a given common name is in no way an indication that this is the standard name. Common names need to be used with much caution. Because there are so many local languages and dialects in the area covered by this book, common names may not be recognized by local inhabitants throughout the area where a palm occurs. The same species may have many different common names, even within one country. I have made no attempt to add accents to common names, especially those of Vietnam. Country or region abbreviations following common names are based on Brummitt (2001): (And)=Andaman Islands, (Ban)=Bangladesh, (Bhu)=Bhutan, (Cbd)=Cambodia, (Chi)=China, (Ind)=India, (Jap)=Japan including the Ryukyu and Bonin Islands, (Lao)=Laos, (Mya)=Myanmar, (Nep)=Nepal, (Ncb)=Nicobar Islands, (Pak)=Pakistan, (Srl)=Sri Lanka, (Tai)=Taiwan, (Tha)=Thailand, (Vie)=Vietnam.

Species descriptions are based on two sources. First, on botanical monographs or floras cited after each genus description, and second on my own experiences with the palms in the herbarium or field. Characters that will enable one to identify a palm in the wild are given priority. For numbers, such as number of leaflets or number of flowering branches, ranges are usually given. For lengths and diameters, the maximum value is usually given.

Following the species description is a section on range and habitat. For range, political divisions (states or provinces) of countries or islands are given. In Laos, Thailand, and Vietnam, where there are many small provinces, larger, nonpolitical divisions are used (e.g., Northern, Central, and Southern for Laos and Vietnam, and North, Northeast, East, Southeast, Central, Southwest, and Peninsular for Thailand).

The most important uses are given. There are so many uses of palms that only a brief selection is possible.

Under synonyms I have included all the synonyms (even if from outside our area) listed in Govaerts and Dransfield (2005), with some minor modifications. Each name is followed by its author, using abbreviations in Govaerts and Dransfield. Illegitimate and invalidly published names, as well as names without descriptions, are excluded.

The maps are designed to show the natural distribution of each species: Dot maps are used, and each dot represents one or more herbarium specimens that I have examined. The data for these maps come from a database containing more than 4400 specimen records. In a few cases, sight records are included, or records from reliable monographs and floras. As can be seen, all palms have patchy distributions. This is most likely a result of uneven collection density, but may also represent real distributions. Deforestation and habitat disturbance are so severe in many areas covered by this guide that many palms that formerly occurred in some area probably no longer do so. In the range and habitat section, political divisions may be given although no dot occurs in that division on the map. Such records are based on reliable literature reports. Dot maps are not given for introduced, cultivated species (*Arenga pinnata*, *Cocos nucifera*, and *Phoenix dactylifera*) or for other widespread species (e.g., *Areca catechu*, *Borassus flabellifer*, and *Trachycarpus fortunei*), or for a few other species with no specimens from our area.

There is at least one color image for each genus, and the number of images per genus is approximately proportional to the number of species. I have tried to illustrate species from countries other than Thailand, especially

Table 1 Position of Southern Asian genera within the classification of Dransfield et al. (2005)

Subfamily	Tribe	Subtribe	Genus
Calamoideae	Eugeissoneae		Eugeissona
	Calameae	Korthalsiinae	Korthalsia
		Salaccinae	Eleiodoxa
			Salacca
		Plectocomiinae	Plectocomia
			Myrialepis
			Plectocomiopsis
		Calaminae	Calamus
			Daemonorops
			Ceratolobus
Nypoideae			Nypa
Coryphoideae	Phoeniceae		Phoenix
	Livistoneae	Raphidinae	Guihaia
			Trachycarpus
			Maxburretia
			Rhapis
		Livistoninae	Livistona
			Licuala
			Johannesteijamannia
			Pholidocarpus
		Chuniophoeniceae	Chuniophoenix
			Kerriodoxa
			Nannorrhops
	Caryoteae		Caryota
			Arenga
			Wallichia
	Corypheae		Corypha
	Borasseae	Hyphaeninae	Hyphaene
		Lataniinae	Borassodendron
			Borassus
Arecoideae	Oranieae		Orania
	Cocoseae	Attaleinae	Cocos
	Areceae	Arecinae	Areca
			Nenga
			Pinanga
		Carpoxylinae	Satakentia
		Oncospermatinae	Oncosperma
		Unplaced Areceae	Bentinckia
			Clinostigma
			Cyrtostachys
			Iguanura
			Loxococcus
			Rhopaloblaste

Myanmar and Vietnam, because the palms of Thailand have been so well illustrated by Hodel (1998) and Vatcharakorn (2005).

Classification of Southern Asian Palms

The most recent classification of the palm family is that of Dransfield et al. (2005). I give the position of Southern Asian genera within that classification in Table 1.

Morphology of Palms

In this section I discuss the morphology of palms, and define all the terms that are used in the descriptions. While I have tried to keep the level of jargon to a minimum, some technical terms are unavoidable. Many important identification features are illustrated. The following discussion refers only to Southern Asian palms.

Stems of individual palms are described as clustered (i.e., an individual plant with several stems forming a clump) or solitary (an individual plant with only one stem). Most palms have free-standing stems—a few have short, subterranean stems and many have slender, climbing stems. Maximum heights and diameters of stems are given.

Leaves of palms are usually spirally arranged around the stem, rarely in one or a few planes.

They are immediately divided into two types, palmate (or fan-shaped) and pinnate (or feather-shaped).

Leaves of palmate-leafed palms are divided into several parts. The basal, sheathing part of the leaf is known as the sheath, and this is often very fibrous. At the apex of the sheath, above the point of insertion of the petiole, there is often a short extension known as the ocrea. The sheath is continuous with the petiole. Thorns occur along the margins of the petioles of many palmate-leafed palms. At the apex of the petiole there is usually a flap of material, where it joins the blade, known as the hastula. Some species of palmate-leafed palm have a short central axis, or rachis, and the leaf is then termed costapalmate.

The blades of palmate-leafed palms are usually divided into leaflets, and only two genera have undivided leaves—*Johannesteijsmannia* and a few species of *Licuala*. The blade may be divided part way or almost to the base. The number of leaflets per blade is given in the descriptions.

Leaflets of all palms are folded, and this folding takes place in two different ways. Most palmate-leafed palms have gutter-shaped folding (V-shaped in cross section, known as induplicate). A very few palmate palms have roof-shaped folding, and this is a useful character for identification. Roof-shaped folding (∧-shaped in cross section, known as

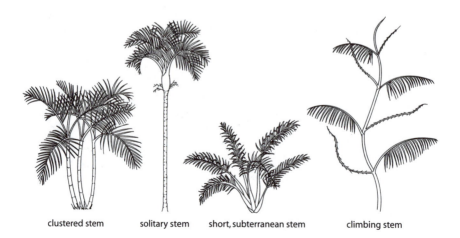

clustered stem   solitary stem   short, subterranean stem   climbing stem

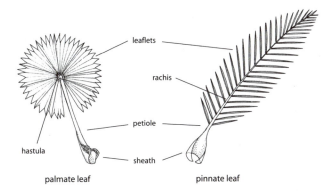

hastula

palmate leaf · pinnate leaf

leaflets

rachis

petiole

sheath

reduplicate) is common in pinnate-leafed palms.

The structure of pinnate-leafed palms is essentially similar to that of palmate-leafed palms, with some modifications. Leaf sheaths

is borne on the leaf sheath, and is actually a modified inflorescence.

The number of leaflets along one side of the rachis is given. Leaflets are arranged in various ways, and the kind of arrangement is a useful

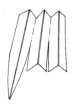

reduplicate folding

induplicate folding

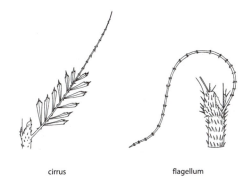

cirrus · flagellum

are always present, but in some species the sheaths are closed and form a structure known as the crownshaft. Ocreas are present in some pinnate palms, especially the rattans, where their form is useful in identification. A feature of the sheath found only in rattans (although not all) is the knee, a swollen projection of the sheath directly below the petiole. Petioles are usually well developed, but the hastula is absent or poorly developed in pinnate-leafed palms. The main axis of the leaf blade of pinnate-leafed palms is the rachis, and the rachis bears the leaflets.

In climbing palms, the rattans, the rachis may be extended into a long, whiplike organ known as the cirrus (plural, cirri). A second organ associated with the climbing habit of rattans is the flagellum (plural, flagella). This

character in identification. Most commonly, leaflets are regularly arranged along the rachis and spread in the same plane. Less commonly, leaflets are irregularly arranged, and leaflets spread in the same or different planes. Occasionally, pinnate leaves do not split, and an undivided leaf results. However, the venation is still pinnate.

The apices of the leaflets are usually pointed, but in a few palms they are jagged or lobed. In a few genera, only the apical few leaflets have lobed apices. Some palms have leaflets that are silvery or gray on the lower surfaces, and this is always a useful identification character. Leaves of many Southern Asian palms are spiny, espe-

| leaflets regularly arranged, spreading in one plane | leaflets regularly arranged, spreading in several planes | leaflets irregularly arranged, spreading in several planes | undivided leaf, with pinnate venation |

cially the rattans. Arrangement of spines, especially on the leaf sheaths, can also be a useful character in identification.

One genus, *Caryota*, has bipinnate leaves, that is, the leaflets themselves are split again into secondary leaflets. Any palm with such leaves must be a *Caryota*.

There are two life-history strategies in palms. The most common strategy, known as iteroparity (also known as pleonanthy), is where an individual stem reproduces (i.e., produces inflorescences) over a relatively long period. The second, less-common strategy is where an individual stem reproduces over a relatively short period, and this is followed by death of the stem. This is known as semelparity (or hapaxanthy). In several semelparous palms, especially *Corypha*, all inflorescences are produced together above the leaves, and appear like one enormous inflorescence. However, like all other palms, these structures consist of several, separate inflorescences.

Many Southern Asian palms, including all the rattans, are dioecious. This means that individual plants of a species bear either male or female flowers.

The structures that bear flowers and fruits are referred to as inflorescences and infructescences, respectively. In a few species the inflorescences are borne below the crownshafts, but in most Southern Asian palms the inflorescences are borne among the leaves. Most palms have a single inflorescence at each node, but occasionally more than one can be produced, in some species of *Arenga*, for example.

| leaflet with jagged margins | apical leaflets with lobed apices | bipinnate leaf |

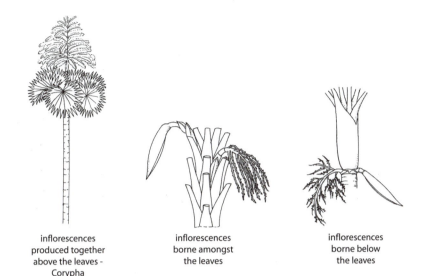

inflorescences
produced together
above the leaves -
Corypha

inflorescences
borne amongst
the leaves

inflorescences
borne below
the leaves

Inflorescences, like the leaves, consist of
several parts. The basal axis, known as the
peduncle, bears from one to many bracts.
The very first bract is known as the prophyll,
and the subsequent bracts on the peduncle
as peduncular bracts. In many palms, particularly the calamoid palms, there are conspicuous bracts subtending all inflorescence
branches. Most inflorescences are branched,
and flowers are borne along the ultimate
branches. Unbranched inflorescences are
referred to as spicate. The arrangement of
flowers along the branches is variable in
palms, from solitary to paired, or commonly
borne in threes of a central female and two
lateral male flowers.

Fruits of palms come in a great variety of
sizes, shapes, and colors. Size ranges from a
few millimeters to almost 20 cm in diameter
(e.g., in *Borassus*). Shape ranges from rounded
(i.e., globose) to ellipsoid (i.e., football-shaped)
to ovoid (i.e., egg-shaped), and there are various
permutations of these shapes. In most palm
fruits the remains of the stigmas (stigmatic remains) persist at the apices of the fruits, but in
a few they are displaced to the base of the
fruits. Almost all palm fruits are green as they
mature, but ripen to a variety of colors, commonly black, yellow, or red.

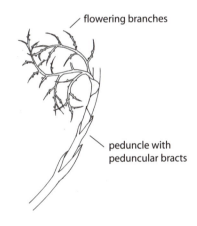

flowering branches

peduncle with
peduncular bracts

inflorescence

The fruits of all calamoid palms are covered
with overlapping scales. Most palm fruits have
one seed, but it is not uncommon to have two-
or three-seeded fruits. The endosperm of
palms is termed either ruminate (i.e., with uneven indentations of the seed coat) or homogeneous (without such indentations). Both conditions are visible only when the seed is cut
in half.

Germination in palms follows one of two pat-
terns. In most species, the seedling develops

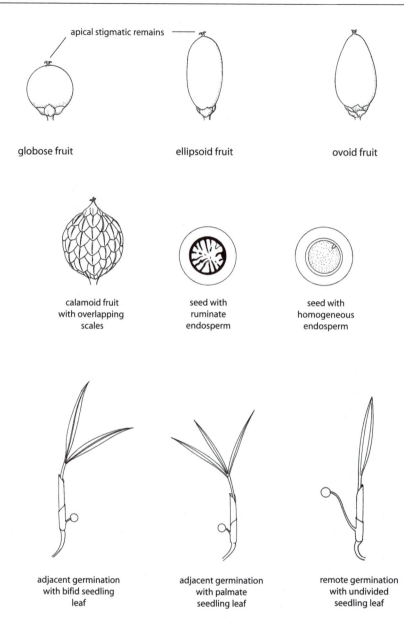

apical stigmatic remains

globose fruit

ellipsoid fruit

ovoid fruit

calamoid fruit
with overlapping
scales

seed with
ruminate
endosperm

seed with
homogeneous
endosperm

adjacent germination
with bifid seedling
leaf

adjacent germination
with palmate
seedling leaf

remote germination
with undivided
seedling leaf

next to the seed, and this is known as adjacent germination. In other species, the seedling develops at some distance from the seed, and this is known as remote germination. The first seedling leaf is either undivided, bifid, or palmate. Most palms with adjacent germination have bifid seedling leaves, and most palms with remote germination have undivided seedling leaves, but there are several exceptions to this.

Key to the Genera of Palms in Southern Asia

1a. Leaves palmate or costapalmate . . . . 2.
1b. Leaves pinnate (or pinnately veined if undivided) or bipinnate . . . . 17.

2a. Leaf blades undivided; Thailand (Peninsular) . . . . 3.
2b. Leaf blades divided into leaflets; all areas including Thailand (Peninsular) . . . . 4.

3a. Leaf blades diamond-shaped . . . . *Johannesteijsmannia.*
3b. Leaf blades rounded . . . . *Licuala* (*L. peltata* var. *sumawongii*).

4a. Hastulas absent . . . . 5.
4b. Hastulas present . . . . 6.

5a. Petioles deeply channeled; China (Hainan) and Vietnam (Northern) . . . . *Chuniophoenix.*
5b. Petioles not deeply channeled; Afghanistan and Pakistan . . . . *Nannorrhops.*

6a. Leaf sheaths smooth, not fibrous, with a triangular cleft at the base . . . . 7.
6b. Leaf sheaths fibrous, not split at the base . . . . 10.

7a. Stems branching dichotomously above ground; India (Guyjarat, Maharashtra) . . . . *Hyphaene.*
7b. Stems not branching; widespread . . . . 8.

8a. Petiole margins without thorns; blades divided almost to the base into numerous
segments, and these again divided into leaflets; Thailand (Peninsular) . . . . *Borassodendron.*
8b. Petiole margins with thorns; blades divided for about half their length into leaflets;
widespread including Thailand (Peninsular) . . . . 9.

9a. Petiole margins with regularly arranged thorns; fruits to 7 cm diameter; inflorescences
produced simultaneously above the leaves, their production ending the life of stem . . . . *Corypha.*
9b. Petiole margins with irregularly arranged thorns; fruits to 20 cm diameter;
inflorescences produced sequentially among the leaves, their production
not ending the life of stem . . . . *Borassus.*

10a. Petiole margins with thorns . . . . 11.
10b. Petiole margins without thorns . . . . 14.

11a. Leaflets split to their bases into multifold, wedge-shaped leaflets with lobed apices . . . . *Licuala.*
11b. Leaflets not or seldom split to their bases, single or multifold, not wedge-shaped, with
pointed or split apices . . . . 12.

12a. Petioles with 2 yellow stripes on the lower surfaces; fruits to 12 cm diameter,
with warty surfaces; Thailand (Peninsular) . . . . *Pholidocarpus.*
12b. Petioles without yellow stripes on the lower surfaces; fruits to 2.5 cm diameter, not warty;
widespread including Thailand (Peninsular) . . . . 13.

13a. Adult leaves markedly costapalmate; petioles with stout thorns along the margins;
fruits globose to ellipsoid, not grooved . . . . *Livistona.*
13b. Adult leaves not costapalmate; petioles with small, blunt teeth along the margins; fruits
kidney-shaped or oblong, grooved . . . . *Trachycarpus.*

14a. Leaflets green on the lower surface, the margins with scarcely visible thorns . . . . *Rhapis.*
14b. Leaflets grayish or silvery white on the lower surface, the margins without thorns . . . . 15.

15a. Leaflets Λ-shaped (reduplicate) in cross section; China (Guangxi, Guangdong)
and Vietnam (Northern) . . . . *Guihaia.*
15b. Leaflets V-shaped (induplicate) in cross section; Thailand (Peninsular). . . . . 16.

16a. Stems clustered, to 8 cm diameter . . . . *Maxburretia.*
16b. Stems solitary, to 20 cm diameter . . . . *Kerriodoxa.*

17a. Leaflets at the base of the leaf modified into into green, straight spines . . . . *Phoenix.*
17b. Leaflets at the base of the leaf not modified into spines . . . . 18.

(continued)

Key to the Genera of Palms in Southern Asia (continued)

18a. Stems, leaves, and inflorescences spiny . . . . 19.
18b. Stems, leaves, and inflorescences not spiny . . . . 30.

19a. Leaf sheaths forming a crownshaft; inflorescences borne below the crownshaft; fruits
smooth, not covered with overlapping scales . . . . *Oncosperma.*
19b. Leaf sheaths not forming a crownshaft; inflorescences borne among the leaves; fruits
covered with overlapping scales . . . . 20.

20a. Stems thin and flexible, climbing, with either flagella or cirri . . . . 21.
20b. Stems stiff and erect, sometimes short and subterranean, not climbing, without flagella or cirri . . . . 27.

21a. Leaflets narrowly to broadly rhomboidal, with jagged apices, usually silvery on the lower
surfaces; climbing stems branching above ground . . . . *Korthalsia.*
21b. Leaflets not rhomboidal, usually with pointed apices, green on the lower surfaces, rarely
silvery; climbing stems branching only at ground level, rarely above ground . . . . 22.

22a. Knees on leaf sheaths absent; inflorescences borne simultaneously at apex of stem, their
production ending life of stem; female flowers solitary . . . . 23.
22b. Knees on leaf sheaths usually present; inflorescences borne sequentially along the stem,
their production not ending life of stem; female flowers paired . . . . 25.

23a. Leaflets usually silvery gray, rarely green on the lower surfaces, without scales; inflorescence
branches covered with prominent, overlapping bracts, these obscuring the flowers . . . . . . *Plectocomia.*
23b. Leaflets green on the lower surfaces, with small, brown scales; inflorescence branches
without prominent, overlapping bracts, the flowers visible . . . . 24.

24a. Leaf sheath spines scattered, sometimes absent; ocreas present; leaflets with
conspicuous, yellow spines on the upper surfaces; fruits covered with
normal-sized scales . . . . *Plectocomiopsis.*
24b. Leaf sheath spines arranged in rows; ocreas absent; leaflets without conspicuous,
yellow spines on the upper surfaces; fruits covered with minute scales . . . . *Myrialepis.*

25a. Inflorescences covered with only 1 bract, this covering the flowers and splitting
as the fruits develop; Thailand (Peninsular) . . . . *Ceratolobus.*
25b. Inflorescences covered with several bracts, these not covering the flowers; widespread
including Thailand (Peninsular) . . . . 26.

26a. Cirri always present; inflorescences not flagellate, usually shorter than the leaves,
with boat-shaped bracts splitting their entire length and then either falling off or
remaining attached and enclosed by the prophyll, without grapnel-like spines . . . . *Daemonorops.*
26b. Cirri present or absent; inflorescences flagellate or nonflagellate, usually longer
than the leaves, with sheathing, tubular bracts not or only briefly splitting and
remaining attached, not enclosed by the prophyll, usually with grapnel-like spines . . . . *Calamus.*

27a. Inflorescences arising from the center of the leaves, stout and erect with no apparent
branches, to 3 m long; stems often with dense stilt roots at the base . . . . *Eugeissona.*
27b. Inflorescences borne among the leaves, not stout and erect, branched, to 2 m long;
stems without stilt roots at the base . . . . 28.

28a. Stems subterranean or erect; ocreas present, often conspicuous . . . . *Calamus.*
28b. Stems always short and subterranean, or creeping; ocreas absent . . . . 29.

29a. Fruits not spiny; leaflets at apex of leaf split, not forming a broad, compound
apical leaflet . . . . *Eleiodoxa.*
29b. Fruits spiny; leaflets at apex of leaf usually forming a broad, compound apical
leaflet, sometimes the apical leaflets split . . . . *Salacca.*

30a. Leaf sheaths closed and forming a crownshaft; inflorescences borne below
the crownshaft . . . . 31.
30b. Leaf sheaths open, not forming a crownshaft; inflorescences borne among the leaves . . . . 40.

The Palms of Southern Asia

ARECA L.

(*Gigliolia* Becc., *Mischophloeus* Scheff.,
Pichisermollia H. C. Monteiro)

Stems are solitary or clustered and range from tall to short or subterranean. They are usually green and ringed with conspicuous leaf scars, and some species have prominent stilt roots at the base. Leaves are pinnate or occasionally undivided and 4–12 in number. Leaf sheaths are closed and form a distinct, green, yellowish, or rarely bright red (not ours) crownshaft, although in some species this does not develop and the leaf sheaths are open. The leaf rachis is sometimes strongly recurved but in most species spreads horizontally. Leaflets are usually regularly arranged along the rachis and always spread in the same plane. They are one- to several-veined and thus can be of different widths. Sometimes, especially at the leaf apex, the leaflets are joined with only short splits at the apices, resulting in compound leaflets with lobed apices.

Inflorescences are branched to three orders (rarely spicate) and are usually borne below the crownshaft, sometimes among the leaves. They are covered in bud with just one bract, the prophyll. After this bract falls away the flowering branches spread or, less often, remain stiffly erect. Flowers are unisexual and are borne in threes of a central female and two lateral males. The female flowers are much larger than the males. Usually these groups of three flowers are borne at the bases of the flowering branches (as are the fruits), and above them are male flowers only. These male flowers may be paired or solitary. This part of the flowering branches, with male flowers only, is often thin and rots away after the flowers are shed, or shrivels and persists as a "tail" as the fruits develop. Fruits are small to moderate in size, ellipsoid to globose or spindle-shaped, commonly beaked, usually bright red, and one-seeded. The seeds of one species, *A. catechu*, are chewed, and the local name for these seeds in southern India is *adeka* or *adaka*, hence the name of the genus. The endosperm is ruminate, germination is adjacent, and the seedling leaf is bifid.

Areca contains about 50 species, naturally occurring from Sri Lanka and northeastern India through Indochina and into Southeast Asia as far east as New Guinea and the Solomon Islands. They are usually small to moderate, understory palms, except for the taller, cultivated *A. catechu*. The genus is most diverse in Southeast Asia, particularly Borneo, and there are only five species in our area (Hodel 1998; Lim & Whitmore 2001a). There is no recent treatment of the genus.

Areca catechu L.
PLATE I

doma (Bhu), pin lang (Chi, Tai), gua, supari (Ind), cun pan, kunti (Mya), mark (Tha), cau (Vie), areca nut palm, betel nut palm

Field characters. Stems solitary, to 20 m tall and 20 cm diameter. Petioles very short; leaf rachis recurved, to 2 m long with to 30 regularly and closely arranged leaflets per side, these stiffly erect. Inflorescences branched to 3 orders; flowering branches yellowish green; male flowers solitary, alternate along flowering branches; stamens 6; fruits ovoid, to 8 cm long and 6 cm diameter, yellow, orange, or red.
Range and habitat. Widely cultivated throughout our area (and also in the Asian tropics and western

Key to the Species of Areca

1a. Stems solitary, to 20 m tall and 20 cm diameter; male flowers solitary, alternate along the flowering branches; cultivated, rarely naturalized . . . . *A. catechu.*

1b. Stems clustered or less often solitary, to 6 m tall and 7 cm diameter; male flowers paired, borne on one side of the flowering branches; naturally occurring, rarely cultivated . . . . 2.

2a. Petioles very short or absent; inflorescences with rigid, erect flowering branches arranged in a fan shape; Thailand (Peninsular) . . . . *A. tunku.*

2b. Petioles usually well developed; inflorescences with flexible, spreading flowering branches not arranged in a fan shape; widespread, including Thailand (Peninsular) . . . . 3.

3a. Sri Lanka . . . . *A. concinna.*

3b. Andaman and Nicobar islands, Bangladesh, Cambodia, India, Laos, Myanmar, Thailand, and Vietnam . . . . 4.

4a. Stamens 3; Andaman and Nicobar islands, Bangladesh, Cambodia, India, Laos, Myanmar, Thailand, and Vietnam . . . . *A. triandra.*

4b. Stamens 6; Laos and Vietnam . . . . *A. laosensis.*

Pacific) and commonly seen around houses, rarely naturalized (no map provided).

Uses. An important, cultivated species. The sliced seeds are chewed as a mild narcotic, and there are many other minor uses.

Synonyms. *Areca cathechu* Burm. f., *Areca faufel* Gaertn., *Areca hortensis* Lour., *Areca himalayana* Griff., *Areca nigra* Giseke, *Sublimia areca* Comm.

Areca concinna Thwaites
lenteri, lenatheriya (Srl)

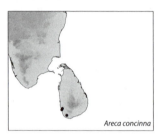

Areca concinna

Field characters. Stems clustered, to 5 m tall and 6 cm diameter. Petioles to 15 cm long; leaf rachis arching, to 1.5 m long with to 20 regularly arranged leaflets per side, these closely to distantly spaced and spreading horizontally. Inflorescences branched to 2 orders; flowering branches yellowish green; male flowers paired, borne on one side of flowering branches; stamens 6; fruits globose to ovoid, to 3 cm long and 1.2 cm diameter, red.

Range and habitat. Sri Lanka; lowland rain forest, often in swampy places at low elevations.

Uses. The seeds are chewed as a substitute for *A. catechu*.

Notes. Difficult to distinguish from *A. triandra*.

Areca laosensis Becc.

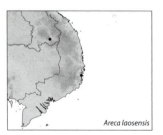

Areca laosensis

Field characters. Stems solitary or clustered, to 2.5 cm diameter, height not known. Petioles to 10 cm long; leaf rachis at least 1 m long with few regularly arranged leaflets per side. Inflorescences branched to 2 orders; flowering branches yellowish green; male flowers paired, borne on one side of flowering branches; stamens 6; fruits not known.

Range and habitat. Laos (Southern) and Vietnam (Southern); lowland rain forest or deciduous forest at low elevations.

Uses. The seeds are used as a substitute for those of *A. catechu*.

Notes. Known only from two old specimens, one collected in Laos in 1877 and the other in Vietnam in 1923. These appear intermediate between *A. triandra*, in their paired male flowers, and *A. catechu*, in their six stamens, and may represent hybrids.

Areca triandra Roxb.   PLATES 1 & 2
abaradah (And, Ncb), khur (Ind), tau kunti, thaung paw conthee (Mya), mark-nang-ling, tao kao (Tha), cau rung (Vie)

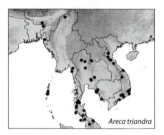

Areca triandra

Field characters. Stems clustered, rarely solitary, to 6 m tall and 7 cm diameter, often with stilt roots. Petioles to 50 cm long; leaf rachis arching, to 2 m long with 10–40 regularly arranged leaflets per side, these distantly spaced and spreading horizontally. Inflorescences branched to 3 orders; flowering branches yellowish green; male flowers paired, borne on one side of flowering branches; stamens 3; fruits ellipsoid to ovoid, to 2.5 cm long and 1.5 cm diameter, red.

Range and habitat. Andaman and Nicobar islands, Bangladesh, Cambodia, India (Assam, Meghalaya, Sikkim), Laos, Myanmar (Kachin, Kayin, Tanintharyi), Thailand (East, North, Peninsular, Southeast, Southwest), and Vietnam (Central, Southern) (also in Borneo, Java, Sumatra, and Peninsular Malaysia); lowland to montane rain forest, rarely cultivated, to 1500 m elevation.

Uses. The seeds are used as a substitute for those of *A. catechu*.

Notes. A widespread and variable species with a scattered distribution. There are many local forms, some with solitary stems, some with clustered stems; some with few broad leaflets, some with numerous narrow leaflets; and some with yellow flowers and some with white flowers. Habitat is also variable, ranging from steep mountain slopes to margins of fast-flowing rivers (rheophytic form).

Synonyms. *Areca aliceae* W. Hill., *Areca borneensis* Becc., *Areca humilis* Blanco, *Areca latiloba* Ridl., *Areca laxa* Buch.-Ham., *Areca montana* Ridl., *Areca nagensis* Griff., *Areca polystachya* (Miq.) H. Wendl., *Areca recurvata* Hodel, *Areca triandra* var. *bancana*

Scheff., *Nenga nagensis* (Griff.) Scheff., *Ptychosperma polystachyum* Miq.

Areca tunku J. Dransf. & C. K. Lim

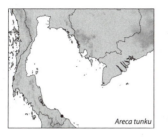

Areca tunku

Field characters. Stems solitary, to 4 m tall and 6 cm diameter, with stilt roots. Petioles very short or absent, the leaf bases trapping leaf litter; leaf rachis arching, to 2.5 m long with 5–24 regularly or slightly irregularly arranged leaflets per side, these spreading horizontally. Inflorescences branched to 1 order (rarely to 2 orders), with thick, rigid, erect, reddish purple flowering branches arranged in a fan shape; male flowers paired or solitary, borne on one side of flowering branches; stamens 6; fruits ovoid or obovoid, to 4.5 cm long and 3 cm diameter, purple-brown.
Range and habitat. Thailand (Peninsular) (also in Sumatra and Peninsular Malaysia); lowland rain forest to 800 m elevation.
Uses. None recorded.
Synonym. *Areca bifaria* Hodel

ARENGA Labill.
(*Saguerus* Steck, *Gomutus* Corrêa, *Blancoa* Blume, *Didymosperma* H. Wendl. & Drude)

Stems are clustered and sometimes spread by stolons, or are less often solitary. They are usually covered with persistent, fibrous leaf bases. Leaves are pinnate (seldom undivided) and 5–30 in number. Leaf sheaths are open and often very fibrous, and the sheaths of dead leaves commonly persist on the stems. Petioles are usually covered with distinctive scales. Leaflets vary in shape from linear to rhomboidal and are sometimes lobed, but they always have jagged apices. The bases of the leaflets in some species have an unusual ear-shaped projection that overlaps the rachis. Leaflets are either regularly or irregularly arranged, but the basal few leaflets are often borne in a cluster, even when the leaflets on the rest of the leaf are regularly arranged. Leaflets are usually silvery gray on the lower surface.

Inflorescences are branched to two orders (rarely spicate) and are borne among the leaves. Number of flowering branches ranges from 1 to more than 100. Flowering behavior in *Arenga* is unusual. Most species are semelparous, but a few species are iteroparous (only one species in our area). Inflorescences are usually solitary at the nodes, although some species can have more than one inflorescence at each node. Inflorescences are covered with several persistent bracts. Flowers are unisexual and are borne in threes of a central female and two lateral males. However, often either female or male flowers of an inflorescence do not develop, giving unisexual inflorescences. Commonly female inflorescences are borne at the apex of the stem, and male ones below. Fruits are usually quite large; ellipsoid, globose, ovoid, or oblong; red, yellowish, or purplish; and one- to three-seeded. The mesocarp contains crystals of calcium oxalate (known as raphides). Although an irritant to humans, these do not deter palm civets and other animals that eat the fruits. The endosperm is homogeneous, germination is remote, and the seedling leaf is either undivided or bifid with jagged margins. The genus gets its name from the Latinized form of a common name for one species, *aren* or *areng*.

Arenga contains about 20 species, widely distributed from India to Southeast Asia, and reaching New Guinea and Australia. Ten species occur in our area (Henderson 2006; Mogea 1991). *Arenga nana* is now included in *Wallichia*, as *W. nana* (Henderson 2007a).

Arenga is distinguished with difficulty from *Wallichia*, based on the form of the sepals of male flowers (Uhl & Dransfield 1987). This character is difficult to observe, and male flowers are seldom available. Most species of *Arenga*, at least in our area, have leaflets that are linear and more or less symmetrical, and are not or scarcely lobed on the margins, in contrast to most *Wallichia* species. Unfortunately there are several exceptions (*A. caudata, A. hastata, A. longicarpa,* and *A. rheophytica*), but these have leaflets with long, pointed apices, unlike those of *Wallichia*. Leaflet shape and size are useful in identification, and these are illustrated in Figure 3. Note that leaflet shape of *A. obtusifolia* (not illustrated) is very similar to that of *A. pinnata*, and that of *A. wightii* is similar to that of *A. micrantha*.

The species of *Arenga* can be divided into two subgenera, and the following key is arranged according to these. Subgenus *Arenga*, at least in our area, contains larger palms and the leaflets are always numerous, linear, and usually have ears at the base. Subgenus *Didymosperma* contains smaller palms and the leaflets are fewer, broader and lobed, and do not have ears at the base.

Arenga caudata (Lour.) H. E. Moore   PLATE 2
tao 'hang (Lao), mimbaw (Mya), rang nu, tan (Tha), dung dinh, bac bo (Vie)

Field characters. Stems clustered, to 1.5 m tall and 2 cm diameter, semelparous. Leaves to 1 m long, ending in a triangular leaflet; leaflets linear to rhomboidal, without basal ears, with elongate apices, regularly or irregularly arranged and spreading in the same plane, to 10 per side of rachis (sometimes blade

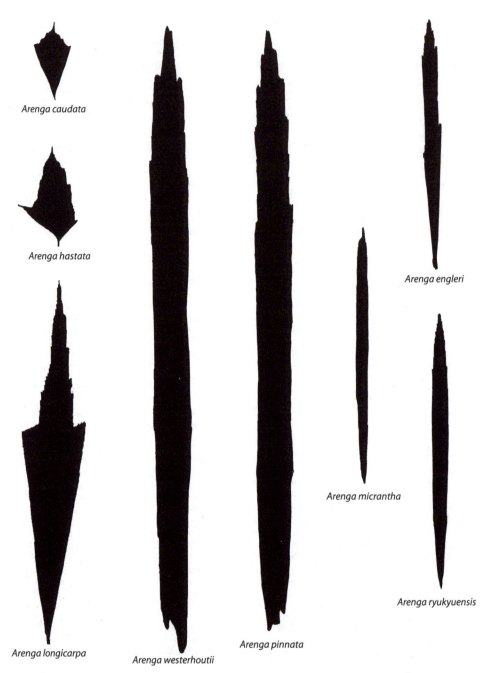

Figure 3. Leaflet shapes of *Arenga* species.

Key to the Species of Arenga

1a. Leaflets numerous, to 150 per side of rachis, linear, usually with ears at the bases
(subgenus *Arenga*) . . . . 2.
1b. Leaflets fewer, to 10 per side of rachis, variously shaped, often rhomboidal or lobed, less
often linear, without ears at the bases (or occasionally leaves undivided) (subgenus
Didymosperma) . . . . 8.

2a. Stems solitary . . . . 3.
2b. Stems clustered . . . . 5.

3a. Stems to 20 m tall; leaflets irregularly arranged and spreading in different planes; usually
cultivated . . . . *A. pinnata.*
3b. Stems to 12 m tall; leaflets regularly arranged and spreading in the same plane, sometimes
slightly irregularly arranged; naturally occurring . . . . 4.

4a. Stems to 12 m tall and 60 cm diameter; leaflets 80–150 per side of rachis; Cambodia, China
(Guangxi, Hainan, Yunnan), Laos, Myanmar, Thailand, and Vietnam . . . . *A. westerhoutii.*
4b. Stems to 2 m tall and 15 cm diameter; leaflets to 35 per side of rachis; Bhutan, China (Tibet),
and northeastern India . . . . *A. micrantha.*

5a. Stems to 20 m tall, with stolons; leaflets spreading in slightly different planes;
Thailand (Peninsular) . . . . *A. obtusifolia.*
5b. Stems to 7 m tall, without stolons; leaflets spreading in the same plane; Ryukyu Islands,
Taiwan, and southwestern India . . . . 6.

6a. Stems to 7 m tall and 30 cm diameter; southwestern India . . . . *A. wightii.*
6b. Stems to 4 m tall and 15 cm diameter; Ryukyu Islands and Taiwan . . . . 7.

7a. Leaflets strongly ribbed on upper surfaces, lobed only near the apices;
Japan (Ryukyu Islands) . . . . *A. ryukyuensis.*
7b. Leaflets flat on upper surfaces, lobed near the middle and at the apices;
Taiwan . . . . *A. engleri.*

8a. Inflorescences with 2–8 flowering branches; China (Guangdong) . . . . *A. longicarpa.*
8b. Inflorescences with 1–3 flowering branches; Cambodia, China (Hainan), Laos,
Myanmar, Thailand, and Vietnam . . . . 9.

9a. Leaves ending in a pair of leaflets; leaflets borne on short stalks, paler green on the lower
surfaces; stems iteroparous . . . . *A. hastata.*
9b. Leaves ending in a single leaflet; leaflets not borne on short stalks, silvery gray on the lower
surfaces; stems semelparous . . . . *A. caudata.*

undivided and lobed), silvery gray on the lower surfaces. Inflorescences solitary (or sometimes male ones multiple at each node), to 0.5 m long, spicate or sometimes with 2 or 3 flowering branches; fruits ellipsoid, to 1.5 cm long and 0.8 cm diameter, red.

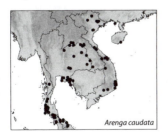

Arenga caudata

Range and habitat. Cambodia, China (Guangxi, Hainan), Laos, Myanmar (Tanintharyi), Thailand (East, Northeast, Southeast), and Vietnam (also in Peninsular Malaysia); lowland rain forest or deciduous forest, sometimes on limestone outcrops, to 700 m elevation.

Uses. The leaves are used to weave hats.

Notes. A common, widespread, and extremely variable species. Four varieties have been recognized (Mogea 1991) but there are many different local forms and the varieties cannot be satisfactorily distinguished. Some of these forms are so distinct that they should probably be recognized at the species level, for example, a rheophytic form from Vietnam (Plate 2). *Arenga caudata* is greatly in need of a modern revision.

Synonyms. *Arenga hookeriana* (Becc.) Whitmore, *Blancoa caudata* (Lour.) Kuntze, *Borassus caudatus* Lour., *Didymosperma caudatum* (Lour.) H. Wendl. & Drude, *Didymosperma caudata* var. *stenophylla* Becc., *Didymosperma caudatum* var. *tonkinense* Becc.,

Didymosperma hookeriana Becc., *Didymosperma tonkinense* (Becc.) Gagnep., *Wallichia caudata* (Lour.) Mart.

Arenga engleri Becc.
shan-tsong, soan-tsang, tsung (Tai)

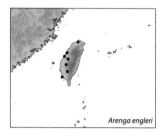

Arenga engleri

Field characters. Stems clustered, to 4 m tall and 15 cm diameter, semelparous. Leaves to 3 m long, ending in a triangular leaflet; leaflets linear, with basal ears but these poorly developed, briefly lobed near the middle and at the apices, regularly arranged and spreading in the same plane, 38–41 per side of rachis, silvery gray on the lower surfaces. Inflorescences solitary at each node, to 0.6 m long, with to 15 flowering branches; fruits globose, to 1.5 cm diameter, orange to reddish.
Range and habitat. Taiwan; western lowlands in open places or lowland rain forest, to 850 m elevation.
Notes. Mogea (1991) confused this species with *A. tremula* from the Philippines. As pointed out by Henderson (2006), *A. engleri* is native to Taiwan, although widely cultivated elsewhere as an ornamental.
Synonyms. *Arenga tremula* var. *engleri* (Becc.) Hatus., *Didymosperma engleri* (Becc.) Warb.

Arenga hastata (Becc.) Whitmore

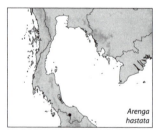

Arenga hastata

Field characters. Stems clustered, to 2 m tall and 1.2 cm diameter, iteroparous. Leaves to 1 m long, ending in a pair of leaflets; leaflets broadly and irregularly triangular, borne on short stalks, without basal ears, regularly arranged and spreading in the same plane, to 5 per side of rachis, paler green on the lower surfaces. Inflorescences solitary at each node, to 0.5 m long, with 1 flowering branch; fruits globose, to 0.7 cm diameter, purple-brown.

Range and habitat. Thailand (Peninsular) (also in Borneo, Peninsular Malaysia, and Sumatra); lowland rain forest to 300 m elevation.
Uses. None recorded.
Notes. The presence of this species in Thailand is doubtful. It is based on a single specimen, possibly misidentified, and the species is not included in the list of Dransfield et al. (2004).
Synomyms. *Arenga borneensis* (Becc.) Dransf., *Blancoa borneensis* (Becc.) Kuntze, *Blancoa hastata* (Becc.) Kuntze, *Didymosperma borneense* Becc., *Didymosperma hastatum* Becc.

Arenga longicarpa C. F. Wei

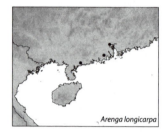

Arenga longicarpa

Field characters. Stems clustered, to 3 m tall and 7 cm diameter, semelparous. Leaves to 2.5 m long, ending in a triangular leaflet; leaflets few, elongate, lobed, without basal ears, regularly arranged and spreading in the same plane, silvery gray on the lower surfaces. Inflorescences solitary at each node, to 0.5 m long, with 2–8 flowering branches; fruits ovoid to oblong, curved, 2-seeded and 1.8 cm long and 1 cm diameter, purple.
Range and habitat. China (Guangdong); lowland rain forest or secondary forest, to 750 m elevation.
Uses. None recorded.

Arenga micrantha C. F. Wei
guanglang (Chi)

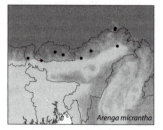

Arenga micrantha

Field characters. Stems solitary, to 2 m tall and 15 cm diameter, semelparous. Leaves to 3 m long, ending in a triangular leaflet; leaflets linear, with basal ears, regularly arranged and spreading in the same plane, to 35 per side of rachis, silvery gray on the lower surfaces. Inflorescences solitary at each node, to 1 m long, with to 100 flowering branches; fruits not known.

Range and habitat. Bhutan, China (Tibet), and India (Arunachal Pradesh, Sikkim, West Bengal); montane rain forest at 1400–2150 m elevation.
Notes. Noltie (2000) considered that this species could be dioecious.

Arenga obtusifolia Mart.
prao nuu (Tha)

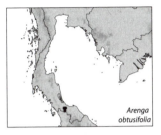

Arenga
obtusifolia

Field characters. Stems clustered, to 20 m tall and 30 cm diameter, with stolons to 15 m long, iteroparous. Leaves to 10 m long, ending in a triangular leaflet; leaflets linear, with basal ears, regularly to somewhat irregularly arranged and spreading in slightly different planes, to 100 per side of rachis, silvery gray on the lower surfaces. Inflorescences solitary at each node, to 2 m long, with to 40 flowering branches; fruits ellipsoid, to 6 cm long and 4 cm diameter, yellowish green.
Range and habitat. Thailand (Peninsular) (also in Java, Peninsular Malaysia, and Sumatra); lowland rain forest or secondary forest, to 700 m elevation.
Notes. In Thailand known only from Khao Namkhang National Park, Songkhla (Pongsattayapipat & Barfod 2005).
Synonym. *Gomotus obtusifolius* Blume

Arenga pinnata (Wurmb) Merr.
taung-ong (Mya), long-chit (Tha), sugar palm

Field characters. Stems solitary, to 20 m tall and 60 cm diameter, semelparous. Leaves to 8 m long, ending in a triangular leaflet; leaflets linear, with basal ears, irregularly arranged and spreading in different planes (sometimes almost regularly arranged on younger plants), to 150 per side of rachis, silvery gray on the lower surfaces. Inflorescences solitary at each node, to 2.5 m long, with to 50 flowering branches; fruits globose to ovoid, to 7 cm long and 6 cm diameter, greenish, yellowish, or orangish.
Range and habitat. Rare in our area (but also in Celebes, Malaysia, New Guinea, Philippines, and Indonesia), usually cultivated near villages or planted as an ornamental, to 700 m elevation, rarely to 1200 m (no map provided).
Uses. The sugar palm was formerly an important source of sugar, especially in Malaysia and Indonesia, derived from tapping the inflorescences. Tapping is still carried out on a local scale. There are many other minor uses.

Notes. *Arenga pinnata* is rare in our area. The only population known from Thailand (Peninsular), between Krabi and Trang, may represent a distinct species or may be a form of *A. westerhoutii*.
Synonyms. *Arenga gomuto* Merr., *Arenga griffithii* Seem., *Arenga saccharifera* Labill., *Borassus gomutus* Lour., *Caryota onusta* Blanco, *Gomutus rumphii* Corrêa, *Gomutus saccharifera* (Labill.) Sprengel, *Gomutus vulgaris* Oken, *Saguerus gamuto* Houtt., *Saguerus saccharifera* (Labill.) Blume, *Saguerus pinnatus* Wurmb, *Saguerus rumphii* (Corrêa) Roxb., *Sagus gomutus* (Lour.) Perr.

Arenga ryukyuensis Henderson
kuro-tsugu, mani (Jap)

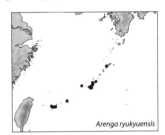

Arenga ryukyuensis

Field characters. Stems clustered, to 2 m tall and 20 cm diameter, semelparous. Leaves to 2 m long, ending in a triangular leaflet; leaflets linear, with basal ears but these poorly developed, briefly lobed only near the apices, regularly arranged and spreading in the same plane, 32–48 per side of rachis, strongly ribbed on the upper surfaces, silvery gray on the lower surfaces. Inflorescences solitary at each node, to 0.5 m long, with to 30 flowering branches; fruits globose, to 1.8 cm diameter, orange to reddish.
Range and habitat. Japan (Ryukyu Islands), and possibly, in historical times, in southern Japan; open places or scrub forest, to 300 m elevation.
Notes. Previously confused with *A. engleri* (Henderson 2006). It has been introduced into the Bonin Islands.

Arenga westerhoutii Griff.   PLATE 3
chok (Cbd), dong dong fen, guanglang (Chi), taw-ohn, toung-on (Mya), long-gupp, rang kai (Tha), bung bang (Vie)

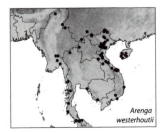

Arenga
westerhoutii

Field characters. Stems solitary, to 12 m tall and 60 cm diameter, semelparous. Leaves to 8 m long, ending in a triangular leaflet; leaflets linear, with basal ears, regularly arranged and spreading in the same plane (rarely slightly irregularly arranged), closely spaced, 80–150 per side of rachis, silvery gray on the lower surfaces. Inflorescences solitary at each node, to 3 m long, with 60–70 flowering branches; fruits globose, to 7 cm diameter, greenish black.
Range and habitat. Cambodia, China (Guangxi, Hainan, Yunnan), Laos, Myanmar, Thailand, and Vietnam (also in Peninsular Malaysia); lowland rain forest, often on limestone hills, to 600 m, rarely to 1400 m elevation.
Uses. The leaves are used for thatching, and the palm heart is occasionally eaten.
Notes. A common and widespread species with several local forms. Plants are usually seen with perfectly regularly arranged leaflets, but populations occur with slightly irregularly arranged leaflets (see notes under *A. pinnata*).
Synonym. *Saguerus westerhoutii* (Griff.) H. Wendl. & Drude

Arenga wightii Griff.   PLATE 4
malamthengu (Ind)

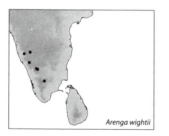

Arenga wightii

Field characters. Stems clustered, to 7 m tall and 30 cm diameter, semelparous. Leaves to 10 m long, ending in a triangular leaflet; leaflets linear, with basal ears, regularly arranged and spreading in the same plane, to 70 per side of rachis, silvery gray on the lower surfaces. Inflorescences solitary at each node, to 1 m long, with to 40 flowering branches; fruits globose to obovoid, to 2.5 cm long and 3 cm diameter, greenish black.
Range and habitat. India (Karnataka, Kerala, Maharashtra, Tamil Nadu); lowland or montane rain forest to 1350 m elevation.
Uses. None recorded.
Synonym. *Saguerus wightii* (Griff.) H. Wendl. & Drude

BENTINCKIA Berry
(*Keppleria* Mart.)

This genus was named for William Henry Cavendish-Bentinck (1774–1839), a colonial governor in India. Stems are tall and solitary, and ringed with conspicuous leaf scars. Leaves are pinnate, 8–12 in number, and dead leaves fall cleanly from the stem. Leaf sheaths are closed and form a prominent, green crownshaft. Petioles are usually very short. Leaflets are numerous, regularly arranged, lanceolate, and spread in the same plane. They tend to project upwards because of the arching of the rachis. The basal few leaflets may be joined, and all leaflets are briefly split at the apex. Leaflets have prominent brown scales on the midrib on the lower surface. Inflorescences are branched to three orders and are borne below the crownshaft. Several inflorescences are usually present at one time, forming a dense mass at the base of the crownshaft.

Inflorescences are covered with two bracts, and these fall before flowering time, leaving two scars. The numerous flowering branches are rather stiff. Flowers are unisexual and are arranged in threes of a central female and two lateral male flowers. Fruits are small, irregularly globose, brown or black, and one-seeded. A distinctive feature of the fruits is the basal stigmatic remains. The endosperm is homogeneous, germination is adjacent, and the seedling leaf is undivided or bifid.

Bentinckia contains two species, distributed in southwestern India and the Nicobar Islands. They occur in lowland or montane rain forest, often in steep rocky places.

Bentinckia condapanna Berry   PLATE 4
kattukamuku, parapakku (Ind)

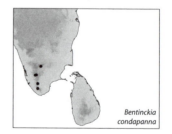

Bentinckia condapanna

Field characters. Stems solitary, to 10 m tall and 15 cm diameter. Leaves arching; leaflets lanceolate,

Key to the Species of *Bentinckia*

1a. Stems to 10 m tall and 15 cm diameter; leaflets to 40 per side of rachis; India
(Kerala, Tamil Nadu) . . . . *B. condapanna.*
1b. Stems to 20 m tall and 25 cm diameter; leaflets to 60 per side of rachis; Nicobar Islands . . . *B. nicobarica.*

to 40 per side of rachis. Inflorescences borne below the leaves; fruits irregularly globose, to 1.5 cm diameter, brown.

Range and habitat. India (Kerala, Tamil Nadu); montane rain forest at 1000–1400 m elevation.

Uses. The palm heart is eaten.

Notes. Reported to be rare in the wild, but still quite common in certain areas.

Bentinckia nicobarica (Kurz) Becc.
hilu'a (Ncb)

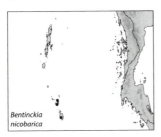

Field characters. Stems solitary, to 20 m tall and 25 cm diameter. Leaves arching; leaflets linear, to 60 per side of rachis. Inflorescences borne below the leaves; fruits irregularly globose to ellipsoid, to 1.5 cm long and 1 cm diameter, brown or black.

Range and habitat. Nicobar Islands (Bompoka, Camorta, Great Nicobar, Nancowry, Trinkat); lowland rain forest at low elevations.

Uses. The stems are used in construction of houses and fences.

Notes. Reported to be rare in the wild.

Synonym. *Orania nicobarica* Kurz

BORASSODENDRON Becc.

This small genus of large palms is closely related to *Borassus*; indeed it gets its name from that genus together with the Greek word *dendron*, meaning tree. Stems are large, solitary, gray, and relatively slender considering the large and dense leaf crown. Leaves are palmate, very large, and 40–50 in number. Leaf sheaths are open and split at the base to give a central triangular cleft. Petioles are elongate and covered with easily removed scales. The margins of the petioles are very hard and razor-sharp. At the apex of the petiole, where it joins the blade, there is a prominent hastula. Blades are divided almost to the base into numerous segments, and these are again divided into leaflets.

Inflorescences are borne among the leaves and are usually pendulous, and individual trees bear either male or female inflorescences (i.e., dioecious). Male inflorescences are branched to two orders, and are covered by several bracts, on both peduncle and rachis. The very thick flowering branches are borne in groups of two to five. They are covered with small overlapping bracts, each bract covering a pit containing two to six male flowers. Female inflorescences are either spicate or with to four branches, and have similar bracts and pits as the male inflorescences. Each pit contains only one female flower, and these are very large, with leathery sepals and petals. They are also very strongly scented. Fruits are large, obovoid, brown or green, and usually three-seeded. The seeds are covered in a thick, bony endocarp, and are grooved longitudinally. Endosperm is homogeneous, germination is remote, and the seedling leaf is palmate.

Borassodendron is closely related to *Borassus* but can be distinguished by its nonthorny petioles and unevenly split leaves. The genus contains two species, one in Peninsular Thailand and Peninsular Malaysia, and the other in Borneo (Dransfield 1972a).

Borassodendron machadonis (Ridl.) Becc.   PLATE 4
chang-hai (Tha)

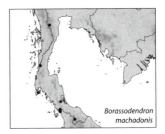

Field characters. Stems solitary, to 20 m tall and 30 cm diameter. Leaves very large; petioles to 4 m long, with very sharp margins; blades dark green on both surfaces, split into to 75 leaflets. Male inflorescences to 2 m long, with 15–20 thick flowering branches; fruits obovoid, to 12 cm long and 10 cm diameter, purple-black.

Range and habitat. Thailand (Peninsular, Southwest) and probably Myanmar (Tanintharyi) (also in Peninsular Malaysia); lowland forest, often on limestone soils, to 700 m elevation.

Synonym. *Borassus machadonis* Ridl.

BORASSUS L.

This small genus is closely related to the last. The name of the genus is from the Greek word *borassos*, which refers, inappropriately, to the date palm. Stems are large, solitary, columnar or swollen, gray, and usually have a large mound of roots at the base. Leaves are very large, costapalmate, and 12–40 in number. Leaf sheaths are open and are split at the base to give a central triangular cleft. Petioles are elongate and the margins are usually covered with irregularly arranged, curved thorns. At the apices of the petioles, where they join the blade, there is a prominent hastula. Blades are divided into numerous leaflets, and these are briefly split at the apices.

Inflorescences are borne among the leaves and are usually pendulous. Individual trees bear either male or female inflorescences (i.e., dioecious). Male inflorescences are branched to two orders, and are covered by several bracts. Flowering branches are borne in groups of one to three, and are very thick. They are covered with small overlapping bracts, each covering a pit containing about 30 male flowers. Female inflorescences are either spicate or with two branches, and have bracts similar to those of the male inflorescences. Each pit contains only one female flower, and these are very large, with leathery sepals and petals. Fruits are large, irregularly globose, brown or green, and one-to three-seeded. The seeds are covered in a thick, bony endocarp, and are grooved longitudinally. The endosperm is homogeneous, germination is remote, and the seedling leaf is undivided.

A genus of five species, widely ranging from Africa to New Guinea. Only one species occurs in our area (Bayton 2007).

Borassus flabellifer L.   PLATE 4

tal (Ban), thnot skar (Cbd), palmyra (Ind), kok mak tan (Lao), htan (Mya), thann (Tha), thot not (Vie)

Field characters. Stems solitary, to 25 m tall and 30 cm diameter. Leaves large, costapalmate; petiole margins with black, curved thorns; leaflets 60–80, stiffly spreading. Inflorescences borne among the leaves; fruits irregularly globose, to 20 cm diameter, yellowish or greenish violet, becoming almost black.
Range and habitat. Bangladesh, Cambodia, China, India, Laos, Myanmar, Sri Lanka, Thailand, and Vietnam (Southern) (also in Indonesia and Peninsular Malaysia); low-lying, flat, disturbed areas, occasionally in hills, to 800 m elevation. A commonly planted palm whose range has been greatly extended by humans (no map provided).
Uses. A widely used and important palm. The leaves are used as paper for writing, as thatching, or for fiber; the immature endosperm is eaten; the mesocarp, seedlings, and heart are eaten; and male inflorescences are tapped for their sweet sap, either drunk fresh, fermented into palm wine, or boiled down and made into sugar.
Synonyms. *Borassus flabelliformis* L., *Borassus sundaicus* Becc., *Borassus tunicatus* Lour., *Lontarus domestica* Gaertn., *Pholidocarpus tunicatus* (Lour.) H. Wendl.

CALAMUS L.

(*Cornera* Furtado, *Rotang* Adans., *Rotanga* Boehm., *Schizospatha* Furtado, *Zalacella* Becc.)

Stems exhibit a great variety of forms. They can be clustered or less often solitary, and most species have slender, climbing stems, often reaching great heights in the forest canopy. The derivation of the name comes from this kind of stems, from the Latin word *calamus*, meaning a reed or cane, itself derived from the Greek word *kalamos*. However, a few species have nonclimbing stems, and these stems are either short and subterranean or free-standing. Leaves are pinnate, spiny, and 10–60 in number. Leaf sheaths are closed in climbing species and open in nonclimbers. Sheaths are variously hairy and spiny, and the nature of these is characteristic for each species. The hairs of young sheaths soon wear off, however, and may not be visible on older sheaths. Spines may be scattered or densely arranged (rarely absent), or arranged in rows, occasionally hairy on the margins, and variously shaped and colored. The apices of the sheaths are usually extended above the point of insertion of the petiole into inconspicuous or prominent ocreas. Just below the petiole is a characteristic swollen part of the sheath, known as the knee. Most species have knees; a few do not, especially the nonclimbers. Another feature of the leaf sheath is the presence or absence of flagella. These arise directly from the sides of the leaf sheaths and consist of a long, slender, whiplike structure that can reach several meters long. They are armed with small, grapnel-like spines, and these cling to surrounding vegetation. A second, similar, climbing organ, the cirrus, is a continuation of the leaf rachis, with grapnel-like spines. In general, species that have flagella do not have cirri, and vice versa, and these are important characters in identification. Leaflets are variously arranged and shaped, and in a few species are whitish or gray on the lower surfaces.

Individual plants of *Calamus* produce either male or female flowers (i.e., dioecious). Inflorescences are usually elongate, and in general male inflorescences are branched to three orders and females to two orders. The inflorescences of some species have whiplike apices, and such inflorescences are referred to as flagellate. The branches of the inflorescences are covered with overlapping, tubular bracts. Inflorescences usually consist of several partial inflorescences, and the form of the bract subtending each partial inflorescence, especially at their apices, is important in identification. Clawed spines are present on the outer surfaces of the bracts, but only in the climbing species. Male flowers are borne along opposite sides of the flowering branches. The female flowers are borne in pairs along opposite sides of the flowering branches; one flower of this pair is sterile. Fruits are mostly small, variously shaped and colored, usually one-seeded, and in some species they are borne on a short stalk. Fruits are always covered with overlapping scales, and these sometimes have a groove down the middle. The endosperm is homogeneous or ruminate, germination is adjacent, and the seedling leaf is bifid or pinnate.

Calamus is the largest genus of palms, containing about 375 species. These are widely distributed from West Africa, India and Sri Lanka, through Southern Asia and Southeast Asia, to Australia and Fiji. There has been only one attempt to revise the whole genus—the remarkable, illustrated works of Beccari (1908, 1913). Although now out of date, these are still the foundation of our systematic knowledge of *Calamus*. One hundred thirty-four species occur in our area (Alam 1990; Amatya 1997; Basu 1992; Beccari 1908, 1913; Chen et al. 2002; de Zoysa 2000; de Zoysa & Vivekanandan 1994; Dransfield 1979a; Evans et al. 2001, 2002; Furtado 1956; Guo Lixiu & Henderson 2007; Henderson 2005; Henderson et al., 2008a; Henderson & Henderson 2007; Hodel 1998; Lakshmana 1993; Noltie 1994; Pei et al. 1991; Renuka 1992, 1995, 1999a, 2000; Wei 1986).

Species of *Calamus* are very similar to the closely related *Daemonorops*, and the two genera are difficult to tell apart. Cirri are present in rather few species of *Calamus*, whereas all *Daemonorops*, except for a few nonclimbing species, have cirri. Most *Calamus* with cirri also have fruits with homogeneous endosperm, at least in our area. A rattan with a cirrus and fruits with ruminate endosperm is very likely to be a *Daemonorops*. Inflorescences of *Calamus* are usually longer than the leaves and often have a flagellate extension. They also have sheathing, tubular bracts that usually do not split, or at least not to the base, and these bracts have grapnel-like spines. Inflorescences of *Daemonorops*, on the other hand, are often short and congested, and the bracts split their entire length, and these either fall off or remain attached and enclosed by the prophyll.

Although there are many of them, *Calamus* species are generally not difficult to identify. The first things to note in identification are whether the stem is climbing or nonclimbing, solitary or clustered, whether a cirrus or flagella is present, and the arrangement of the leaflets. Based on these characters, and especially on the form of the leaf sheaths (spines, knees, and ocreas), it should not be difficult to key out any species. Indeed, it is often possible to identify species just from the leaf sheaths. In the following key and descriptions, note that young plants, and plants whose stems have been repeatedly cut, may produce thickets, and these may appear to be nonclimbing. Also, cirri and flagella may not be present on younger or cut plants. The keys are by country or region, in alphabetical order. In the descriptions, stem diameter includes the leaf sheaths.

Key to the Species of *Calamus* by Country or Region

Andaman and Nicobar Islands

1a. Cirri present; flagella absent . . . . 2.
1b. Cirri absent, rarely short and vestigial; flagella present . . . . 6.

2a. Leaflets irregularly arranged, often in distant, alternate clusters of 2–4 leaflets . . . . *C. palustris.*
2b. Leaflets regularly arranged . . . . 3.

3a. Stems clustered; leaf sheath spines densely covering the sheath . . . . *C. dilaceratus.*
3b. Stems solitary; leaf sheath spines not completely covering the sheath . . . . 4.

4a. Leaflets broadly lanceolate, 15–20 per side of rachis . . . . *C. unifarius.*
4b. Leaflets linear or linear-lanceolate, more than 20 per side of rachis . . . . 5.

5a. Basal parts of stems erect; stems to 15 m long . . . . *C. semierectus.*
5b. Basal parts of stems flexible and climbing; stems to 24 m long . . . . *C. andamanicus.*

6a. Leaves with short and vestigial cirri . . . . *C. basui.*
6b. Leaves without cirri . . . . 7.

7a. Leaflets irregularly arranged or clustered and spreading in different planes . . . . 8.
7b. Leaflets regularly arranged and spreading in the same plane . . . . 9.

8a. Leaf sheaths with scattered, to 4.5-cm-long spines; leaf rachis to 1.3 m long . . . . *C. viminalis.*
8b. Leaf sheaths with densely arranged or short rows of to 6-cm-long spines,
these interspersed among very short spines; leaf rachis to 4 m long . . . . *C. longisetus.*

9a. Leaf sheaths without spines or with very few spines . . . . *C. baratangensis.*
9b. Leaf sheaths with densely arranged spines . . . . 10.

10a. Leaf sheath spines longer at sheath apices . . . . *C. pseudorivalis.*
10b. Leaf sheath spines not longer at sheath apices . . . . *C. nicobaricus.*

Bangladesh

1a. Stems nonclimbing, free-standing; knees, flagella, and cirri absent;
inflorescence bracts without clawed spines; petioles and rachis
with whorls of yellow spines . . . . *C. erectus.*
1b. Stems climbing; knees, flagella, and/or cirri usually present; inflorescence bracts
with clawed spines; petioles and rachis without whorls of yellow spines. . . . . 2.

Key to the Species of *Calamus* by Country or Region (continued)

2a. Flagella absent; cirri present . . . . *C. nambariensis.*
2b. Flagella present; cirri absent . . . . 3.

3a. Leaflets few, 14–21 per side of rachis, the apical ones inserted close together in a fan shape . . . . . . 4.
3b. Leaflets numerous, 27–75 per side of rachis, the apical ones not inserted close together
in a fan shape . . . . 5.

4a. Leaf sheaths without spines or with scattered, black-tipped, conical-based, to 0.5-cm-long
spines; ocreas not bristly; petioles very short; leaflets curled over at the tips . . . . *C. gracilis.*
4b. Leaf sheaths with densely arranged, brown, flattened spines, interspersed with black,
needlelike, to 4-cm-long spines; ocreas densely bristly; petioles present;
leaflets not curled over at the tips . . . . *C. floribundus.*

5a. Leaflets irregularly arranged or clustered and spreading in different planes . . . . 6.
5b. Leaflets regularly arranged and spreading in the same plane . . . . 7.

6a. Leaf sheaths with scattered, to 4.5-cm-long spines; leaf rachis to 1.3 m long . . . . *C. viminalis.*
6b. Leaf sheaths with densely arranged or short rows of to 6-cm-long spines,
these interspersed among very short spines; leaf rachis to 4 m long . . . . *C. longisetus.*

7a. Leaf sheath spines not longer at sheath apices; ocreas very small; leaf sheaths
often ridged . . . . *C. tenuis.*
7b. Leaf sheath spines longer at sheath apices; ocreas prominent; leaf sheaths not
ridged . . . . 8.

8a. Leaf sheaths with upward-pointing spines; inflorescence bracts not sheathing,
split open and flat, brown . . . . *C. guruba.*
8b. Leaf sheath spines not upward-pointing; inflorescence bracts
not split open and flat, nor brown . . . . 9.

9a. Stems to 2 cm diameter; leaf sheath spines to 2.5 (to 5 at sheath apices) cm long,
those at sheath apices needlelike . . . . *C. leptospadix.*
9b. Stems to 5 cm diameter; leaf sheath spines to 5.5 (sometimes to 10 at sheath apices)
cm long, those at sheath apices flattened . . . . *C. flagellum.*

Bhutan and Nepal

1a. Stems nonclimbing, free-standing; knees, flagella, and cirri absent; inflorescence
bracts without clawed spines; petioles and rachis with whorls of yellow spines . . . . *C. erectus.*
1b. Stems climbing; knees, flagella, and/or cirri usually present; inflorescence bracts
with clawed spines; petioles and rachis without whorls of yellow spines . . . . 2.

2a. Flagella absent; cirri present . . . . *C. nambariensis.*
2b. Flagella present; cirri absent . . . . 3.

3a. Leaflets 8–15 per side of rachis, broadly lanceolate . . . . *C. acanthospathus.*
3b. Leaflets 27–65 per side of rachis, linear or lanceolate . . . . 4.

4b. Leaf sheath spines not longer at sheath apices; ocreas very small; leaf sheaths
often ridged . . . . *C. tenuis.*
4a. Leaf sheath spines longer at sheath apices; ocreas prominent; leaf sheaths not ridged . . . . 5.

5a. Leaf sheaths with upward-pointing spines; inflorescence bracts not sheathing,
split open and flat, brown . . . . *C. guruba.*
5b. Leaf sheath spines not upward-pointing; inflorescence bracts not split open
and flat, nor brown . . . . 6.

6a. Stems to 2 cm diameter; leaf sheath spines to 2.5 (to 5 at sheath apices) cm long,
those at sheath apices needlelike . . . . *C. leptospadix.*
6b. Stems to 5 cm diameter; leaf sheath spines to 5.5 (sometimes to 10 at sheath apices)
cm long, those at sheath apices flattened . . . . *C. flagellum.*

Cambodia

1a. Stems nonclimbing, free-standing, scrambling, or short and subterranean; knees, flagella, and
   cirri usually absent, rarely vestigial flagella present; inflorescence bracts without clawed spines . . . . . 2.
1b. Stems climbing; knees, flagella, and/or cirri usually present; inflorescence bracts with
   clawed spines. . . . . 3.

2a. Stems free-standing or scrambling, to 2 m long; leaflets light gray-green on the lower
   surfaces . . . . *C. salicifolius.*
2b. Stems short and subterranean; leaflets green on the lower surfaces. . . . . *C. acanthophyllus.*

3a. Flagella absent; cirri present . . . . 4.
3b. Flagella present; cirri absent . . . . 5.

4a. Leaflets about 65 per side of rachis, linear, pendulous, regularly arranged;
   mangrove forest and other places near the sea . . . . *C. erinaceus.*
4b. Leaflets 12–25 per side of rachis, broadly lanceolate, not pendulous, irregularly arranged,
   often in distant, alternate clusters of 2–4 leaflets; lowland or montane rain forest . . . . *C. palustris.*

5a. Leaflets rhomboidal . . . . *C. bousigonii.*
5b. Leaflets linear, linear-lanceolate, or lanceolate . . . . 6.

6a. Leaf rachis to 0.5 m long with 8–13 leaflets per side, the apical ones inserted
   close together in a fan shape, the apical pair joined at their bases . . . . *C. tetradactylus.*
6b. Leaf rachis 1–3 m long with 16–65 leaflets per side, the apical ones not inserted
   close together in a fan shape, the apical pair not joined at their bases . . . . 7.

7a. Leaflets distinctly clustered, spreading in different planes . . . . *C. viminalis.*
7b. Leaflets regularly arranged, or regularly arranged but with gaps, spreading in the same
   plane . . . . 8.

8a. Petioles short or absent; leaflets grayish green on the lower surfaces; basal leaflets
   often swept back across the sheath; leaf sheath spines not longer at the sheath apices . . . . *C. godefroyi.*
8b. Petioles present; leaflets green on the lower surfaces; basal leaflets not swept back
   across the sheath; leaf sheath spines sometimes longer at the sheath apices . . . . 9.

9a. Leaf sheaths without spines, or with a few spines to 0.7 cm long; endosperm ruminate . . . . . *C. lateralis.*
9b. Leaf sheaths with spines to 2 cm or more long; endosperm not or only slightly ruminate . . . . 10.

10a. Leaf sheaths often with ridges, with scattered or rows of to 2-cm-long spines
   with oblique, crescent-shaped bases . . . . *C. tenuis.*
10b. Leaf sheaths without ridges, with scattered to densely arranged to 6-cm-long spines
   without with oblique, crescent-shaped bases . . . . 11.

11a. Stems to 7 cm diameter; leaf sheaths with densely arranged rows of yellowish to black,
   to 6 (to 15 at sheath apices)-cm-long spines . . . . *C. rudentum.*
11b. Stems to 3.5 cm diameter; leaf sheaths with scattered to densely arranged,
   dark brown, to 4.5 (sometimes to 10 at sheath apices)-cm-long spines . . . . 12.

12a. Ocreas conspicuous, tattering and soon falling; inflorescence bracts not sheathing,
   split open and flat, brown . . . . *C. guruba.*
12b. Ocreas inconspicuous; inflorescence bracts tubular . . . . *C. siamensis.*

China and Taiwan

1a. Taiwan. . . . . 2.
1b. China . . . . 4.

2a. Flagella present; cirri absent . . . . *C. beccarii.*
2b. Flagella absent; cirri present . . . . 3.

3a. Stems solitary; Lanyu Island . . . . *C. siphonospathus.*
3b. Stems clustered; all other areas . . . . *C. formosanus.*

(continued)

Key to the Species of *Calamus* by Country or Region (continued)

4a. Stems nonclimbing, free-standing or short and subterranean; knees, flagella, and cirri usually absent; inflorescence bracts without clawed spines . . . . 5.
4b. Stems climbing; knees, flagella, and/or cirri usually present; inflorescence bracts with clawed spines . . . . 9.

5a. Leaflets whitish on the lower surfaces . . . . 6.
5b. Leaflets green on the lower surfaces . . . . 7.

6a. Leaflets 11–15 per side of rachis, lanceolate to broadly lanceolate, irregularly arranged in distant clusters . . . . *C. oxycarpus.*
6b. Leaflets 30–45 per side of rachis, linear, regularly arranged but with gaps . . . . *C. macrorhynchus.*

7a. Petioles and rachis with whorls of yellow spines . . . . *C. erectus.*
7b. Petioles and rachis without whorls of yellow spines . . . . 8.

8a. Leaflets regularly arranged and spreading in the same plane . . . .*C. dianbaiensis.*
8b. Leaflets irregularly arranged in remote clusters and spreading in different planes . . . . *C. thysanolepis.*

9a. Flagella absent; cirri present . . . . 10.
9b. Flagella present; cirri absent . . . . 14.

10a. Leaflets 3–10 per side of rachis . . . . 11.
10b. Leaflets 14–40 per side of rachis . . . . 12.

11a. Leaflets to 5 per side of rachis, regularly arranged; fruits globose to ellipsoid, to 1 cm long and 0.8 cm diameter, not stalked, the scales not grooved . . . . *C. compsostachys.*
11b. Leaflets to 10 per side of rachis, clustered in alternate pairs; fruits ovoid to ellipsoid, to 1.8 cm long and 1.2 cm diameter, stalked, with grooved scales . . . . *C. austroguanxiensis.*

12a. Leaflets 36–40 per side of rachis; Yunnan . . . . *C. nambariensis.*
12b. Leaflets 14–22 per side of rachis; Hainan . . . . 13.

13a. Leaflets clustered in alternate groups of 2 or 3 . . . .*C. egregius.*
13b. Leaflets regularly arranged . . . . *C. simplicifolius.*

14a. Leaflets 3–16 per side of rachis, usually irregularly arranged, the apical ones inserted close together in a fan shape, the apical pair free or joined at their bases . . . . 15.
14b. Leaflets 27–70 per side of rachis, the apical ones not inserted close together in a fan shape, the apical pair not joined at their bases . . . . 21.

15a. Leaflets whitish on the lower surfaces . . . . *C. albidus.*
15b. Leaflets green on the lower surfaces . . . . 16.

16a. Stems to 5 cm diameter; petioles very short or absent; ocreas densely bristly; leaflets broadly lanceolate . . . .*C. acanthospathus.*
16b. Stems to 2 cm diameter; petioles usually present and well developed; ocreas not or rarely densely bristly; leaflets linear to lanceolate, not broadly lanceolate . . . . 17.

17a. Leaflets regularly arranged but with wide gaps between groups, shiny green, curled over at the tips . . . . 18.
17b. Leaflets regularly arranged or clustered, dull green, not curled over at the tips . . . . 19.

18a. Fruits to 2 cm long and 1 cm diameter; Yunnan . . . . *C. gracilis.*
18b. Fruits to 2.7 cm long and 2 cm diameter; Hainan . . . . *C. hainanensis.*

19a. Leaf sheath spines triangular, not longer at the sheath apices (rarely spines absent); Guangdong, Guangxi, Hainan, Hong Kong, and possibly Fujian and Yunnan . . . . *C. tetradactylus.*
19b. Leaf sheath spines needlelike, longer at the sheath apices; Hainan . . . . 20.

20a. Leaflets broadly lanceolate . . . .*C. pulchellus.*
20b. Leaflets linear-lanceolate . . . . *C. tetradactyloides.*

21a. Leaf sheaths with densely arranged, oblique rows of glossy, black or brown,
  flattened, to 4 (to 10 at sheath apices)-cm-long spines . . . . *C. rhabdocladus.*
21b. Leaf sheath spines not in rows . . . . 22.

22a. Leaflets strongly clustered, spreading in different planes . . . . 23.
22b. Leaflets not strongly clustered, spreading in the same plane . . . . 25.

23a. Fruits black; Guangxi . . . .*C. melanochrous.*
23b. Fruits brown, whitish, or yellowish; Yunnan . . . . 24.

24a. Ocreas short; knees present; fruits to 1 cm diameter . . . .*C. viminalis.*
24b. Ocreas to 35 cm long, soon tattering; knees absent; fruits to 2.5 cm diameter . . . . . *C. wuliangshanensis.*

25a. Leaf sheath spines upward-pointing; ocreas conspicuous, tattering and soon falling;
  inflorescence bracts not sheathing, split open and flat, brown . . . . *C. guruba.*
25b. Leaf sheath spines not upward-pointing; ocreas short, inconspicuous;
  inflorescence bracts not split open and flat, nor brown . . . . 26.

26a. Leaf sheath spines densely arranged, to 5.5 (sometimes to 10 at sheath apices)
  cm long, interspersed with shorter spines . . . . *C. flagellum.*
26b. Leaf sheath spines scattered, to 2.5 (sometimes to 7 at sheath apices) cm long,
  usually not interspersed with shorter spines . . . . 27.

27a. Ocreas densely bristly; leaf sheath spines not longer at sheath apices; inflorescence
  bracts not tattering . . . . *C. walkeri.*
27b. Ocreas not densely bristly; leaf sheath spines sometimes longer at sheath apices;
  inflorescence bracts tattering . . . . 28.

28a. Leaf sheaths with to 2 (sometimes to 7 at sheath apices)-cm-long spines; Guangxi,
  Yunnan, and just reaching Sichuan . . . . *C. henryanus.*
28b. Leaf sheaths with to 1.5 (sometimes to 3 at sheath apices)-cm-long spines; Hainan . . . . *C. multispicatus.*

India

1a. Southern India (Andhra Pradesh, Goa, Karnataka, Kerala, Maharastra, Tamil Nadu) . . . . 2.
1b. Northern India (Arunachal Pradesh, Assam, Bihar, Himachal Pradesh, Madhya Pradesh,
  Manipur, Meghalaya, Mizoram, Nagaland, Orissa, Sikkim, Tripura, Uttar Pradesh,
  Uttarakhand, West Bengal) . . . . 25.

2a. Flagella absent; cirri present . . . . 3.
2b. Flagella present; cirri absent . . . . 4.

3a. Leaflets regularly arranged, linear, pendulous; Karnataka, Kerala . . . . *C. nagbettai.*
3b. Leaflets clustered, lanceolate, not pendulous; Andhra Pradesh . . . . *C. nambariensis.*

4a. Leaflets few, 15 or less per side of rachis, clustered, the apical ones inserted close
  together in a fan shape, the apical pair usually joined at their bases . . . . 5.
4b. Leaflets numerous, more than 15 per side of rachis, usually regularly arranged, the apical
  ones not inserted close together in a fan shape, not or rarely joined at their bases . . . . 10.

5a. Stems spreading by stolons . . . . *C. stoloniferus.*
5b. Stems not spreading by stolons . . . . 6.

6a. Leaflets about 3 per side of rachis . . . . *C. pseudofeanus.*
6b. Leaflets to 15 per side of rachis . . . . 7.

7a. Leaf sheath spines longer at sheath apices; leaflets linear or lanceolate . . . . 8.
7b. Leaf sheath spines not longer at sheath apices; leaflets broadly lanceolate . . . . 9.

8a. Inflorescence bracts tubular; fruits ovoid, to 1.8 cm long, not stalked . . . .*C. brandisii.*
8b. Inflorescence bracts split and open at the apices; fruits globose, to 1 cm long, stalked . . . *C. travancoricus.*

9a. Leaf sheaths with to 1.5-cm-long spines . . . . *C. rheedei.*
9b. Leaf sheaths with to 2-cm-long spines . . . .*C. vattayila.*

(continued)

Key to the Species of *Calamus* by Country or Region (continued)

10a. Leaflets irregularly arranged and spreading in different planes . . . . 11.
10b. Leaflets regularly arranged and spreading in the same plane . . . . 12.

11a. Leaf sheaths with ridges of black spines . . . . *C. thwaitesii.*
11b. Leaf sheaths without ridges, the spines greenish or brownish . . . . *C. viminalis.*

12a. Leaf sheaths spines longer at sheath apices, sometimes only a few spines longer
but then ocreas prominent, to 10 cm long . . . . 13.
12b. Leaf sheath spines not longer at sheath apices; ocreas seldom prominent . . . . 14.

13a. Leaf sheath spines longer at sheath apices, arranged in a fan; ocreas
inconspicuous . . . .*C. hookerianus.*
13b. Leaf sheath spines not arranged in a fan at the sheath apices, usually
only a few spines longer; ocreas well developed, to 10 cm long . . . . *C. pseudotenuis.*

14a. Stems often forming thickets; apical leaflets very small; leaflets without long hairs
on upper and lower surfaces; wet areas (river margins, marshes, coastal swamps) . . . . *C. rotang.*
14b. Stems climbing; apical leaflets not very small; leaflets usually with long hairs on upper and/or
lower surfaces; lowland or montane rain forests . . . . 15.

15a. Stems solitary . . . . 16.
15b. Stems clustered . . . . 19.

16a. Petioles and rachis exuding a milky latex when cut . . . .*C. prasinus.*
16b. Petioles and rachis not exuding a milky latex when cut . . . . 17.

17a. Leaf sheaths green with few, scattered spines . . . . *C. dransfieldii.*
17b. Leaf sheaths darker green, without hairs, with more densely arranged spines. . . . . 18.

18a. Leaf sheath spines to 1 cm long . . . . *C. neelagiricus.*
18b. Leaf sheath spines to 2 cm long . . . . *C. delessertianus.*

19a. Flagella rooting at the apices and forming new plants . . . . *C. lacciferus.*
19b. Flagella not rooting at the apices . . . . 20.

20a. Leaf sheaths, petioles, rachis, and inflorescence axes densely covered with red-brown
or gray hairs initially; petioles very short, less than 5 cm long . . . . *C. metzianus.*
20b. Leaf sheaths, rachis, and inflorescence axes not densely covered with hairs initially;
petioles elongate, to 30 cm long . . . . 21.

21a. Leaflets without long hair on the veins above and below; fruits brown or black with
black-fringed scales . . . .*C. wightii.*
21b. Leaflets with long hairs on the veins above and below; fruits yellow or green,
without fringed scales . . . . 22.

22a. Ocreas prominent, spiny; leaf sheath spines sometimes to 4 cm long at sheath apices;
apical leaflets united at their bases . . . .*C. karnatakensis.*
22b. Ocreas inconspicuous, not spiny; leaf sheath spines not longer at sheath apices; apical
leaflets not or only briefly joined at their bases . . . . 23.

23a. Leaf sheaths with scattered to densely arranged, upward-pointing spines;
fruits not stalked . . . .*C. lakshmanae.*
23b. Leaf sheaths with very few or scattered, horizontally spreading spines; fruits stalked . . . . 24.

24a. Leaf sheaths with very few, black-tipped, to 1-cm-long spines; apical pair of leaflets
briefly joined at their bases . . . . *C. shendurunii.*
24b. Leaf sheaths with scattered, greenish, to 1.5-cm-long spines; apical pair of leaflets
not joined at their bases . . . . *C. gamblei.*

25a. Stems nonclimbing, free-standing; knees, flagella, and cirri absent; inflorescence bracts
without clawed spines; petioles and rachis with whorls of yellow spines . . . . *C. erectus.*
25b. Stems climbing; knees, flagella, and/or cirri usually present; inflorescence bracts
with clawed spines; petioles and rachis without whorls of yellow spines . . . . 26.

26a. Flagella absent; cirri present . . . . *C. nambariensis.*
26b. Flagella present; cirri absent . . . . 27.

27a. Leaflets few, 4–21 per side of rachis, usually irregularly arranged, the apical ones inserted
    close together in a fan shape, the apical pair free or often joined at their bases . . . . 28.
27b. Leaflets numerous, 27–65 per side of rachis, usually regularly arranged, the apical ones not
    inserted close together in a fan shape, not or rarely joined at their bases . . . . 32.

28a. Stems to 5 cm diameter, solitary or weakly clustered; leaf sheath spines with sinuous
    margins and densely hairy initially; leaflets broadly lanceolate . . . . *C. acanthospathus.*
28b. Stems to 2.5 cm diameter, usually clustered; leaf sheath spines not with sinuous margins
    and densely hairy initially; leaflets linear or lanceolate . . . . 29.

29a. Leaflets 11–21 per side of rachis; leaf sheath spines of 2 kinds, 1 flattened, brown,
    the other needlelike, black, both kinds to 4 cm long . . . . *C. floribundus.*
29b. Leaflets 4–15 per side of rachis; leaf sheath spines of 1 kind only, to 1 cm long . . . . 30.

30a. Leaflets 8–15 per side of rachis; leaf sheaths without spines or with conical-based,
    to 0.5-cm-long spines; fruits ovoid to ellipsoid, to 2 cm long and 1 cm diameter . . . . *C. gracilis.*
30b. Leaflets 4–6 per side of rachis; leaf sheaths with spines to 1 cm long, without conical bases;
    fruits globose, to 1 cm diameter . . . . 31.

31a. Leaf rachis to 0.6 m long with to 6 leaflets per side; leaf sheaths with densely arranged,
    greenish spines, these sometimes in short rows . . . . *C. kingianus.*
31b. Leaf rachis to 0.3 m long with 4 or 5 leaflets per side; leaf sheaths sparsely covered
    with brown spines, not in short rows . . . . *C. meghalayensis.*

32a. Leaflets irregularly arranged or clustered and spreading in different planes . . . . *C. viminalis.*
32b. Leaflets regularly arranged and spreading in the same plane . . . . 33.

33a. Leaf sheath spines not longer at sheath apices, spines with oblique, crescent-shaped bases;
    ocreas very small; leaf sheaths often ridged . . . . *C. tenuis.*
33b. Leaf sheath spines longer at sheath apices, spines not with oblique, crescent-shaped bases;
    ocreas prominent; leaf sheaths not ridged . . . . 34.

34a. Leaf sheaths with upward-pointing spines; inflorescence bracts not sheathing,
    split open and flat, brown . . . . *C. guruba.*
34b. Leaf sheaths spines not upward-pointing; inflorescence bracts not split open and flat, nor brown . . . . 35.

35a. Stems to 2 cm diameter; leaf sheath spines to 2.5 (to 5 at sheath apices)-cm-long spines,
    those at sheath apices needlelike . . . . *C. leptospadix.*
35b. Stems to 5 cm diameter; leaf sheath spines to 5.5 (sometimes to 10 at
    sheath apices)-cm-long spines, those at sheath apices flattened . . . . *C. flagellum.*

Laos
1a. Stems nonclimbing, free-standing or short and subterranean; knees, flagella,
    and cirri usually absent; inflorescence bracts without clawed spines . . . . 2.
1b. Stems climbing; knees, flagella, and/or cirri usually present; inflorescence bracts with clawed spines . . 4.

2a. Stems short and subterranean; petiole spines scattered, not in whorls . . . . *C. acanthophyllus.*
2b. Stems to 6 m long; petiole spines in whorls . . . . 3.

3a. Stems to 6 m long; leaf rachis to 3 m long; fruits to 5 cm long and 2.5 cm diameter . . . . *C. erectus.*
3b. Stems to 1 m long; leaf rachis to 1 m long; fruits to 1.2 cm long and 0.9 cm diameter . . . . . . *C. harmandii.*

4a. Flagella absent; cirri present . . . . 5.
4b. Flagella usually present; cirri absent or rarely short and vestigial . . . . 6.

5a. Female flowering branches to 7 cm long, straight; fruits not stalked, usually less than
    1.2 cm long, the scales not grooved; leaflets usually less than 35 cm long . . . . *C. palustris.*
5b. Female flowering branches to 10 cm long, zigzag; fruits stalked, to 2.4 cm long,
    rarely more, the scales grooved; leaflets usually more than 40 cm long . . . . *C. nambariensis.*

(continued)

Key to the Species of *Calamus* by Country or Region (continued)

6a. Leaflets rhomboidal . . . . *C. bousigonii.*
6b. Leaflets linear, linear-lanceolate, lanceolate, or broadly lanceolate . . . . 7.

7a. Leaflets 3–15 per side of rachis, the apical ones inserted close together in a fan shape
(or occasionally vestigial cirri present), the apical pair free or often joined at their bases . . . . 8.
7b. Leaflets 15–65 per side of rachis, the apical ones not inserted close together in a fan shape
(vestigial cirri absent), nor the apical pair joined at their bases . . . . 15.

8a. Stems to 5 cm diameter, solitary or weakly clustered; leaf sheath spines with sinuous
margins and densely hairy initially; leaflets broadly lanceolate . . . .*C. acanthospathus.*
8b. Stems to 2 cm diameter, usually clustered; leaf sheath spines not with sinuous margins
nor densely hairy initially; leaflets linear or lanceolate . . . . 9.

9a. Leaflets gray on the lower surfaces . . . . *C. minor.*
9b. Leaflets green on the lower surfaces . . . . 10.

10a. Leaves with vestigial cirri . . . . *C. bimaniferus.*
10b. Leaves without vestigial cirri . . . . 11.

11a. Leaf sheaths without spines or with scattered, black-tipped, conical-based,
to 0.5-cm-long spines; petioles very short; leaflets curled over at the tips. . . . . *C. gracilis.*
11b. Leaf sheath spines not as above; petioles usually well developed; leaflets not curled
over at the tips . . . . 12.

12a. Stems solitary . . . . *C. solitarius.*
12b. Stems clustered . . . . 13.

13a. Apical pair of leaflets not joined at their bases . . . .*C. evansii.*
13b. Apical pair of leaflets joined at their bases . . . . 14.

14a. Leaf sheath spines triangular, to 1.5 cm long, or spines absent; partial inflorescences
more than 20 cm long . . . . *C. tetradactylus.*
14b. Leaf sheath spines needlelike, to 0.7 cm long; partial inflorescences less than
10 cm long . . . . *C. oligostachys.*

15a. Leaflets whitish on the lower surfaces . . . . *C. laoensis.*
15b. Leaflets green on the lower surfaces. . . . . 16.

16a. Stems solitary . . . . *C. poilanei.*
16b. Stems clustered . . . . 17.

17a. Leaflets clustered, spreading in different planes . . . .*C. viminalis.*
17b. Leaflets regularly arranged, or regularly arranged but with gaps, spreading in the
same plane. . . . . 18.

18a. Leaf sheath spines conspicuously longer at sheath apices . . . . 19.
18b. Leaf sheath spines not longer at sheath apices (sometimes only a few spines longer) . . . . 21.

19a. Leaf sheath spines scattered, not in rows . . . . *C. flagellum.*
19b. Leaf sheaths with rows of spines . . . . 20.

20a. Leaf sheaths with rows of yellowish to black, to 6 (to 15 at sheath apices)-cm-long
spines, the rows borne on ridges interspersed with shorter, needlelike spines; leaf
rachis to 3 m long . . . .*C. rudentum.*
20b. Leaf sheaths with oblique rows of glossy, black or brown, to 4
(to 10 at sheath apices)-cm-long spines; leaf rachis to 1.5 m long . . . .*C. rhabdocladus.*

21a. Petioles short or absent; basal few leaflets often swept back across the sheath . . . . *C. godefroyi.*
21b. Petioles usually elongate, rarely short or absent; basal few leaflets
not swept back across the sheath . . . . 22.

22a. Leaf sheaths often with ridges; leaf sheath spines with oblique, crescent-shaped bases . . . . . .*C. tenuis.*
22b. Leaf sheaths without ridges; leaf sheath spines not with oblique, crescent-shaped bases . . . . 23.

23a. Leaf sheaths with to 4.5 (sometimes a few spines to 7 at sheath apices)-cm-long spines,
 interspersed among shorter spines; inflorescence bracts tubular . . . . *C. siamensis.*
23b. Leaf sheaths with to 2 (sometimes a few spines to 7 at sheath apices)-cm-long spines,
 not interspersed with shorter spines; inflorescence bracts tattering at the apices . . . . *C. henryanus.*

Myanmar

1a. Stems nonclimbing, free-standing; knees, flagella, and cirri absent; inflorescence bracts
 without clawed spines . . . . 2.
1b. Stems climbing; knees, flagella, and/or cirri usually present; inflorescence bracts
 with clawed spines . . . . 4.

2a. Leaflets whitish on the lower surfaces . . . . *C. arborescens.*
2b. Leaflets green on the lower surfaces . . . . 3.

3a. Petioles and rachis with whorls of yellow spines; leaflets regularly arranged; Kachin,
 Sagaing, Shan . . . . *C. erectus.*
3b. Petioles and rachis without whorls of yellow spines; leaflets clustered; Tanintharyi . . . . *C. concinnus.*

4a. Flagella absent; cirri present . . . . 5.
4b. Flagella present; cirri absent . . . . 8.

5a. Upper surfaces of petioles not or scarcely spiny . . . . 6.
5b. Upper surfaces of petioles spiny . . . . 7.

6a. Petioles present, with spines along the margins; leaflets with yellowish bases . . . . *C. oxleyanus.*
6b. Petioles very short, sparsely spiny; leaflets green at the base . . . . *C. axillaris.*

7a. Female flowering branches to 7 cm long, straight; fruits not stalked, usually less
 than 1.2 cm long, the scales not grooved; leaflets usually less than 35 cm long . . . . *C. palustris.*
7b. Female flowering branches to 10 cm long, zigzag; fruits stalked, to 2.4 cm long,
 rarely more, the scales grooved; leaflets usually more than 40 cm long . . . . *C. nambariensis.*

8a. Leaflets 4–21 per side of rachis, usually irregularly arranged, the apical ones
 usually inserted close together in a fan shape, the apical pair free or often joined
 at their bases . . . . 9.
8b. Leaflets 27–75 per side of rachis, usually regularly arranged, the apical ones not inserted
 close together in a fan shape, nor the apical pair joined at their bases . . . . 19.

9a. Stems to 5 cm diameter, solitary or weakly clustered; leaf sheath spines with sinuous
 margins and densely hairy initially; leaflets broadly lanceolate; Kachin . . . . *C. acanthospathus.*
9b. Stems to 2 cm diameter, usually clustered; leaf sheath spines not with sinuous margins
 nor densely hairy initially; leaflets linear or lanceolate; widespread . . . . 10.

10a. Leaflets grayish or whitish on the lower surfaces . . . . 11.
10b. Leaflets green on the lower surfaces . . . . 13.

11a. Basal pair of leaflets swept back across the sheath . . . . *C. griseus.*
11b. Basal pair of leaflets not swept back across the sheath . . . . 12.

12a. Ocreas very short; leaf sheath spines to 0.5 cm long, not longer at the sheath apices. . . . . . *C. hypoleucus.*
12b. Ocreas to 5 cm long; leaf sheath spines to 2 cm long, those at the sheath apices
 to 5 cm long . . . . *C. platyspathus.*

13a. Basal pair of leaflets often swept back across the sheath . . . . *C. javensis.*
13b. Basal pair of leaflets not swept back across the sheath . . . . 14.

14a. Petioles very short or absent; leaf sheaths without spines or with conical-based,
 to 0.5-cm-long spines . . . . 15.
14b. Petioles present; leaf sheath spines to 1 cm or more long, not conical-based . . . . 16.

(continued)

Key to the Species of *Calamus* by Country or Region (continued)

15a. Leaflets to 8 per side of rachis, not curled over at the apices, the apical pair joined
at their bases; Tanintharyi . . . .*C. pandanosmus.*
15b. Leaflets 8–15 per side of rachis, curled over at the tips, the apical pair not joined
at their bases; Kachin, Sagaing, Shan . . . . *C. gracilis.*

16a. Leaf sheaths spines often downward-pointing; leaflets regularly but distantly arranged;
Tanintharyi . . . .*C. luridus.*
16b. Leaf sheath spines horizontally spreading; leaflets irregularly arranged, sometimes
in distant groups; Kachin, Sagaing . . . . 17.

17a. Leaflets 14–21 per side of rachis; leaf sheath spines of 2 kinds, 1 flattened, brown,
the other needlelike, black, both kinds to 4 cm long . . . . *C. floribundus.*
17b. Leaflets 3–10 per side of rachis; leaf sheath spines of 1 kind only, flattened, to 1 cm long. . . . . 18.

18a. Rachis to 0.7 m long with 4–10 leaflets per side, the apical pair free or briefly joined
at their bases; inflorescence bracts without bristles at the apices . . . .*C. spicatus.*
18b. Rachis to 0.3 m long with 4–6 leaflets per side, the apical pair joined at their bases;
inflorescence bracts with the apical margins densely covered with bristles . . . . *C. hukaungensis.*

19a. Leaflets clustered, spreading in different planes . . . . 20.
19b. Leaflets regularly arranged, or regularly arranged but with gaps, spreading in the same plane . . . . . . 21.

20a. Leaf sheaths with densely arranged or short rows of to 6-cm-long spines (sometimes
to 10 cm long at sheath apices), these interspersed among very short spines . . . . *C. longisetus.*
20b. Leaf sheaths with scattered, to 4.5-cm-long spines, not interspersed with short spines . . . . .*C. viminalis.*

21a. Stems solitary . . . .*C. peregrinus.*
21b. Stems clustered . . . . 22.

22a. Leaf sheath spines longer at sheath apices . . . . 23.
22b. Leaf sheath spines not longer at sheath apices (sometimes only a few spines longer). . . . . 26.

23a. Leaf sheaths with densely arranged rows of spines, the rows borne on ridges;
ocreas inconspicuous; Tanintharyi . . . . *C. rudentum.*
23b. Leaf sheath spines not in rows; ocreas prominent; widespread. 24.

24a. Leaf sheaths with upward-pointing spines; inflorescence bracts not sheathing,
split open and flat, brown . . . . C. guruba.
24b. Leaf sheath spines not upward-pointing; inflorescence bracts not split open and flat,
nor brown . . . . 25.

25a. Stems to 2 cm diameter; leaf sheath spines to 2.5 (to 5 at sheath apices) cm long,
those at sheath apices needlelike . . . . C. leptospadix.
25b. Stems to 5 cm diameter; leaf sheath spines to 5.5 (sometimes to 10 at sheath apices)
cm long, those at sheath apices flattened . . . . C. flagellum.

26a. Leaf sheath spines upward-pointing, to 1 cm long; fruits to 2.5 cm long, stalked . . . . . C. melanacanthus.
26b. Leaf sheath spines horizontally spreading, to 4.5 cm or more long; fruits to 1.5 cm long,
not stalked . . . . 27.

27a. Leaf sheath spines with oblique, crescent-shaped bases; leaf sheaths often with ridges . . . . . . C. tenuis.
27b. Leaf sheath spines not with oblique, crescent-shaped bases; leaf sheaths without ridges . . . . 28.

28a. Leaf sheaths green, with brown hairs, with brown, to 4.5 (sometimes to 7
at sheath apices)-cm-long spines, interspersed among shorter spines . . . . C. siamensis.
28b. Leaf sheaths with mottled, reddish brown hairs, with black-tipped, to 2
(sometimes to 7 at sheath apices)-cm-long spines . . . . .C. henryanus.

Sri Lanka

1a. Flagella absent; cirri present . . . . 2.
1b. Flagella present; cirri absent . . . . 3.

2a. Leaf sheaths with well-spaced rings of spines; leaflets green on lower surfaces . . . . *C. zeylanicus.*
2b. Leaf sheaths with closely spaced rings of spines; leaflets whitish on lower surfaces . . . . *C. ovoideus.*

3a. Leaflets few, 6 or less per side of rachis, the apical pair usually joined at their bases . . . . 4.
3b. Leaflets numerous, more than 15 per side of rachis, the apical pair not joined at their
bases . . . . 6.

4a. At least 1 pair of basal leaflets present, the others arranged in a fan shape at apices of rachis . . . . *C. pachystemonus.*
4b. All leaflets at apices of rachis, arranged in a fan shape . . . . 5.

5a. Leaflets linear; petioles with short, recurved spines only . . . . *C. radiatus.*
5b. Leaflets broadly lanceolate; petioles with short recurved spines and straight spines
to 1.7 cm long . . . . *C. digitatus.*

6a. Leaflets irregularly arranged and spreading in different planes; leaf sheaths with ridges;
inflorescence bracts tattering at the apices . . . . *C. thwaitesii.*
6b. Leaflets regularly arranged and spreading in the same plane; leaf sheaths without ridges;
inflorescence bracts not tattering at the apices . . . . 7.

7a. Petioles short or absent; spines at sheath apices not longer than others; stems often
forming thickets or climbing; palms of wet areas (river margins, marshes, coastal swamps) . . . . 8.
7b. Petioles well developed; spines at sheath apices usually longer than others; stems climbing;
palms of lowland or montane rain forests . . . . 9.

8a. Sheaths green, without hairs; apical leaflets very small . . . . *C. rotang.*
8b. Sheaths with dense, red-brown hairs; apical leaflets not very small . . . . *C. metzianus.*

9a. Ocreas short, less than 1 cm long; leaf sheath spines dense at sheath apices . . . . *C. deliculatus.*
9a. Ocreas well developed, to 10 cm long; leaf sheath spines few at sheath apices . . . . *C. pseudotenuis.*

Thailand

1a. Stems nonclimbing, free-standing or short and subterranean; knees, flagella,
and cirri usually absent; inflorescence bracts without clawed spines . . . . 2.
1b. Stems climbing; knees, flagella, and/or cirri usually present; inflorescence bracts
with clawed spines . . . . 9.

2a. Leaflets dull gray or whitish on the lower surfaces . . . . 3.
2b. Leaflets green on the lower surfaces . . . . 4.

3a. Stems creeping, usually subterranean, sometimes erect, to 1.5 m long and 20 cm diameter;
Peninsular . . . . *C. castaneus.*
3b. Stems free-standing, to 10 m long and 6.5 cm diameter; Southwest . . . . *C. arborescens.*

4a. Petioles and rachis with whorls of yellow spines . . . . *C. erectus.*
4b. Petioles and rachis without whorls of yellow spines . . . . 5.

5a. Stems solitary; leaf sheath spines to 45 cm long at sheath apices; leaflets strongly folded,
regularly arranged . . . . *C. sedens.*
5b. Stems usually clustered; leaf sheaths spines not longer at sheath apices; leaflets not
strongly folded, irregularly arranged, or regularly arranged but with gaps . . . . 6.

6a. Stems to 1.5 cm diameter; vestigial cirri sometimes present . . . . *C. viridispinus.*
6b. Stems to 8 cm diameter; cirri never present . . . . 7.

7a. Ocreas elongate, tattering; Peninsular . . . . *C. concinnus.*
7b. Ocreas not elongate, short and inconspicuous; East, Northeast . . . . 8.

8a. Stems short and subterranean; leaf sheath spines scattered, not in rows . . . . *C. acanthophyllus.*
8b. Stems aerial, to 5 m long; leaf sheath spines in short rows . . . . *C. temii.*

9a. Flagella absent; cirri present . . . . 10.
9b. Flagella present; cirri absent, or rarely short and vestigial . . . . 18.

(continued)

Key to the Species of *Calamus* by Country or Region (continued)

10a. Leaflets whitish on the lower surfaces . . . . *C. caesius.*
10b. Leaflets green on the lower surfaces . . . . 11.

11a. Leaflets 45–65 per side of rachis, regularly arranged, pendulous, and linear or
linear-lanceolate . . . . 12.
11b. Leaflets not as above . . . . 13.

12a. Leaflets linear; stems clustered; wet places near the sea . . . . *C. erinaceus.*
12b. Leaflets linear-lanceolate; stems solitary; steep slopes in forest . . . . *C. manan.*

13a. Basal leaflets swept back across the sheath; stems solitary . . . . *C. laevigatus.*
13b. Basal leaflets not swept back across the sheath; stems usually clustered. . . . . 14.

14a. Upper surfaces of petioles not or scarcely spiny . . . . 15.
14b. Upper surfaces of petioles spiny . . . . 17.

15a. Leaflets arranged in groups of 2–5 on alternate sides of rachis. . . . . *C. viridispinus.*
15b. Leaflets irregularly arranged, often in pairs, or borne in remote groups and spreading
in slightly different planes . . . . 16.

16a. Petioles present, with spines along the margins; leaflets with yellowish bases . . . . *C. oxleyanus.*
16b. Petioles very short, scarcely spiny on upper surfaces; leaflets green at the base . . . . *C. axillaris.*

17a. Female flowering branches to 7 cm long, straight; fruits not stalked, usually less than
1.2 cm long, the scales not grooved; leaflets usually less than 35 cm long . . . . *C. palustris.*
17b. Female flowering branches to 10 cm long, zigzag; fruits stalked, to 2.4 cm long,
rarely more, the scales grooved; leaflets usually more than 40 cm long . . . . *C. nambariensis.*

18a. Leaflets rhomboidal . . . . 19.
18b. Leaflets linear, lanceolate, linear-lanceolate, or broadly lanceolate . . . . 21.

19a. Leaf sheaths with mottled brown hairs, with sparsely to densely arranged, yellowish
brown, flattened, to 1.3-cm-long spines . . . . *C. bousigonii.*
19b. Leaf sheaths with silvery, gray, or black hairs, with scattered, swollen-based, upward-pointing,
to 0.5-cm-long spines (sometimes spines absent) . . . . 20.

20a. Stems solitary or clustered, to 60 m long and 2 cm diameter . . . . *C. blumei.*
20b. Stems clustered, to 20 m long and 2.5 cm diameter . . . . *C. tomentosus.*

21a. Leaflets 4–15 per side of rachis, usually irregularly arranged, the apical ones often inserted
close together in a fan shape, the apical pair free or often joined at their bases . . . . 22.
21b. Leaflets 15–90 per side of rachis, often regularly arranged, the apical ones not inserted
close together in a fan shape, nor the apical pair joined at their bases . . . . 33.

22a. Leaflets broadly lanceolate, almost oblong, leathery . . . . *C. insignis.*
22b. Leaflets lanceolate, rarely broadly lanceolate but then not oblong, nor leathery . . . . 23.

23a. Stems to 5 cm diameter, solitary or weakly clustered; leaf sheath spines with
sinuous margins, densely hairy initially; leaflets broadly lanceolate; North . . . . *C. acanthospathus.*
23b. Stems to 2 cm diameter, usually clustered; leaf sheath spines not with sinuous margins
and densely hairy initially; leaflets linear or lanceolate; widespread . . . . 24.

24a. Leaflets whitish or gray on the lower surfaces . . . . 25.
24b. Leaflets green on the lower surfaces . . . . 26.

25a. Basal pair of leaflets swept back across the sheath; leaf sheath spines not longer
at sheath apices . . . . *C. griseus.*
25b. Basal pair of leaflets not swept back across the sheath; leaf sheath spines longer
at sheath apices . . . . *C. platyspathus.*

26a. Cirri present, vestigial, to 0.2 m long . . . . *C. bimaniferus.*
26b. Cirri absent . . . . 27.

27a. Leaf sheaths with scattered swellings, sometimes these with very small spines . . . . *C. pandanosmus.*
27b. Leaf sheaths without swellings . . . . 28.

(continued)

Key to the Species of *Calamus* by Country or Region (continued)

45a. Stems very large, to 60 m long and 8 cm diameter . . . . 46.
45b. Stems medium sized, to 35 m long and 4 cm diameter . . . . 47.

46a. Leaf sheaths with downward-pointing spines; apical leaflets very small . . . . *C. ornatus.*
46b. Leaf sheaths with horizontal spines; apical leaflets not very small . . . . *C. scipionum.*

47a. Petioles short or absent; basal few leaflets often swept back across
the sheath . . . . *C. godefroyi.*
47b. Petioles usually elongate, rarely short or absent; basal few leaflets not swept back
across the sheath . . . . 48.

48a. Leaf sheaths often with ridges; leaf sheath spines with oblique, crescent-shaped bases . . . . . . *C. tenuis.*
48b. Leaf sheaths without ridges; leaf sheath spines not with oblique, crescent-shaped bases . . . . 49.

49a. Petioles usually absent in adult plants; leaf sheaths with dense, black hairs . . . . *C. densiflorus.*
49b. Petioles present; leaf sheaths with brown hairs . . . . 50.

50a. Stems to 2 cm diameter; leaflets regularly arranged or regularly arranged but with gaps;
a few spines sometimes longer at sheath apices . . . . 51.
50b. Stems to 4 cm diameter; leaflets always regularly arranged; spines not longer at
sheath apices . . . . 52.

51a. Leaf sheaths with to 4.5 (sometimes a few to 7 at sheath apices)-cm-long spines;
inflorescence bracts tubular . . . . *C. siamensis.*
51b. Leaf sheaths with to 2 (sometimes a few to 7 at sheath apices)-cm-long spines;
inflorescence bracts tattering at the apices . . . . *C. henryanus.*

52a. Leaf rachis with 30–50 linear leaflets per side; usually near the sea, in scrub forest
or sand bars behind beaches, at low elevations . . . . *C. burkillianus.*
52b. Leaf rachis with 26–35 lanceolate leaflets per side; lowland rain forest to 800 m
elevation . . . . *C. diepenhorstii.*

Vietnam

1a. Stems nonclimbing, free-standing, scrambling, or short and subterranean; knees,
flagella, and cirri usually absent; inflorescence bracts without clawed spines . . . . 2.
1b. Stems climbing; knees, flagella, and/or cirri usually present; inflorescence bracts with
clawed spines . . . . 7.

2a. Stems to 0.8 cm diameter; leaflets to 12 per side of rachis, light gray-green on the lower
surfaces . . . . *C. salicifolius.*
2b. Stems to 5 cm diameter; leaflets 14–49 per side of rachis, green on the lower surfaces . . . . 3.

3a. Stems short and subterranean . . . . 4.
3b. Stems aerial . . . . 5.

4a. Stems solitary; apical pair of leaflets joined almost for their entire length . . . . *C. acaulis.*
4b. Stems clustered; apical pair of leaflets not joined . . . . *C. dongnaiensis.*

5a. Leaflets strongly clustered and spreading in different planes; Northern . . . . *C. thysanolepis.*
5b. Leaflets regularly arranged, sometimes with gaps, spreading in the same plane . . . . 6.

6a. Stems clustered; inflorescences to 0.5 m long, erect among the leaves; Central . . . . *C. modestus.*
6b. Stems solitary; inflorescences to 1.5 m long, arching below the leaves; Southern . . . . . . *C. nuichuaensis.*

7a. Flagella absent; cirri present . . . . 8.
7b. Flagella present; cirri absent . . . . 12.

8a. Small palms with stems to 1 cm diameter; leaflets 3–13 per side of rachis . . . . 9.
8b. Large palms with stems to 6 cm diameter; leaflets 12–40 per side of rachis . . . . 11.

9a. Basal pair of leaflets not swept back across the sheaths; inflorescence bracts splitting
almost to the bases . . . . *C. fissilis.*
9b. Basal pair of leaflets swept back across the sheaths; inflorescence bracts not splitting . . . . 10.

10a. Ocreas spiny; sheaths with bulbous-based groups of spines . . . . *C. spiralis.*
10b. Ocreas not spiny; sheath spines not bulbous-based . . . . *C. centralis.*

11a. Female flowering branches to 7 cm long, straight; fruits not stalked, usually less than
     1.2 cm long, the scales not grooved; leaflets usually less than 35 cm long . . . . *C. palustris.*
11b. Female flowering branches to 10 cm long, zigzag; fruits stalked, to 2.4 cm long,
     rarely more, the scales grooved; leaflets usually more than 40 cm long . . . . *C. nambariensis.*

12a. Leaflets rhomboidal . . . . *C. bousigonii.*
12b. Leaflets linear, lanceolate, linear-lanceolate, or broadly lanceolate . . . . 13.

13a. Leaflets 4–15 per side of rachis, usually irregularly arranged, the apical ones often
     inserted close together in a fan shape, the apical pair free or often joined at their bases . . . . 14.
13b. Leaflets 15–90 per side of rachis, often regularly arranged, the apical ones not
     inserted close together in a fan shape, nor the apical pair joined at their bases . . . . 19.

14a. Stems to 5 cm diameter, solitary or weakly clustered; leaf sheath spines
     with sinuous margins, densely hairy initially; leaflets broadly lanceolate; Northern . . . . *C. acanthospathus.*
14b. Stems less than 2 cm diameter, usually clustered; leaf sheath spines not with sinuous
     margins and densely hairy initially; leaflets linear or lanceolate; Central and Southern . . . . 15.

15a. Apical pair of leaflets split to their bases . . . . *C. dioicus.*
15a. Apical pair of leaflets joined at their bases . . . . 16.

16a. Leaf sheaths densely covered with reddish brown spines; ocreas densely spiny
     as the sheath but with longer spines . . . . *C. bachmaensis.*
16b. Leaf sheath spines not reddish brown; ocreas not densely spiny . . . . 17.

17a. Inflorescence bracts splitting to the base, tattering . . . . *C. kontumensis.*
17b. Inflorescence bracts tubular, not splitting . . . . 18.

18a. Basal pair of leaflets swept back across the sheaths; petioles absent; leaflets conspicuously
     bristly on the margins, curled over at the apices . . . . *C. crispus.*
18b. Basal pair of leaflets not swept back across the sheaths; petioles present; leaflets
     not conspicuously bristly on the margins, not curled over at the apices . . . . *C. tetradactylus.*

19a. Fruits borne on conspicuous, slender stalks . . . . *C. ceratophorus.*
19b. Fruits not borne on conspicuous, slender stalks . . . . 20.

20a. Stems solitary . . . . 21.
20b. Stems clustered . . . . 22.

21a. Leaf sheaths with to 3.5-cm-long spines, sometimes without spines; leaf rachis
     to 3.4 m long; endosperm homogeneous . . . . *C. poilanei.*
21b. Leaf sheaths without spines, or with a few spines to 0.7 cm long; leaf rachis to 1.4 m long;
     endosperm ruminate . . . . *C. lateralis.*

22a. Leaflets clustered and spreading in different planes . . . . *C. viminalis.*
22b. Leaflets regularly arranged, or regularly arranged but with gaps, spreading in the same plane . . . . . . 23.

23a. Leaf sheath spines conspicuously longer at sheath apices . . . . 24.
23b. Leaf sheath spines not longer at sheath apices (sometimes only a few spines longer) . . . . 27.

24a. Leaf sheaths with rows of spines . . . . 25.
24b. Leaf sheath spines scattered, not in rows . . . . 26.

25a. Leaf sheaths split open, not tubular; upper surface of petioles without spines. . . . . *C. rudentum.*
25b. Leaf sheaths closed for their entire length; upper surface of petioles
     with rings of spines . . . . *C. rhabdocladus.*

26a. Leaf sheaths with scattered to densely arranged, dark brown, upward-pointing,
     to 3.5-cm-long spines; inflorescence bracts not sheathing, split open and flat, brown . . . . . . *C. guruba.*
26b. Leaf sheaths with densely arranged, black, brownish, or yellowish, to 5.5-cm-long spines,
     interspersed with shorter spines; inflorescence bracts tubular, tattering at the apices . . . . . *C. flagellum.*

(continued)

Key to the Species of *Calamus* by Country or Region (continued)

27a. Ocreas densely bristly with black bristles . . . . *C. walkeri.*
27b. Ocreas not bristly   . . . . 28.

28a. Leaf sheath spines with oblique, crescent-shaped bases; leaf sheaths often with ridges. . . . .*C. tenuis.*
28b. Leaf sheaths spines not with oblique, crescent-shaped bases; leaf sheaths without ridges . . .*C. henryanus.*

Calamus acanthophyllus Becc.
wai tia (Lao), wai nang, wai pum (Tha)

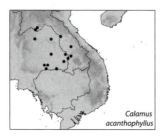

Calamus
acanthophyllus

Field characters. Stems clustered, nonclimbing, short and subterranean. Petioles greenish brown with brown hairs, with scattered, yellowish, flattened, to 1 cm long spines; ocreas present, earlike; knees absent; flagella absent; leaf rachis to 1.5 m long with 15–20 linear-lanceolate leaflets per side, these clustered and spreading in different planes; cirri absent. Inflorescences to 1.1 m long, erect, not flagellate; bracts tubular, swollen; fruits globose-ellipsoid, to 1.2 cm long and 0.9 cm diameter, whitish.
Range and habitat. Cambodia, Laos (Central, Southern), and Thailand (East, Northeast); dry, deciduous, open forest to 250 m elevation.
Uses. The fruits are eaten and the roots used medicinally.
Notes. Unusual in being tolerant of burning (Evans & Sengdala 2001).

Calamus acanthospathus Griff.   PLATE 5
gauri bet (Bhu, Nep), lengni (Chi), jouribet (Ind), wai hom (Lao), wai hawm (Tha)

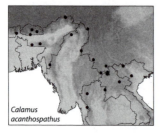

Calamus
acanthospathus

Field characters. Stems solitary or weakly clustered, climbing, to 30 m long and 5 cm diameter. Leaf sheaths green with brown hairs, with sparsely to densely arranged, sometimes in short rows, brown,

flattened, to 1-cm-long spines, these with sinuous margins, densely hairy initially; ocreas present, densely bristly; knees present; flagella present, to 5.6 m long; petioles very short or absent; leaf rachis to 1.4 m long with 8–15 broadly lanceolate leaflets per side, these regularly arranged, sometimes somewhat irregularly, especially near base of leaves; cirri absent. Inflorescences to 3 m long, flagellate; bracts tubular; flowering branches short and strongly recurved; fruits ovoid to ellipsoid, to 2.5 cm long and 1.5 cm diameter, yellowish brown, with grooved scales.
Range and habitat. Bhutan, China (Yunnan, Tibet), northeastern India (Arunachal Pradesh, Assam, Manipur, Meghayala, Nagaland, Sikkim, West Bengal), Laos (Northern), Myanmar (Kachin, Sagaing, Shan, Tanintharyi), Nepal, Thailand (North), and Vietnam (Northern); lowland or montane rain forest at 850–2400 m elevation, mostly at higher elevations.
Uses. Provides a cane used in basketry and furniture making.
Synonyms. *Calamus feanus* Becc., *Calamus feanus* var. *medogensis* S. J. Pei & S. Y. Chen, *Calamus montanus* T. Anderson, *Calamus yunnanensis* Govaerts, *Calamus yunnanensis* var. *densiflorus* S. J. Pei & S. Y. Chen, *Calamus yunnanensis* var. *intermedius* S. J. Pei & S. Y. Chen, *Palmijuncus acanthospathus* (Griff.) Kuntze, *Palmijuncus montanus* (T. Anderson) Kuntze

Calamus acaulis Henderson,   PLATE 5
N. K. Ban & N. Q. Dung
may (Vie)

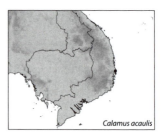

Calamus acaulis

Field characters. Stems solitary, nonclimbing, short and subterranean, to 3.5 cm diameter. Leaf sheaths green with brown hairs, with scattered, yellowish spines to 6 cm long; ocreas prominent, to 10 cm long, bristly; knees absent; flagella absent; leaf rachis to 0.7 m long with 21–25 lanceolate leaflets per side, these irregularly arranged in distant clusters of 2–6

leaflets and spreading in different planes, yellowish at their bases, the apical pair joined for almost their entire length; cirri absent. Inflorescences to 1 m long, not flagellate; bracts tubular; fruits not seen.
Range and habitat. Vietnam (Southern); dry, scrub forest at low elevations.
Uses. None recorded.

Calamus albidus (S. Y. Chen ex K. L. Wang) Guo & Henderson
fan teng (Chi)

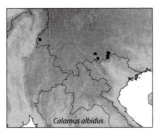
Calamus albidus

Field characters. Stems clustered, climbing, to 6 m long and 4 cm diameter. Leaf sheaths brown with brown hairs, densely covered with gray or black, flattened spines to 2 cm long; ocreas prominent, to 10 cm long, spiny, fibrous, disintegrating; knees absent; flagella present; leaf rachis to 0.5 m long with 15 or 16 linear to lanceolate leaflets per side, these irregularly arranged in distant clusters of 2 or 3 leaflets, whitish on the lower surfaces; cirri absent. Inflorescences to 2 m long, not flagellate; bracts tattering from the base; fruits ovoid to pear-shaped, to 2.5 cm long and 1.5 cm diameter, brownish, the scales fringed with dense, brown hairs.
Range and habitat. China (Yunnan) and probably Vietnam (Northern); broadleaf forest, 1000–1850 m elevation.
Uses. None recorded.
Notes. This species is similar to both *C. oxycarpus* and *C. macrorhynchus*, and the three have been confused (Guo Lixiu & Henderson 2007).
Synonym. *Calamus oxycarpus* var. *angustifolius* S. Y. Chen & K. L. Wang

Calamus andamanicus Kurz
chowdah, motta beth (And, Ncb)

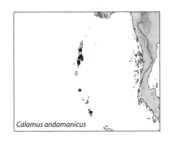
Calamus andamanicus

Field characters. Stems solitary, climbing, to 24 m long and 10 cm diameter. Leaf sheaths yellowish with brown hairs, with many, oblique, low, interrupted ridges, these with black, needlelike, to 0.3-cm-long spines, the apices of sheath with denser spines to 1.2 cm long; ocreas present, very short; knees present; flagella absent; leaf rachis to 2 m long with numerous pendulous, linear-lanceolate leaflets per side, these regularly arranged; cirri present, to 2 m long. Inflorescences to 1.3 m long, flagellate or sometimes not flagellate; bracts tubular; fruits ellipsoid, to 1.8 cm long and 1.1 cm diameter, brown, the scale apices elongate and fringed.
Range and habitat. Andaman and Nicobar islands, and Coco Island; lowland rain forest at low elevations.
Uses. Provides a good-quality cane used in furniture making.
Synonyms. *Calamus andamanicus* var. *nicobaricus* Becc., *Palmijuncus andamanicus* (Kurz) Kuntze

Calamus arborescens Griff.   PLATES 5 & 6
danon, danote, danoug (Mya), bo talow, wai baw talung, wai tha-nong (Tha)

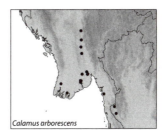
Calamus arborescens

Field characters. Stems clustered, nonclimbing, free-standing, to 10 m long and 6.5 cm diameter. Leaf sheaths open, green, with densely arranged or short rows of black, flattened, to 4-cm-long spines; ocreas present; knees absent; flagella absent; leaf rachis to 4 m long with 36–86 lanceolate leaflets per side, these regularly arranged and whitish on the lower surfaces; cirri absent. Inflorescences to 2.5 m long, not flagellate; bracts tubular, split, tattering at the apices; fruits obovoid to ellipsoid, to 2.2 cm long and 1.5 cm diameter, yellowish or reddish brown.
Range and habitat. Myanmar (Ayeyarwady, Bago, Yangon) and Thailand (Southwest); lowland rain forest, now mostly in disturbed areas near villages, but still common in the Pegu Yoma, Myanmar, especially in wet places, below 400 m elevation.
Uses. The leaves are used for thatching.
Notes. Published reports of this species from Bangladesh, India, and Peninsular Malaysia may not be correct, and are not documented by specimens. It has been grown for many years in the India Botanic Garden, Howrah, Calcutta.
Synonyms. *Calamus hostilis* Wall., *Palmijuncus arborescens* (Griff.) Kuntze

Calamus austroguangxiensis
S. J. Pei & S. Y. Chen
kai t'ang (Chi)

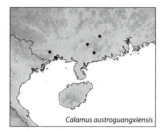

Calamus austroguangxiensis

Field characters. Stems clustered, climbing, to 10 m long and to 1.5 cm diameter. Leaf sheaths green with brown hairs, with scattered, yellowish, flattened, to 1.5-cm-long spines; ocreas present, short, spiny; knees present; flagella absent; leaf rachis to 0.9 m long with to 10 broadly lanceolate leaflets per side, these clustered in distantly spaced, alternate pairs; cirri present, to 1 m long. Inflorescences to 1 m long, not flagellate; bracts tubular; fruits ovoid to ellipsoid, to 1.8 cm long and 1.2 cm diameter, yellowish brown, stalked, with grooved scales.
Range and habitat. China (Guangdong, Guangxi); lowland rain forest at low elevations.
Uses. The stems are used in furniture making.
Notes. Included here are specimens that have been identified as *C. melanoloma* Mart., and described as *C. distichus* var. *shangsiensis* S. J. Pei & S. Y. Chen. *Calamus melanoloma* does not occur in our area, and although *C. distichus* var. *shangsiensis* was considered by Govaerts and Dransfield (2005) as a synonym of *C. viridispinus*, I believe it should be included here.
Synonym. *Calamus distichus* var. *shangsiensis* S. J. Pei & S. Y. Chen

Calamus axillaris Becc.
wai sam (Tha)

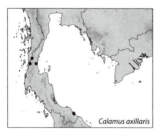

Calamus axillaris

Field characters. Stems clustered, climbing, to 40 m long and 2.5 cm diameter. Leaf sheaths green, without hairs or with sparse, brown hairs, with scattered, black-tipped, flattened, to 2.5-cm-long spines; ocreas present; knees present; flagella absent; petioles very short, grooved and scarcely spiny on upper surfaces; leaf rachis to 1.5 m long with 15–20 broadly

lanceolate leaflets per side, these irregularly arranged, often in pairs; cirri present, to 0.8 m long. Inflorescences to 1.5 m long, not flagellate; bracts tubular, open and spreading at the apices; fruits ovoid, to 1.1 cm long and 0.9 cm diameter, yellowish.
Range and habitat. Thailand (Peninsular) and probably Myanmar (Tanintharyi) (also in Peninsular Malaysia); wet areas in lowland rain forest to 600 m elevation.
Uses. Provides a good-quality cane used in furniture making.
Synonyms. *Calamus hendersonii* Furtado, *Calamus riparius* Furtado

Calamus bachmaensis Henderson,   PLATE 6
N. K. Ban & N. Q. Dung
may tre, may cam tre (Vie)

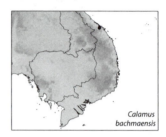

Calamus bachmaensis

Field characters. Stems clustered, climbing, to 10 m long and 1.3 cm diameter. Leaf sheaths green, without hairs, densely covered with reddish brown, flattened, to 1-cm-long spines; ocreas present, densely spiny as the sheath but with longer spines; knees present; flagella present, to 1 m long; leaf rachis to 0.3 m long with 4–6 lanceolate leaflets per side, these clustered, the apical pair joined at their bases; cirri absent. Inflorescences to 1 m long, flagellate; bracts tubular; fruits globose, to 1 cm diameter, brown.
Range and habitat. Vietnam (Central); lowland rain forest to 800 m elevation.
Uses. Provides a thin cane for tying and basketry.

Calamus balingensis Furtado   PLATE 6
wai ng wai (Tha)

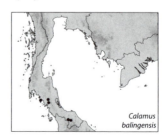

Calamus balingensis

Field characters. Stems usually solitary, sometimes clustered, climbing, to 15 m long and 5 cm diameter.

Leaf sheaths green with brown hairs, with densely arranged brown, flattened, to 5 (to 10 at sheath apices)-cm-long spines, interspersed with short spines; ocreas present; knees present; flagella present, to 3.5 m long; leaf rachis to 1.8 m long with 50–90 linear leaflets per side, these regularly and closely arranged; cirri absent. Inflorescences to 3.5 m long, flagellate; bracts tubular; fruits globose, to 1.2 cm diameter, greenish.

Range and habitat. Thailand (Peninsular) (also in Peninsular Malaysia); lowland rain forest, often on limestone, to 900 m elevation.

Uses. None recorded.

Calamus baratangensis Renuka & Vijayakumaran
malay beth (And)

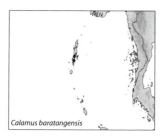

Calamus baratangensis

Field characters. Stems clustered, climbing, to 25 m long and 2 cm diameter. Leaf sheaths green with brown hairs, without spines or with few, brown, flattened, to 2-cm-long spines; ocreas present; knees present; flagella present; leaf rachis to 1 m long with numerous lanceolate leaflets per side, these regularly arranged; cirri absent. Inflorescences elongate, flagellate; bracts tubular; fruits ovoid, to 1.3 cm long and 0.9 cm diameter, whitish.

Range and habitat. Andaman Islands; lowland rain forest at low elevations.

Uses. Provides a cane used in furniture making.

Calamus basui Renuka & Vijayakumaran
safed beth (And)

Calamus basui

Field characters. Stems clustered, climbing, to 20 m long and 3 cm diameter. Leaf sheaths green with scattered, green, flattened, to 1-cm-long spines;

ocreas present; knees present; flagella present; petioles very short; leaf rachis to 1 m long with about 20 lanceolate leaflets per side, these regularly arranged; cirri present, short and vestigial. Inflorescences elongate, flagellate; bracts tubular; fruits ovoid, 1.5 cm long and 1 cm diameter, brown.

Range and habitat. Andaman Islands (Little Andaman); lowland rain forest at low elevations.

Uses. Provides a cane for use in furniture making.

Calamus beccarii Henderson
tu-teng (Tai)

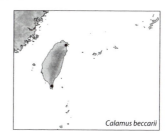

Calamus beccarii

Field characters. Stems clustered, climbing, to 50 m long and 4 cm diameter. Leaf sheaths brown with brown hairs, with densely arranged, in short rows, black, needlelike, to 2.5-cm-long spines, these interspersed with shorter spines; ocreas present; knees present, inconspicuous; flagella present, to 2.5 m long; leaf rachis to 0.8 m long with 30–62 linear leaflets per side, these regularly and closely arranged; cirri absent. Inflorescences to 3 m long, flagellate; bracts tubular; fruits globose-ellipsoid, to 12 cm long and 1.2 cm diameter, yellowish brown.

Range and habitat. Taiwan; lowland rain forest or drier forest at low elevations.

Uses. None recorded.

Notes. This species has been confused with *C. formosanus* (Henderson 2005).

Calamus bimaniferus T. Evans, K. Sengdala, O. Viengkham, B. Thammavong & J. Dransf.
wai hangnou (Lao)

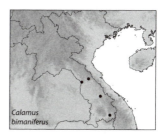

Calamus bimaniferus

Field characters. Stems clustered, climbing, to 3 m long and 1 cm diameter. Leaf sheaths green with brown hairs, without spines or with scattered, black-tipped,

flattened, to 0.7-cm-long spines; ocreas present; knees present; flagella present, to 0.5 m long; leaf rachis to 0.4 m long with 4–6 lanceolate leaflets per side, these irregularly arranged, often in pairs; cirri present, vestigial, to 0.2 m long. Inflorescences to 0.7 m long, not flagellate; bracts tubular; fruits globose, 0.8 cm diameter, yellowish brown.
Range and habitat. Laos (Central, Southern) and possibly adjacent Thailand; lowland rain forest to 530 m elevation.
Uses. Provides a cane used in handicraft making.

Calamus blumei Becc.
wai-ki-punng (Tha)

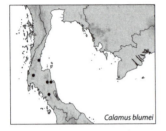

Calamus blumei

Field characters. Stems solitary or clustered, climbing, to 60 m long and 2 cm diameter. Leaf sheaths mottled green with gray or black hairs, without spines or with scattered, swollen-based, upward-pointing, to 0.5-cm-long spines; ocreas present; knees present; flagella present, to 1.5 m long; leaf rachis to 1 m long with 4–8 rhomboidal leaflets per side, these regularly arranged; cirri absent. Inflorescences to 1.5 m long, flagellate; bracts tubular; fruits globose-ellipsoid, 2.2 cm long and 1.7 cm diameter, whitish or yellowish.
Range and habitat. Thailand (Peninsular) (also in Borneo, Sumatra, and Peninsular Malaysia); lowland rain forest, usually in wet places, at low elevations.
Uses. None recorded.
Synonyms. *Calamus mawaiensis* Furtado, *Calamus penibukanensis* Furtado, *Calamus slootenii* Furtado

Calamus bousigonii Becc.   PLATES 6 & 7
phdav arech (Cbd), wai huadio (Tha), may la rong (Vie)

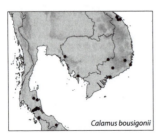

Calamus bousigonii

Field characters. Stems clustered or sometimes solitary, climbing, to 20 m long and 1.6 cm diameter.

Leaf sheaths green with mottled brown hairs, with sparsely to densely arranged, yellowish brown, flattened, to 1.3-cm-long spines; ocreas present; knees present; flagella present, to 1.5 m long; leaf rachis to 1 m long with 5–8 rhomboidal leaflets per side, these regularly arranged; cirri absent. Inflorescences to 1 m long, flagellate; bracts tubular or split open and spreading; fruits ovoid to ellipsoid, to 1.8 cm long and 1.4 cm diameter, yellowish.
Range and habitat. Cambodia, Thailand (Peninsular, Southeast), and Vietnam (Central, Southern); lowland or montane rain forest to 1100 m elevation.
Uses. None recorded.
Notes. Two subspecies are recognized: subsp. *bousigonii*, with tubular inflorescence bracts, from Cambodia, Thailand (Southeast), and Vietnam (Central, Southern); and subsp. *smitinandii* J. Dransf., with deeply split inflorescence bracts, from Thailand (Peninsular).

Calamus brandisii Becc.
vanthal (Ind)

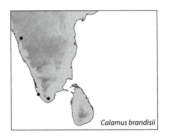

Calamus brandisii

Field characters. Stems clustered, climbing, to 15 m long and 1.5 cm diameter. Leaf sheaths green with brown hairs, with scattered, black, needlelike, to 2.5 (to 6 at sheath apices)-cm-long spines; ocreas very short; knees present; flagella present; leaf rachis to 0.7 m long with 6–15 lanceolate leaflets per side, these in distinct clusters, the apical ones inserted close together in a fan shape; cirri absent. Inflorescences to 1.5 m long, flagellate; bracts tubular; fruits ovoid, to 1.8 cm long and 1 cm diameter, brown.
Range and habitat. Southwestern India (Karnataka, Kerala, Tamil Nadu); montane rain forest at 1000–1500 m elevation.
Uses. Provides a good-quality cane used in furniture making.

Calamus burkillianus Becc.
wai kradat (Tha)

Field characters. Stems clustered, climbing, to 20 m long and 4 cm diameter. Leaf sheaths green with reddish brown hairs, with scattered, black-tipped, flattened, to 2-cm-long spines; ocreas present; knees present; flagella present, to 4 m long; leaf rachis to 1.5 m long with 30–50 linear leaflets per side, these regularly arranged; cirri absent. Inflorescences to 4 m long, flagellate; bracts tubular; fruits ellipsoid, to 1.2 cm long and 0.6 cm diameter, whitish.

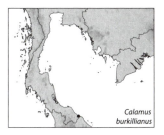
Calamus burkillianus

Range and habitat. Thailand (Peninsular) (also in Peninsular Malaysia); usually near the sea, in scrub forest or sand bars behind beaches at low elevations.
Uses. None recorded.
Synonym. *Calamus chibehensis* Furtado

Calamus caesius Blume PLATE 7
rotan sako ma, wai-tha-ka-tong (Tha)

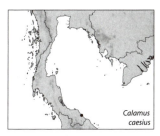
Calamus caesius

Field characters. Stems clustered, climbing, to 100 m long and 2 cm diameter. Leaf sheaths green with gray hairs, with scattered, pale brown, triangular, to 5-cm-long spines; ocreas very short; knees present; flagella absent; petioles short or absent; leaf rachis to 1.5 m long with 7–15 lanceolate leaflets per side, these clustered, often in pairs, whitish on the lower surfaces; cirri present, to 0.8 m long. Inflorescences to 2 m long, not flagellate; bracts tubular, open near apices; fruits ellipsoid, to 1.5 cm long and 1 cm diameter, greenish white.
Range and habitat. Thailand (Peninsular) (also in Borneo, the Philippines, Sumatra, and Peninsular Malaysia); lowland rain forest in low-lying, wet places, at low elevations.
Uses. Provides an important, medium-sized, high-quality cane used in furniture making. It has been introduced to various places for trial plantings.
Synonyms. *Calamus glaucescens* Blume, *Palmijuncus caesius* (Blume) Kuntze, *Palmijuncus glaucescens* (Blume) Kuntze, *Rotang caesius* (Blume) Baill.

Calamus castaneus Griff. PLATE 8
jark-khao (Tha)

Field characters. Stems clustered or sometimes solitary, nonclimbing, creeping, usually subterra-

nean, sometimes erect, to 1.5 m long and 20 cm diameter. Leaf sheaths green with grayish brown hairs, with scattered, grouped, gray or black, flattened, to 6-cm-long spines; ocreas present, densely bristly; knees absent; flagella absent; leaf rachis to 4.5 m long with 30–60 linear leaflets per side, these regularly arranged, dull gray on the lower surfaces; cirri absent. Inflorescences to 1 m long, not flagellate; bracts tubular, slightly swollen near apices; fruits ellipsoid, to 2.5 cm long and 1.8 cm diameter, brown.

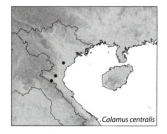
Calamus castaneus

Range and habitat. Thailand (Peninsular) (also in Peninsular Malaysia and Sumatra); lowland rain forest to 800 m elevation.
Uses. The fruits are used medicinally.
Synonyms. *Calamus castaneus* var. *griffithianus* (Mart.) Furtado, *Calamus griffithianus* Mart., *Palmijuncus griffith*ianus (Mart.) Kuntze

Calamus centralis Henderson, PLATE 8
N. K. Ban & N. Q. Dung
may, may mat (Vie)

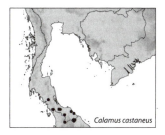
Calamus centralis

Field characters. Stems clustered, climbing, to 20 m long and 1 cm diameter. Leaf sheaths green without hairs or with mottled, brown hairs, with scattered, yellowish green or brown, flattened, to 2-cm-long spines; ocreas present; knees present; flagella absent; petioles short or absent; leaf rachis to 0.8 m long with 3–7 linear-lanceolate leaflets per side, these distantly and irregularly arranged, the basal ones swept back across the sheath; cirri to 0.8 m long. Inflorescences to 0.4 m long, not flagellate, erect or arching; bracts tubular; fruits not known.
Range and habitat. Vietnam (Central); lowland rain forest, often on karst limestone hills, to 800 m elevation.
Uses. None recorded.

Calamus ceratophorus Conrard
may sung, ui song (Vie)

Field characters. Stem branching not known, climbing, to 30 m long and 3 cm diameter. Leaf sheaths green with dark brown hairs, with scattered, yellowish, flattened, downward-pointing, to 2-cm-long spines; ocreas present; knees present; flagella present; leaf rachis to 1.5 m long with 25–30 lanceolate leaflets per side, these regularly arranged; cirri absent. Inflorescences to 4 m long, flagellate; bracts tubular; fruits borne on conspicuous, slender stalks, ellipsoid, to 1.9 cm long and 0.8 cm diameter, yellowish.
Range and habitat. Vietnam (Southern); montane rain forest at 1000–1200 m elevation.
Uses. Produces a cane used in furniture making.
Notes. A poorly understood species, known only from the original collection made in 1922. Although Evans et al. (2002) considered that this species had a cirrus, this seems not to be the case.

Calamus compsostachys Burret
kai t'ang (Chi)

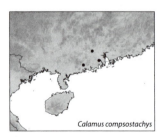

Field characters. Stems clustered, climbing, to 10 m long and to 1 cm diameter. Leaf sheaths greenish brown with scattered, dark brown, needlelike, to 0.5-cm-long spines, or spines absent; ocreas present; knees present; flagella absent; leaf rachis to 0.7 m long with 3–10 lanceolate leaflets per side, these distantly spaced; cirri present, to 0.5 m long. Inflorescences to 0.6 m long, not flagellate; bracts tubular; fruits globose to ellipsoid, to 1 cm long and 0.8 cm diameter, yellowish.
Range and habitat. China (Guangdong, Guangxi); lowland rain forest at low elevations.
Uses. None recorded.

Calamus concinnus Mart.   PLATE 9
wai nong (Tha)

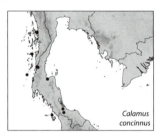

Field characters. Stems clustered, nonclimbing, short and subterranean or creeping, to 6 m long and 8 cm diameter. Leaf sheaths open, green, with scattered, yellowish, triangular, to 4-cm-long spines; ocreas present, elongate, to 75 cm long, tattering; knees absent; flagella absent; leaf rachis to 3.5 m long with 35–65 lanceolate leaflets per side, these irregularly arranged in groups of 2–7; cirri absent. Inflorescences to 2 m long, not flagellate; bracts tubular, tattering at apices; fruits globose, to 0.8 cm diameter, yellowish.
Range and habitat. Myanmar (Tanintharyi) and Thailand (Peninsular) (also in Peninsular Malaysia); lowland rain forest, often near the sea or rivers, at low elevations.
Uses. None recorded.
Synonyms. *Palmijuncus concinnus* (Mart.) Kuntze, *Plectocomiopsis ferox* Ridl.

Calamus crispus Henderson,   PLATE 9
N. K. Ban & N. Q. Dung
may tat, may tom (Vie)

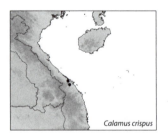

Field characters. Stem clustered, climbing, to 10 m long and 1.8 cm diameter. Leaf sheaths green with brown hairs, with scattered, yellowish green, downward-pointing, flattened, to 1-cm-long spines; ocreas present; knees present; flagella present; petioles absent; leaf rachis to 0.4 m long with 9 or 10 lanceolate leaflets per side, these clustered in alternate groups of 2 or 3, leathery, conspicuously spiny along the margins, curled over at the apices, the basal pair swept back across the sheath, the apical pair joined for about half their length; cirri absent. Inflorescences to 1.3 m long, flagellate; bracts tubular; fruits not known.

Range and habitat. Vietnam (Central); lowland rain forest at 200–600 m elevation.
Uses. None recorded.

Calamus delessertianus Becc.
paccha chural (Ind)

Field characters. Stems solitary, climbing, to 40 m long and 5 cm diameter. Leaf sheaths dark green, without hairs, with green, flattened, bulbous-based, to 2-cm-long spines; ocreas absent; knees present; flagella present, to 3 m long; leaf rachis to 2 m long with to 60 linear-lanceolate leaflets per side, these regularly arranged and with long hairs on the veins above and below; cirri absent. Inflorescences to 3 m long, flagellate; bracts tubular; fruits globose, to 1.5 cm diameter, yellowish.
Range and habitat. Southwestern India (Karnataka, Kerala, Maharashtra, Tamil Nadu); lowland rain forest to 1000 m elevation.
Uses. Provides a good-quality cane used in furniture making.
Notes. Beccari (1913; see also Evans & Sengdala 2002) considered that *C. delessertianus* was conspecific with *C. tenuis*, a view not shared by Renuka (1999b). No specimens of *C. delessertianus* have been seen nor are precise localities given in the literature, and no map is provided.

Calamus deliculatus Thwaites
nara wel (Srl)

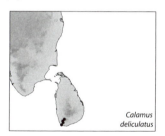

Calamus
deliculatus

Field characters. Stems clustered, climbing, to 10 m long and 2 cm diameter. Leaf sheaths yellowish green with reddish brown hairs, with scattered to densely arranged, greenish brown, flattened, to 4 (to 12 at sheath apices)-cm-long spines, these hairy on the margins and denser at sheath apices; ocreas present, inconspicuous; knees inconspicuous or absent; flagella present, to 2 m long; leaf rachis to 1 m long with 25–26, linear-lanceolate leaflets per side, these regularly arranged; cirri absent. Inflorescences to 0.5 m long, flagellate; bracts tubular; fruits globose, to 1 cm diameter, yellow.
Range and habitat. Sri Lanka; lowland rain forest to 1000 m elevation.
Uses. Provides a good-quality cane used in basketry.
Synonym. *Palmijuncus deliculatus* (Thwaites) Kuntze

Calamus densiflorus Becc.   PLATE 10
wai-ki-lay, wai kaerae (Tha)

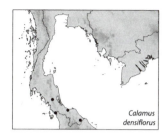

Calamus
densiflorus

Field characters. Stems clustered, climbing, to 40 m long and 4 cm diameter. Leaf sheaths yellowish green with dense, black hairs, with densely arranged, brownish, flattened, to 4-cm-long spines, these usually with hairy margins; ocreas present; knees present; flagella present, to 5 m long; petioles usually absent in adult plants; leaf rachis to 2 m long with 50–60 linear leaflets per side, these regularly and closely arranged; cirri absent. Inflorescences to 5 m long, flagellate; bracts tubular; fruits ovoid, to 2 cm long and 1.2 cm diameter, yellowish.
Range and habitat. Thailand (Peninsular) (also in Peninsular Malaysia and Singapore); lowland rain forest to 600 m elevation.
Uses. Provides a medium-quality cane used in furniture making.
Synonym. *Calamus neglectus* Becc.

Calamus dianbaiensis C. F. Wei
dian bai shen teng (Chi)

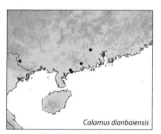

Calamus dianbaiensis

Field characters. Stems clustered, nonclimbing, free-standing or creeping, to 4 m long and 7 cm diameter. Leaf sheaths yellowish brown with brown hairs, with short, oblique rows of yellowish, flattened, to 3-cm-long spines; ocreas present, to 20 cm long, fibrous; knees absent; flagella absent; leaf rachis to 3 m long with to 30 linear-lanceolate leaflets per side, these regularly arranged; cirri absent. Inflorescences to 1 m long, not flagellate; bracts split open and tattering at the apices; fruits globose to ellipsoid, to 2 cm long and 1.5 cm diameter, brownish, with grooved scales.
Range and habitat. China (Guangxi, Guangdong); lowland rain forest at low elevations.

Uses. None recorded.
Synonyms. *Calamus guangxiensis* C. F. Wei, *Calamus yuangchunensis* C. F. Wei

Calamus diepenhorstii Miq.
wai-tam-dek (Tha)

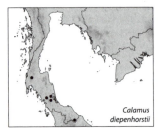

Calamus
diepenhorstii

Field characters. Stems clustered, climbing, to 20 m long and 3.5 cm diameter. Leaf sheaths green with brownish hairs, with scattered to densely arranged, often in rows, black, flattened, to 2-cm-long spines, these with hairy margins; ocreas obscure or absent; knees present; flagella present, to 6 m long; leaf rachis to 1.8 m long with 26–35 lanceolate leaflets per side, these regularly arranged; cirri absent. Inflorescences to 6 m long, flagellate; bracts tubular; fruits globose, to 2 cm diameter, brownish or yellowish.
Range and habitat. Thailand (Peninsular) (also in Borneo, Peninsular Malaysia, the Philippines, and Singapore); lowland rain forest to 800 m elevation.
Uses. Provides a medium-quality cane used in furniture making.
Notes. Three varieties are recognized: var. *diepenhorstii* from Singapore, Thailand, and Peninsular Malaysia; var. *exulans* Becc. from the Philippines; and var. *major* J. Dransf. from Borneo.
Synonyms. *Calamus diepenhorstii* var. *kemamanensis* Furtado, *Calamus diepenhorstii* var. *singaporensis* (Becc.) Becc., *Calamus pacificus* Ridl., *Calamus singaporensis* Becc., *Palmijuncus diepenhorstii* (Miq.) Kuntze

Calamus digitatus Becc.
kukulu wel (Srl)

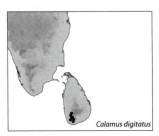

Calamus digitatus

Field characters. Stems clustered, climbing, to 5 m long and 1 cm diameter. Leaf sheaths green with

brown hairs, sometimes with ridges, almost spineless or with scattered, greenish brown, flattened, to 1.5-cm-long spines; ocreas present; knees present; flagella present, to 2 m long; leaf rachis to 0.05 m long with 2 or 3 broadly lanceolate leaflets per side, these inserted close together in a fan shape, the apical pair joined at their bases; cirri absent. Inflorescences to 1.3 m long, flagellate; bracts tubular; fruits globose, to 1 cm diameter, yellow.
Range and habitat. Sri Lanka; lowland or montane rain forest, to 1500 m elevation.
Uses. Provides a good-quality cane used in basketry.
Notes. Very similar to *C. pachystemonus* and especially to *C. radiatus*, the three species forming a related group. *Calamus digitatus* can be distinguished by its petioles with straight spines to 1.7 cm long; *C. pachystemonus* and *C. radiatus* have petioles with short recurved spines only.

Calamus dilaceratus Becc.

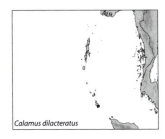

Calamus dilacteratus

Field characters. Stems clustered, climbing, to 20 m long and 4 cm diameter. Leaf sheaths green with whitish hairs, densely covered with reddish brown, needlelike, to 4-cm-long spines; ocreas present, very short; knees present; flagella absent; leaf rachis to 2 m long with numerous lanceolate leaflets per side, these regularly arranged; cirri present, to 1.5 m long. Inflorescences elongate, not flagellate; bracts split open and tattering at the apices; fruits ovoid, to 1 cm long and 0.8 cm diameter, yellow.
Range and habitat. Nicobar Islands (Great Nicobar); lowland rain forest at low elevations.
Uses. Provides a cane used in furniture making.

Calamus dioicus Lour.   PLATE 10
may chi (Vie)

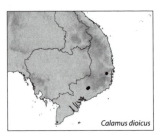

Calamus dioicus

Field characters. Stems clustered, climbing, to 10 m long and 0.4 cm diameter. Leaf sheaths green with patches of brown hairs, moderately covered with yellowish, black-tipped, flattened, to 0.6-cm-long spines; ocreas present, to 4 cm long, membranous and soon falling, with needlelike spines at the bases; knees present; flagella present, to 1 m long; petioles absent; leaf rachis to 0.2 m long with 5 lanceolate leaflets per side, these irregularly and distantly arranged in three groups, the basal pair swept back across the sheath, the apical pair split to their bases; cirri absent. Inflorescences to 1.5 m long, not flagellate; bracts tubular; fruits globose, to 0.8 cm diameter, yellowish white.
Range and habitat. Vietnam (Southern); lowland rain forest at low elevations.
Uses. Produces a good-quality cane for tying.
Notes. Evans et al. (2002) included specimens from Bac Ma National Park in central Vietnam in their description of *C. dioicus*. However, these are quite distinct from *C. dioicus* and are recognized as a separate species, *C. bachmaensis*.
Synonym. *Palmijuncus dioicus* (Lour.) Kuntze

Calamus dongnaiensis Becc.
may dong nai (Vie)

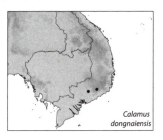

Calamus dongnaiensis

Field characters. Stems clustered, nonclimbing, short and subterranean. Leaf sheaths greenish brown with brown hairs, with scattered, yellowish, flattened spines; ocreas and knees not known; flagella absent; leaf rachis with about 14 broadly lanceolate, leathery leaflets per side, these irregularly arranged; cirri absent. Inflorescences to 2.5 m long, not flagellate; bracts split open and tattering at the apices; fruits ovoid, to 3 cm long and 1.5 cm diameter, brown, the scale margins whitish.
Range and habitat. Vietnam (Southern); lowland rain forest at low elevations.
Uses. The fruits are eaten.
Notes. A poorly known species.

Calamus dransfieldii Renuka
meesebetha (Ind)

Field characters. Stems solitary, climbing, to 22 m long and 3.5 cm diameter. Leaf sheaths green with greenish hairs, with scattered, greenish, bulbous-based, to 2.2-cm-long spines; ocreas absent; knees present; flagella present, to 6 m long; leaf rachis to 1.5 m long with to 60 lanceolate leaflets per side,

these regularly arranged and with long hairs on the veins above and below; cirri absent. Inflorescences to 3.5 m long, flagellate; bracts tubular; fruits globose, to 1.8 cm diameter, stalked, yellow.

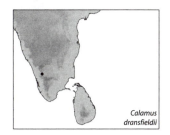

Calamus dransfieldii

Range and habitat. Southwestern India (Kerala); lowland rain forest or deciduous forest at 300-700 m elevation.
Uses. Provides a good-quality, large-diameter cane used in furniture making and basketry.
Notes. Very similar to *C. gamblei*, and known from only one locality in the Dhoni Hills. However, it may occur in other localities, farther to the north in Karnataka.

Calamus egregius Burret   PLATE 10
liteng (Chi)

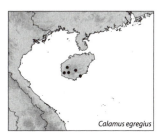

Calamus egregius

Field characters. Stems clustered, climbing, to 50 m long and to 5 cm diameter. Leaf sheaths yellowish green with brown hairs, with scattered, brownish, flattened, to 2-cm-long spines; ocreas present, to 10 cm long, disintegrating; knees present; flagella absent; leaf rachis to 1.5 m long with to 20 lanceolate leaflets per side, these clustered in alternate groups of 2 or 3; cirri present, to 1 m long. Inflorescences to 1 m long, not flagellate; bracts tubular; fruits ovoid, to 2 cm long and 1.6 cm diameter, brown, stalked, with grooved scales.
Range and habitat. China (Hainan); lowland rain forest to 1000 m elevation.
Uses. Provides a high-quality cane for binding and weaving; the palm hearts are eaten.

Calamus erectus Roxb.   PLATE 11
kadam bet (Ban), pekri (Bhu), zhi li sheng teng (Chi), rong (Ind), wai namsay (Lao), mauk chee kyein, soo-patle, thaing kyaing, (Mya), kheersing (Nep), wai khom (Tha)

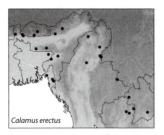

Calamus erectus

Field characters. Stems clustered, nonclimbing, free-standing or sometimes leaning, to 6 m long and 5 cm diameter. Leaf sheaths dark green with dark brown hairs, with short rows of brown, flattened, to 3.5-cm-long spines; ocreas present, with rows of short spines, split into 2, soon falling; knees absent; flagella absent; petioles and rachis with whorls of yellow spines; leaf rachis to 3 m long with to 40 lanceolate leaflets per side, these regularly arranged; cirri absent. Inflorescences to 2 m long, not flagellate; bracts tubular, tattering at the apices; fruits ellipsoid, to 5 cm long and 2.5 cm diameter, greenish or reddish brown, with grooved scales.

Range and habitat. Bangladesh, Bhutan, China (Yunnan), northeastern India (Arunachal Pradesh, Assam, Manipur, Meghalaya, Manipur, Sikkim, Tripura, West Bengal), Laos (Central, Northern), Myanmar (Kachin, Sagaing, Shan), Nepal, and Thailand (North, Southwest); lowland or montane rain forest or drier forest, usually on steep slopes, to 1400 m elevation.

Uses. Provides a short, thick, nonflexible cane used in construction and furniture making.

Synonyms. *Calamus collinus* Griff., *Calamus erectus* var. *birmanicus* Becc., *Calamus erectus* var. *collinus* (Griff.) Becc., *Calamus erectus* var. *macrocarpus* (Griff.) Becc., *Calamus erectus* var. *schizospathus* (Griff.) Becc., *Calamus macrocarpus* Griff., *Calamus schizospathus* Griff., *Palmijuncus collinus* (Griff.) Kuntze, *Palmijuncus erectus* (Roxb.) Kuntze, *Palmijuncus macrocarpus* (Griff.) Kuntze, *Palmijuncus schizospathus* (Griff.) Kuntze

Calamus erinaceus (Becc.) J. Dransf.   PLATE 11
wai pangka (Tha)

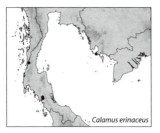

Calamus erinaceus

Field characters. Stems clustered, climbing, to 15 m long and 6 cm diameter. Leaf sheaths yellowish green with gray hairs, with densely arranged, oblique rows of brown, needlelike or flattened, to 3.5 (to 10 at sheath apices)-cm-long spines; ocreas very short or absent; knees present, orange-yellow; flagella absent; leaf rachis to 2.5 m long with about 65 linear leaflets per side, these regularly arranged and pendulous; cirri present, to 2 m long. Inflorescences to 1.5 m long, not flagellate; bracts tubular; fruits globose, to 1 cm diameter, yellowish.

Range and habitat. Cambodia and Thailand (Peninsular) (also in Borneo, the Philippines, Singapore, Sumatra, and Peninsular Malaysia); mangrove forest and other places near the sea at low elevations.

Uses. None recorded.

Synonyms. *Calamus aquatilis* Ridl., *Daemonorops erinacea* Becc.

Calamus evansii Henderson
leum, wai leum (Lao)

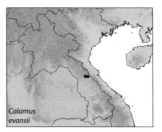

Calamus evansii

Field characters. Stems clustered, climbing, to 7 m long and 1.3 cm diameter. Leaf sheaths green with white hairs, with sparsely to densely arranged brown, black-tipped, flattened, horizontally spreading spines to 1 cm long, sometimes with many short spines interspersed; knees present; ocreas present, densely bristly; flagella present; leaf rachis to 0.5 m long with 3–6 lanceolate leaflets per side, these arranged in distant groups or solitary, the apical pair free or only briefly joined at their bases; cirri absent. Inflorescences to 3 m long, flagellate; bracts tubular; fruits not seen.

Range and habitat. Laos (Central); lowland forest at 520–530 m elevation.

Uses. The stems are used for handicrafts.

Notes. Evans et al. (2002) recognized a widespread *C. kingianus* occurring in both Laos and northeastern India. Henderson and Henderson (2007) separated the Laos population as *C. evansii*.

Calamus exilis Griff.
wai phra ram (Tha)

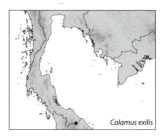

Calamus exilis

Plate 1. *Areca catechu*; habit; Vietnam (top left). *Areca triandra*; habit; Vietnam (top right). *Areca triandra*; habit of rheophytic form; Vietnam (bottom left). *Areca triandra*; inflorescence; Thailand (bottom right).

Plate 2. *Areca triandra*; inflorescence; Vietnam (top left). *Arenga caudata*; habit, *Arenga wester-houtii* in background; Thailand (top right). *Arenga caudata*; habit of form with undivided leaves; Vietnam (bottom left). *Arenga caudata*; male flowers of rheophytic form; Vietnam (bottom right).

Plate 3. *Arenga westerhoutii*; habit; Vietnam (top left). *Arenga westerhoutii*; ears at bases of leaflets; Myanmar (top right). *Arenga westerhoutii*; inflorescence with male flowers; Myanmar (bottom left). *Arenga westerhoutii*; inflorescence with male flowers; Vietnam (bottom right).

Plate 4. *Arenga wightii*; habit; India (top left). *Bentinckia condapanna*; habit; cultivated, India (top right). *Borassodendron machadonis*; habit; Thailand (bottom left). *Borassus flabellifer*; habit; Myanmar (bottom right).

Plate 5. *Calamus acanthospathus*; leaf sheath; Myanmar (top left). *Calamus acaulis*; petioles; Vietnam (top right). *Calamus arborescens*; habit; Myanmar (bottom left). *Calamus arborescens*; lower surfaces of leaflets; Myanmar (bottom right).

Plate 6. *Calamus arborescens*; fruits; Myanmar (top left). *Calamus bachmaensis*; leaf sheath; Vietnam (top right). *Calamus balingensis*; habit; Thailand (bottom left). *Calamus bousigonii* subsp. *smitinandii*; leaflets; Thailand (bottom right).

Plate 7. *Calamus bousigonii* subsp. *smitinandii*; leaf sheath; Thailand (top left). *Calamus bousigonii* subsp. *bousigonii*; leaf sheath; Vietnam (top right). *Calamus caesius*; leaf sheath; Thailand (bottom left). *Calamus caesius*; lower surface of leaflets and cirrus; Thailand (bottom right).

Plate 8. *Calamus castaneus*; habit; Thailand (top left). *Calamus castaneus*; leaf sheaths; Thailand (top right). *Calamus castaneus*; fruits; Thailand (bottom left). *Calamus centralis*; leaf sheath; Vietnam (bottom right).

Plate 9. *Calamus concinnus*; leaflets; Thailand (top left). *Calamus concinnus*; leaf bases, ocreas, and old inflorescences; Thailand (top right). *Calamus crispus*; leaf sheath; Vietnam (bottom left). *Calamus crispus*; leaflets; Vietnam (bottom right).

Plate 10. *Calamus densiflorus*; leaf sheath; Thailand (top left). *Calamus dioicus*; leaf sheath; Vietnam (top right). *Calamus dioicus*; fruits; Vietnam (bottom left). *Calamus egregius*; leaf; China (bottom right).

Plate 11. *Calamus erectus*; habit; Myanmar (top left). *Calamus erectus*; petioles; Myanmar (top right). *Calamus erectus*; fruits; Myanmar (bottom left). *Calamus erinaceus*; leaf sheath; Thailand (bottom right).

Plate 12. *Calamus fissilis*; leaf sheath; Vietnam (top left). *Calamus flagellum* var. *flagellum*; habit; Myanmar (top right). *Calamus flagellum* var. *flagellum*; leaf sheath; Myanmar (bottom left). *Calamus flagellum* var. *flagellum*; fruits; Myanmar (bottom right).

Plate 13. *Calamus floribundus*; habit; India (top left). *Calamus floribundus*; leaf sheath; Myanmar (top right). *Calamus guruba*; leaf sheath; Myanmar (bottom left). *Calamus hainanensis*; leaf; China (bottom right).

Plate 14. *Calamus hainanensis*; leaf sheath; China (top left). *Calamus henryanus*; leaf sheath; Myanmar (top right). *Calamus henryanus*; leaf; Myanmar (bottom left). *Calamus hookerianus*; leaf sheath; India (bottom right).

Plate 15. *Calamus hukaungensis*; leaf sheath; Myanmar (top left). *Calamus insignis* var. *insignis*; leaf sheath; Thailand (top right). *Calamus insignis* var. *insignis*; leaflets; Thailand (bottom left). *Calamus javensis*; leaf; Myanmar (bottom right).

Plate 16. *Calamus lateralis*; leaf sheath and fruits; Vietnam (top left). *Calamus leptospadix*; leaf sheath; India (top right). *Calamus longisetus*; habit; Myanmar (bottom left). *Calamus longisetus*; leaf sheath; Myanmar (bottom right).

Field characters. Stems solitary or clustered, climbing, to 15 m long and 2.5 cm diameter. Leaf sheaths green, with densely arranged, minute, triangular, reflexed spines, giving a rough feel to the sheath, sometimes with scattered, brown, to 1.2-cm-long spines also present; ocreas present; knees present; flagella present, to 1.8 m long; leaf rachis to 0.7 m long with 20–30 linear leaflets per side, these regularly arranged, closely spaced, and densely covered with fine hairs; cirri absent. Inflorescences to 0.8 m long, flagellate; bracts tubular; fruits ovoid, stalked, to 1.6 cm long and 1.2 cm diameter, yellowish.
Range and habitat. Thailand (Peninsular) (also in Sumatra and Peninsular Malaysia); lowland rain forest to 700 m elevation.
Uses. Provides a slender cane used in tying.
Synonyms. *Calamus ciliaris* var. *peninsularis* Furtado, *Calamus curtisii* Ridl., *Palmijuncus exilis* (Griff.) Kuntze

Calamus fissilis Henderson, N. K. Ban & N. Q. Dung
may cam (Vie)

PLATE 12

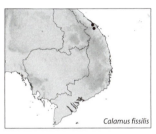

Calamus fissilis

Field characters. Stems clustered, climbing, to 10 m long and 1 cm diameter. Leaf sheaths green with reddish brown hairs, with reddish brown, flattened spines to 1 cm long, arranged in small, horizontally spreading groups; ocreas present; knees present; flagella absent; petioles short or absent; leaf rachis to 0.3 m long with 9–11 linear-lanceolate leaflets per side, these regularly arranged; cirri present, to 0.5 m long. Inflorescences erect or arching, to 0.4 m long, not flagellate; bracts splitting almost to their bases; fruits not known.
Range and habitat. Vietnam (Central); lowland rain forest to 800 m elevation.
Uses. The canes are used for tying.

Calamus flagellum Griff.
rhim (Bhu), da teng mie, shengteng (Chi), putli bet, reem (Ind), wai kom, wai lao (Lao), mauk chee kyein (Mya), may roi (Vie)

PLATE 12

Field characters. Stems clustered, climbing, to 30 m long and 5 cm diameter. Leaf sheaths greenish yellow with dark brown hairs, with densely arranged, black, brownish, or yellowish, flattened, to 5.5 (sometimes to 10 at sheath apices)-cm-long spines, interspersed with shorter spines; ocreas present, fibrous, soon falling;

knees present, inconspicuous; flagella present, to 7 m long; leaf rachis to 3 m long with 27–35 linear-lanceolate leaflets per side, these regularly or sometimes irregularly arranged; cirri absent. Inflorescences to 7 m long, flagellate; bracts tubular, tattering at the apices; fruits ovoid, to 3 cm long and 2.2 cm diameter, yellowish or brownish, with grooved scales.

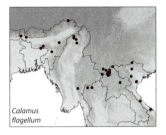

Calamus flagellum

Range and habitat. Bangladesh, Bhutan, China (Guangxi, Yunnan, Tibet), Laos (Northern), Myanmar (Kachin, Sagaing, Shan), Nepal, northeastern India (Arunachal Pradesh, Assam, Manipur, Meghalaya, Sikkim, West Bengal), Thailand (North), and Vietnam (Central, Northern); lowland or montane rain forest, to 1500 m elevation.
Uses. The hearts are eaten.
Notes. A widespread and variable species. Two varieties are recognized: var. *flagellum*; and var. *furvifuraceus* S. J. Pei & S. Y. Chen, with darker leaf hairs and some of the lower leaflets clustered, from China (Yunnan).
Synonyms. *Calamus flagellum* var. *karinensis* Becc., *Calamus jenkinsianus* Griff., *Calamus karinensis* (Becc.) S. J. Pei & S. Y. Chen, *Calamus polygamus* Roxb., *Palmijuncus flagellum* (Griff.) Kuntze, *Palmijuncus jenkinsianus* (Griff.) Kuntze, *Palmijuncus polygamus* (Roxb.) Kuntze

Calamus floribundus Griff.
chota bet, moksoma kyein (Ind), maukye, ye-kyaing (Mya)

PLATE 13

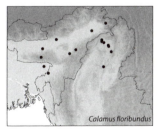

Calamus floribundus

Field characters. Stems clustered, climbing, to 6 m long and 2.5 cm diameter. Leaf sheaths greenish brown with brown hairs, with densely arranged spines of 2 kinds, 1 brown and flattened, the other black and needlelike, both to 4 cm long, interspersed with many short, black spines; ocreas present, densely bristly; knees present; flagella present; leaf rachis to 0.6 m long with 11–21 lanceolate leaflets per side, these irregularly arranged, the apical ones inserted close together in a fan shape, the apical pair free or joined at their bases; cirri absent. Inflorescences to 2.5 m long, flagellate; bracts tubular; fruits globose to ellipsoid, to 1.2 cm long and 1 cm diameter, yellowish.

Range and habitat. Bangladesh, northeastern India (Arunachal Pradesh, Assam, Manipur, Meghalaya, Nagaland, Tripura, West Bengal), and Myanmar (Kachin, Sagaing); lowland rain forest on river flood-plains or other flat areas, or often in disturbed places, to 1000 m but usually at lower elevations.

Uses. The canes are used for tying and the fruits are eaten.

Synonyms. *Calamus mishmeensis* Griff., *Palmijuncus floribundus* (Griff.) Kuntze, *Palmijuncus mishmeensis* (Griff.) Kuntze

Calamus formosanus Becc.
shui-teng (Tai)

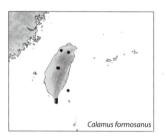

Calamus formosanus

Field characters. Stems clustered, climbing, to 20 m long and to 5 cm diameter. Leaf sheaths yellowish brown with brown hairs, with densely arranged, yellowish, flattened, upward-pointing, to 2-cm-long spines; ocreas present, small and papery; knees present; flagella absent; petioles short or absent; leaf rachis to 2 m long with 18 or 19 broadly lanceolate leaflets per side, these irregularly and distantly arranged; cirri present, to 3 m long. Inflorescences elongate, flagellate; bracts tubular; fruits ellipsoid, to 2 cm long and 1 cm diameter, brownish or yellowish.

Range and habitat. Taiwan; lowland rain forest to 1000 m elevation.

Uses. None recorded.

Synonyms. *Calamus orientalis* C. E. Chang, *Calamus quinquesetinervius* Burret

Calamus gamblei Becc.
hasirubetha (Ind)

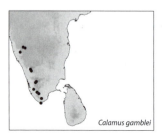

Calamus gamblei

Field characters. Stems clustered, to 30 m long and 2.5 cm diameter. Leaf sheaths green with dark brown hairs, with scattered, greenish, bulbous-based, to 1.5-cm-long spines; ocreas present; knees present; flagella present, to 4 m long; leaf rachis to 1 m long with numerous linear-lanceolate leaflets per side, these regularly arranged and with long hairs on the veins above and below; cirri absent. Inflorescences to 3 m long, flagellate; bracts tubular; fruits globose to obovoid, to 2 cm diameter, stalked, yellow.

Range and habitat. Southwestern India (Karnataka, Kerala, Tamil Nadu); lowland or montane rain forest at 600–2000 m elevation.

Uses. Provides a good-quality cane used in furniture making and basketry.

Synonym. *Calamus gamblei* var. *sphaerocarpus* Becc.

Calamus godefroyi Becc.
wai nong (Lao)

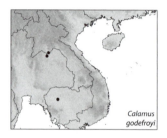

Calamus godefroyi

Field characters. Stems clustered, climbing, to 30 m long and 1.5 cm diameter. Leaf sheaths green with brown hairs, with scattered to densely arranged, black-tipped, flattened, triangular, to 2-cm-long spines; ocreas present; knees present; flagella present, elongate; petioles short or absent; leaf rachis to 1 m long with 15–20 linear-lanceolate leaflets per side, these regularly arranged and grayish green on the lower surface, with the basal few leaflets often swept back across the sheath; cirri absent. Inflorescences to 1.3 m long, flagellate; bracts tubular; fruits globose to ellipsoid, to 1.6 cm long and 1.2 cm diameter, yellowish or whitish.

Range and habitat. Cambodia, Laos (Central), and Thailand (Northeast); marshy areas in flooded forest at low elevations.

Uses. None recorded.

Notes. Evans et al. (2002) considered that this species may be synonymous with *C. rotang*.

Calamus gracilis Roxb.
mapuri bet (Ban, Ind), wai nan (Chi), wai hom (Lao), kyetu kyein (Mya)

Field characters. Stems clustered, climbing, to 30 m long and 2 cm diameter. Leaf sheaths green with mottled, dark brown and whitish hairs, without spines or with scattered, black-tipped, conical-based, to 0.5-cm-long spines; ocreas present, small;

knees present, obscure; flagella present; petioles very short; leaf rachis to 0.7 m long with 8–5 linear or lanceolate leaflets per side, these regularly arranged but with wide gaps between groups, shiny green, curled over at the tips, the apical ones inserted close together in a fan shape, the apical pair not joined at their bases; cirri absent. Inflorescences to 0.7 m long, flagellate; bracts tubular; fruits ovoid to ellipsoid, to 2 cm long and 1 cm diameter, yellowish or orange, with grooved scales, stalked.

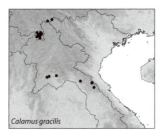

Range and habitat. Bangladesh, China (Yunnan), northeastern India (Arunachal Pradesh, Assam, Meghalaya), Laos (Northern, Central), and Myanmar (Kachin, Sagaing, Shan); lowland or montane rain forest at 850–1500 m elevation.
Uses. None recorded.
Notes. Plants from Hainan are often included in *C. gracilis*, but here are recognized as a separate species, *C. hainanensis*.
Synonym. *Palmijuncus gracilis* (Roxb.) Kuntze

Calamus griseus J. Dransf.
wai chumpawn (Tha)

Field characters. Stems clustered, climbing, to 5 m long and 0.8 cm diameter. Leaf sheaths green with brown hairs, with scattered, green, triangular, to 0.6-cm-long spines; ocreas present, inconspicuous; knees present; flagella present, to 0.6 m long; leaf rachis to 0.3 m long with 5 or 6 broadly lanceolate leaflets per side, these irregularly arranged and whitish on the lower surfaces, the basal pair swept back across the sheath, the apical pair joined for about half their length; cirri absent. Inflorescences to 1.1 m long, flagellate; bracts tubular; fruits ellipsoid, 0.7 cm long and 0.4 cm diameter, brown.
Range and habitat. Thailand (Peninsular) and probably Myanmar (Tanintharyi) (also in Peninsular

Malaysia and Sumatra); lowland rain forest at low elevations.
Uses. None recorded.

Calamus guruba Buch.-Ham.   PLATE 13
sundi bet, teeta bet (Ban, Ind), wai deng (Lao), kyaing-ni, kyein-ni (Mya), dute bet (Nep), wai khi kai (Tha)

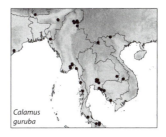

Field characters. Stems clustered, climbing or forming thickets, to 20 m long and 3 cm diameter. Leaf sheaths dull green with rusty brown or light brown hairs, with scattered to densely arranged, brown, flattened, upward-pointing, to 3.5 (sometimes to 10 at sheath apices)-cm-long spines; ocreas present, conspicuous, tattering and soon falling; knees present; flagella present, to 3 m long; leaf rachis to 1.3 m long with 30–65 linear-lanceolate leaflets per side, these regularly arranged, the apical ones smaller than the others; cirri absent. Inflorescences to 3 m long, flagellate, bracts not sheathing, split open and flat, brown; fruits globose, to 0.8 cm diameter, yellowish or brown.
Range and habitat. Bangladesh, Bhutan, Cambodia, China (Yunnan), eastern and northeastern India (Assam, Bihar, Manipur, Meghalaya, Nagaland, Orissa, Sikkim, Tripura, West Bengal), Laos (Southern), Myanmar (Ayeyarwady, Bago, Kachin, Sagaing, Yangon), Thailand (East, Peninsular, Southeast), and possibly Vietnam (also in Peninsular Malaysia); lowland and montane rain forest, scrub forest, dry forest, and in disturbed places, especially roadsides, to 1200 m elevation, rarely more.
Uses. Provides a good-quality cane used in basketry and furniture making.
Synonyms. *Calamus guruba* var. *ellipsoideus* S. Y. Chen & K. L. Wang, *Calamus mastersianus* Griff., *Calamus multirameus* Ridl., *Calamus nitidus* Mart., *Daemonorops guruba* (Buch.-Ham.) Mart., *Daemonorops guruba* var. *hamiltonianus* Mart., *Daemonorops guruba* var. *mastersianus* (Griff.) Mart., *Palmijuncus guruba* (Buch.-Ham.) Kuntze, *Palmijuncus nitidus* (Mart.) Kuntze

Calamus hainanensis   PLATES 13 & 14
C. C. Chang & L. G. Xu

Field characters. Stems clustered, climbing, to 15 m long and 1 cm diameter. Leaf sheaths green with brown and whitish hairs, without spines or with scattered, conical-based, to 0.5-cm-long spines;

ocreas present, small; knees inconspicuous or absent; flagella present; petioles very short; leaf rachis to 0.4 m long with 12–14 linear leaflets per side, these regularly arranged but with wide gaps between groups, shiny green, curled over at the tips, the apical ones inserted close together in a fan shape, the apical pair not joined at their bases; cirri absent. Inflorescences to 0.7 m long, flagellate; bracts tubular; fruits ellipsoid, to 2.7 cm long and 2 cm diameter, yellowish or orange, with grooved scales, stalked.

Range and habitat. China (Hainan); lowland rain forest to 1000 m elevation.
Uses. None recorded.
Notes. Very similar to *C. gracilis*, and sometimes included there. However, it appears distinct in its larger fruits.

Calamus harmandii Pierre
nyaa seui (Lao)

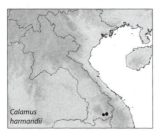

Field characters. Stems solitary, nonclimbing, freestanding, to 1.1 m long and 4 cm diameter. Leaf sheaths open, green with scattered, yellowish, flattened, to 3-cm-long spines; ocreas present, prominent, spiny; knees absent; flagella absent; petioles with whorls of yellow spines; leaf rachis to 1 m long with 30–37 linear leaflets per side, these regularly arranged; cirri absent. Inflorescences to 1.4 m long, erect, not flagellate; bracts split, open and tattering at the apices; partial inflorescences unbranched; fruits globose-ellipsoid, to 1.2 cm long and 0.9 cm diameter, brown.
Range and habitat. Laos (Southern) and possibly Thailand (North) and Vietnam (Central); lowland rain forest at low elevations.
Uses. The fruits are eaten.
Notes. Evans (2000) has given an account of the recent rediscovery of this species.
Synonym. *Zalacella harmandii* (Pierre) Becc.

Calamus henryanus Becc.   PLATE 14
dian nan sheng teng, mao-teng (Chi), wai namlee (Lao), mauk chee kyein (Mya), wai bun (Tha)

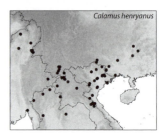

Field characters. Stems clustered, climbing, to 20 m long and 1.8 cm diameter. Leaf sheaths with mottled, reddish brown hairs, with scattered, yellowish, flattened, triangular, to 2 (sometimes a few spines to 7 at sheath apices)-cm-long spines; ocreas present, very small, sometimes spiny; knees present; flagella present, to 4 m long; leaf rachis to 1.3 m long with 30–45 linear leaflets per side, these regularly arranged, or often regularly arranged but with gaps; cirri absent. Inflorescences to 4.5 m long, flagellate; bracts tattering at apices; fruits globose to ellipsoid, to 1.5 cm long and 1 cm diameter, yellowish brown.
Range and habitat. China (Guangxi, Yunnan, and just reaching Sichuan), Laos (Central, Northern), Myanmar (Kachin, Mon, Shan), Thailand (North, Northeast), and Vietnam (Central, Northern); lowland or montane rain forest, or scrub forest, to 1700 m elevation.
Uses. Provides a cane used in furniture making.
Notes. Specimens of this species have been identified as *C. rugosus* Becc. (Chen et al. 2002). However, these identifications appear to be mistaken, and *C. rugosus* probably does not occur in our area. *Calamus henryanus* is similar to *C. multispicatus*, but differs in its partial inflorescences with elongate terminal flowering branches.
Synonyms. *Calamus balansaeanus* Becc., *Calamus balansaeanus* var. *castanolepis* (C. F. Wei) S. J. Pei & S. Y. Chen, *Calamus henryanus* var. *castanolepis* C. F. Wei

Calamus hookerianus Becc.   PLATE 14
velichural (Ind)

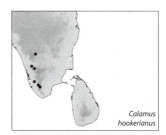

Field characters. Stems clustered, climbing, to 10 m long and 4 cm diameter. Leaf sheaths brownish green with brown hairs, with densely spaced, brownish, triangular, to 2.5 (to 18 at sheath apices, these arranged in a fan)-cm-long spines; ocreas present; knees present; flagella present, to 5 m long; leaf rachis to 1.3 m long with to 40 linear leaflets per side, these regularly arranged; cirri absent. Inflorescences to 5 m long, flagellate; bracts tubular; fruits globose, to 1 cm diameter, yellowish brown.

Range and habitat. Southwestern India (Karnataka, Kerala, Tamil Nadu); lowland rain forest to 1000 m elevation.

Uses. Provides a medium-quality cane used in furniture making and basketry.

Calamus hukaungensis Henderson   PLATE 15
htin phu (Mya)

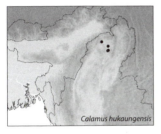
Calamus hukaungensis

Field characters. Stems clustered, climbing, to 4 m long and 1 cm diameter. Leaf sheaths greenish brown with whitish hairs, with densely arranged, reddish brown, flattened, horizontally spreading spines to 1 cm long; knees present; ocreas present, densely bristly; flagella present, to 1.5 m long; leaf rachis to 0.3 m long with 4–6 lanceolate leaflets per side, these arranged in distant groups, the apical pair joined at their bases; cirri absent. Inflorescences to 2 m long, flagellate; bracts loosely sheathing, the apical margins densely covered with bristles; fruits not known.

Range and habitat. Myanmar (Kachin); lowland forest on flat land at 190–285 m elevation.

Uses. The stems are used for weaving.

Calamus hypoleucus (Kurz) Kurz

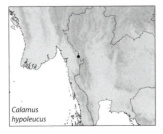
Calamus hypoleucus

Field characters. Stems climbing, to 0.8 cm diameter. Leaf sheaths greenish brown with brown hairs, with sparsely arranged, brown, flattened, recurved spines to 0.5 cm long; knees present; ocreas present, very short;

flagella absent; leaf rachis to 0.3 m long with about 8 broadly lanceolate leaflets per side, these arranged in distant pairs, gray on the lower surfaces, the apical pair free or briefly joined at their bases; cirri absent. Inflorescences to 0.15 m long, not flagellate; bracts open, not sheathing the main axis; fruits not known.

Range and habitat. Myanmar (Kayin); lowland forest at low elevations.

Uses. None recorded.

Notes. This poorly known rattan has been collected in only one locality in Myanmar, the Thoungyinn River near Myawadi in Kayin State. Evans et al. (2002) recognized a widespread *C. hypoleucus* occurring in both Laos and Myanmar. Henderson and Henderson (2007) separated the Laos population as *C. minor*.

Synonyms. *Daemonorops hypoleuca* Kurz, *Palmijuncus hypoleucus* (Kurz) Kuntze

Calamus insignis Griff.   PLATE 15
wai-hin (Tha)

Calamus insignis

Field characters. Stems solitary or clustered, climbing, to 40 m long and 2 cm diameter. Leaf sheaths green with reddish brown hairs, with scattered to densely arranged, yellowish, black-tipped, flattened, to 2.5-cm-long spines, these often upward-pointing; ocreas present; knees present; flagella present, to 2 m long; leaf rachis to 2 m long with 4–15 broadly lanceolate, almost oblong, leathery leaflets per side, these regularly arranged, the apical pair usually joined at their bases; cirri absent. Inflorescences to 2 m long, flagellate; bracts tubular; fruits ellipsoid, to 1.2 cm long and 0.7 cm diameter, yellowish.

Range and habitat. Thailand (Peninsular) (also in Peninsular Malaysia and Sumatra); lowland rain forest to 1000 m elevation.

Uses. Provides a good-quality cane used in basketry and furniture making.

Notes. A variable species in which three varieties are recognized: var. *insignis* from Thailand and Peninsular Malaysia; var. *longispinosus* J. Dransf., with longer leaf sheath spines, from Sumatra, Thailand and Peninsular Malaysia; and var. *robustus* (Becc.) J. Dransf., with larger stems, leaves, and inflorescences, from Thailand and Peninsular Malaysia.

Synonyms. *Calamus spathulatus* Becc., *Calamus spathulatus* var. *robustus* Becc., *Calamus subspathulatus* Ridl., *Palmijuncus insignis* (Griff.) Kuntze

Calamus javensis Blume

PLATE 15

kyein (Mya), wai kuan, wai-lek (Tha)

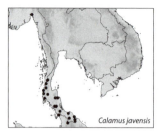

Calamus javensis

Field characters. Stems clustered, climbing, to 10 m long and 1 cm diameter. Leaf sheaths green, without spines or with scattered to densely arranged, brown, flattened or bulbous-based, to 0.5-cm-long spines; ocreas present; knees present; flagella present, to 1.3 m long; petioles short; leaf rachis to 0.6 m long with 5–10 lanceolate to broadly lanceolate leaflets per side, these irregularly arranged, the basal pair often swept back across the sheath, the apical pair joined for most of their length; cirri absent. Inflorescences to 1.5 m long, flagellate; bracts tubular, briefly split open and flat at the apex; fruits ellipsoid, to 1.5 cm long and 1.2 cm diameter, whitish.
Range and habitat. Myanmar (Mon, Tanintharyi) and Thailand (Peninsular) (also in Borneo, Java, Singapore, Sumatra, and Peninsular Malaysia); lowland or montane rain forest, to 1200 m elevation.
Uses. Provides a thin cane for tying and basketry; the hearts are eaten.
Synonyms. *Calamus amplectens* Becc., *Calamus borneensis* Miq., *Calamus equestris* Blume, *Calamus filiformis* Becc., *Calamus javensis* var. *acicularis* Becc., *Calamus javensis* var. *intermedius* Becc., *Calamus javensis* var. *peninsularis* Becc., *Calamus javensis* var. *polyphyllus* Becc., *Calamus javensis* var. *sublaevis* Becc., *Calamus javensis* var. *tenuissimus* Becc., *Calamus javensis* var. *tetrastichus* Becc., *Calamus javensis* var. *peninsularis* subvar. *pinangianus* Becc., *Calamus javensis* var. *peninsularis* subvar. *purpurascens* Becc., *Calamus javensis* var. *tetrastichus* subvar. *mollispinus* Becc., *Calamus javensis* subvar. *exilis* Becc., *Calamus javensis* subvar. *intermedius* Becc., *Calamus javensis* subvar. *penangianus* Becc., *Calamus javensis* subvar. *polyphyllus* Becc., *Calamus javensis* subvar. *purpurascens* Becc., *Calamus kemamanensis* Furtado, *Calamus tetrastichus* Blume, *Palmijuncus amplectens* (Becc.) Kuntze, *Palmijuncus borneensis* (Miq.) Kuntze, *Palmijuncus javensis* (Blume) Kuntze, *Palmijuncus penicellatus* (Roxb.) Kuntze, *Palmijuncus tetrastichus* (Blume) Kuntze

Calamus karnatakensis Renuka & Lakshmana

handibetha (Ind)

Field characters. Stems clustered, climbing, to 35 m long and 3 cm diameter. Leaf sheaths yellow-ish green with brown hairs, with scattered or rings of black, flattened, upward-pointing, to 2.5 (sometimes to 4 at sheath apices)-cm-long spines; ocreas present, to 6 cm long, spiny; knees present; flagella present; leaf rachis to 1.2 m long with numerous linear-lanceolate leaflets per side, these regularly arranged and with long hairs on the veins above and below, the apical pair joined at their bases; cirri absent. Inflorescences elongate, flagellate; bracts tubular; fruits globose, to 0.8 cm diameter, yellow.

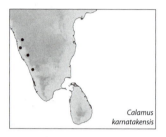

Calamus karnatakensis

Range and habitat. Southwestern India (Karnataka, possibly Goa and Kerala); lowland or montane rain forest at 500–1200 m elevation.
Uses. Provides a good-quality cane used in furniture making.

Calamus kingianus Becc.

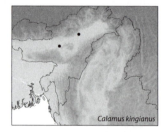

Calamus kingianus

Field characters. Stems clustered, climbing, to 5 m long and 1.2 cm diameter. Leaf sheaths green with brown hairs, with densely arranged, greenish, flattened, to 1-cm-long spines, these sometimes in short rows; ocreas present, bristly; knees present; flagella not seen, possibly absent; leaf rachis to 0.6 m long with about 6 lanceolate leaflets per side, these in distinct clusters, the apical pair briefly joined at their bases; cirri absent. Inflorescences elongate, flagellate; bracts tubular; fruits globose, to 1 cm diameter, yellowish.
Range and habitat. Northeastern India (Assam); lowland rain forest to 500 m elevation.
Uses. The fruits are eaten.
Notes. Evans et al. (2002) recognized a widespread *C. kingianus* occurring in both Laos and northeastern India. Henderson and Henderson (2007) separated the Laos population as *C. evansii*.

Calamus kontumensis Henderson, N. K. Ban & N. Q. Dung

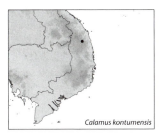
Calamus kontumensis

Field characters. Stem branching not known, climbing, to 3 m long and 0.9 cm diameter. Leaf sheaths green with brown hairs, with scattered, yellowish, black-tipped, flattened, to 1-cm-long spines, sometimes spines absent; ocreas present; knees present; flagella to 0.2 m long; leaf rachis to 0.3 m long with 5 or 6 lanceolate leaflets per side, these in distinct clusters, the apical pair briefly joined at their bases; cirri absent. Inflorescences to 0.5 m long, briefly flagellate, bracts splitting to the base, tattering; fruits globose, to 0.7 cm diameter, brown.
Range and habitat. Vietnam (Central); montane rain forest at 1100–1200 m elevation.
Uses. None recorded.

Calamus lacciferus Lakshmana & Renuka
neerubetha (Ind)

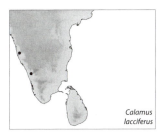
Calamus lacciferus

Field characters. Stems clustered, to 15 m long and 4 cm diameter. Leaf sheaths grayish green with brown hairs, with scattered or rings of greenish, bulbous-based, to 0.5-cm-long spines; ocreas present, inconspicuous; knees present; flagella elongate; petioles and rachis exuding a milky latex when cut; leaf rachis to 1.6 m long with numerous linear-lanceolate leaflets, these regularly arranged and with long hairs on the veins above and below; cirri absent. Inflorescences elongate, flagellate, rooting at the apices and forming new plants; bracts tubular; fruits globose, to 2 cm diameter, stalked, yellow.
Range and habitat. Southwestern India (Karnataka, Kerala); lowland rain forest to 950 m elevation.
Uses. None recorded.

Calamus laevigatus Mart.
wai kri ya (Tha)

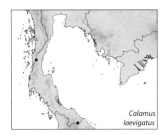
Calamus laevigatus

Field characters. Stems solitary, climbing, to 30 m long and 2 cm diameter. Leaf sheaths green with brown hairs, with scattered, green, triangular, to 1-cm-long spines; ocreas very short or absent; knees present; flagella absent; petioles short or absent; leaf rachis to 1 m long with to 20 lanceolate leaflets per side, these clustered, the basal leaflets swept back across the sheath and often forming ant chambers; cirri present, to 0.7 cm long. Inflorescences to 1 m long, not flagellate; bracts tubular; fruits globose, to 1.2 cm diameter, yellowish.
Range and habitat. Thailand (Peninsular) (also in Borneo, Peninsular Malaysia, Singapore, and Sumatra); lowland rain forest to 800 m elevation.
Uses. Provides a good-quality cane for use in furniture making.
Notes. Three varieties are recognized: var. *laevigatus* from Thailand, Peninsular Malaysia, and Singapore; var. *mucronatus* (Becc.) J. Dransf., with few, broadly lanceolate leaflets, from Borneo and Sumatra; and var. *serpentinus* J. Dransf., with few, narrowly linear leaflets, from Borneo.
Synonyms. *Calamus mucronatus* Becc., *Calamus pallidulus* Becc., *Calamus retrophyllus* Becc., *Ceratolobus laevigatus* (Mart.) Becc. & Hook. f., *Palmijuncus laevigatus* (Mart.) Kuntze

Calamus lakshmanae Renuka
halubetha (Ind)

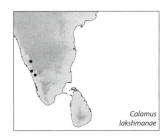
Calamus lakshmanae

Field characters. Stems clustered, climbing, to 20 m long and 2.5 cm diameter. Leaf sheaths yellowish green with brown hairs, with scattered to densely arranged, yellowish, bulbous-based, upward-pointing, to 2-cm-long spines; ocreas present, inconspicuous; knees present; flagella present;

leaf rachis to 1.4 m long with to 36 linear-lanceolate leaflets per side, these regularly arranged and with long hairs on the veins above and below; cirri absent. Inflorescences elongate, flagellate; bracts tubular; fruits globose to ovoid, to 1 cm long and 0.7 cm diameter, brownish yellow.

Range and habitat. Southwestern India (Karnataka, Kerala); lowland rain forest to 1000 m elevation.

Uses. Provides a medium-quality cane used in furniture making.

Calamus laoensis T. Evans, K. Sengdala, O. Viengkham, B. Thammavong & J. Dransf.
wai leum (Lao)

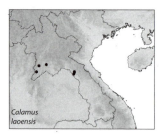

Calamus
laoensis

Field characters. Stems clustered, climbing, to 40 m long and 5 cm diameter. Leaf sheaths dark green with brown hairs, with densely arranged, brown, black-tipped, flattened, triangular, to 6-cm-long spines, interspersed with many small spines; ocreas present, spiny; knees present; flagella present, elongate; leaf rachis to 2 m long with to 50 lanceolate leaflets per side, these clustered in groups of 2–5 and spreading in different planes, whitish on lower surfaces; cirri absent. Inflorescences to 6 m long, flagellate; bracts tubular, split, open and spreading at the apices; fruits ellipsoid, to 2 cm long and 1.2 cm diameter, brown, with grooved scales.

Range and habitat. Laos (Central); lowland rain forest at low elevations.

Uses. Provides a cane used in furniture making and basketry.

Calamus lateralis Henderson, N. K. Ban & N. Q. Dung   PLATE 16
may tu, may xanh (Vie)

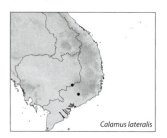

Calamus lateralis

Field characters. Stems solitary, climbing, to 70 m long and 5.5 cm diameter. Leaf sheaths green with dark reddish brown hairs initially, without spines or with a few, hooked, to 1-cm-long spines; ocreas very small, membranous; knees present; flagella present, to 5 m long; leaf rachis to 1.4 m long with 39–51 lanceolate leaflets per side, these regularly arranged; cirri absent. Inflorescences to 2.8 m long, flagellate (male ones not flagellate); bracts tubular; fruits ellipsoid, to 3.5 cm long and 2 cm diameter, orange.

Range and habitat. Cambodia and Vietnam (Southern); lowland rain forest or semievergreen forest at low elevations.

Uses. Provides a high-quality cane used in furniture making.

Notes. It is distinguished from the similar *C. poilanei* by its ruminate endosperm.

Calamus leptospadix Griff.   PLATE 16
kukhre bet (Bhu), lat, takik (Ind), dhangri bet (Ind, Nep), moke-soe-ma (Mya)

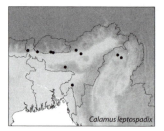

Calamus leptospadix

Field characters. Stems clustered, climbing, to 25 m long and 2 cm diameter. Leaf sheaths green with grayish brown hairs, with scattered to densely arranged, brownish, flattened, to 2.5 (to 5 at sheath apices)-cm-long spines, those at sheath apices needlelike, yellowish; ocreas present, to 1.5 cm long, densely bristly, with long, needlelike spines; knees present; flagella present; leaf rachis to 2 m long with 50–55 linear leaflets per side, these regularly arranged; cirri absent. Inflorescences to 4 m long, flagellate; bracts tubular, briefly open and spreading at the apices; flowering branches very short; fruits globose, to 1.5 cm diameter, white or yellowish.

Range and habitat. Bangladesh, Bhutan, northeastern India (Arunachal Pradesh, Assam, Manipur, Meghalaya, Nagaland, Sikkim, Tripura, West Bengal), Myanmar (Kachin), and Nepal; lowland or montane rain forest, often along river margins, to 1300 m elevation.

Uses. Provides a low-quality cane used in basketry and furniture making.

Synonym. *Palmijuncus leptospadix* (Griff.) Kuntze

Calamus longisetus Griff.   PLATE 16
jungli bet, umdah (And, Ncb), udum bet (Ban), la mei, lémé (Mya), wai pong, waigum-puon (Tha)

Plate 17. *Calamus luridus*; leaf sheath; Thailand (top left). *Calamus manan*; leaf sheath; Thailand (top right). *Calamus modestus*; habit; Vietnam (bottom left). *Calamus modestus*; leaf sheath; Vietnam (bottom right).

Plate 18. *Calamus multispicatus*; leaf and inflorescence; China (top left). *Calamus nambariensis*; leaf sheath; Myanmar (top right). *Calamus nambariensis*; leaf sheath; Myanmar (bottom left). *Calamus nambariensis*; fruits; Vietnam (bottom right).

Plate 19. *Calamus nuichuaensis*; habit; Vietnam (top left). *Calamus nuichuaensis*; infructescence; Vietnam (top right). *Calamus ornatus* var. *ornatus*; leaf sheath; Thailand (bottom left). *Calamus ovoideus*; leaf sheath; Sri Lanka (bottom right).

Plate 20. *Calamus oxleyanus* var. *oxleyanus*; leaf sheath; Thailand (top left). *Calamus palustris*; leaf sheath; Myanmar (top right). *Calamus peregrinus*; leaf sheath and male flowers; Thailand (bottom left). *Calamus poilanei*; leaf sheath; Vietnam (bottom right).

Plate 21. *Calamus rhabdocladus*; young leaf; China (top left). *Calamus rhabdocladus*; leaf sheath; Vietnam (top right). *Calamus rudentum*; habit; Vietnam (bottom left). *Calamus rudentum*; leaf sheath; Vietnam (bottom right).

Plate 22. *Calamus rudentum*; fruits; Vietnam (top left). *Calamus scipionum*; leaf sheath; Thailand (top right). *Calamus spiralis*; leaf sheath; Vietnam (bottom left). *Calamus tenuis*; habit; India (bottom right).

Plate 23. *Calamus tenuis*; leaf sheath; Myanmar (top left). *Calamus tetradactyloides*; leaf sheath; China (top right). *Calamus tetradactylus*; apical leaflets; China (bottom left). *Calamus tetradactylus*; leaf sheath; Vietnam (bottom right).

Plate 24. *Calamus thwaitesii*; leaf sheath; India (top left). *Calamus thysanolepis*; leaflets; China (top right). *Calamus travancoricus*; leaf sheath; India (bottom left). *Calamus viminalis*; leaf sheath; Myanmar (bottom right).

Plate 25. *Calamus walkeri*; habit; Vietnam (top left). *Calamus walkeri*; leaf sheath; Vietnam (top right). *Calamus wuliangshanensis* var. *wuliangshanensis*; leaflets; China (bottom left). *Calamus zeylanicus*; habit; Sri Lanka (bottom right).

Plate 26. *Caryota maxima*; habit; Vietnam (top left). *Caryota mitis*; infructescences; Vietnam (top right). *Caryota monostachya*; flowers; Vietnam (bottom left). *Caryota obtusa*; habit; China (bottom right).

Plate 27. *Caryota sympetala*; habit; Vietnam (top left). *Caryota sympetala*; inflorescence; Vietnam (top right). *Caryota urens*; habit; Sri Lanka (bottom left). *Ceratolobus subangulatus*; infructescence; West Malaysia (bottom right).

Plate 28. *Chuniophoenix hainanensis*; habit; China (top left). *Chuniophoenix hainanensis*; flowers; China (top right). *Chuniophoenix humilis*; habit; China (bottom left). *Chuniophoenix nana*; habit; Vietnam (bottom right).

Plate 29. *Clinostigma savoryanum*; habit; Bonin Islands (top left). *Corypha lecomtei*; habit; Vietnam (top right). *Corypha umbraculifera*; habit; Sri Lanka (bottom left). *Corypha utan*; habit; Thailand (bottom right).

Plate 30. *Cyrtostachus renda*; habit; Thailand (top left). *Daemonorops angustifolia*; habit; Thailand (top right). *Daemonorops angustifolia*; infructescence; Thailand (bottom left). *Daemonorops didymophylla*; infructescence; Thailand (bottom right).

Plate 31. *Daemonorops didymophylla*; leaflets; Thailand (top left). *Daemonorops jenkinsiana*; habit; China (top right). *Daemonorops jenkinsiana*; inflorescence; Vietnam (bottom left). *Daemonorops kunstleri*; leaf sheath; Thailand (bottom right).

Plate 32. *Daemonorops poilanei*; inflorescences; Vietnam (top left). *Daemonorops poilanei*; leaf sheath; Vietnam (top right). *Daemonorops sabut*; leaflets; Thailand (bottom left). *Daemonorops sabut*; leaf sheath; Thailand (bottom right).

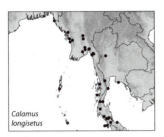

Calamus
longisetus

Field characters. Stems clustered, climbing, to 50 m long and 10 cm diameter. Leaf sheaths green with brownish hairs, with densely arranged or short rows of brown, flattened, to 6 (sometimes to 10 at sheath apices)-cm-long spines, these interspersed among very short spines; ocreas present, inconspicuous; knees present, inconspicuous; flagella present, to 13 m long; leaf rachis to 4 m long with 30–75 lanceolate leaflets per side, these irregularly arranged in clusters and spreading in different planes; cirri absent. Inflorescences to 10 m long, flagellate; bracts tubular, splitting and tattering at the apices; fruits ellipsoid, to 3.5 cm long and 2 cm diameter, the scales dark brown with paler brown, lacerated fringes.

Range and habitat. Andaman and Nicobar islands, Bangladesh, Myanmar (Bago, Kayin, Mon, Rakhine, Tanintharyi, Yangon), and Thailand (Peninsular, Southeast, Southwest) (also in Peninsular Malaysia); lowland rain forest or more open places, persisting in disturbed areas, at low elevations.

Uses. Provides a low-quality cane used in furniture making. The leaves are used for thatching and the fruits are eaten.

Synonyms. *Calamus tigrinus* Kurz, *Palmijuncus longisetus* (Griff.) Kuntze, *Palmijuncus trigrinus* (Kurz) Kuntze

Calamus luridus Becc.   PLATE 17
wai sai (Tha)

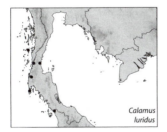

Calamus
luridus

Field characters. Stems clustered, climbing, to 20 m long and 2 cm diameter. Leaf sheaths green with brown hairs, with scattered to densely arranged, green, flattened, often downward-pointing, to 1-cm-long spines; ocreas present; knees present; flagella present, to 2.3 m long; leaf rachis to 1.3 m long with 6–12 lanceolate leaflets per side, these regularly arranged and distantly spaced; cirri absent. Inflores-

cences to 2 m long, flagellate; bracts tubular; fruits ellipsoid, 1 cm long and 0.8 cm diameter, yellowish.

Range and habitat. Myanmar (Tanintharyi) and Thailand (Peninsular) (also in Peninsular Malaysia and Singapore); lowland or montane rain forest to 1400 m elevation.

Uses. Provides a medium-quality cane used in furniture making.

Notes. The few specimens from Myanmar and Thailand have 6–12 lanceolate leaflets per side of the rachis, although in Peninsular Malaysia the species is reported to have as many as 50 linear leaflets per side of the rachis (Dransfield 1979a).

Synonyms. *Calamus belumutensis* Furtado, *Calamus distans* Ridl., *Calamus laxiflorus* Becc.

Calamus macrorhynchus Burret
da hui sheng teng (Chi)

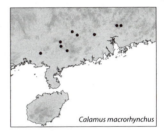

Calamus macrorhynchus

Field characters. Stems clustered, nonclimbing, to 3 m long and 4 cm diameter. Leaf sheaths brown with brown hairs, with short rows of yellowish, flattened, to 2.5-cm-long spines; ocreas present, to 15 cm long, spiny, elongate, fibrous and tattering; knees absent; flagella absent; leaf rachis to 1 m long with 30–45 linear leaflets per side, these regularly arranged but with gaps, whitish on lower surfaces; cirri absent. Inflorescences to 1 m long, not flagellate; bracts tattering from the base; fruits ovoid or pear-shaped, to 2.7 cm long and 1.5 cm diameter, reddish brown, the scales fringed with dense, brown hairs.

Range and habitat. China (Guangdong, Guangxi); lowland or montane rain forest or bamboo forest, in hilly places usually near streams, 460–1350 m elevation.

Uses. None recorded.

Notes. This species is similar to both *C. oxycarpus* and *C. albidus*, and the three have been confused (Guo Lixiu & Henderson 2007).

Calamus manan Miq.   PLATE 17
wai-bu-bo (Tha)

Field characters. Stems solitary, climbing, to 100 m long and 11 cm diameter. Leaf sheaths gray-green with white waxy hairs, with scattered or grouped, black, flattened, triangular, to 3-cm-long spines; ocreas very small or absent; knees present; flagella absent; leaf rachis to 5 m long with 45–60 linear-lanceolate leaflets per side, these regularly arranged, pendulous; cirri present, to 3 m long. Inflorescences to 2.5 m long, not flagellate; bracts tubular; fruits globose-ellipsoid, to 2.8 cm long and 2 cm diameter, yellowish.

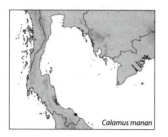

Calamus manan

Range and habitat. Thailand (Peninsular) (also in Borneo, Sumatra, and Peninsular Malaysia); on steep slopes in lowland rain forest to 1000 m elevation.
Uses. Provides one of the highest-quality, large-diameter canes for furniture making.
Synonyms. *Calamus giganteus* Becc., *Palmijuncus manan* (Miq.) Kuntze, *Rotang manan* (Miq.) Baill.

Calamus meghalayensis Henderson
risigin, tairu, rita (Ind)

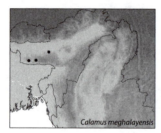

Calamus meghalayensis

Field characters. Stems to 2 m long and 0.6 cm diameter. Leaf sheaths green with brown hairs, sparsely covered with brown, flattened, horizontally spreading spines to 1 cm long; knees present; ocreas present, densely bristly; flagella present, to 2 m long; rachis to 0.3 m long with 4 or 5 lanceolate leaflets per side, these arranged in distant groups or solitary, the apical pair free or briefly joined at their bases; cirri absent. Inflorescences to 1 m long, flagellate; bracts tubular, bristly at the apices; fruits globose, to 1 cm diameter, yellowish.
Range and habitat. Northeastern India (Meghalaya); lowland forest at low elevations in the Khasi Hills.
Uses. None recorded.
Synonym. *Calamus floribundus* var. *depauperatus* Becc.

Calamus melanacanthus Mart.
medan (Mya)

Field characters. Stems clustered, climbing, to 25 m long and 2.5 cm diameter. Leaf sheaths green,

with dense, brown hairs, with scattered, light brown, hairy, flattened, upward-pointing, to 1-cm-long spines; ocreas present, very short; knees present; flagella present, to 4 m long; leaf rachis to 1 m long with 34–38 linear-lanceolate leaflets per side, these regularly arranged; cirri absent. Inflorescences elongate, flagellate; bracts tubular; fruits ovoid-ellipsoid, to 2.5 cm long and 1.5 cm diameter, yellowish, stalked.

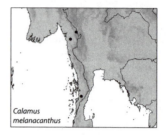

Calamus melanacanthus

Range and habitat. Myanmar (Tanintharyi); lowland rain forest at low elevations.
Uses. None recorded.
Notes. A poorly known species, represented by only a few specimens.
Synonym. *Palmijuncus melanacanthus* (Mart.) Kuntze

Calamus melanochrous Burret

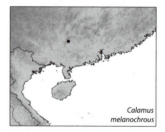

Calamus melanochrous

Field characters. Stems not known. Leaf sheaths not known; leaf rachis with to 36 linear leaflets per side, these clustered and spreading in different planes; cirri absent. Bracts tattering at the base; fruits ovoid, to 2.4 cm long and 1.8 cm diameter, black.
Range and habitat. China (Guangxi); lowland rain forest at low elevations.
Uses. None recorded.
Notes. A poorly known species, based on a single, incomplete specimen.

Calamus metzianus Schltdl.
odiyan-chural (Ind), ela wewel, kaha wewel (Srl)

Field characters. Stems clustered, climbing or forming thickets, to 15 m long and 2 cm diameter. Leaf sheaths green with dense red-brown or gray hairs, with scattered to densely arranged (sometimes in rings), yellowish or greenish triangular, to 3-cm-long spines, these hairy on the margins; ocreas present; knees present; petioles short; flagella present, to 2.5 m long; leaf rachis to 1.5 m long with 26–30 linear-lanceolate leaflets per side, these regularly arranged; cirri absent. Inflorescences to 2 m long, flagellate; bracts tubular; fruits ovoid, to 1.7 cm long and 1.1 cm diameter, yellow.

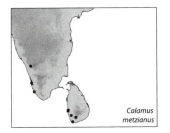

Calamus metzianus

Range and habitat. Southwestern India (Karnataka, Kerala, Tamil Nadu) and Sri Lanka; lowland rain forest or deciduous forest, often in wet areas, river margins, marshes, or disturbed places, at low elevations. **Uses.** Provides a medium-quality cane used in basketry.
Synonyms. *Calamus rivalis* Thwaites, *Calamus rudentum* Mart., *Palmijuncus rivalis* (Thwaites) Kuntze

Calamus minor Henderson
wai deng, wai hangnou (Lao)

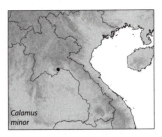

Calamus minor

Field characters. Stems clustered, to 3 m long and 1 cm diameter. Leaf sheaths greenish yellow, sparsely covered with brown, black-tipped, flattened, horizontally or upward-spreading spines to 1.4 cm (sometimes to 2.5 cm at sheath apices) long; knees present; ocreas present, fibrous, disintegrating; flagella absent; rachis to 0.7 m long with 5 or 6 lanceolate leaflets per side, these regularly but distantly arranged, gray on the lower surfaces, the apical pair briefly joined at their bases; cirri absent. Inflorescences to 0.4 m long, briefly or not flagellate; inflorescences bracts open and not sheathing; fruits not known.
Range and habitat. Laos (Northern); scrub forest or bamboo forest at 140–160 m elevation.
Uses. The shoot is edible and the stems are used for handicrafts.
Notes. Evans et al. (2002) recognized a widespread *C. hypoleucus* occurring in both Laos and Myanmar.

Henderson and Henderson (2007) separated the Laos population as *C. minor.*

Calamus modestus T. Evans & T. P. Anh   PLATE 17
heo da, song da (Vie)

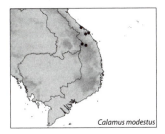

Calamus modestus

Field characters. Stems clustered, to 1.5 m tall and 2 cm diameter, nonclimbing, free-standing, to 4 m long and 2.5 cm diameter. Leaf sheaths greenish brown with whitish hairs, with rows of black, flattened, to 2.5-cm-long spines borne on ridges, interspersed with shorter spines; ocreas prominent; knees absent; flagella absent; leaf rachis to 0.8 m long with 23–34 linear leaflets per side, these regularly arranged but sometimes with gaps; cirri absent. Inflorescences to 0.5 m long, not flagellate; bracts splitting and tattering; fruits ovoid, to 1.5 cm long and 0.6 cm diameter, orange-brown.
Range and habitat. Vietnam (Central); montane rain forest at 1100–2000 m elevation.
Uses. The hearts are eaten.

Calamus multispicatus Burret   PLATE 18
lie bao shengteng (Chi)

Calamus multispicatus

Field characters. Stems clustered, climbing, to 5 m long and 1.5 cm diameter. Leaf sheaths with brown hairs, with scattered, brown, flattened, to 1.5 (sometimes to 3 at sheath apices)-cm-long spines; ocreas present, small; knees present; flagella present, to 2 m long; leaf rachis to 1.3 m long with 33–45 linear leaflets per side, these regularly arranged; cirri absent. Inflorescences to 2 m long, flagellate; bracts tattering; fruits globose, to 1 cm diameter, yellowish brown.
Range and habitat. China (Hainan); lowland rain forest to 600 m elevation.
Uses. Provides a cane used in furniture making.

Notes. *Calamus multispicatus* is similar to *C. henryanus*, but differs in its partial inflorescences with short, terminal flowering branches.

Calamus nagbettai R. R. Fernandez & Dey
nagbetta (Ind)

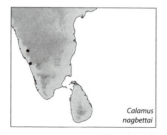

Calamus nagbettai

Field characters. Stems clustered, climbing, to 25 m long and 10 cm diameter. Leaf sheaths yellowish green with brown hairs, with densely arranged, grouped, dark brown, flattened, triangular, to 4-cm-long spines, these in rows; ocreas not known; knees present; flagella absent; leaf rachis to 3 m long with to 75 linear leaflets per side, these regularly arranged and pendulous; cirri present, to 2.5 m long. Inflorescences to 0.7 m long, not flagellate; bracts tubular; fruits ovoid, to 1.6 cm long and 1 cm diameter, brown.
Range and habitat. Southwestern India (Karnataka, Kerala); lowland or montane rain forest, to 1500 m elevation.
Uses. Provides a good-quality, mottled cane used in basketry and for walking sticks.
Notes. Similar to the Sri Lankan *C. zeylanicus* and *C. ovoideus*.

Calamus nambariensis Becc.   PLATE 18
korak bet, rong (Ban, Ind), da hong, wong t'ang (Chi), hoka-bhet (Ind), wai nwn (Lao), ya-ma-lha-kyaing, ya-ma-ta (Mya), wai hok nam kao (Tha), song mat (Vie)

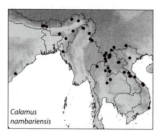

Calamus nambariensis

Field characters. Stems clustered, climbing, to 30 m long and 6 cm diameter. Leaf sheaths green with light brown hairs, with scattered to densely arranged, yellowish brown, triangular, flattened, downward-pointing, to 3.5 (rarely to 9)-cm-long spines, often interspersed among shorter spines, or sometimes spines absent; ocreas present; knees present, prominent; flagella absent; leaf rachis to 4 m

long with 36–40 lanceolate leaflets per side, these clustered or less often regularly arranged; cirri present, to 2.5 m long. Inflorescences to 2 m long, not flagellate; bracts tubular; fruits globose to ovoid or ellipsoid, to 2.4 cm long and 2.5 cm diameter (rarely to 3.4 cm long), whitish to yellowish brown, stalked, with grooved scales.
Range and habitat. Bangladesh, Bhutan, China (Yunnan), northeastern India (Arunachal Pradesh, Assam, Manipur, Meghalaya, Nagaland, Sikkim, West Bengal, with an outlier in Andhra Pradesh), Laos (Central, Northern), Myanmar (Kachin, Sagaing), Nepal, Thailand (North), and Vietnam (Central, Northern); lowland or montane rain forest, to 2000 m elevation.
Uses. Provides a high-quality cane used in furniture making and binding. It has been introduced into other areas for trial plantings.
Notes. *Calamus nambariensis* is morphologically similar to *C. palustris*, and the two can be distinguished reliably only with the female inflorescences and fruits. *Calamus nambariensis* has longer leaflets (usually more than 40 cm long and sometimes regularly arranged), longer (to 10 cm long), zigzag female flowering branches, and larger (to 2.5 cm long, rarely to 3.4 cm long) fruits that are stalked and have grooved scales. *Calamus palustris* has shorter leaflets (usually less than 35 cm long and arranged in distant, alternate clusters of 2–4 leaflets), shorter (to 7 cm long), straight female flowering branches, and smaller (to 1.2 cm long, rarely longer) fruits that are not stalked and do not have grooved scales.

The habitat and distribution of the two species also differ, although there is some overlap. *Calamus nambariensis* occurs mostly in montane forests at higher elevations (to 2000 m, but sometimes below 1000 m) in the northern part of the Southern Asian region, in mountainous regions of Bangladesh, Bhutan, China, northeastern India (with an outlier in Andhra Pradesh), Laos, Myanmar, Nepal, Thailand, and Vietnam. *Calamus palustris* occurs at lower elevations (to 1300 m, usually below 1000 m) in lowland forests in the southern parts of the region, in the Andaman Islands, Bangladesh, Cambodia, Laos, Myanmar, Thailand, and Vietnam.

Calamus nambariensis is very variable and difficult taxonomically. Indeed, it is probably the most variable species of *Calamus* in the Southern Asian region. It may be viewed as a species complex, that is, a widespread and variable species that may contain several distinct, local forms, appearing and apparently behaving as distinct species. However, at larger scales these local forms cannot be separated morphologically from one another because of intermediates.

Calamus nambariensis has been treated in local floras as consisting of several distinct species (e.g., Basu 1992; Evans et al. 2001; Hodel 1998; Pei et al. 1991). The characters used to separate these species are based mostly on leaf sheath spines or their absence, leaflet arrangement, and fruit size. The most distinctive local forms that have been recognized at the species level are *C. inermis*, without leaf sheath spines, from northeastern India and Yunnan; *C. obovoideus*, with fruits to 3.4 cm long, from Yunnan; *C. platyacanthoides*, with long spines on the leaf sheaths, from China, Laos, and Vietnam; and *C. wailong*, with regularly arranged leaflets, from Laos, Thailand, and Yunnan.

While these local flora treatments may work on a limited scale, they do not work throughout the range of the species. For this reason I recognize only one species, *C. nambariensis*, while at the same time pointing out that many local forms are likely to be encountered (at least where these economically important rattans have not been overharvested), and that the complex is greatly in need of a modern revision. There are also nomenclatural problems. The widely accepted name used here, *C. nambariensis*, is not the oldest name, which is *C. inermis* T. Anderson. However, I follow Evans et al. (2002) and continue to use this name pending a revision of the whole complex. **Synonyms.** *Calamus doriaei* Becc., *Calamus giganteus* var. *robustus* S. J. Pei & S. Y. Chen, *Calamus inermis* T. Anderson, *Calamus inermis* var. *menghaiensis* S. Y. Chen, S. J. Pei & K. L. Wang, *Calamus khasianus* Becc., *Calamus multinervis* var. *menglaensis* S. Y. Chen, S. J. Pei & K. L. Wang, *Calamus nambariensis* var. *alpinus* S. J. Pei & S. Y. Chen, *Calamus nambariensis* var. *furfuraceus* S. J. Pei & S. Y. Chen, *Calamus nambariensis* var. *menglongensis* S. J. Pei & S. Y. Chen, *Calamus nambariensis* var. *xishuangbannaensis* S. J. Pei & S. Y. Chen, *Calamus nambariensis* var. *yingjiangensis* S. J. Pei & S. Y. Chen, *Calamus obovoideus* S. J. Pei & S. Y. Chen, *Calamus palustris* var. *longistachys* S. J. Pei & S. Y. Chen, *Calamus platyacanthoides* Merr., *Calamus platyacanthus* Warb., *Calamus platyacanthus* var. *longicarpus* S. Y. Chen & K. L. Wang, *Calamus platyacanthus* var. *mediostachys* S. J. Pei & S. Y. Chen, *Calamus polydesmus* Becc., *Calamus wailong* S. J. Pei & S. Y. Chen, *Palmijuncus inermis* (T. Anderson) Kuntze

Calamus neelagiricus Renuka

Calamus
neelagiricus

Field characters. Stems solitary, climbing, to 25 m long and 5 cm diameter. Leaf sheaths green, without hairs, with scattered, green, bulbous-based, to 1-cm-long spines; ocreas present; knees present; flagella present, to 4 m long; leaf rachis to 1.8 m long with numerous linear-lanceolate leaflets per side, these regularly arranged and with long hairs on the veins above and below; cirri absent. Inflorescences to 2.5 m long,

flagellate; bracts tubular; fruits depressed globose, to 1 cm long and 0.5 cm diameter, stalked, yellowish. **Range and habitat.** Southwestern India (Kerala); montane rain forest at 1100 elevation. **Uses.** Provides a good-quality cane used in furniture making.

Calamus nicobaricus Becc.
dahya (Ncb)

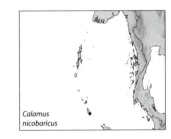

Calamus
nicobaricus

Field characters. Stems clustered, climbing, to 1.4 cm diameter. Leaf sheaths green with brown hairs, with densely arranged, brown, flattened, downward-pointing, to 2.5-cm-long spines, these interspersed among many shorter spines; ocreas present; knees present; flagella present; leaf rachis to 0.9 m long with numerous linear leaflets per side, these regularly arranged; cirri absent. Inflorescences not known. **Range and habitat.** Nicobar Islands (Great Nicobar); scrub forest at low elevations. **Uses.** None recorded. **Notes.** A poorly known species that is not known from recent collections.

Calamus nuichuaensis Henderson, PLATE 19
N. K. Ban & N. Q. Dung
sui (Vie)

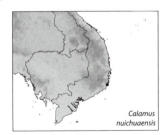

Calamus
nuichuaensis

Field characters. Stems solitary, nonclimbing, to 5 m long and 3 cm diameter. Leaf sheaths brown with brown hairs, with densely arranged, yellowish brown, flat, to 6-cm-long spines; ocreas present; knees absent; flagella absent; leaf rachis to 1 m long with about 33 lanceolate leaflets per side, these regularly arranged and spreading in the same plane; cirri absent. Inflorescences to 1.5 m long, arching below the leaves, not flagellate; bracts open; fruits globose, 2 cm diameter, reddish brown.

Range and habitat. Vietnam (Southern); lowland rain forest at 800 m elevation.
Uses. None recorded.
Notes. Only known from higher elevations in Nui Chua National Park.

Calamus oligostachys T. Evans, K. Sengdala, O. Viengkham, B. Thammavong & J. Dransf.
wai kating (Lao, Tha)

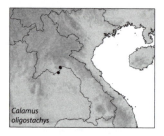

Field characters. Stems clustered, climbing, to 7 m long and 1 cm diameter. Leaf sheaths green with scattered, brown, needlelike, to 0.7-cm-long spines; ocreas present; knees present; flagella present, to 1.8 m long; leaf rachis to 0.6 m long with 5–9 lanceolate leaflets per side, these clustered, the apical ones close together in a fan shape, the apical pair joined at their bases; cirri absent. Inflorescences to 2.2 m long, flagellate; bracts tubular; fruits globose, to 0.7 cm diameter, yellowish.
Range and habitat. Laos (Central) and Thailand (Northeast); lowland rain forest at low elevations.
Uses. Provides a cane used in making handicraft making.
Synonym. *Calamus pauciflorus* T. Evans, K. Sengdala, O. Viengkham, B. Thammavong & J. Dransf.

Calamus ornatus Blume   PLATE 19
wai chaang, wai-khao-dom (Tha)

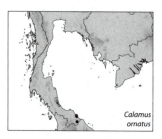

Field characters. Stems clustered, climbing, to 60 m long and 8 cm diameter. Leaf sheaths green with brown hairs, with scattered, dark brown, flattened, triangular, downward-pointing, to 4-cm-long spines; ocreas present; knees present; flagella present, to 10 m long; leaf rachis to 4 m long with 20–30 lanceolate leaflets per side, these regularly arranged, the apical ones very small; cirri absent. Inflores-

cences to 8 m long, flagellate; bracts tubular; fruits ellipsoid, to 3 cm long and 2 cm diameter, black.
Range and habitat. Thailand (Peninsular) (also in Borneo, Celebes, Java, Peninsular Malaysia, the Philippines, and Singapore); lowland rain forest or secondary forest, at low elevations.
Uses. Provides a poor-quality cane used in furniture making.
Notes. Two varieties are recognized: var. *ornatus* from Thailand, Borneo, Celebes, Java, Singapore, and Peninsular Malaysia; and var. *pulverulentus* Fernando, without spines on the leaf sheath and inflorescences with powdery hairs, from the Philippines.
Synonyms. *Calamus aureus* Reinw., *Calamus ornatus* var. *celebicus* Becc., *Calamus ornatus* var. *horridus* Becc., *Calamus ornatus* var. *philippinensis* Becc., *Calamus ovatus* Reinw., *Palmijuncus aureus* (Reinw.) Kuntze, *Palmijuncus ornatus* (Blume) Kuntze, *Rotang ornatus* (Blume) Baill.

Calamus ovoideus Thwaites   PLATE 19
sudu wewel, thudarena (Srl)

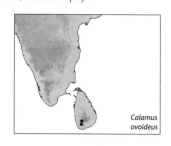

Field characters. Stems clustered, climbing, to 100 m long and 8 cm diameter. Leaf sheaths brownish with brown hairs, with closely spaced, densely arranged rings of dark brown, flattened, to 4-cm-long spines; ocreas inconspicuous; knees present; flagella absent; leaf rachis to 4 m long with 50–65 linear leaflets per side, these regularly arranged, pendulous, and whitish on lower surfaces; cirri present, to 2.5 m long. Inflorescences to 2.5 m long, not flagellate; bracts tubular; fruits ovoid, to 1.6 cm long and 1 cm diameter, yellowish green.
Range and habitat. Sri Lanka; lowland or montane rain forest in wet places, to 1500 m elevation.
Uses. Provides a high-quality, large-diameter cane used in furniture making and basketry.
Notes. Difficult to distinguish from *C. zeylanicus*, with which it occurs.
Synonym. *Palmijuncus ovoideus* (Thwaites) Kuntze

Calamus oxleyanus Teijsm. & Binn.   PLATE 20
kyein bya, kyein dan (Mya), wai dum, wai-lum-dio (Tha)

Field characters. Stems clustered or solitary, climbing to 15 m long and 3 cm diameter. Leaf sheaths green with brown hairs, with scattered, black or brown, flattened, to 5-cm-long spines; ocreas present; knees present; flagella absent; leaf rachis to 2.5 m long with 30–50 lanceolate leaflets per side, these borne in remote groups and spreading in slightly different planes, dark green with yellowish bases; cirri present, to 1.25 m long. Inflorescences to 1.3 m long, not flagellate; bracts tubular; fruits globose to ovoid, to 1.4 cm long and 1 cm diameter, yellowish brown.

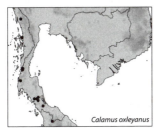
Calamus oxleyanus

Range and habitat. Myanmar (Tanintharyi) and Thailand (Peninsular) (also in Bangka Island, Peninsular Malaysia Singapore, and Sumatra); lowland rain forest at low elevations.
Uses. The canes are used to make walking sticks.
Notes. Two varieties are recognized: var. *montanus* Furtado, with broader leaflets, from Thailand and Peninsular Malaysia; and var. *oxleyanus* from Bangka Island, Myanmar, Singapore, Sumatra, Thailand, and Peninsular Malaysia.
Synonyms. *Calamus aggregatus* Burret, *Calamus diffusus* Becc., *Calamus helferianus* Kurz, *Calamus leiospathus* Bartlett, *Calamus fernandezii* H. Wendl., *Calamus oxleyanus* var. *diffusus* Becc., *Calamus oxleyanus* var. *obovatus* Becc., *Daemonorops fasciculata* Mart., *Palmijuncus fernandezii* (H. Wendl.) Kuntze, *Palmijuncus helferianus* (Kurz) Kuntze, *Palmijuncus oxleyanus* (Teijsm. & Binn.) Kuntze

Calamus oxycarpus Becc.
jian guo sheng teng (Chi)

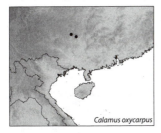
Calamus oxycarpus

Field characters. Stems clustered, nonclimbing, free-standing, to 3 m long and 2 cm diameter. Leaf sheaths not seen; ocreas not seen; knees absent; flagella absent; leaf rachis to 0.5 m long with 11–15 lanceolate or broadly lanceolate leaflets per side, these remotely clustered, whitish on the lower surfaces; cirri absent. Inflorescences to 1 m long, not flagellate; bracts tattering from the base; fruits ovoid to pear-shaped, to 3 cm long and 1.7 cm diameter,

reddish brown, the scales fringed with dense, brown hairs.
Range and habitat. China (Guangxi, Guizhou); lowland or montane rain forest on steep slopes at 880–1100 m elevation.
Uses. None recorded.
Notes. See notes under *C. macrorhynchus.*

Calamus pachystemonus Thwaites
kukulu wel (Srl)

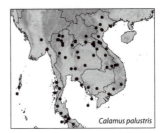
Calamus pachystemonus

Field characters. Stems clustered, climbing, to 15 m long and 1 cm diameter. Leaf sheaths green, without hairs, with scattered, dark brown, needlelike, to 0.8-cm-long spines (or spines absent), sometimes with ridges; ocreas present; knees present; flagella present; leaf rachis to 20 cm long with 3–6 broadly lanceolate leaflets per side, the apical pair joined at their bases; cirri absent. Inflorescences to 1 m long, flagellate; bracts tubular; fruits globose, to 0.5 cm diameter, brown.
Range and habitat. Sri Lanka; lowland rain forest at low elevations.
Uses. Provides a good-quality cane used in basketry.
Notes. Very similar to both *C. digitatus* and *C. radiatus.*
Synonym. *Palmijuncus pachystemonus* (Thwaites) Kuntze

Calamus palustris Griff.   PLATE 20
dunda beth (And), wai hangnou (Lao), la-me-kyein, ying kyein, ya-ma-lha-kyaing, ya-ma-ta (Mya), wai kot, wai-ling (Tha), may nuoc, may tau (Vie)

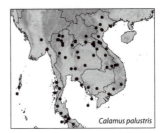
Calamus palustris

Field characters. Stems clustered or sometimes solitary, to 30 m long and 5 cm diameter. Leaf sheaths green with whitish or brownish hairs, with scattered or sometimes in partial rows, brownish, to 5-cm-long spines, these often curving downwards; ocreas present; knees present, prominent; flagella absent; petioles short, flat and spiny on upper surfaces; leaf rachis to 2 m long with 12–25 broadly lanceolate leaflets per side, these irregularly arranged, usually in distant, alternate clusters of 2–4 leaflets; cirri present, to 2 m long. Inflorescences to 1.7 m long, not flagellate; erect; bracts tubular; fruits ellipsoid to ovoid, to 1.2 cm long (rarely more) and 1 cm diameter, yellowish, with a pronounced nipple at the tip and flattened perianth at the base, the scales not grooved.

Range and habitat. Andaman Islands (and possibly Nicobar Islands), Cambodia, Laos, Myanmar (Bago, Tanintharyi), Thailand, and Vietnam (also in Peninsular Malaysia); lowland or montane rain forest, disturbed areas, and sometimes by villages, to 1300 m elevation.

Uses. Provides a good-quality cane used in furniture making, and the palm hearts are eaten.

Notes. It has been reported from other Southern Asian countries—Bangladesh, China (Yunnan), northern Myanmar, and northeastern India—but I have seen no reliable, fertile specimens from these areas. *Calamus palustris* is closely related to *C. nambariensis*—see notes under that species. The widely accepted name *C. palustris* is used here, although it may not be the oldest name. However, I continue to use this name pending a revision of the whole complex.

Synonyms. *Calamus dumetorum* Ridl., *Calamus extensus* Roxb., *Calamus gregisectus* Burret, *Calamus humilis* Roxb., *Calamus kerrianus* Becc., *Calamus latifolius* Kurz, *Calamus latifolius* Roxb., *Calamus latifolius* var. *marmoratus* Becc., *Calamus loiensis* Hodel, *Calamus macracanthus* T. Anderson, *Calamus palustris* var. *amplissimus* Becc., *Calamus palustris* var. *cochinchinensis* Becc., *Calamus palustris* var. *malaccensis* Becc., *Calamus quinquenervius* Roxb., *Palmijuncus extensus* (Roxb.) Kuntze, *Palmijuncus humilis* (Roxb.) Kuntze, *Palmijuncus latifolius* (Roxb.) Kuntze, *Palmijuncus macracanthus* (T. Anderson) Kuntze, *Palmijuncus palustris* (Griff.) Kuntze, *Palmijuncus quinquenervius* (Roxb.) Kuntze

Calamus pandanosmus Furtado
wai hawn (Tha)

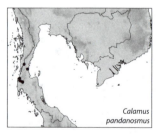

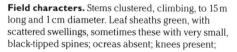

Field characters. Stems clustered, climbing, to 15 m long and 1 cm diameter. Leaf sheaths green, with scattered swellings, sometimes these with very small, black-tipped spines; ocreas absent; knees present;

flagella present, to 0.8 m long; petioles short or absent; leaf rachis to 0.5 m long with 6–8 lanceolate leaflets per side, these irregularly arranged, the apical ones inserted close together in a fan shape, the apical pair joined at their bases; cirri absent. Inflorescences to 1 m long, not flagellate; bracts tubular; fruits globose, to 1.5 cm diameter, brownish.

Range and habitat. Thailand (Peninsular) and probably Myanmar (Tanintharyi) (also in Borneo, Peninsular Malaysia, and Sumatra); lowland rain forest at low elevations.

Uses. Provides a cane used in furniture making.

Notes. The leaflets omit a fetid smell when crushed, hence the common name, meaning "smelly palm."

Calamus peregrinus Furtado   PLATE 20
wai-ngouy (Tha)

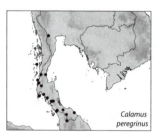

Field characters. Stems solitary, climbing, to 40 m long and 9 cm diameter. Leaf sheaths mottled green and yellow, with scattered or short rows of yellowish, black-tipped, flattened, triangular, to 4-cm-long spines, these with hairy margins; ocreas present; knees present, swollen; flagella present, to 6 m long; leaf rachis to 3.5 m long with 45–60 linear-lanceolate leaflets per side, these regularly arranged; cirri absent. Inflorescences to 6 m long, flagellate, the 2 or 3 partial inflorescences borne close to the base of the inflorescence; bracts becoming tattered and splitting lengthwise; fruits globose to obovoid, to 2 cm long and 1.6 cm diameter, stalked, reddish brown.

Range and habitat. Myanmar (Tanintharyi) and Thailand (Peninsular, Southwest) (also in Peninsular Malaysia); lowland rain forest at low elevations.

Uses. None recorded.

Calamus platyspathus Mart.
kyein bok (Mya), wai ki kai (Tha)

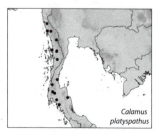

Field characters. Stems clustered, to 25 m long and 1.2 cm diameter. Leaf sheaths green with brown hairs, with densely arranged, brown, flattened, upward-pointing spines to 2 (to 5 at sheath apices) cm long, these sometimes with spines on the margins; knees present; ocreas present, fibrous and soon disintegrating; flagella present, to 1.5 m long; rachis to 0.8 m long with 4–7 broadly lanceolate leaflets per side, these regularly but distantly arranged, gray on the lower surfaces, the apical pair free or joined for about half their length; cirri absent. Inflorescences to 2 m long, flagellate; bracts open, not sheathing; fruits globose, to 0.8 cm diameter, whitish.
Range and habitat. Myanmar (Kayin, Tanintharyi) and Thailand (Peninsular); lowland forest at low elevations.
Uses. None recorded. The common name in Myanmar means "bad cane" because it is of little use.
Synonyms. *Calamus leucotes* Becc., *Calamus myrianthus* Becc., *Daemonorops platyspatha* (Mart.) Mart., *Palmijuncus platyspathus* (Mart.) Kuntze

Calamus poilanei Conrard   PLATE 20
wai thoon (Lao), wai kruh (Tha), song bot (Vie)

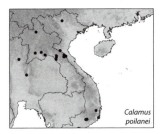

*Calamus
poilanei*

Field characters. Stems solitary, climbing, to 150 m long and 7.5 cm diameter. Leaf sheaths green or yellowish with patches or stripes of brown hairs, with scattered, greenish, flattened, triangular, to 3.5-cm-long spines (sometimes spines absent); ocreas present; knees present; flagella present, to 6 m long; leaf rachis to 3.4 m long with 40–50 linear leaflets per side, these regularly arranged; cirri absent. Inflorescences to 6 m long, flagellate; bracts tubular; fruits ellipsoid, 2 cm long and 1.4 cm diameter, brown.
Range and habitat. Laos (Central, Northern), Thailand (North, Northeast), Vietnam (Central, Southern), and probably Cambodia; lowland or montane rain forest to 1300 m elevation.
Uses. Provides a high-quality, large-diameter cane used in furniture making.
Notes. It is distinguished from the similar *C. lateralis* by its homogeneous endosperm.

Calamus prasinus Lakshmana & Renuka
ontibetha (Ind)

Field characters. Stems solitary, climbing, height not known, to 3 cm diameter. Leaf sheaths yellowish

green, with densely arranged, to 1-cm-long spines; ocreas not known; knees present; flagella present; petioles and rachis exuding a milky latex when cut; leaf rachis to 2.2 m long with numerous leaflets per side, these regularly arranged and with long hairs on the veins above and below; cirri absent. Inflorescences length not known; bracts tubular; fruits globose, stalked, yellow.

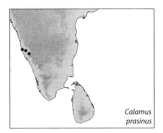

*Calamus
prasinus*

Range and habitat. Southwestern India (Karnataka); lowland rain forest to 500 m elevation.
Uses. Provides a good-quality cane used in furniture making.

Calamus pseudofeanus Basu

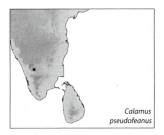

*Calamus
pseudofeanus*

Field characters. Stem branching and height not known, to 1.5 cm diameter. Leaf sheaths not known; leaf rachis with about 3 broadly lanceolate leaflets per side, these irregularly arranged, the apical pair joined at their bases; cirri absent. Inflorescences elongate, flagellate; bracts tubular; fruits ellipsoid, to 1.5 cm long and 1 cm diameter, yellow.
Range and habitat. Southwestern India (Tamil Nadu); lowland rain forest at low elevations.
Uses. None recorded.

Calamus pseudorivalis Becc.
china bet (Ncb)

Field characters. Stems clustered, climbing, to 30 m long and 3 cm diameter. Leaf sheaths green with brown hairs, with densely arranged, dark brown, flattened, triangular, to 0.8 (to 2 at sheath apices)-cm-long spines; ocreas present, very short; knees present; flagella present, elongate; leaf rachis to 1 m long with numerous linear-lanceolate leaflets per side, these regularly arranged; cirri absent. Inflorescences elongate, flagellate; bracts tubular; fruits ovoid, to 1.5 cm long and 1 cm diameter, yellowish.

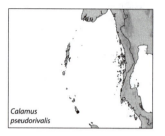

Range and habitat. Nicobar Islands (Great Nicobar); lowland rain forest in inland areas, at low elevations.
Uses. Provides a good-quality cane used in furniture making.

Calamus pseudotenuis Becc.
perumperambu, koala hangala (Ind), heen wewel (Srl)

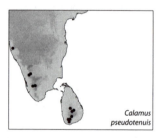

Field characters. Stems clustered, climbing, to 15 m long and 5 cm diameter. Leaf sheaths yellowish green with brown hairs, with scattered, greenish, needle-like to flattened, to 3.5 (to 12 at sheath apices)-cm-long spines, these densely hairy on the margins; ocreas present, well developed, to 10 cm long; knees present; flagella present, to 3 m long; leaf rachis to 1.5 m long with 25–40 linear-lanceolate leaflets per side, these regularly arranged; cirri absent. Inflorescences to 3 m long, flagellate; bracts tubular; fruits globose, to 1.5 cm diameter, yellow.
Range and habitat. Southwestern India (Andhra Pradesh, Karnataka, Kerala, Tamil Nadu) and Sri Lanka; lowland or montane rain forest to 1500 m elevation.
Uses. Provides a good-quality cane used in furniture making and basketry.

Calamus pulchellus Burret
mao teng (Chi)

Field characters. Stems clustered, climbing, to 6 m long and 1 cm diameter. Leaf sheaths brown with densely arranged, brown, needlelike, to 1 (to 1.5 at sheath apices)-cm-long spines; ocreas present; knees inconspicuous or absent; flagella present, to 1 m long; leaf rachis to 0.5 m long with 3–5 broadly lanceolate leaflets per side, these regularly but distantly arranged,

the apical ones inserted close together in a fan shape; cirri absent. Inflorescences to 0.7 m long, flagellate; bracts tubular; fruits not known.

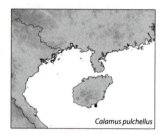

Range and habitat. China (Hainan); lowland rain forest at low elevations.
Uses. None recorded.
Notes. A rare species, known from only one collection from Hainan.

Calamus radiatus Thwaites
kukulu wel (Srl)

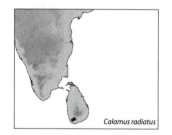

Field characters. Stems clustered, climbing, to 5 m long and 0.7 cm diameter. Leaf sheaths green with scattered to densely arranged, greenish, flattened, to 0.8-cm-long spines; ocreas present; knees present; flagella present, to 1.5 m long; leaf rachis to 2 cm long with 3 or 4 linear leaflets per side, these inserted close together in a fan shape, the apical pair briefly joined at their bases; cirri absent. Inflorescences to 1 m long, flagellate; bracts tubular; fruits globose, to 1.2 cm diameter, yellow.
Range and habitat. Sri Lanka; lowland rain forest to 1000 m elevation.
Uses. Provides a good-quality cane used in basketry.
Notes. Very similar to *C. pachystemonus* and especially to *C. digitatus*.
Synonym. *Palmijuncus radiatus* (Thwaites) Kuntze

Calamus rhabdocladus Burret   PLATE 21
da guang teng, wong teng, zhang teng (Chi), wai wan (Lao), may thuan, r'sui (Vie)

Field characters. Stems clustered, climbing (sometimes only shortly climbing or erect), to 40 m long and 6 cm diameter. Leaf sheaths green with reddish brown hairs, with densely arranged, oblique rows of glossy, black or brown, flattened, to 4 (to 10 at sheath apices)-cm-long spines; ocreas present; knees inconspicuous or absent; flagella present, to 5 m long; petioles with rings of spines; leaf rachis to 1.5 m long with to 60 linear leaflets per side, these regularly arranged (young plants regularly arranged but with gaps); cirri absent. Inflorescences to 8 m long, flagellate; bracts tubular; fruits globose, ellipsoid, or ovoid, to 1.4 cm long and 0.8 cm diameter, reddish or yellowish.

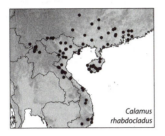

Range and habitat. China (Fujian, Guangxi, Guangdong, Guizhou, Hainan, Yunnan), Laos (Central, Northern), and Vietnam (throughout); lowland or montane rain forest, to 1600 m elevation.
Uses. Provides a cane of medium quality for furniture making, and the palm hearts and fruits are eaten.
Notes. A very common and widespread species.
Synonyms. *Calamus pseudoscutellaris* Conrard, *Calamus pseudoscutellaris* var. *cylindrocarpus* Conrard, *Calamus rhabdocladus* var. *globulosus* S. J. Pei & S. Y. Chen

Calamus rheedei Griff.
kattu chooral (Ind)

Field characters. Stems clustered, climbing, height not known, to 1.3 cm diameter. Leaf sheaths with scattered, to 1.5-cm-long spines; ocreas not known; knees present; flagella present; leaf rachis to 0.7 m long with to 12 broadly lanceolate leaflet per side, these in distinct clusters, the apical ones inserted close together in a fan shape; cirri absent. Inflorescences to 1 m long, not flagellate; bracts tubular, funnel-shaped at the apices; fruits ovoid or ellipsoid, to 2.2 cm long and 1.5 cm diameter, stalked, brown, with spinelike scales.
Range and habitat. Southwestern India (Kerala, Tamil Nadu); lowland rain forest.
Uses. None recorded.
Notes. A poorly known species, not known from any precise locality, and no map is provided. Very similar to *C. vattaliya.*
Synonyms. *Daemonorops rheedei* (Griff.) Mart., *Palmijuncus rheedei* (Griff.) Kuntze

Calamus rotang L.
betambu, perambu (Ind), polonnaru wewel, wewel (Srl)

Field characters. Stems clustered, forming thickets or climbing, to 30 m long and 2 cm diameter. Leaf

sheaths green, without hairs, with scattered, greenish to black, needlelike or flattened, to 1.5-cm-long spines; ocreas present, inconspicuous; knees present; flagella present, to 2.5 m long; petioles short or absent; leaf rachis to 0.8 m long with 30–40 linear-lanceolate leaflets per side, these regularly arranged, the apical ones very small; cirri absent. Inflorescences to 3 m long, flagellate; bracts tubular; fruits globose to ellipsoid, to 1.5 cm diameter, orange.

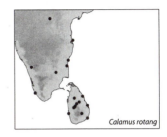

Range and habitat. Southern India (Andhra Pradesh, Kerala, Tamil Nadu, possibly north to Orissa) and Sri Lanka; open places, river margins, and coastal swamps, usually in drier regions, at low elevations.
Uses. Provides a good-quality cane used in furniture making and basketry.
Synonyms. *Calamus monoecus* Roxb., *Calamus roxburghii* Griff., *Palmijuncus monoecus* (Roxb.) Kuntze, *Rotang linnaei* Baill., *Rotanga calamus* Crantz

Calamus rudentum Lour.   PLATES 21 & 22
wai boun (Lao), kyien ni (Mya), wai-pong (Tha), cay may song, may da (Vie)

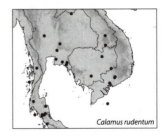

Field characters. Stems clustered, climbing, to 75 m long and 7 cm diameter. Leaf sheaths split open, not tubular, yellowish green with brown hairs, with densely arranged rows of yellowish to black, flattened, to 6 (to 15 at sheath apices)-cm-long spines, the rows borne on ridges interspersed with shorter, needlelike spines; ocreas present; knees inconspicuous or absent; flagella present, to 10 m long; upper surface of petioles without spines, deeply channeled; leaf rachis to 3 m long with 45–50 lanceolate leaflets per side, these regularly arranged; cirri absent. Inflorescences to 10 m long, flagellate; bracts tubular; fruits globose-ellipsoid, to 2 cm long and 1.5 cm diameter, yellowish, with grooved scales.

Range and habitat. Cambodia, Laos (Central, Southern), Myanmar (Tanintharyi), Thailand (Central, East, North, Peninsular, Southeast), and Vietnam (Southern); lowland rain forest and disturbed areas, at 100–500 m elevation.

Uses. Provides a high-quality cane used in furniture making.

Synonyms. *Palmijuncus rudentum* (Lour.) Kuntze, *Rotang rudentum* (Lour.) Baill.

Calamus salicifolius Becc.
lopiek, ropiek (Cbd), may la lieu (Vie)

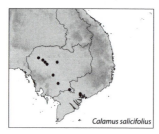

Calamus salicifolius

Field characters. Stems clustered, nonclimbing, free-standing or scrambling, to 2 m long and 0.8 cm diameter. Leaf sheaths green, with scattered, bulbous-based, black, to 1-cm-long spines, occasionally without spines; ocreas present; knees present; flagella sometimes present but very short; petioles very short; leaf rachis to 0.3 m long with to 12 very small, lanceolate leaflets per side, these strongly clustered and spreading in different planes, the apical ones smaller still, light gray-green on the lower surfaces; cirri absent. Inflorescences to 0.3 m long, not flagellate; bracts split open and briefly spreading at the apices; fruits globose, to 1 cm diameter, yellowish brown.

Range and habitat. Cambodia and Vietnam (Southern); lowland rain forest, especially river margins, at low elevations.

Uses. Provides a cane used in basketry.

Synonym. *Calamus salicifolius* var. *leiophyllus* Becc.

Calamus scipionum Lour.   PLATE 22
wai-ba-mu, wai gum (Tha)

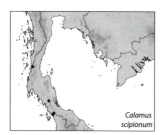

Calamus scipionum

Field characters. Stems clustered, climbing, to 50 m long and 7 cm diameter. Leaf sheaths green with whitish hairs, with scattered, black-tipped, flattened, to

5-cm-long spines, sometimes spines absent; ocreas present; knees present, conspicuous; flagella present, to 7 m long; leaf rachis to 2.3 m long with 23–30 lanceolate leaflets per side, these regularly arranged; cirri absent. Inflorescences to 7 m long, flagellate; bracts tubular; fruits ovoid, to 1.4 cm long and 0.9 cm diameter, greenish.

Range and habitat. Thailand (Peninsular) (also in Borneo, the Philippines, Sumatra, Singapore, and Peninsular Malaysia); lowland rain forest at low elevations.

Uses. Provides a good-quality cane used in furniture making and also for malacca canes.

Synonyms. *Palmijuncus scipionum* (Lour.) Kuntze, *Rotang scipionum* (Lour.) Baill.

Calamus sedens J. Dransf.
waai nang yong (Tha)

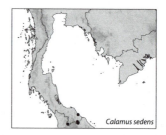

Calamus sedens

Field characters. Stems solitary, nonclimbing, usually short and subterranean or to 4 m long and 6 cm diameter. Leaf sheaths green with brown hairs, with densely arranged, green, flattened, to 4 (to 45 at sheath apices)-cm-long spines; ocreas present; knees absent; flagella absent; leaf rachis to 2 m long with 20–30 broadly lanceolate leaflets per side, these regularly arranged and strongly folded; cirri absent. Inflorescences to 1.5 m long, not flagellate; bracts not sheathing, split open and flat, soon decaying; fruits globose, to 0.8 cm diameter, red-brown.

Range and habitat. Thailand (Peninsular) (also in Peninsular Malaysia); lowland or montane rain forest to 1100 m elevation.

Uses. The canes are used to make walking sticks.

Calamus semierectus Renuka & Vijayakumaran

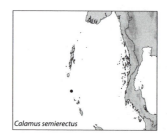

Calamus semierectus

Field characters. Stems solitary, basal part erect, upper part flexible and climbing, to 15 m long and

5 cm diameter. Leaf sheaths yellowish with brown hairs, with oblique, low ridges, these with black, needlelike, to 0.3-cm-long spines, the apices of sheath with denser spines to 1.2 cm long; ocreas inconspicuous; knees present; flagella absent; leaf rachis elongate with numerous linear leaflets per side, these regularly arranged; cirri present. Inflorescences elongate, flagellate; bracts tubular; fruits ellipsoid, to 1.5 cm long and 1 cm diameter, brown.
Range and habitat. Nicobar Islands (Car Nicobar); lowland rain forest at low elevations.
Uses. The stems are used in house construction.

Calamus setulosus J. Dransf.

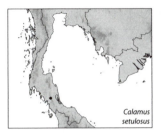

Calamus setulosus

Field characters. Stems clustered, climbing, height not known, to 1.1 cm diameter. Leaf sheaths green, with scattered, to 1 (to 3 at sheath apices)-cm-long spines; ocreas present; knees present; flagella present, to 0.6 cm long; leaf rachis to 0.8 m long with about 60 linear leaflets per side, these regularly arranged; cirri absent. Inflorescences to 1 m long, flagellate; bracts tubular; fruits not known.
Range and habitat. Thailand (Peninsular) (also in Peninsular Malaysia); lowland rain forest at low elevations.
Uses. None recorded.

Calamus shendurunii Anto, Renuka & Sreek.

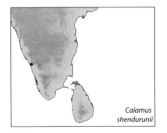

Calamus shendurunii

Field characters. Stems clustered, climbing, to 20 m long and 2 cm diameter. Leaf sheaths green with very few, black-tipped, bulbous-based, to 1-cm-long spines; ocreas not known; knees present; flagella present, to 2 m long; leaf rachis to 1 m long with numerous linear-lanceolate leaflets per side, these regularly arranged and with long hairs on the veins above and below, the apical pair briefly joined at their

bases; cirri absent. Inflorescences to 2 m long, flagellate; bracts tubular; fruits globose, to 1.8 cm diameter, stalked, greenish.
Range and habitat. Southwestern India (Kerala); lowland rain forest at 300 m elevation.
Uses. None recorded.

Calamus siamensis Becc.
wai khom (Lao)

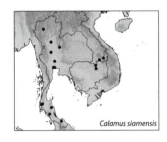

Calamus siamensis

Field characters. Stems clustered, climbing, to 25 m long and 2 cm diameter, or often forming thickets. Leaf sheaths green, with brown hairs, with scattered, brown, flattened, to 4.5 (sometimes a few spines to 7 at sheath apices)-cm-long spines, interspersed among shorter spines; ocreas present, inconspicuous; knees present; flagella present, to 3 m long; leaf rachis to 1.5 m long with 30–50 linear leaflets per side, these regularly arranged, sometimes with gaps; cirri absent. Inflorescences to 2.5 m long, flagellate; bracts tubular; fruits globose, 0.8 cm diameter, whitish or yellowish, sometimes borne in pairs.
Range and habitat. Cambodia, Laos (Southern), Thailand (Central, North, Northeast, Peninsular), and probably Myanmar (also in Peninsular Malaysia); lowland rain forest, scrub forest, or disturbed areas, at low elevations.
Uses. Provides a cane for use in furniture making; planted for its palm heart.
Notes. Similar to *C. viminalis* but differing in its regularly arranged leaflets.
Synonym. *Calamus siamensis* var. *malaianus* Furtado

Calamus simplicifolius C. F. Wei
danye shengteng (Chi)

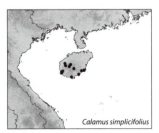

Calamus simplicifolius

Field characters. Stems clustered, climbing, to 50 m long and to 6 cm diameter. Leaf sheaths green

with brown hairs, with densely arranged, yellowish, flattened, triangular, downward-pointing, to 4-cm-long spines; ocreas absent; knees present; flagella absent; leaf rachis to 2 m long with 14–22 broadly lanceolate leaflets per side, these regularly arranged, tending to be irregular on younger leaves; cirri present, to 1.5 m long. Inflorescences to 1 m long, not flagellate; bracts tubular; fruits globose, to 3 cm long and 2.3 cm diameter, yellowish.
Range and habitat. China (Hainan); lowland rain forest at low elevations.
Uses. Provides a high-quality cane used in furniture making and binding. It has been introduced into other areas of China for trial plantings.

Calamus siphonospathus Mart.
lanyu sheng-teng (Tai)

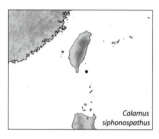

Field characters. Stems solitary, climbing, to 30 m long and 6 cm diameter. Leaf sheaths yellowish, without hairs, with rows of brown, triangular, to 1-cm-long spines; ocreas present, elongate; knees present; flagella absent; leaf rachis to 1.5 m long with to 50 lanceolate leaflets per side, these regularly arranged; cirri present, to 1 m long. Inflorescences to 0.6 m long, flagellate or not flagellate; bracts tubular, open and inflated near the apices; fruits ellipsoid, to 0.6 cm long and 0.4 cm diameter, yellowish brown.
Range and habitat. Taiwan (Lanyu Island) (also in the Philippines and Sulawesi); scrub forest to 400 m elevation.
Uses. None recorded.
Notes. Six varieties are recognized, all from the Philippines and Sulawesi; var. *siphonospathus* just reaches Taiwan, on Lanyu Island.
Synonyms. *Calamus inflatus* Warb., *Palmijuncus siphonospathus* (Mart.) Kuntze

Calamus solitarius T. Evans, K. Sengdala, O. Viengkham, B. Thammavong & J. Dransf.
wai thork (Lao, Tha)

Field characters. Stems solitary, climbing, to 50 m long and 1.5 cm diameter. Leaf sheaths green with gray hairs, with scattered to densely arranged, green, needlelike, to 2-cm-long spines; ocreas present; knees present; flagella present, to 1 m long; leaf rachis to 0.9 m long with 9–14 lanceolate leaflets per side, these distinctly clustered, the apical ones close together in a fan shape, the apical pair joined at

their bases; cirri absent. Inflorescences to 5 m long, flagellate; bracts tubular; fruits globose, to 0.8 cm diameter, yellowish.

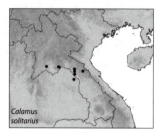

Range and habitat. Laos (Central) and Thailand (Northeast); lowland rain forest at low elevations.
Uses. Provides a high-quality cane used in furniture making and basketry.

Calamus speciosissimus Furtado
wai-tieng (Tha)

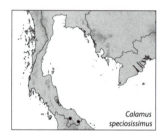

Field characters. Stems clustered, climbing, to 25 m long and 4 cm diameter. Leaf sheaths green, without spines or with scattered to densely arranged, green, flattened, to 2-cm-long spines; ocreas present; knees present; flagella present, to 4 m long; leaf rachis to 1.5 m long with 10–14 broadly lanceolate leaflets per side, these regularly arranged; cirri absent. Inflorescences to 4 m long, not flagellate; bracts tubular; fruits globose, 1 cm diameter, greenish.
Range and habitat. Thailand (Peninsular) (also in Peninsular Malaysia); lowland rain forest at low elevations.
Uses. Produces a good-quality cane used in furniture making.

Calamus spectatissimus Furtado
wai ng woi (Tha)

Field characters. Stems clustered, climbing, to 20 m long and 1.7 cm diameter. Leaf sheaths green with brown hairs, with sparsely to densely arranged, green, flattened, to 1.5-cm-long spines; ocreas present; knees present; flagella present, to 1.5 m long; leaf rachis to 0.7 m long with about 40 linear leaflets per side, these regularly arranged with dense, short bristles on the lower surfaces; cirri absent. Inflorescences to 1 m long with 3–6 partial inflorescences, flagellate; bracts loose and open at the apices; fruits globose, to 2 cm diameter, dark brown.

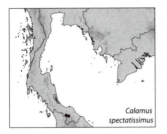

Range and habitat. Thailand (Peninsular) (also in Borneo, Peninsular Malaysia, and Sumatra); lowland rain forest at low elevations.
Uses. None recorded.

Calamus spicatus Henderson
kyetu kyein (Mya)

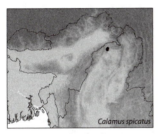

Field characters. Stems clustered, to 4 m long and 1 cm diameter. Leaf sheaths green with reddish brown hairs, sparsely to densely covered with brown or black, flattened, horizontally spreading spines to 1 cm long; knees present; ocreas present, spiny; flagella not seen, possibly absent; rachis to 0.7 m long with 4–10 lanceolate leaflets per side, these solitary or arranged in distant groups, the apical pair free or briefly joined at their bases; cirri absent. Inflorescences to 2 m long, flagellate; bracts closely sheathing, becoming split; fruits not seen.
Range and habitat. Myanmar (Kachin, Sagaing); lowland forest at 500–1040 m elevation.
Uses. None recorded.

Calamus spiralis Henderson,   PLATE 22
N. K. Ban & N. Q. Dung
may cam mo (Vie)

Field characters. Stems clustered, to 15 m long and 0.7 cm diameter. Leaf sheaths green with gray hairs, sparsely covered with bulbous-based groups of 3 black spines to 0.3 cm long, these longer at sheath apices; knees present; ocreas present, bristly; flagella absent; petioles absent; rachis to 0.2 m long with 3 linear-lanceolate leaflets per side, the basal pair

swept back across the sheath; cirri present, to 0.6 m long. Inflorescences to 0.4 m long, not flagellate; bracts tubular; fruits ellipsoid, 2.3 cm long and 1.4 cm diameter, reddish brown.

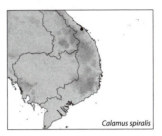

Range and habitat. Vietnam (Central); lowland forest at 400 m elevation.
Uses. The canes are used for tying.

Calamus stoloniferus Renuka
jeddubetha (Ind)

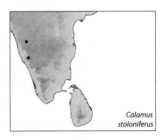

Field characters. Stems clustered, spreading by stolons, climbing, height not known, to 3 cm diameter. Leaf sheaths green, with scattered, to 2-cm-long spines; ocreas present; knees present; flagella present; leaf rachis to 1 m long with few lanceolate leaflets per side, these in distinct clusters, the apical ones inserted close together in a fan shape, the apical pair joined at their bases; cirri absent. Inflorescence length not known, flagellate; bracts tubular; fruits globose, to 1 cm diameter, yellow.
Range and habitat. Southwestern India (Karnataka); lowland rain forest at low elevations.
Uses. Provides a good-quality cane used in furniture making.

Calamus temii T. Evans
wai ton (Tha)

Field characters. Stems clustered or solitary, non-climbing, free-standing, to 5 m long and to 5 cm diameter. Leaf sheaths brown with oblique rows of black, flattened, to 3-cm-long spines; ocreas not known; knees absent; flagella absent; leaf rachis to 2 m long with numerous linear leaflets per side, these regularly arranged but with gaps and spreading in different planes; cirri absent. Inflorescences to 1 m long, not flagellate; bracts tattering at the base; fruits ellipsoid, to 2 cm long and 1.5 cm diameter, dark brown.

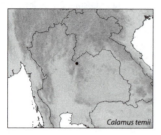

Calamus temii

Range and habitat. Thailand (Northeast); montane rain forest at 1300–1550 m elevation.
Uses. None recorded.

Calamus tenuis Roxb.   PLATES 22 & 23
bet (Ban), jati bet (Ind), wai nyair (Lao), htan-ye-li-kyiang, kyien dui, ye kyein (Mya), pani bet (Nep), wai kaerae, wai khom (Tha), may dang (Vie)

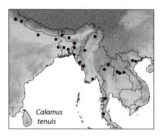

Calamus tenuis

Field characters. Stems clustered, often forming thickets, climbing, to 20 m long and 2.5 cm diameter. Leaf sheaths green with brownish white hairs, often with ridges, with scattered or rows of greenish brown or black, flattened, to 2-cm-long spines, with oblique, crescent-shaped bases and hairy margins; ocreas present, very small and papery; knees present; flagella present, to 2.5 m long; leaf rachis to 1 m long with 31–42 linear or linear-lanceolate leaflets per side, these regularly and closely arranged; cirri absent. Inflorescences to 2.5 m long, flagellate; bracts tubular; fruits globose to ellipsoid, to 1.6 cm long and 1.2 cm diameter, whitish or yellowish brown.
Range and habitat. Bangladesh, Bhutan, northern and northeastern India (Arunachal Pradesh, Assam, Bihar, Manipur, Meghalaya, Mizoram, Nagaland, Tripura, Uttarakhand, Uttar Pradesh, West Bengal, possibly farther south in Madhya Pradesh), Laos (Central), Nepal, Myanmar (Kachin, Rakhine, Sagaing, Tanintharyi, Yangon), Thailand (North, Peninsular), Vietnam (Northern), and probably Cambodia (also in Java and Sumatra); lowland rain forest, in swampy or flooded areas, often cultivated or persisting near villages, to 300 m elevation.
Uses. Provides a medium-quality cane used in basketry and weaving. The palm heart is eaten in some areas.

Notes. One of the most widespread species of *Calamus*. A few specimens from Peninsular Thailand have been identified as *C. radulosus* Becc., but appear to belong to *C. tenuis*. Beccari (1913; see also Evans & Sengdala 2002) considered that *C. delessertianus* Becc. from southwestern India may be conspecific with *C. tenuis*, a view not shared by Renuka (1999b).
Synonyms. *Calamus amarus* Lour., *Calamus royleanus* Griff., *Calamus heliotropium* Buch.-Ham., *Calamus horrens* Blume, *Calamus stoloniferus* Teijsm. & Binn., *Palmijuncus amarus* (Lour.) Kuntze, *Palmijuncus heliotropium* (Buch.-Ham.) Kuntze, *Palmijuncus horrens* (Blume) Kuntze, *Palmijuncus royleanus* (Griff.) Kuntze, *Palmijuncus tenuis* (Roxb.) Kuntze, *Rotang royleanus* (Griff.) Baill.

Calamus tetradactyloides Burret   PLATE 23
duo ci ji teng (Chi)

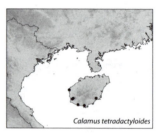

Calamus tetradactyloides

Field characters. Stems clustered, climbing, to 5 m long and 1 cm diameter. Leaf sheaths greenish brown with brown hairs, with densely arranged, brown, needlelike, to 1 (to 2 at sheath apices)-cm-long spines; ocreas present, short and densely bristly; knees present; flagella present, to 1 m long; leaf rachis to 0.4 m long with 4–6 (to 12 on young plants) linear-lanceolate leaflets per side, these irregularly arranged, the apical ones close together in a fan shape; cirri absent. Inflorescences to 0.7 m long, not flagellate; bracts tubular; fruits subglobose, to 1.5 cm long and 1 cm diameter, whitish.
Range and habitat. China (Hainan); lowland rain forest at low elevations.
Uses. None recorded.

Calamus tetradactylus Hance   PLATE 23
phdau-dan (Cbd), kai t'ang, paak t'ang (Chi), wai hang-nou (Lao), wai krit (Tha), cay mai, may tat (Vie)

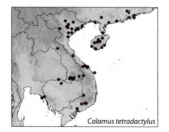

Calamus tetradactylus

Field characters. Stems clustered, climbing, to 6 m long and 1.8 cm diameter. Leaf sheaths green, without hairs, with scattered, yellowish brown, triangular, to 1.5-cm-long spines, or spines absent; ocreas present, prominent, membranous; knees present; flagella present, to 1 m long; leaf rachis to 0.6 m long with 8–13 lanceolate leaflets per side, these clustered, the apical ones close together in a fan shape, the apical pair joined at their bases, sometimes grayish on the lower surfaces; cirri absent. Inflorescences to 1.8 m long, usually flagellate; bracts tubular; fruits globose, to 0.9 cm diameter, yellowish, borne on short stalks.
Range and habitat. Cambodia, China (Guangdong, Guangxi, Hainan, Hong Kong, possibly Fujian and Yunnan), Laos (Central, Southern), Thailand (East, Southeast), and Vietnam; lowland rain forest, scrub forest, disturbed places, and often planted in small-holdings, to 1000 m elevation.
Uses. The stems provide a cane commonly used in weaving and basketry.
Notes. A widespread, common, and variable species, widely planted for its useful cane.
Synonyms. *Calamus bonianus* Becc., *Calamus cambojensis* Becc., *Calamus tetradactylus* var. *bonianus* (Becc.) Conrard, *Palmijuncus tetradactylus* (Hance) Kuntze

Calamus thwaitesii Becc.   PLATE 24
handibetha, pannichural (Ind), ma wewel, periya pirambu (Srl)

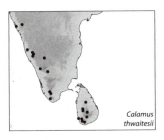

Calamus thwaitesii

Field characters. Stems clustered, climbing, to 50 m long and 6 cm diameter. Leaf sheaths yellow-green with brown hairs, with ridges of black, strongly flattened, to 4-cm-long spines, interspersed among many short spines; ocreas absent; knees absent; flagella present, to 9 m long; leaf rachis to 3 m long with to 30 lanceolate leaflets per side, these irregularly arranged; cirri absent. Inflorescences to 7 m long, flagellate; bracts tattering at the apices; fruits ovoid, to 2.5 cm long and 1.5 cm diameter, dull orange or yellowish brown.
Range and habitat. Southwestern India (Andhra Pradesh, Goa, Karnataka, Kerala, Maharastra, Tamil Nadu) and central and southern Sri Lanka; lowland or montane rain forest or deciduous forest, persisting in disturbed places, to 1500 m elevation.
Uses. Provides a medium-quality, large-diameter cane used in furniture making and basketry.
Synonym. *Calamus thwaitesii* var. *canaranus* Becc.

Calamus thysanolepis Hance   PLATE 24
paak t'ang, qi linxue teng, yeh chung shu (Chi), may tua (Vie)

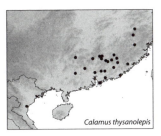

Calamus thysanolepis

Field characters. Stems clustered, nonclimbing, short and subterranean or free-standing, to 5 m long and 5 cm diameter. Leaf sheaths greenish brown with brown hairs, with densely arranged, black, needlelike, to 2-cm-long spines; ocreas present, to 40 cm long, spiny, fibrous and soon disintegrating; knees absent; flagella absent; leaf rachis to 1.5 m long with 28–49 lanceolate leaflets per side, these strongly clustered and spreading in different planes; cirri absent. Inflorescences to 1 m long, erect, not flagellate; bracts split open and tattering; fruits ovoid or ellipsoid, to 1.5 cm long and 1 cm diameter, reddish brown.
Range and habitat. China (Fujian, Guangdong, Guangxi, Hong Kong, Hunan, Jiangxi, Zhejiang) and Vietnam (Northern); lowland rain forest to 800 m elevation.
Uses. The fruits are eaten.
Notes. The record from Vietnam is doubtful, and is based on fruits only, which came from a local market.
Synonyms. *Calamus hoplites* Dunn, *Calamus sculletaris* Becc., *Calamus thysanolepis* var. *polylepis* C. F. Wei, *Palmijuncus thysanolepis* (Hance) Kuntze

Calamus tomentosus Becc.
wai tao (Tha)

Field characters. Stems clustered, climbing, to 20 m long and 2.5 cm diameter. Leaf sheaths green with silvery hairs, with scattered, black, swollen-based, upward-pointing, to 0.2-cm-long spines; ocreas present; knees present; flagella present, to 1.8 m long; leaf rachis to 1 m long with 5–7 rhomboidal leaflets per side, these regularly arranged; cirri absent. Inflorescences to 0.8 m long, flagellate; bracts tubular; fruits globose-ellipsoid, to 2.5 cm long and 2.2 cm diameter, brown.
Range and habitat. Thailand (Peninsular) (also in Borneo and Peninsular Malaysia); lowland rain forest to 800 m elevation.
Uses. None recorded.
Notes. Reported to occur in Peninsular Thailand (Dransfield et al. 2004), but no specimens from there have been seen and no map is provided.
Synonyms. *Calamus tomentosus* var. *intermedius* Becc., *Calamus tomentosus* var. *korthalsiaefolius* Becc.

Calamus travancoricus Bedd.

PLATE 24

kiribetha (Ind)

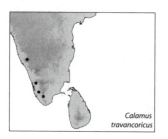

Calamus travancoricus

Field characters. Stems clustered, climbing, to 15 m
long and 1 cm diameter. Leaf sheaths green with
brown hairs, with scattered, black, needlelike, to 2
(to 5 at sheath apices)-cm-long spines; ocreas present; knees absent; flagella present, to 1.3 m long; leaf
rachis to 0.5 m long with to 15 lanceolate leaflets per
side, these in distant clusters, the apical ones inserted
close together in a fan shape; cirri absent. Inflorescences to 1.1 m long, flagellate; bracts split and open
at the apices; fruits globose, to 1 cm diameter,
stalked, yellowish brown.
Range and habitat. Southwestern India (Karnataka,
Kerala, Tamil Nadu); lowland rain forest at 200–500 m
elevation.
Uses. Provides a good-quality cane used in basketry
and furniture making.

Calamus unifarius H.Wendl.

hara beth (Ncb)

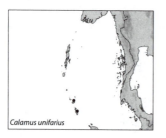

Calamus unifarius

Field characters. Stems solitary, climbing, to 20 m
long and 5 cm diameter. Leaf sheaths green with rusty
brown hairs, with scattered, brown, bulbous-based, to
0.5-cm-long spines; ocreas present; knees present;
flagella absent; leaf rachis to 2 m long with 15–20
broadly lanceolate leaflets per side, these regularly
arranged; cirri present. Inflorescences elongate, flagellate; bracts tubular; fruits ellipsoid, 1.5 cm long and
1 cm diameter, whitish.
Range and habitat. Nicobar Islands (Camorta,
Great Nicobar); lowland rain forest, often near the
sea, at low elevations.
Uses. Provides a cane used in furniture making.
Notes. Two varieties are recognized: var. *pentong*
Becc., with regularly arranged leaflets, from the
Nicobar Islands; and var. *unifarius*, with somewhat

irregularly arranged leaflets, from Java and
Sumatra.
Synonym. *Palmijuncus unifarius* (H. Wendl.) Kuntze

Calamus vattayila Renuka

vattayilayan (Ind)

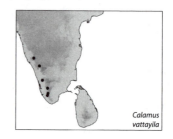

Calamus vattayila

Field characters. Stems solitary, climbing, to 30 m
long and 2.5 cm diameter. Leaf sheaths dark green,
without hairs, with scattered, green, to 2-cm-long
spines; ocreas present; knees present; flagella present, to 4 m long; leaf rachis to 0.8 m long with to 12
broadly lanceolate leaflets per side, these irregularly
arranged, the apical pair joined for about half their
length; cirri absent. Inflorescences to 1 m long, flagellate; bracts tubular; fruits ellipsoid, to 2.5 cm long
and 0.8 cm diameter, brown.
Range and habitat. Southwestern India (Karnataka,
Kerala, Tamil Nadu); lowland rain forest at 200–750 m
elevation.
Uses. Provides a good-quality cane used in furniture
making.

Calamus viminalis Willd.

PLATE 24

*jungli beth (And), bara bet (Ban), phdau, phdau kree
(Cbd), huang ci teng, wai-chi-ling (Chi), boro bet, golla
bet (Ind), wai ton (Lao), kyaing-kha, taung kyein (Mya),
wai komm (Tha), may cat (Vie)*

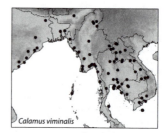

Calamus viminalis

Field characters. Stems clustered, climbing or often
forming thickets, to 35 m long and 4 cm diameter. Leaf
sheaths green with dense covering of grayish or brownish hairs, with scattered, greenish or brownish, triangular, flattened, to 4.5-cm-long spines; ocreas present;
knees present; flagella present, to 5 m long; leaf rachis
to 1.3 m long with 32–55 lanceolate leaflets per side,
these gray-green, distinctly clustered and spreading in
different planes, the apical ones usually smaller than
the others; cirri absent. Inflorescences to 3 m long,

flagellate, bracts tubular; fruits globose, to 1 cm diameter, whitish or yellowish, sometimes borne in pairs.
Range and habitat. Andaman Islands, Bangladesh, Cambodia, China (Yunnan), India (Andhra Pradesh, Bihar, Jharkhand, Orissa, Sikkim, Tripura, West Bengal), Laos, Myanmar (Ayeyarwady, Bago, Kachin, Kayin, Mon, Tanintharyi, Yangon), Thailand, and Vietnam (Central, Southern) (also in Bali, Java, and Peninsular Malaysia); lowland rain forest or deciduous forest, persisting in cleared areas and often present near villages, sometimes planted, to 600 m elevation.
Uses. Provides a widely used cane for basketry and furniture making, and the palm heart and fruits are eaten.
Notes. Evans et al. (2002) reported this species from Uttar Pradesh in India, but no specimens from there have been seen. A variable and widespread species, similar to *C. siamensis.*
Synonyms. *Calamus extensus* Mart., *Calamus fasciculatus* Roxb., *Calamus litoralis* Blume, *Calamus pseudorotang* Mart., *Calamus viminalis* var. *fasciculatus* (Roxb.) Becc., *Calamus viminalis* var. *fasciculatus* subvar. *andamanicus* Becc., *Calamus viminalis* var. *fasciculatus* subvar. *bengalensis* Becc., *Calamus viminalis* var. *fasciculatus* subvar. *cochinchinensis* Becc., *Calamus viminalis* var. *fasciculatus* subvar. *pinangianus* Becc., *Palmijuncus fasciculatus* (Roxb.) Kuntze, *Palmijuncus litoralis* (Blume) Kuntze, *Palmijuncus pseudorotang* (Mart.) Kuntze, *Palmijuncus viminalis* (Willd.) Kuntze, *Rotang viminalis* (Willd.) Baill.

Calamus viridispinus Becc.
whai (Tha)

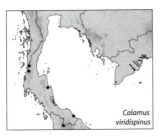

Calamus
viridispinus

Field characters. Stems clustered, erect and non-climbing or climbing, to 15 m long and 1.5 cm diameter. Leaf sheaths green with gray hairs, with scattered to densely arranged, yellow-based, black, flattened, to 3-cm-long spines; ocreas present; knees present in climbing plants; flagella absent; leaf rachis to 0.8 m long with 5–40 lanceolate leaflets per side, these arranged in groups of 2–5 leaflets on alternate sides of the rachis; cirri present in climbing plants, sometimes vestigial in nonclimbing plants. Inflorescences to 1 m long, not flagellate; bracts tubular; fruits ovoid, to 1 cm long and 0.6 cm diameter, brown.
Range and habitat. Thailand (Peninsular) (also in Peninsular Malaysia and Sumatra); montane rain forest, 800–1500 m elevation.

Uses. Produces a good-quality cane used in tying.
Notes. Two varieties are recognized: var. *sumatranus* Becc., with less-pointed leaflets, from Sumatra; and var. *viridispinus* from Thailand (Peninsular) and Peninsular Malaysia. *Calamus viridispinus* var. *viridispinus* is variable; the Thai plants have only 5–15 leaflets per side of the rachis.
Synonyms. *Calamus benomensis* Furtado, *Calamus brevispadix* Ridl., *Calamus bubuensis* Becc., *Calamus distichoideus* Furtado, *Calamus distichus* Ridl., *Calamus elegans* Becc., *Calamus koribanus* Furtado, *Calamus oreophilus* Furtado

Calamus walkeri Hance   PLATE 25
ku-teng, wong teng (Chi), may dang (Vie)

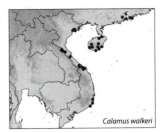

Calamus walkeri

Field characters. Stems clustered, climbing, to 15 m long and 3 cm diameter. Leaf sheaths green with gray-brown hairs, with scattered, yellowish, black-tipped, flattened, to 2.5-cm-long spines; ocreas present, densely bristly; knees present; flagella present, to 5 m long; leaf rachis to 1.5 m long with to 40 linear-lanceolate leaflets per side, these regularly arranged; cirri absent. Inflorescences to 5.5 m long, flagellate; bracts tubular; fruits ovoid, to 1.2 cm long and 1 cm diameter, yellowish.
Range and habitat. China (Guangdong, Hainan, Hong Kong) and Vietnam (throughout); lowland rain forest at low elevations.
Uses. The fruits are eaten.
Synonyms. *Calamus faberi* Becc., *Calamus faberi* var. *brevispicatus* (C. F. Wei) S. J. Pei & S. Y. Chen, *Calamus tonkinensis* Becc., *Calamus tonkinensis* var. *brevispicatus* C. F. Wei, *Palmijuncus walkeri* (Hance) Kuntze

Calamus wightii Griff.
soojibetha (Ind)

Field characters. Stems clustered, climbing, to 30 m long and 3 cm diameter. Leaf sheaths brownish green with brown hairs, with scattered or short rows of brownish, triangular, to 1.5-cm-long spines; ocreas present; knees present; flagella present; leaf rachis to 1.7 m long with numerous linear-lanceolate leaflets per side, these regularly arranged; cirri absent. Inflorescences elongate, flagellate; bracts tubular; fruits globose, to 1.8 cm diameter, stalked, brown or black with black-fringed scales.

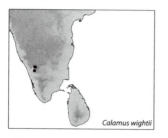

Calamus wightii

Range and habitat. Southwestern India (Karnataka, Kerala, Tamil Nadu); montane rain forest at 1300–2000 m elevation.

Uses. Provides a cane used in furniture making and basketry.

Notes. Previously known as *C. huegelianus*.

Synonyms. *Calamus huegelianus* Mart., *Calamus melanolepis* (Mart.) H. Wendl., *Daemonorops melanolepis* Mart., *Palmijuncus huegelianus* (Mart.) Kuntze, *Palmijuncus melanolepis* (Mart.) Kuntze, *Palmijuncus wightii* (Griff.) Kuntze

Calamus wuliangshanensis S. Y. Chen, PLATE 25
K. L. Wang & S. J. Pei
waqu (Chi)

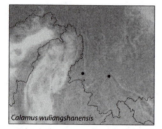

Calamus wuliangshanensis

Field characters. Stems clustered, climbing, to 15 m long and 3.5 cm diameter. Leaf sheaths gray or brown, with gray hairs, with scattered or densely arranged, yellowish brown, flattened, to 2.5-cm-long spines; ocreas present, to 35 cm long, soon tattering; knees absent; flagella present; leaf rachis to 2.8 m long with 45–70 lanceolate leaflets per side, these in distant clusters and spreading in different planes; cirri absent. Inflorescences to 5 m long, flagellate; bracts tubular; fruits ellipsoid to globose, to 2.7 cm long and 2.5 cm diameter, brownish, with densely hairy scale margins.

Range and habitat. China (Yunnan); montane rain forest at 2000–2400 m elevation.

Uses. None recorded.

Notes. Two varieties are recognized: var. *sphaerocarpus* S. Y. Chen & K. L. Wang, with larger, rounder fruits; and var. *wuliangshanensis*, with smaller fruits, both from Yunnan.

Calamus zeylanicus Becc.   PLATE 25
thambotu wel (Srl)

Field characters. Stems clustered, climbing, to 50 m long and 5 cm diameter. Leaf sheaths copper-colored with brown hairs, with well-spaced ridges of dark brown, flattened, to 1-cm-long spines; ocreas absent; knees present; flagella absent; leaf rachis to 2 m long with 35–50 linear leaflets per side, these regularly arranged and pendulous; cirri present, to 1.7 m long. Inflorescences to 1.8 m long, not flagellate; bracts tubular; fruits globose, to 2 cm diameter, brownish.

Calamus zeylanicus

Range and habitat. Sri Lanka; lowland rain forest to 1000 m elevation.

Uses. Provides a high-quality, large-diameter cane used in furniture making and basketry.

Notes. Difficult to distinguish from *C. ovoideus*, with which it occurs.

CARYOTA L.
(Schunda-Pana Adans., *Thuessinkia* Korth.)

Stems are small to very large, solitary or clustered, columnar or swollen, and usually ringed with conspicuous leaf scars. Leaves are 4–20 in number and are usually spread out along the stem, although in a few species they are borne in a compact crown at the top of the stem. Leaf sheaths are closed but do not form a crownshaft. Petioles are short or elongate and then rounded in cross section. They are usually covered with whitish or brownish hairs, and in some species they are attractively striped. The leaves of *Caryota* are unique among palms in being bipinnate—any palm with a bipinnate leaf must be a *Caryota*. Each primary leaflet is made up of several secondary leaflets borne on a secondary rachis, and this rachis is terminated by a leaflet. Individual secondary leaflets are triangular and have jagged outer margins—hence the common English name, fishtail palm. The leaflets often spread in different planes, giving the leaves a three-dimensional appearance.

Caryota is semelparous. Stems will grow vegetatively for many years, but not flower. Then, over a short period of time (usually less than five years), leaf production stops and flowering and fruiting begin. The first inflorescence to develop and flower is the topmost one, and flowering (and fruiting) proceeds toward the base of the stem. In a reproductive plant a whole series of inflorescences at different stages may be visible along the stem. After the final fruits have formed the whole stem dies. This means that in solitary-stemmed plants the whole plant dies, but in clustered-stemmed plants only the flowering stem dies after flowering. Inflorescences are usually branched to one order, rarely spicate. They are borne either among or below the leaves, and are covered in numerous, persistent bracts. The peduncle bears a prophyll and several penduncular bracts. Flowering branches are usually numerous, long, and pendulous (although in one species there are only a few branches). Flowers are unisexual, and are borne in threes of one central female and two lateral males. Male flowers have either yellow or purplish petals, and this is a useful character in species identification. There are 6–150 stamens. Fruits are medium-sized; usually more or less globose;

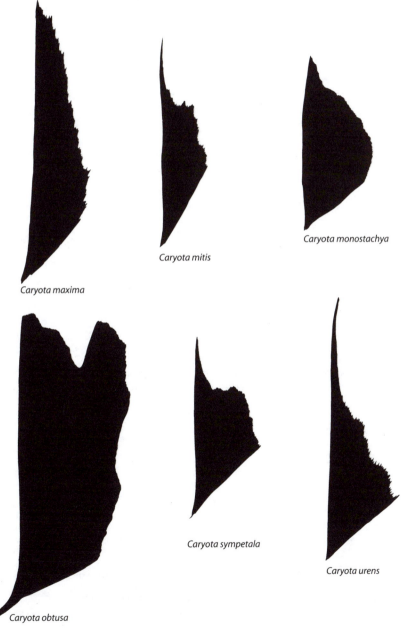

Caryota maxima

Caryota mitis

Caryota monostachya

Caryota obtusa

Caryota sympetala

Caryota urens

Figure 4. Leaflet shapes of *Caryota* species.

Key to the Species of *Caryota*

1a. Stems clustered; leaves borne along half or more of the stems; flowers purple to maroon; fruits
purple, purple-black, or brownish purple . . . . 2.
1b. Stems solitary; leaves borne along the upper half or third of the stem, or in a compact crown at
the top of the stems; flowers yellowish, rarely reddish brown to purple; fruits reddish, orange,
or rarely purple . . . . 4.

2a. Inflorescences with to 60 flowering branches; Andaman and Nicobar islands, Cambodia, China,
Myanmar, Thailand, and Vietnam . . . . *C. mitis.*
2b. Inflorescences with 1–20 flowering branches; China, Laos, and Vietnam . . . . 3.

3a. Inflorescences with 1–3 flowering branches; China and Vietnam . . . . *C. monostachya.*
3b. Inflorescences with 5–20 flowering branches; Laos and Vietnam . . . . *C. sympetala.*

4a. Flowers reddish brown to purple; fruits purple; southern India and Sri Lanka . . . . *C. urens.*
4b. Flowers yellowish; fruits reddish to orange; all other areas . . . . 5.

5a. Leaves borne along the upper half of the stems; primary leaflets pendulous . . . . *C. maxima.*
5b. Leaves borne in a compact crown at the top of the stems; primary leaflets spreading . . . . 6.

6a. Inflorescences to 2.5 m long; seedling leaves pinnate; Thailand (Peninsular) . . . . *C. kiriwongensis.*
6b. Inflorescences to 6 m long; seedling leaves bifid; China, India, Laos, Myanmar, Thailand (North),
and Vietnam . . . . *C. obtusa.*

orange, red, or purple; and one- to two-seeded. The genus gets its name from the Greek word *caryon*, meaning nutlike, in reference to the fruits. The mesocarp of the fruits contains crystals of calcium oxalate. Although highly irritant to humans, the fruits are eaten by palm civets, birds, and other animals. The endosperm is ruminate (homogeneous in one species), germination is remote, and the seedling leaf is bifid (pinnate in one species) with jagged margins.

Caryota contains 13 species, widely distributed from India throughout Southeast Asia and the western Pacific to Vanuatu. Seven species occur in our area (Hahn 1993, 1999; Hodel 1998). Secondary leaflet shape and size are useful in identification, and these are illustrated in Figure 4. Leaflet shape of *C. kiriwongensis* (not illustrated) is very similar to that of *C. obtusa*.

Caryota kiriwongensis Hodel
tao rang yak (Tha)

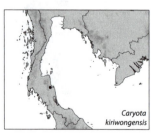

Caryota
kiriwongensis

Field characters. Stems solitary, to 35 m tall and 85 cm diameter, slightly swollen. Leaves borne in a compact crown at the top of the stems; primary leaflets to 25 per side of rachis, secondary leaflets with

scarcely jagged margins and blunt apices. Inflorescences borne below the leaves, to 2.5 m long, with numerous flowering branches; flowers yellowish; fruits globose, to 3.3 cm diameter, reddish, with homogeneous endosperm.
Range and habitat. Thailand (Peninsular); montane rain forest at 1000–1200 m elevation.
Notes. Unusual in having pinnate seedling leaves.

Caryota maxima Blume   PLATE 26
rungbong (Bhu), qing zong (Chi), siwa, tamak (Ind), kyauk minbaw, min-baw (Mya), taou-rung-yak (Tha), cay moc (Vie)

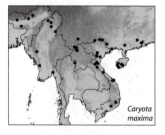

Caryota
maxima

Field characters. Stems solitary, to 30 m tall and 65 cm diameter, columnar. Leaves borne along the upper half of the stems; primary leaflets to 27 per side of rachis, pendulous, secondary leaflets with deeply jagged margins. Inflorescences borne among the leaves, to 3.5 m or more long, with to 170 flowering branches; flowers yellowish; fruits globose, to 2.5 cm diameter, dull reddish or orange.
Range and habitat. Bhutan, China (Guangdong, Guangxi, Hainan, Hong Kong, Yunnan), India (Arunachal Pradesh, Assam, Sikkim), Laos (Northern), Myanmar (Bago, Chin, Kachin, Mon, Rakhine, Sa-

gaing), Thailand (North), and Vietnam (throughout) (also in Java, Sumatra, and Peninsular Malaysia); lowland to montane rain forest or disturbed places, often planted or naturalized, 200–1800 m elevation.
Uses. The palm heart is eaten, the stems are used to make implements, and the sheath fibers are used for tinder.
Notes. The tall, solitary stems and pendulous leaflets are distinctive, as are the very long inflorescences. Smaller plants, from limestone areas in Thailand and elsewhere, may represent a distinct species, and have been identified as *C. bacsonensis*.
Synonyms. *Caryota aequatorialis* (Becc.) Ridl., *Caryota bacsonensis* Magalon, *Caryota furfuracea* var. *caudata* Blume, *Caryota furfuracea* var. *furcata* Blume, *Caryota macrantha* Burret, *Caryota obtusa* var. *aequatorialis* Becc., *Caryota ochlandra* Hance, *Caryota rumphiana* var. *javanica* Becc., *Caryota rumphiana* var. *oxydonta* Becc., *Caryota rumphiana* var. *philippinensis* Becc.

Caryota mitis Lour.   PLATE 26
minbaw (Mya), taou-rung-dang (Tha), dung dinh (Vie)

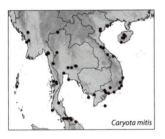

Caryota mitis

Field characters. Stems clustered, to 10 m tall and 20 cm diameter, columnar. Leaves usually borne along upper half of the stems; primary leaflets to 23 per side of rachis, secondary leaflets with jagged margins and elongate apices. Inflorescences borne among or below the leaves, to 1.5 m long, with to 60 flowering branches; flowers purple to maroon; fruits globose, to 2 cm diameter, purple-black or reddish.
Range and habitat. Andaman and Nicobar islands, Cambodia, China (Hainan, Guangdong, Guangxi), Myanmar (Bago, Magway, Mon, Rakhine, Tanintharyi), Thailand, and Vietnam (also in Borneo, Java, Peninsular Malaysia, the Philippines, Singapore, Sulawesi, and Sumatra); lowland rain forest, secondary forest, disturbed places, and often cultivated, below 1000 m elevation.
Uses. Widely planted as an ornamental.
Synonyms. *Caryota furfuracea* Blume, *Caryota griffithii* Becc., *Caryota griffithii* var. *selebica* Becc., *Caryota javanica* Zipp., *Caryota minor* Wall., *Caryota nana* Linden, *Caryota propinqua* Blume, *Caryota sobolifera* Wall., *Caryota speciosa* Linden, *Drymophloeus zippellii* Hassk., *Thuessinkia speciosa* Korth.

Caryota monostachya Becc.   PLATE 26
danshui yuweiqui (Chi), cay dong dinh, mot buong (Vie)

Field characters. Stems clustered, to 3 m tall and 4 cm diameter, not swollen. Leaves borne almost all along the stems; primary leaflets to 9 per side of rachis, secondary leaflets with scarcely jagged margins and short apices. Inflorescences borne among the leaves, to 1 m long, with 1–3 flowering branches; flowers purple or maroon; fruits globose, to 3.5 cm diameter, brownish purple.

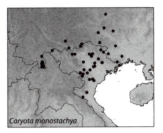

Caryota monostachya

Range and habitat. China (Guangxi, Guizhou, Yunnan), Vietnam (Northern), and probably Laos (Northern); lowland to montane rain forest, often on limestone soils, to 1400 m elevation.
Uses. None recorded.

Caryota obtusa Griff.   PLATE 26
dong zong (Chi), tao raang yak (Tha), moc (Vie)

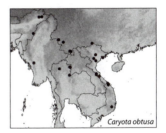

Caryota obtusa

Field characters. Stems solitary, to 40 m tall and 90 cm diameter, swollen. Leaves borne in a compact crown at the top of the stems; primary leaflets to 22 per side of rachis, secondary leaflets with scarcely jagged margins and blunt apices. Inflorescences borne below the leaves, to 6 m long, with to 200 flowering branches; flowers yellowish; fruits globose, to 3.5 cm diameter, reddish.
Range and habitat. Southern China (Yunnan), India (Arunachal Pradesh, Manipur), Laos (Northern), Myanmar (Rakhine), Thailand (North), Vietnam (throughout), and probably Cambodia; scattered localities in montane rain forest, usually on limestone soils, at 1400–1800 m elevation.
Uses. None reported.
Synonyms. *Caryota gigas* Hahn, *Caryota obtusidentata* Griff., *Caryota rumphiana* var. *indica* Becc.

Caryota sympetala Gagnep.   PLATE 27
dung dinh, canh dinh (Vie)

Field characters. Stems clustered, to 6 m tall and 6 cm diameter, not swollen. Leaves borne almost all along the stems; primary leaflets about 10 per side of rachis, secondary leaflets with jagged margins and elongate apices. Inflorescences borne among the leaves, to 0.5 m long, with 5–20 flowering branches; flowers purple to maroon; fruits globose, to 3 cm diameter, purple.

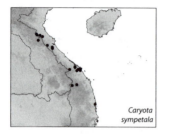

Caryota sympetala

Range and habitat. Laos (Central) and Vietnam (Central); lowland rain forest at low elevations, rarely to 1400 m.

Uses. None recorded.

Notes. Plants usually consist of large clumps of stemless shoots, with few, short flowering stems emerging from the center of the clump.

Caryota urens L.   PLATE 27
choonda pana, toddy (Ind), kitul (Srl)

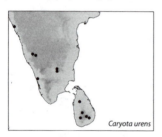

Caryota urens

Field characters. Stems solitary, to 20 m tall and 65 cm diameter, columnar. Leaves borne along the upper third of the stems; primary leaflets to 20 per side of rachis, secondary leaflets with jagged margins and elongate apices. Inflorescences borne among and below the leaves, to 3 m long, with to 190 flowering branches; flowers reddish brown to purple; fruits globose, to 2 cm diameter, purple.

Range and habitat. Southern India (Goa, Karnataka, Kerala, Maharashtra, Tamil Nadu) and Sri Lanka; widely cultivated.

Uses. Planted in gardens and smallholdings for a wide variety of products made from the sap, which is tapped, including syrup, sugar, palm wine, and vinegar. Fibers from the leaf sheaths are also important for weaving various items, the leaves are used for thatching and elephant fodder, and the stems are used in construction.

Notes. Almost indistinguishable from the Southeast Asian *C. rumphiana*, and possibly only an in-

troduced, naturalized form of that species (Hahn 1993).

CERATOLOBUS Blume

The stems of this rattan genus are always clustered and usually slender and seldom reach great heights in the forest. Leaves are pinnate, numerous, and spirally arranged. Leaf sheaths are closed, spiny, and have knees and small ocreas. The leaf rachis, at least in adult leaves, terminates in a long cirrus, lacking leaflets but with grapnel-like spines, and this serves as a climbing organ. There is great variation in leaflets, especially for such a small genus. Some species have linear or lanceolate leaflets, others have rhomboidal leaflets with jagged margins. The latter can be whitish gray on the lower surface.

Individual plants bear either male or female flowers (i.e., dioecious). Inflorescences are branched to three orders, and are either short and erect or borne on a long peduncle and then pendulous. The whole inflorescence is covered by one large bract, and at flowering time this opens only by two narrow, lateral slits. The bract is finally split completely open by the developing fruits. The generic name is derived from the form of this bract, from the Greek words *keras*, meaning horn, and *lobos*, meaning pod. Male flowers are borne singly along the short flowering branches. Female flowers are borne in pairs with a sterile male flower, and these pairs are borne rather loosely along the flowering branches. Fruits are globose to ellipsoid, brown, usually one-seeded, and are covered with overlapping scales. The endosperm is homogeneous or ruminate, germination is adjacent, and the seedling leaf is palmate.

Ceratolobus contains six species, distributed in Borneo, Java, Sumatra, Thailand, and Peninsular Malaysia. They are not as economically important as other rattans because of their weak stems. The genus differs from other closely related rattan genera, such as *Calamus* and *Daemonorops*, by its unusual, single inflorescence bract with a small opening.

One species occurs in our area (Dransfield 1979b; Hodel 1998). Hodel (1998) recorded *C. glaucescens* for Peninsular Thailand, but Dransfield et al. (2004) considered this unlikely.

Ceratolobus subangulatus (Miq.)   PLATE 27
Becc.

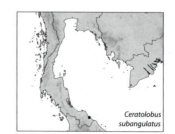

Ceratolobus subangulatus

Field characters. Stems clustered, climbing, to 15 m long and 1.7 cm diameter (including leaf sheaths). Leaf sheaths green with brown scales, with scattered, green, flattened, to 1.1-cm-long spines; knees present; leaf rachis to 0.6 m long with to 16 lanceolate leaflets per side of rachis, these clustered, the lower ones swept back across the sheaths; cirri to 0.5 m long. Inflorescences to 0.3 m long, erect; fruits globose, to 1.5 cm diameter, brown.

Range and habitat. Thailand (Peninsular) (also in Borneo, Peninsular Malaysia, Singapore, and Sumatra); lowland rain forest in well-drained places, to 1000 m elevation.

Uses. None recorded.

Synonyms. *Calamus subangulatus* Miq., *Ceratolobus laevigatus* (Mart.) Becc., *Ceratolobus laevigatus* var. *angustifolius* Becc., *Ceratolobus laevigatus* var. *borneensis* Becc., *Ceratolobus laevigatus* var. *divaricatus* Becc., *Ceratolobus laevigatus* var. *major* Becc., *Ceratolobus laevigatus* var. *regularis* Becc., *Ceratolobus laevigatus* var. *subangulatus* (Miq.) Becc., *Palmijuncus subangulatus* (Miq.) Kuntze

CHUNIOPHOENIX Burret

This small genus was named after Woon-Young Chun (1890–1971), a Chinese scientist who established the South China Institute of Botany in 1929. Stems are small to moderate and clustered. Leaves are briefly costapalmate, 15–20 in number, and are borne on slender, elongate, smooth-margined, deeply channeled petioles. These channeled petioles are characteristic of the genus. Leaf sheaths are open and on older plants may split at the base to give a central triangular cleft. There is no hastula at the apex of the petiole, as there is in most other coryphoid palms. Blades are irregularly divided into few to numerous leaflets of varying widths, and these are green on both surfaces.

Inflorescences are spicate or branched to three orders, and are borne among the leaves. There are several persistent, tubular bracts covering the peduncle and rachis. Flowers are bisexual and usually occur in small groups, their bases covered by small, tubular bracts. Fruits are small; globose, obovoid, or pear-shaped; red; orange, or purple; and one-seeded. The endosperm is ruminate or homogeneous, germination is remote, and the seedling leaf is undivided.

Two species of *Chuniophoenix* are usually recognized (Zona 1998), but here three species are accepted, occurring in southern China and northern Vietnam.

Chuniophoenix hainanensis Burret   PLATE 28
qiong zong (Chi)

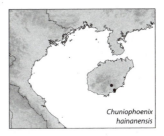

Chuniophoenix hainanensis

Field characters. Stems clustered, to 5 m tall and 6 cm diameter. Leaf blades divided into 36–45 leaflets. Inflorescences to 2 m long, with many flowering branches; fruits obovoid to pear-shaped, to 2.5 cm long and 2.2 cm diameter, red, orange, or purple, borne on short stalks.

Range and habitat. China (Hainan); lowland rain forest at low elevations.

Uses. None recorded.

Chuniophoenix humilis C. Z. Tang   PLATE 28
& T. L. Wu
ai qiong zong, xiao qiong zong (Chi)

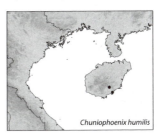

Chuniophoenix humilis

Field characters. Stems clustered, to 2 m tall and 2 cm diameter. Leaf blades divided into 4–6 leaflets, these broad and hooded. Inflorescences to 0.4 m long with 1–4 flowering branches; fruits globose, to 1.6 cm diameter, red.

Key to the Species of *Chuniophoenix*

1a. Stems to 4 m tall and 10 cm diameter; leaf blades divided into 36–45 leaflets; inflorescences with many flowering branches; China (Hainan) . . . . *C. hainanensis.*

1b. Stems to 2 m tall and 2 cm diameter; leaf blades divided into 4–6 leaflets; inflorescences with 1–4 flowering branches; China (Hainan) and Vietnam (Northern) . . . . 2.

2a. Leaflets broad and hooded; China (Hainan) . . . . *C. humilis.*

2b. Leaflets narrow, not hooded; Vietnam . . . . *C. nana.*

Range and habitat. China (Hainan); lowland rain forest at low elevations.
Uses. None recorded.

Bonin Islands to Micronesia, Fiji, Samoa, and the Solomon Islands. One species occurs in our area, on the Bonin Islands (Moore & Fosberg 1956).

Chuniophoenix nana Burret   PLATE 28
cha (Vie)

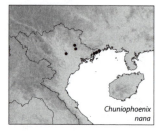

Chuniophoenix nana

Field characters. Stems clustered, to 2 m tall and 2 cm diameter. Leaf blades divided into 4–7 leaflets, these narrow, not hooded. Inflorescences to 0.4 m long with 1–4 flowering branches; fruits globose, to 1.6 cm diameter, red.
Range and habitat. Vietnam (Northern); lowland rain forest at low elevations.
Uses. None recorded.
Notes. Usually included in *C. humilis*, but here recognized as a separate species, based on its distinctive leaves.

CLINOSTIGMA H. Wendl.
(Exorrhiza Becc.)

Stems are tall, solitary, columnar, and ringed with conspicuous leaf scars. These scars are not parallel as a result of uneven internode expansion. Occasionally stems are supported by stilt roots. Leaves are pinnate and 8–16 in number. Leaf sheaths are closed and form a prominent, grayish green crownshaft. Petioles are short. Leaflets are regularly and closely arranged along the rachis and spread in the same plane. They can be arched or pendulous, and are linear or lanceolate and one-veined. Often they have prominent, brown scales on the lower surface.

Inflorescences are borne below the crownshaft and are branched to three orders. They are covered with two bracts, and these fall before flowering. The peduncle is short and flat, and the flowering branches are long and slender. Flowers are unisexual and are borne in threes of a central female and two lateral males. Fruits are small, ovoid to ellipsoid, red or black, and one-seeded. This genus gets its name from the Greek words *klenein*, meaning to bend, and *stigma*, meaning a spot or mark, in reference to the position of the stigmatic remains on the fruit. The endosperm is homogeneous, germination is adjacent, and the seedling leaf is bifid or undivided.

Clinostigma contains 11 species, widely distributed on islands across the western Pacific, from the

Clinostigma savoryanum (Rheder   PLATE 29
& E. H. Wilson) H. E. Moore & Fosberg
noyashi (Jap)

Clinostigma savoryanum

Field characters. Stems solitary, to 16 m tall and 15 cm diameter. Leaf sheaths forming a grayish green crownshaft; rachis to 3 m long with to 60 pendulous, linear leaflets per side. Inflorescences borne below the leaves, to 0.7 m long; fruits globose to ellipsoid, to 1.5 cm long and 1 cm diameter, black.
Range and habitat. Bonin Islands (Ogasawara Islands—Mukojima, Chichijima, and Hahajima chains); deciduous forest on steep, rocky slopes in coastal areas, at low elevations.
Uses. The palm heart is edible.
Synonyms. *Bentinckiopsis savoryana* (Rehder & E. H. Wilson) Becc., *Cyphokentia savoryana* Rehder & E. H. Wilson, *Exorrhiza savoryana* (Rehder & E. H. Wilson) Burret

COCOS L.
(Calappa Steck, *Coccos* Gaertn., *Coccus* Mill.)

Stems are large and solitary, gray, and often leaning. Leaves are pinnate, 25–30 in number, and form a graceful crown. Leaf sheaths are open and very fibrous. Leaflets are linear, one-veined, numerous, regularly arranged along the rachis, and spread in the same plane.

Inflorescences are branched to one order, and are borne among the leaves. They are covered by two persistent bracts, the second of which is somewhat woody. Flowers are unisexual and are borne in threes of one central female and two lateral males at the base of the flowering branches, where the large female flowers are easily visible. The one-seeded fruits are very distinctive, mostly because of their large size. The origin of the name is from the Portuguese or Spanish word *coco*, meaning a nut or a seed. The outer layer is green, orange, or yellow, depending on the variety. Inside is a fibrous layer and this gives coconuts their ability to float. A thick bony endocarp protects the inner layer of endosperm. The inside of the seed is hollow and contains liquid endosperm. Germination is adjacent, and the seedling leaf is undivided.

A genus of one species, which is widely cultivated throughout tropical areas of the world, especially along sandy coasts. The origin of the coconut palm is not known.

Cocos nucifera L.
doeum dong (Cbd), kok p'haou (Lao), own pan, thai (Mya), coco, ma-prow (Tha), cay dua (Vie)

Field characters. Stems solitary, often leaning, to 20 m tall and 30 cm or more diameter. Leaflets to 100 per side, regularly arranged and stiffly spreading in the same plane. Inflorescences borne among the leaves; fruits ovoid to irregularly globose, to 30 cm long and 20 cm diameter, green, yellowish, or reddish brown. **Range and habitat.** Commonly planted throughout our area (and in other tropical regions), usually at low elevations but occasionally seen up to 1000 m elevation (no map provided). **Uses.** The coconut is an important commercial crop, producing coconut oil, coir, and toddy. Coconut oil is obtained from the dried endosperm (known as copra) and has been used in the manufacture of soap and margarine. Coir is obtained from the fibrous mesocarp and is used to weave mats and rugs. Toddy is sugar-containing sap that is tapped from unopened inflorescences and often fermented into an alcoholic drink. Apart from these major uses, the coconut has a host of minor uses, especially as an ornamental plant. **Synonyms.** *Cocos indica* Royle, *Cocos nana* Griff.

CORYPHA L.
(Bessia Raf., *Codda-pana* Adans., *Dendrema* Raf., *Gembanga* Blume, *Taliera* Mart.)

Stems are massive, solitary, and are covered, at least when young, with persistent leaf bases. After the leaves fall, some species have a distinctive spiral pattern of leaf scars around the stem. Leaves are palmate and very large (probably the largest of any palmate-leafed palm), and 15–35 in number. Leaf sheaths are open and split at the base to give a central triangular cleft. Petioles are elongate and are covered on their margins with stout, black thorns. Sometimes the petioles are covered with dense, white hairs. At the base of the petiole, where it joins the leaf sheath, there is sometimes a pair of earlike flaps. At the apex of the petiole there is a prominent hastula. The blade is divided to about half its length into numerous, stiff leaflets.

Corypha is semelparous—all inflorescences are produced together at the apex of the stem after a period of vegetative growth, and after flowering and fruiting the stem dies. At first glance, these inflorescences appear as one gigantic inflorescence emerging from above the leaves, but in reality they are separate inflorescences, just as in other palms, each one emerging from the axil of a reduced leaf. The genus gets its name from the position of the inflorescences above the leaves, and comes from the Greek work *koryphe*, meaning a summit or peak. Inflorescences are branched to four orders, and have numerous, long flowering branches. Flowers are small and bisexual, and are borne in small groups. Fruits are globose, usually brownish, and one-seeded. The endosperm is homogeneous, germination is remote, and the seedling leaf is undivided.

There is no recent revision of *Corypha*, and the genus remains poorly known. Six species are recognized, four of which occur in our area (Basu 1987; Beccari 1933; Hodel 1998). *Corypha* is commonly seen in the Southern Asian region, especially in towns or villages, but most are planted or naturalized.

Corypha lecomtei Becc. ex Lecomte   PLATE 29
treang (Cbd), lan (Tha), la buong (Vie)

Field characters. Stems solitary, to 5 m tall and 100 cm diameter, smooth or often covered with persistent leaf bases, without spiral furrows. Petioles green with black margins, the bases without conspicuous earlike flaps; blades spherical in outline, divided into about 140 stiff leaflets. Inflorescences to 12 m long; individual inflorescences emerging from the mouths of the subtending leaf sheaths, not splitting them; fruits globose, to 7 cm diameter, brownish.

Key to the Species of *Corypha*

1a. Petioles green, the bases with 2, conspicuous earlike flaps . . . . 2.
1b. Petioles green or with white hairs, the bases without conspicuous earlike
flaps . . . . 3.

2a. Individual inflorescences emerging through splits in the subtending leaf sheaths; India (Karnataka, Kerala, Tamil Nadu) and Sri Lanka . . . . *C. umbraculifera.*
2b. Individual inflorescences emerging from the mouths of the subtending leaf sheaths; Bangladesh and India (West Bengal) . . . . *C. taliera.*

3a. Petioles green, with black margins; stems without a spiral furrow; Cambodia, Laos, Thailand (East, Southeast), and Vietnam (Southern) . . . . *C. lecomtei.*
3b. Petioles with whitish hairs, without black margins; stems with a faint, spiral furrow; Andaman and Nicobar islands, Myanmar (Tanintharyi), and Thailand (Peninsular) . . . . *C. utan.*

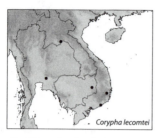

Range and habitat. Cambodia, Laos, Thailand (East, Southeast), and Vietnam (Southern); dry forest or open areas along rivers, commonly persisting in disturbed places, at low elevations.
Uses. None recorded.

Corypha taliera Roxb.
talier (Ban), tali, tara (Ind)

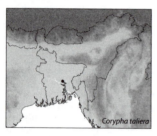

Field characters. Stems solitary, to 10 m tall and 70 cm diameter, without spiral furrows. Petioles green, the bases with 2 conspicuous earlike flaps; blades spherical in outline, divided into about 100 stiff leaflets. Inflorescences to 10 m long; individual inflorescences emerging from the mouths of the subtending leaf sheaths, not splitting them; fruits globose, to 4 cm diameter, brown or yellowish.
Range and habitat. Bangladesh and India (West Bengal); not known with certainty from the wild, usually found in disturbed places or planted as an ornamental, at low elevations.
Uses. The leaves are used as paper for writing.
Notes. Similar to, and perhaps not distinct from, *C. umbraculifera*.
Synonyms. *Corypha careyana* Becc., *Corypha martiana* Becc. ex Hook. f., *Taliera bengalensis* Spreng., *Taliera tali* Mart. ex Blume in J. J. Roemer & J. A. Schultes

Corypha umbraculifera L.   PLATE 29
conda pani, talipot (Ind, Srl), tala (Srl)

Field characters. Stems solitary, to 25 m tall and 100 cm diameter, without spiral furrows. Petioles green, without white hairs, the bases with 2 conspicuous earlike flaps; blades spherical in outline, divided into 80–110 stiff leaflets. Inflorescences to 6 m long; individual inflorescences emerging through splits in

the subtending leaf sheaths; fruits globose, to 4 cm diameter, greenish brown.

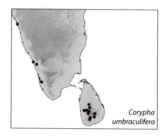

Range and habitat. India (Karnataka, Kerala, Maharashtra, Tamil Nadu) and Sri Lanka; low-lying areas, often near the sea and in disturbed places.
Uses. There are many local uses, notably the leaves as umbrellas and as writing paper. Starch is extracted from the stems. Widely cultivated as an ornamental.
Notes. The range of this species has been greatly influenced by humans, and possibly it is always cultivated in India and Sri Lanka. It is widely planted in other parts of our area.
Synonyms. *Bessia sanguinolenta* Raf., *Corypha guineensis* L.

Corypha utan Lam.   PLATE 29
dondah (And, Ncb), pae (Mya), lan pru (Tha)

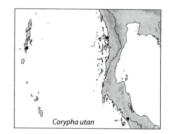

Field characters. Stems solitary, to 30 m tall and 90 cm diameter, with faint, spiral furrows. Petioles green, with whitish hairs, the bases without conspicuous earlike flaps; blades hemispherical in outline, divided into 100 or more stiff leaflets. Inflorescences to 3.5 m long; individual inflorescences emerging from the mouths of the subtending leaf sheaths, not splitting them; fruits globose, to 2.5 cm diameter, greenish brown.
Range and habitat. Andaman and Nicobar islands, Myanmar (Tanintharyi), and Thailand (Peninsular) (also in Australia, Indonesia, Malaysia [Sabah], Papua New Guinea, and the Philippines); low-lying places, savannas, floodplains, often in disturbed areas, usually near the sea, seldom to 500 m elevation.
Uses. This is a very important species. Leaves are used for thatching and for weaving into various items such as mats and baskets; the sap from the base of the inflorescence is tapped and used to make sugar

or fermented into an alcoholic drink; and there are many other uses.

Synonyms. *Corypha elata* Roxb., *Corypha gebang* Mart., *Corypha gembanga* (Blume) Blume, *Corypha griffithiana* Becc., *Corypha macrophylla* Roster, *Corypha macropoda* Kurz ex Linden, *Corypha macropoda* Linden ex Kurz, *Corypha macropoda* Kurz ex Linden, *Corypha sylvestris* (Blume) Mart., *Gembanga rotundifolia* Blume, *Livistona vidalii* Becc., *Taliera elata* (Roxb.) Wall., *Taliera gembanga* Blume in J. J. Roemer & J. A. Schultes, *Taliera sylvestris* Blume in J. J. Roemer & J. A. Schultes

CYRTOSTACHYS Blume

Stems are solitary or clustered, moderate to tall, and ringed with conspicuous leaf scars. There is often a prominent mass of roots at the base. Leaves are pinnate and four to seven in number. Leaf sheaths are closed and form prominent crownshafts, and in one species these are red or orange. Leaflets are regularly arranged along the rachis and spread in the same plane. They are linear and one-veined.

Inflorescences are branched to three orders and are borne below the crownshaft. They are covered with two bracts, and these fall before flowering. Flowers are unisexual and are borne in threes of a central female and two lateral males. These groups of flowers are usually sunken in slight depressions in the flowering branches. The name of the genus is apparently derived from the male flowers, from the Greek word *cyrtos*, meaning curved, and *stachys*, meaning a grain. Fruits are usually rather small, ellipsoid, black, and one-seeded. The endosperm is homogeneous, germination is adjacent, and the seedling leaf if bifid.

Cyrtostachys contains 11 species, naturally occurring from Thailand to New Guinea and the Solomon Islands. One species occurs in our area (Hodel 1998).

Cyrtostachys renda Blume   PLATE 30
kap deng, mark-dang (Tha)

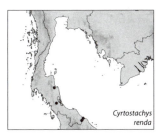

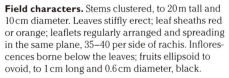

Field characters. Stems clustered, to 20 m tall and 10 cm diameter. Leaves stiffly erect; leaf sheaths red or orange; leaflets regularly arranged and spreading in the same plane, 35–40 per side of rachis. Inflorescences borne below the leaves; fruits ellipsoid to ovoid, to 1 cm long and 0.6 cm diameter, black.

Range and habitat. Thailand (Peninsular) (also in Borneo, Peninsular Malaysia, and Sumatra); low-lying swamp forest to 125 m elevation.

Uses. Widely cultivated as an ornamental.

Synonyms. *Areca erythrocarpa* H. Wendl., *Areca erythropoda* Miq., *Bentinckia renda* (Blume) Mart., *Cyrtostachys lakka* Becc., *Pinanga purpurea* Miq., *Pinanga rubricaulis* Linden, *Ptychosperma coccinea* Teijsm. & Binn.

DAEMONOROPS Blume

Stems of the majority of species are slender and climbing, and can be clustered or less often solitary. Sometimes stems are nonclimbing or even short and subterranean. Leaves are pinnate, spiny, and 13–30 in number. The generic name is based on the spines, and comes from the Greek words *daimon*, a devil or demon, and *rhops*, a bush. Leaf sheaths are closed in climbing species and open in nonclimbing ones. Sheaths are covered in various hairs and spines, and this covering is characteristic for each species. Spines may be scattered (rarely absent) to densely arranged, or arranged in rows, and are variously shaped and colored. Sometimes, and most remarkably, spines are arranged in overlapping, interlocking rings, and these form chambers where ants make their homes. The apex of the sheath is rarely extended above the point of insertion of the petiole into a tubular structure known as an ocrea. Just below the petiole is the knee, a swollen projection of the sheath. Most species have knees, a few, especially nonclimbers, do not. The climbing organ is termed the cirrus. This long, whip-like structure, present in all except the nonclimbing species (and juvenile leaves), is a continuation of the leaf rachis, without leaflets but with grapnel-like spines. Leaflets are variously arranged and shaped.

Species of *Daemonorops* are dioecious. Some species are semelparous; all inflorescences are produced and flower together over a short period of time, and after fruiting the stem dies. Most species, however, are iteroparous and reproduce over long periods. Inflorescences are branched to three orders, and male inflorescences tend to be more branched than female ones. The branches of the inflorescences are covered with overlapping bracts, and the form of these bracts is important in identification. In some species, inflorescence bracts are persistent, swollen, and split lengthwise to reveal the flowering branches. At flowering time, the apices of all bracts are included within the first bract, or prophyll. In other species, the inflorescence bracts fall from the elongating inflorescence, and only the basal bract persists. Male flowers are usually arranged distichously along the flowering branches. The female flowers are paired, each pair consisting of a female flower and a sterile male flower. Fruits are variously shaped and colored and are usually one-seeded. They are always covered with overlapping scales and are usually borne on short stalks. In some species, a red resin, called "dragon's blood," is exuded from the scales and is used medicinally. The endosperm is ruminate, germination is adjacent, and the seedling leaf is pinnate, rarely palmate.

Daemonorops contains approximately 100 species, widely distributed from northeastern India through Indochina, the Philippines, Malaysia, Indonesia, and just reaching New Guinea. Twenty-two species occur in our area (Beccari 1911; Dransfield 1979a, 2001; Evans et al. 2001, 2002; Hodel 1998).

Species of *Daemonorops* are very similar to the closely related *Calamus*, and the two genera are difficult to tell apart. All *Daemonorops*, except for a few nonclimbing species, have cirri, whereas cirri are present in rather few species of *Calamus*. Most *Calamus* with cirri also have fruits with homogeneous endosperm, at least in our area. A rattan with a cirrus and fruits with ruminate endosperm is very likely to be a *Daemonorops*. Inflorescences of *Daemonorops* are usually shorter than the leaves and are not elongate, as in many *Calamus*. They do not have sheathing bracts and do not have grapnel-like spines on the bracts, nor the flagellate extension that is so common in *Calamus*.

Daemonorops can be divided into two groups of species; one has persistent inflorescence bracts (although on infructescences with well-developed fruits the bracts tend to fall). This is known as section *Daemonorops* and in our area includes *D. angustifolia*, *D. aurea*, *D. grandis*, *D. jenkinsiana*, *D. kurziana*, *D. lewisiana*, *D. manii*, *D. melanochaetes*, *D. monticola*, *D. rarispinosa*, *D. sepal*, and *D. wrightmyoensis*. In the other group of species, section *Piptospatha*, the inflorescence bracts fall from the elongating infructescences, and only the basal bract persists. In our area this section includes *D. didymophylla*, *D. geniculata*, *D. kunstleri*, *D. leptopus*, *D. macrophylla*, *D. mollispina*, *D. poilanei*, *D. propinqua*, *D. sabut*, and *D. verticillaris*.

In the species descriptions, stem diameters include the leaf sheaths. Note that many climbing species of *Daemonorops* often form dense thickets before they begin to climb or if longer canes are constantly harvested.

Key to the Species of *Daemonorops*

1a. Andaman Islands . . . . 2.
1b. Bangladesh, Bhutan, Cambodia, China, India, Laos, Myanmar, Nepal, Thailand, and
    Vietnam . . . . 6.

2a. Leaf sheath spines longer at sheath apices . . . . 3.
2b. Leaf sheath spines not longer at sheath apices . . . . 4.

3a. Leaflets green on lower surface; leaf sheaths with partial rows of spines . . . . *D. kurziana*.
3b. Leaflets whitish on lower surface; leaf sheaths with scattered spines . . . . *D. wrightmyoensis*.

4a. Leaf sheath spines to 1.5 cm long; Little Andaman . . . . *D. rarispinosa*.
4b. Leaf sheath spines to 3 cm long; South Andaman . . . . 5.

5a. Leaf sheath spines very few, scattered, brownish . . . . *D. aurea*.
5b. Leaf sheath spines scattered, black . . . . *D. manii*.

6a. Vietnam . . . . 7.
6b. Bangladesh, Bhutan, Cambodia, China, India, Laos, Myanmar, Nepal, and Thailand . . . . 9.

7a. Inflorescence bracts persistent, swollen, splitting lengthwise to reveal the
    flowering branches . . . . *D. jenkinsiana*.
7b. Inflorescence bracts falling from the elongating inflorescences, only the basal bract
    persistent . . . . 8.

8a. Leaf sheath spines longer at sheath apices; ocreas obscure . . . . *D. mollispina*.
8b. Leaf sheath spines not longer at sheath apices; ocreas prominent . . . . *D. poilanei*.

9a. Bangladesh, Bhutan, Cambodia, China, India, Laos, Myanmar (excluding Tanintharyi),
    Nepal, and Thailand (East, North, Northeast, Southeast, Southwest) . . . . *D. jenkinsiana*.
9b. Myanmar (Tanintharyi) and Thailand (Peninsular) . . . . 10.

10a. Leaf sheath spines from some rows pointing either upwards or downwards, the overlapping spines
     forming ant chambers . . . . 11.
10b. Leaf sheath spines not forming ant chambers . . . . 13.

11a. Basal leaflets much longer and wider than the others . . . . *D. macrophylla*.
11b. Basal leaflets the same size as the others . . . . 12.

12a. Leaflets 40–60 per side of rachis, regularly arranged . . . . *D. verticillaris*.
12b. Leaflets 10–17 per side of rachis, arranged in distant clusters . . . . *D. sabut*.

13a. Sheaths, petioles, and rachis mottled . . . . *D. leptopus.*
13b. Sheaths, petioles, and rachis not mottled . . . . 14.

14a. Leaves subtending inflorescences smaller than others; inflorescences produced simultaneously,
the stem dying after fruiting . . . . 15.
14b. Leaves subtending inflorescences not smaller than others; inflorescences produced sequentially,
the stem not dying after fruiting . . . . 16.

15a. Leaf sheath spines scattered; stems to 3 m long, not climbing . . . . *D. lewisiana.*
15b. Leaf sheath spines in rows; stems to 5 m long, climbing . . . . *D. monticola.*

16a. Leaflets irregularly arranged in diverging pairs . . . . *D. didymophylla.*
16b. Leaflets not so arranged . . . . 17.

17a. Leaf sheaths and outer inflorescence bracts with densely arranged, needlelike spines . . . . 18.
17b. Leaf sheaths and outer inflorescence bracts not with densely arranged, needlelike spines . . . . 19.

18a. Leaf sheath spines to 3 cm long; montane rain forest, at higher elevations . . . . *D. sepal.*
18b. Leaf sheath spines to 7 cm long; lowland rain forest, often near the sea,
at low elevations . . . . *D. melanochaetes.*

19a. Inflorescence bracts persistent, swollen, splitting lengthwise to reveal the flowering
branches. . . . . 20.
19b. Inflorescence bracts falling from the elongating inflorescences, only the basal bract
persistent . . . . 23.

20a. Leaf sheath spines longer at sheath apices . . . . *D. kurziana.*
20b. Leaf sheath spines not longer at sheath apices . . . . 21.

21a. Leaflets 18–60 per side of rachis, lanceolate, regularly or slightly irregularly arranged
and distantly spaced . . . . *D. grandis.*
21b. Leaflets to 100 per side of rachis, linear, regularly arranged and closely spaced . . . . 22.

22a. Leaf sheath spines to 4 cm long; leaflets not closely arranged, linear or lanceolate . . . . . . *D. jenkinsiana.*
22b. Leaf sheath spines to 2.5 cm long; leaflets closely arranged, linear . . . . *D. angustifolia.*

23a. Leaf sheath spines not longer at sheath apices and petiole margins; leaflets
13–20 per side of rachis . . . . *D. propinqua.*
23b. Leaf sheath spines longer at sheath apices and often on petiole margins; leaflets 35 or more
per side of rachis . . . . 24.

24a. Leaflets about 65 per side of rachis, linear, regularly arranged . . . . *D. kunstleri.*
24b. Leaflets 35–40 per side of rachis, lanceolate, irregularly arranged in groups of 3–10 leaflets,
or sometimes regularly arranged . . . . *D. geniculata.*

Daemonorops angustifolia (Griff.) Mart.

PLATE 30

wai-nam, waai som (Tha)

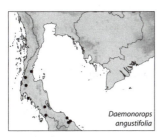

Daemonorops angustifolia

Field characters. Stems clustered, climbing, to 40 m long and 4 cm diameter. Leaf sheaths yellowish green with brown or reddish black hairs, with black, flattened, triangular, to 2.5-cm-long spines; ocreas obscure; knees present, conspicuous; leaf rachis to 2 m long with 80–100 linear leaflets per side, these regularly and closely arranged; cirri present, to 1.3 m long; inflorescences to 0.5 m long, erect; bracts persistent, swollen, splitting lengthwise to reveal the flowering branches; fruits globose, to 1.8 cm diameter, brownish.

Range and habitat. Thailand (Peninsular) (also in Peninsular Malaysia); lowland rain forest especially along streams and other wet places, or more open areas, to 1000 m elevation.

Uses. Provides a cane used in furniture making.

Notes. This species, together with *D. grandis, D. jenkinsiana, D. kurziana, D. manii, D. melanochaetes,* and *D. sepal,* form a closely related group, perhaps

better treated as a single, complex species. Three species from the Andaman Islands (*D. aurea, D. rarispinosa*, and *D. wrightmyoensis*) may also be part of this complex, but tend to have less-spiny leaf sheaths.
Synonyms. *Calamus angustifolius* Griff., *Calamus hygrophilus* Griff., *Daemonorops angustispatha* Furtado, *Daemonorops carcharodon* Ridl., *Daemonorops hygrophila* (Griff.) Mart., *Palmijuncus hygrophilus* (Griff.) Kuntze

Daemonorops aurea Renuka & Vijayak.

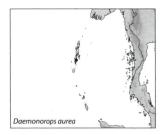

Daemonorops aurea

Field characters. Stems clustered, climbing, to 20 m long and 3.5 cm diameter. Leaf sheaths yellowish green without hairs, with very few, scattered, brownish, flattened, to 3-cm-long spines; ocreas obscure; knees present; leaf rachis to 1.7 m long with numerous, linear leaflets per side, these regularly arranged; cirri present, to 1.5 m long. Inflorescences to 0.3 m long; bracts persistent, swollen, splitting lengthwise to reveal the flowering branches; fruits globose, to 1.5 cm diameter, yellow.
Range and habitat. Andaman Islands (South Andaman); lowland rain forest at low elevations.
Uses. Provides a cane used in furniture making.

Daemonorops didymophylla Becc.
PLATES 30 & 31
wai-ki-ped (Tha)

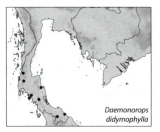

Daemonorops didymophylla

Field characters. Stems clustered, sometimes solitary, climbing, to 20 m long and 3.5 cm diameter. Leaf sheaths green to yellowish green, without hairs, with scattered or rows of black, yellow-based, flattened, triangular, to 3.5-cm-long spines; ocreas obscure; knees present, conspicuous; leaf rachis to 2.3 m long with 12–20 lanceolate to broadly lanceo-

late leaflets per side, these irregularly arranged in diverging pairs; cirri present, to 1 m long. Inflorescences to 0.5 m long, pendulous; bracts falling from the elongating infructescence, only the basal bract persistent; fruits ovoid, to 2.5 cm long and 2 cm diameter, brown, with dragon's blood.
Range and habitat. Thailand (Peninsular) (also in Borneo, Peninsular Malaysia, Singapore, and Sumatra); lowland rain forest to 1000 m elevation.
Uses. Provides a cane used in furniture making, and the fruits are a source of dye and used medicinally.
Synonyms. *Calamus cochleatus* Miq., *Calamus didymophyllus* (Becc.) Ridl., *Daemonorops cochleata* Teijsm. & Binn., *Daemonorops mattanensis* Becc., *Daemonorops motleyi* Becc., *Palmijuncus cochleatus* (Miq.) Kuntze

Daemonorops geniculata (Griff.) Mart.
wai ta no (Tha)

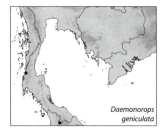

Daemonorops geniculata

Field characters. Stems usually solitary, climbing, to 20 m long and 4.5 cm diameter. Leaf sheaths green with gray-brown hairs, with rows of black, flattened or needlelike, to 4 (to 10 at sheath apices)-cm-long spines, borne on ridges; ocreas absent; knees obscure; petioles with paler, to 10-cm-long spines along the margins; leaf rachis to 3 m long with 35–40 lanceolate leaflets per side, these irregularly arranged in groups of 3–10 leaflets, or sometimes regularly arranged; cirri present, to 1 m long. Inflorescences to 0.8 m long, pendulous; bracts falling from the elongating infructescence, only the basal bract persistent; fruits globose, to 2.2 cm diameter, yellowish brown.
Range and habitat. Thailand (Peninsular) (also in Peninsular Malaysia and Singapore); lowland rain forest to 1000 m elevation.
Uses. None recorded.
Synonyms. *Calamus geniculatus* Griff., *Palmijuncus geniculatus* (Griff.) Kuntze

Daemonorops grandis (Griff.) Mart.
wai-jark (Tha)

Field characters. Stems clustered, climbing, to 20 m long and 5 cm diameter. Leaf sheaths green with brown hairs, with scattered or rows of black, triangular, to 5-cm-long spines, mixed with some needlelike spines; ocreas obscure; knees present, conspicuous;

Plate 33. *Daemonorops verticillaris*; leaf sheath; Thailand (top left). *Eleiodoxa conferta*; leaf bases; Thailand (top right). *Eleiodoxa conferta*; fruits; Thailand (bottom left). *Eugeissona tristis*; fruits; Thailand (bottom right).

Plate 34. *Guihaia argyrata*; habit; China (top left). *Guihaia grossifibrosa*; habit; Vietnam (top right). *Hyphaene dichotoma*; habit; cultivation, Florida (bottom left). *Iguanura bicornis*; fruits; Thailand (bottom right).

Plate 35. *Iguanura thalangensis*; infructescence; Thailand (top left). *Iguanura wallichiana* var. *wallichiana*; habit; Thailand (top right). *Johannesteijsmannia altifrons*; habit; Thailand (bottom left). *Johannesteijsmannia altifrons*; inflorescence; Thailand (bottom right).

Plate 36. *Kerriodoxa elegans*; habit; Thailand (top left). *Kerriodoxa elegans*; inflorescences; Thailand (top right). *Korthalsia flagellaris*; lower surface of leaflets; Thailand (bottom left). *Korthalsia laciniosa*; habit; Thailand (bottom right).

Plate 37. *Korthalsia laciniosa*; lower surface of leaflets; Thailand (top left). *Korthalsia laciniosa*; eaf sheath; Thailand (top right). *Korthalsia laciniosa*; fruits; Vietnam (bottom left). *Licuala acaulis*; female flowers; Vietnam (bottom right).

Plate 38. *Licuala atroviridis*; habit; Vietnam (top left). *Licuala bachmaensis*; habit; Vietnam (top right). *Licuala bidoupensis*; leaves; Vietnam (bottom left). *Licuala calciphila*; habit; Vietnam (bottom right).

Plate 39. *Licuala cattienensis*; habit; Vietnam (top left). *Licuala cattiensis*; fruits; Vietnam (top right). *Licuala centralis*; habit; Vietnam (bottom left). *Licuala dasyantha*; habit; Vietnam (bottom right).

Plate 40. *Licuala dasyantha*; inflorescences; Vietnam (top left). *Licuala distans*; habit; Thailand (top right). *Licuala fordiana*; habit; China (bottom left). *Licuala fordiana*; inflorescences; China (bottom right).

Plate 41. *Licuala hainanensis*; habit; China (top left). *Licuala hexasepala*; habit; Vietnam (top right). *Licuala magalonii*; habit; Vietnam (bottom left). *Licuala merguensis*; habit; Thailand (bottom right).

Plate 42. *Licuala peltata* var. *peltata*; habit; Myanmar (top left). *Licuala peltata* var. *peltata*; flowers; Thailand (top right). *Licuala robinsoniana*; habit; Vietnam (bottom left). *Licuala robinsoniana*; inflorescences; Vietnam (bottom right).

Plate 43. *Livistona chinensis*; leaves; cultivated, Vietnam (top left). *Livistona halongensis*; habit; Vietnam (top right). *Livistona jenkinsiana*; inflorescences; Myanmar (bottom left). *Livistona jenkinsiana*; infructescence; India (bottom right).

Plate 44. *Loxococcus rupicola*; habit; Sri Lanka (top left). *Maxburretia furtadoana*; habit; Thailand (top right). *Maxburretia furtadoana*; leaf bases; Thailand (bottom left). *Myrialepis paradoxa*; fruits; Vietnam (bottom right).

Plate 45. *Nannorrhops ritchiana*; habit; Oman (top left). *Nenga banaensis*; habit; Vietnam (top right). *Nenga banaensis*; inflorescence; Vietnam (bottom left). *Nenga pumila* var. *pachystachya*; habit; Thailand (bottom right).

Plate 46. *Nenga pumila* var. *pachystachya*; infructescences; Thailand (top left). *Nypa fruticans*; habit; Vietnam (top right). *Nypa fruitcans*; inflorescence; Myanmar (bottom left). *Oncosperma fasciculatum*; habit; Sri Lanka (bottom right).

Plate 47. *Oncosperma tigillarium*, with *Nypa fruticans* in foreground; habit; Thailand (top left). *Orania sylvicola*; habit; Thailand (top right). *Phoenix loureiroi* var. *loureiroi*; habit; Vietnam (bottom left). *Phoenix paludosa*; habit; Thailand (bottom right).

Plate 48. *Phoenix pusilla*; habit; Sri Lanka (top left). *Phoenix roebelinii*; habit; Vietnam (top right). *Phoenix rupicola*; habit; India (bottom left). *Phoenix sylvestris*; habit; India (bottom right).

leaf rachis to 3.5 m long with 18–60 lanceolate leaflets per side, these regularly or slightly irregularly and distantly arranged; cirri present, to 1.75 m long. Inflorescences erect, to 0.7 m long; bracts persistent, swollen, splitting lengthwise to reveal the flowering branches; fruits globose, to 2.5 cm diameter, yellowish brown.

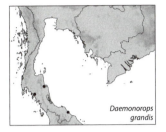

Range and habitat. Thailand (Peninsular) (also in Singapore and Peninsular Malaysia); lowland rain forest to 800 m elevation.
Uses. Provides a poor-quality cane, which is seldom used; the palm hearts are used medicinally.
Notes. See notes under *D. angustifolia.*
Synonyms. *Calamus acanthopis* Griff., *Calamus grandis* Griff., *Calamus intermedius* Griff., *Daemonorops grandis* var. *megacarpus* Furtado, *Daemonorops intermedia* (Griff.) Mart., *Daemonorops intermedia* var. *nudinervis* Becc., *Daemonorops kirtong* Griff., *Daemonorops laciniata* Furtado, *Daemonorops malaccensis* Mart., *Palmijuncus grandis* (Griff.) Kuntze, *Palmijuncus intermedius* (Griff.) Kuntze, *Palmijuncus malaccensis* (Mart.) Kuntze

Daemonorops jenkinsiana (Griff.) Mart.   PLATE 31
gola (Ban), huang teng, paak t'ang (Chi), cheka bet, golak bet (Ind), boun (Lao), kyien-yea taung (Mya), dhangru (Nep), wai-somm (Tha), may rut (Vie)

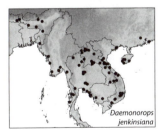

Field characters. Stems clustered, climbing or often forming thickets, to 25 m long and 6 cm diameter. Leaf sheaths yellowish green with gray, brown, or reddish black hairs, with scattered or rows of black, flattened, triangular, to 4-cm-long spines, mixed with some needlelike spines; ocreas obscure; knees present, conspicuous; leaf rachis to 3 m long with 55–100 linear or lanceolate leaflets per side, these regularly arranged; cirri present, to 2 m long. Inflorescences to

0.8 m long, erect; bracts persistent, swollen, splitting lengthwise to reveal the flowering branches; fruits globose to ellipsoid, to 2 cm long and 2 cm diameter, yellowish brown.
Range and habitat. Bangladesh, Bhutan, Cambodia, China (Guangdong, Guangxi, Hainan, Hong Kong), northeastern India (Assam, Manipur, Meghalaya, Sikkim, West Bengal), Laos (Central, Northern, Southern), Myanmar (Bago, Rakhine, Tanintharyi, Yangon), Nepal, Thailand (East, North, Northeast, Southeast, Southwest), and Vietnam; lowland rain forest, often persisting in disturbed areas, to 1000 m elevation.
Uses. Provides a cane used in furniture making, and leaves for thatching.
Notes. A widespread, common, and extremely variable species. See notes under *D. angustifolia.*
Synonyms. *Calamus jenkinsianus* Griff., *Calamus margaritae* Hance, *Calamus nutantiflorus* Griff., *Daemonorops jenkinsiana* var. *tenasserimica* Becc., *Daemonorops margaritae* (Hance) Becc., *Daemonorops margaritae* var. *palawanica* Becc., *Daemonorops nutantiflora* (Griff.) Mart., *Daemonorops pierreana* Becc., *Daemonorops schmidtiana* Becc., *Palmijuncus jenkinsianus* (Griff.) Kuntze, *Palmijuncus margaritae* (Hance) Kuntze, *Palmijuncus nutantiflorus* (Griff.) Kuntze

Daemonorops kunstleri Becc.   PLATE 31
wai hang sûa, wai-ki-lay (Tha)

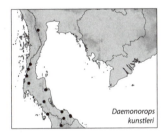

Field characters. Stems clustered, climbing or non-climbing and then short and erect, to 15 m long and 4 cm diameter. Leaf sheaths brownish green with brown hairs, with densely arranged rows of dark brown, flattened, to 4 (to 15 at sheath apex)-cm-long spines; ocreas obscure; knees present, absent in nonclimbing plants; petioles with paler, to 10-cm-long spines along the margins; leaf rachis to 2 m long with about 65 linear leaflets per side, these regularly arranged; cirri present, to 1 m long, very short in nonclimbing forms. Inflorescences to 0.7 m long, arching; bracts falling from the elongating infructescence, only the basal bract persistent; fruits globose, to 1.8 cm diameter, brown.
Range and habitat. Thailand (Peninsular, Southwest) (also in Singapore and Peninsular Malaysia, and possibly Sumatra); lowland or montane rain forest, 50–1000 m, rarely to 1400 m elevation.
Uses. None recorded.
Synonym. *Daemonorops vagans* Becc.

Daemonorops kurziana Hook. f. ex Becc.
sanda beth (And), kyien kalah (Mya)

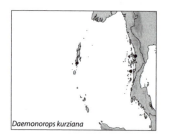

Daemonorops kurziana

Field characters. Stems clustered, climbing, to 25 m long and 6 cm diameter. Leaf sheaths yellowish green without hairs, with partial rows of black, triangular, to 4 (to 6 at sheath apex)-cm-long spines; ocreas obscure; knees present; leaf rachis to 2.5 m long with to 45 lanceolate leaflets per side, these regularly arranged; cirri present, to 1 m long. Inflorescences to 0.6 m long, erect; bracts persistent, swollen, splitting lengthwise to reveal the flowering branches; fruits globose, to 2 cm diameter, brown.
Range and habitat. Andaman Islands (South Andamans), Myanmar (Tanintharyi), and probably Thailand (Southwest); lowland rain forest at low elevations.
Uses. Provides a cane used in furniture making.
Notes. See notes under *D. angustifolia.*

Daemonorops leptopus (Griff.) Mart.

Field characters. Stems clustered, climbing, to 20 m long and 6 cm diameter. Leaf sheaths green, mottled with black, yellow, or purple patches, with scattered, dark brown, triangular, to 4-cm-long spines; ocreas obscure; knees present, conspicuous; petiole mottled as the sheath; leaf rachis mottled as the petiole, to 2.5 m long with about 40 linear leaflets per side, these regularly arranged and pendulous; cirri present, to 2.5 m long. Inflorescences to 1 m long, pendulous; bracts falling from the elongating infructescence, only the basal bract persistent; fruits ovoid, to 1.8 cm long and 1 cm diameter, brown.
Range and habitat. Thailand (Peninsular) (also in Singapore and Peninsular Malaysia); lowland rain forest to 1000 m elevation.
Uses. None recorded.
Notes. Reported to occur in Peninsular Thailand (Dransfield et al. 2004), but no specimens from there have been seen and no map is provided.
Synonyms. *Calamus leptopus* Griff., *Daemonorops congesta* Ridl., *Palmijuncus leptopus* (Griff.) Kuntze

Daemonorops lewisiana (Griff.) Mart.

Field characters. Stems clustered, rarely solitary, nonclimbing, forming thickets, to 3 m long and 7 cm diameter. Leaf sheaths green with brown hairs, with

scattered, black, triangular, to 3-cm-long spines; ocreas obscure; knees absent or obscure; leaf rachis to 2.5 m long with about 80 linear leaflets per side, these regularly arranged; leaves subtending inflorescences much smaller than others; cirri absent or short, to 0.2 m long on older leaves. Inflorescences to 0.2 m long, produced at the same time, the stem dying after flowering; bracts persistent, swollen, splitting lengthwise to reveal the flowering branches; fruits globose, to 2 cm diameter, brown.

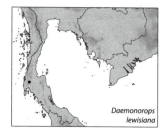

Daemonorops
lewisiana

Range and habitat. Thailand (Peninsular) (also in Peninsular Malaysia, Singapore, and Sumatra); lowland rain forest at low elevations.
Uses. None recorded.
Notes. Close to, and perhaps not distinct from, *D. monticola* (Dransfield 1979a; Hodel 1998).
Synonyms. *Calamus lewisianus* Griff., *Daemonorops bakauensis* Becc., *Daemonorops curtisii* Furtado, *Daemonorops pseudosepal* Becc., *Daemonorops tabacina* Becc., *Palmijuncus lewisianus* (Griff.) Kuntze

Daemonorops macrophylla Becc.
wai loe bae lek (Tha)

Field characters. Stems clustered, climbing, to 20 m long and 3 cm diameter. Leaf sheaths green with brown hairs, with rows of dark brown, needlelike, to 5-cm-long spines, borne on ridges, spines from some rows pointing either upwards or downwards, the overlap forming ant chambers; ocreas obscure; knees present, obscure; leaf rachis to 1 m long with 8–10 lanceolate leaflets per side, these clustered, the basal ones much longer and wider than the others; cirri present, to 1.3 m long. Inflorescences to 1 m long, pendulous; bracts falling from the elongating infructescence, only the basal bract persistent; fruits ovoid, to 2.1 cm long and 1.5 cm diameter, yellowish brown.
Range and habitat. Thailand (Peninsular) (also in Peninsular Malaysia); lowland rain forest to 800 m elevation.
Uses. Provides a medium-quality cane used in furniture making.
Notes. Reported to occur in Peninsular Thailand (Dransfield et al. 2004), but no specimens from there have been seen and no map is provided. Close to, and perhaps not distinct from, *D. sabut* (Dransfield 1979a).

Daemonorops manii Becc.
châng bet (And)

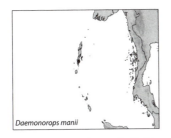

Daemonorops manii

Field characters. Stems clustered, climbing, to 20 m long and 3 cm diameter. Leaf sheaths yellowish with brown hairs, with scattered, black, flattened, triangular, to 3-cm-long spines; ocreas obscure; knees present; leaf rachis to 2 m long with numerous linear leaflets per side, these regularly arranged; cirri present, to 1.5 m long. Inflorescences to 0.3 m long, erect; bracts persistent, swollen, splitting lengthwise to reveal the flowering branches; fruits globose, to 1.8 cm diameter, brown.
Range and habitat. Andaman Islands (South Andaman) and possibly Nicobars; lowland rain forest at low elevations.
Uses. The leaves are used for thatching.
Notes. See notes under *D. angustifolia*. Beccari (1911) considered this species to be a geographic form of *D. jenkinsiana*.

Daemonorops melanochaetes Blume
wai jark (Tha)

Field characters. Stems clustered, forming thickets, climbing, to 30 m long and 7 cm diameter. Leaf sheaths brownish green with light brown hairs, with densely arranged, black, needlelike or flattened, to 7-cm-long spines; ocreas obscure; knees present, conspicuous; leaf rachis to 3 m long with 65–80 linear leaflets per side, these regularly and closely arranged; cirri present, to 1.25 m long. Inflorescences to 0.4 m long, erect; bracts persistent, swollen, splitting lengthwise to reveal the flowering branches; outer inflorescence bract with densely arranged, needlelike spines; fruits globose, 0.7–1 cm diameter, reddish brown.
Range and habitat. Thailand (Peninsular) (also in Java, Peninsular Malaysia, and Sumatra); lowland rain forest, often near the sea, at low elevations.
Uses. None recorded.
Notes. Reported to occur in Peninsular Thailand (Dransfield et al. 2004), but no specimens from there have been seen and no map is provided. See notes under *D. angustifolia*.
Synonyms. *Calamus melanochaetes* (Blume) Miq., *Daemonorops javanica* Furtado, *Daemonorops melanochaetes* var. *depresseglobus* Teijsm., *Daemonorops melanochaetes* var. *macrocarpus* Becc., *Daemonorops melanochaetes* var. *macrocymbus* Becc., *Daemonorops melanochaetes* var. *microcarpus* Teijsm., *Daemonorops melanochaetes* var. *padangensis* Becc.

Daemonorops mollispina J. Dransf.
may heo (Vie)

Daemonorops mollispina

Field characters. Stems clustered, climbing, to 8 m long and 5 cm diameter. Leaf sheaths brownish, with densely arranged, yellowish, black-tipped, triangular, to 4.5 (to 18 at sheath apex)-cm-long spines, with gray or brown hairs; ocreas obscure; knees absent; leaf rachis to 2 m long with about 60 linear leaflets per side, these regularly arranged; cirri present, to 1.5 m long. Inflorescences to 1 m long, arching; bracts falling from the elongating infructescence, only the basal bract persistent; fruits globose, to 1.5 cm diameter, brown.
Range and habitat. Vietnam (Central); lowland or montane rain forest, to 1900 m elevation.
Uses. None recorded.

Daemonorops monticola (Griff.) Mart.

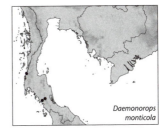

Daemonorops monticola

Field characters. Stems clustered, climbing, to 5 m long and 3.5 cm diameter. Leaf sheaths green with brown hairs, with rows of black, triangular, to 1-cm-long spines; ocreas obscure; knees present, obscure; leaf rachis to 1.7 m long with 30–60 linear leaflets per side, these regularly arranged; leaves subtending inflorescences much smaller than others; cirri present, to 0.75 m long. Inflorescences to 0.75 m long, produced at the same time, the stem dying after flowering; bracts persistent, swollen, splitting lengthwise to reveal the flowering branches; fruits globose, to 1.5 cm diameter, reddish brown.

Range and habitat. Thailand (Peninsular) (also in Peninsular Malaysia); lowland rain forest at low elevations.

Uses. None recorded.

Notes. See notes under *D. lewisiana*.

Synonyms. *Calamus monticola* Griff., *Palmijuncus monticula* (Griff.) Kuntze

Daemonorops poilanei J. Dransf.   PLATE 32
may nuoc (Vie)

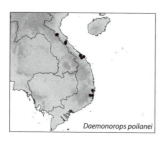

Daemonorops poilanei

Field characters. Stems clustered, climbing, to 10 m long and 2.5 cm diameter. Leaf sheaths yellowish green with brown hairs, with densely arranged, brown, triangular, flattened, to 4.5-cm-long spines; knees present, obscure; ocrea prominent; leaf rachis to 3 m long with to 36 linear-lanceolate leaflets per side, these irregularly arranged in groups, sometimes appearing almost regularly arranged; cirri present, to 1.5 m long. Inflorescences to 0.7 m long, arching; bracts falling from the elongating infructescence, only the basal bract persistent; fruits globose, to 2.5 cm diameter, brown.

Range and habitat. Vietnam (Central, Southern); lowland rain forest, usually along streams and rivers, to 600 m elevation.

Uses. Provides a cane used in furniture making.

Daemonorops propinqua Becc.

Field characters. Stems clustered, climbing or thicket forming, to 5 m long and 4 cm diameter. Leaf sheaths green without hairs, with scattered or arranged in short rows, black-tipped, flattened, to 3-cm-long spines; ocreas obscure; knees present, obscure; leaf rachis to 1.6 m long with 13–20 lanceolate leaflets per side, these well spaced, regularly or slightly irregularly arranged; cirri present, to 1 m long. Inflorescences to 0.6 m long, pendulous; bracts falling from the elongating infructescence, only the basal bract persistent; fruits ellipsoid, to 2.5 cm long and 2 cm diameter, reddish, with dragon's blood.

Range and habitat. Thailand (Peninsular) (also in Sumatra and Peninsular Malaysia); lowland rain forest, usually in wet places, at low elevations.

Uses. The fruits are a source of dye.

Notes. Reported to occur in Peninsular Thailand (Dransfield et al. 2004), but no specimens from there have been seen and no map is provided.

Daemonorops rarispinosa Renuka & Vijayak.

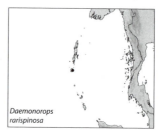

Daemonorops rarispinosa

Field characters. Stems clustered, climbing, to 20 m long and 2.5 cm diameter. Leaf sheaths yellowish without hairs, with scattered, flattened, triangular, to 1.5-cm-long spines; ocreas obscure; knees present; leaf rachis to 1 m long with numerous linear leaflets per side, these regularly arranged; cirri present, to 1.5 m long. Inflorescences to 0.4 m long, erect; bracts persistent, swollen, splitting lengthwise to reveal the flowering branches; fruits globose, to 1.3 cm diameter, yellow.

Range and habitat. Andaman Islands (Little Andaman Island); lowland rain forest at low elevations.

Uses. Provides a cane used in furniture making.

Notes. See notes under *D. angustifolia*.

Daemonorops sabut Becc.   PLATE 32
wai pon, wai-pun-kun-nom (Tha)

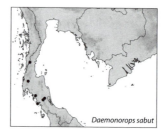

Daemonorops sabut

Field characters. Stems clustered, climbing, to 20 m long and 3 cm diameter. Leaf sheaths green with dark brown hairs, with rows of dark brown, needlelike, to 6-cm-long spines, borne on ridges, spines from some rows pointing either upwards or downwards, the overlap forming ant chambers; knees present, conspicuous; leaf rachis to 1.5 m long with 5–17 lanceolate leaflets per side, these arranged in distant clusters; cirri present, to 1.3 m long. Inflorescences to 1 m long, pendulous; bracts falling from the elongating infructescence, only the basal bract persistent; fruits globose to ovoid, to 1.6 cm long and 1.2 cm diameter, yellowish.

Range and habitat. Thailand (Peninsular) (also in Borneo, Peninsular Malaysia, Singapore, and possibly Sumatra); lowland rain forest, often near rivers or in other wet places, at low elevations.

Uses. Provides a moderate-quality cane used in furniture making.

Notes. See notes under *D. macrophylla*.
Synonyms. *Daemonorops annulata* Becc., *Daemonorops pseudomirabilis* Becc., *Daemonorops turbinata* Becc.

Daemonorops sepal Becc.
chak nam (Tha)

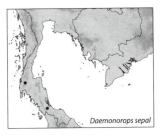

Daemonorops sepal

Field characters. Stems clustered, climbing, to 15 m long and 6 cm diameter. Leaf sheaths green with light brown hairs, with densely arranged, brown, needlelike, to 3-cm-long spines; ocreas obscure; knees present, conspicuous; leaf rachis to 2 m long with to 80 linear leaflets per side, these regularly and closely arranged; cirri present, to 1.3 m long. Inflorescences to 0.4 m long, erect; bracts persistent, swollen, splitting lengthwise to reveal the flowering branches; outer inflorescence bract with densely arranged, needlelike spines; fruits globose, to 3 cm diameter, brown.
Range and habitat. Thailand (Peninsular) (also in Peninsular Malaysia); lowland or montane rain forest, at low to medium elevations.
Uses. None recorded.
Notes. Although sometimes reported to occur at higher elevations, the few specimens from Peninsular Thailand have been collected at low elevations. See notes under *D. angustifolia*.
Synonyms. *Daemonorops aciculata* Ridl., *Daemonorops imbellis* Becc., *Daemonorops kiahii* Furtado, *Daemonorops nurii* Furtado, *Daemonorops scortechinii* Becc.

Daemonorops verticillaris (Griff.) Mart.   PLATE 33
wai taplu (Tha)

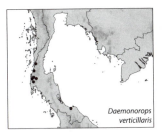

Daemonorops verticillaris

Field characters. Stems usually solitary, climbing, to 15 m long and 5 cm diameter. Leaf sheaths green with

brown hairs, with rows of dark brown, needlelike or flattened, to 2-cm-long spines, borne on ridges, spines from some rows pointing either upwards or downwards, the overlap forming ant chambers, some spines at sheath apex flattened, to 11 cm long; ocreas obscure; knees present, obscure; leaf rachis to 1.5 m long with 40–60 lanceolate leaflets per side, these closely spaced and regularly arranged; cirri present, to 1 m long. Inflorescences to 2 m long, pendulous; bracts falling from the elongating infructescence, only the basal bract persistent; fruits globose, to 1.5 cm diameter, brownish.
Range and habitat. Thailand (Peninsular) (also in Borneo, Peninsular Malaysia, and Sumatra); lowland rain forest to 1000 m elevation.
Uses. Provides a low-quality cane.
Synonyms. *Calamus verticillaris* Griff., *Daemonorops setigera* Ridl., *Daemonorops stipitata* Furtado, *Daemonorops verticillaris* var. *stramineus* Furtado, *Palmijuncus verticillaris* (Griff.) Kuntze

Daemonorops wrightmyoensis Renuka & Vijayak.
sanka beth (And)

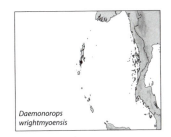

Daemonorops wrightmyoensis

Field characters. Stems clustered, climbing, to 20 m long and 4.5 cm diameter. Leaf sheaths yellowish without hairs, with scattered, black or brown, flattened, triangular, to 4 (to 6 at sheath apex)-cm-long spines; knees present; leaf rachis to 2 m long with numerous linear leaflets per side, these regularly arranged and whitish on the lower surface; cirri present, to 1.5 m long. Inflorescences to 0.8 m long, erect; bracts persistent, swollen, splitting lengthwise to reveal the flowering branches; fruits ellipsoid, to 1.5 cm long and 1 cm diameter, brownish.
Range and habitat. Andaman Islands (South Andaman); lowland rain forest at low elevations.
Uses. Provides a cane used in furniture making.
Notes. See notes under *D. angustifolia*.

ELEIODOXA (Becc.) Burret

The genus name is derived from the swampy habitat of this palm, from the Greek words *eleio*, meaning wet, and *doxa*, meaning at home in. Stems are clustered, short and subterranean, and mostly obscured by the persistent leaf bases. Short breathing roots are produced from the stems, and these protrude above the soil level. Leaves are pinnate, spiny, and five to eight per stem in number. Leaf sheaths are open and do not form crownshafts. Sheaths and petioles are elongate and are covered with short rows of stout, brown or black, needlelike spines, and these spread in different directions. Leaflets are lanceolate and are regularly arranged and spread in the same plane. The leaflets at the apex of the leaf are not joined together, unlike those of the closely related genus *Salacca*.

Eleiodoxa is semelparous and also dioecious. Inflorescences are branched to two orders and are covered in numerous, persistent, sheathing bracts. Unlike the leaves, inflorescences are not spiny. Male and female inflorescences are congested. In male inflorescences, flowers are borne in densely arranged pairs on short, thick flowering branches. In female inflorescences, flowers are borne in pairs, also densely arranged, consisting of one female flower and one sterile male flower. Fruits are obovoid, brown or reddish brown, one- to three-seeded, and are covered in numerous scales. The endosperm is homogeneous, germination is adjacent, and the seedling leaf is bifid.

Eleiodoxa contains one species occurring in Peninsular Thailand, Peninsular Malaysia, Sumatra, and Borneo (Hodel 1998). It is not easily distinguished from *Salacca*, and the two genera need reassessing (Henderson 2008).

Eleiodoxa conferta (Griff.) Burret   PLATE 33
lumpee (Tha)

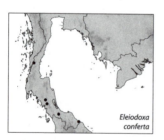

Eleiodoxa conferta

Field characters. Stems short and subterranean, clustered, forming large thickets. Sheaths and petioles with short rows of black or brown (becoming lighter with age), needlelike, to 8-cm-long spines; leaf rachis to 4 m long, with 25–35 lanceolate leaflets per side, these regularly arranged and spreading in the same plane. Inflorescences congested among leaf bases, the males and females similar; fruits obovoid, 1-seeded, to 2.5 cm long and 2.5 cm diameter, reddish brown, not spiny.
Range and habitat. Thailand (Peninsular) and probably adjacent Myanmar (also in Borneo, Peninsular Malaysia, and Sumatra); lowland rain forest in swamps, often near the coast, at low elevations.

Uses. The fruits are edible.
Synonyms. *Eleiodoxa microcarpa* Burret, *Eleiodoxa orthoschista* Burret, *Eleiodoxa scortechinii* (Becc.) Burret, *Eleiodoxa xantholepis* Burret, *Salacca conferta* Griff., *Salacca scortechinii* Becc.

EUGEISSONA Griff.

Stems are clustered, short and subterranean and then either erect or creeping, or taller and aerial. Roots are often conspicuous. In one species stems are borne on the top of long stilt roots, and in another modified roots occur as spines on the stem. Leaves are pinnate, spiny, 6–25 in number, and are spirally arranged or borne in three series. The leaves are used for thatching, hence the name of the genus, from the Greek words *eu*, meaning good, and *geisson*, meaning a roof cornice. Leaf sheaths are open and do not form crownshafts, and petioles are usually very long; both are covered in flat, black spines. Leaflets are linear to broadly lanceolate and are regularly arranged or clustered along the rachis.

Eugeissona is semelparous. After a relatively short period of vegetative growth, the stem greatly elongates and several inflorescences are produced simultaneously along this stem in the axils of much reduced leaves. The whole structure appears as a large, terminal inflorescence. After flowering and fruiting the stem dies. Inflorescences are branched to four orders and are covered in sheathing bracts. Flowers are borne in pairs of a male flower and a bisexual flower. Flowers are unusual among palms in having large, woody petals, and male flowers have colored anthers and pollen. Fruits are ovoid, brownish, one-seeded, and are covered in numerous, small scales. Unlike all other scaly-fruited palms, fruits have a hard, stony inner layer. The endosperm is homogeneous (although penetrated by the stony layer), germination is remote, and the seedling leaf is pinnate.

Eugeissona contains six species, distributed in Borneo, Peninsular Malaysia, and Peninsular Thailand. Only one species occurs in our area (Dransfield 1970; Hodel 1998).

Eugeissona tristis Griff.   PLATE 33
jark-khao (Tha)

Field characters. Stems short and subterranean (but elongating at flowering time), creeping, clustered, forming large thickets, often with dense stilt roots at the base. Leaf rachis to 3 m long, with to 100 regularly arranged, linear leaflets per side, these with soft spines on upper surface. Inflorescences stout, erect, to 3 m long, with no apparent branches; male flowers brown with purple-brown anthers and pollen;

fruits ovoid to almost oblong, to 9 cm long and 5 cm diameter, dark brown.

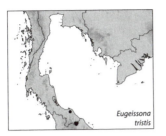

Range and habitat. Thailand (Peninsular) (also in Peninsular Malaysia); lowland rain forest on ridges and slopes, rarely in swamps, to 900 m elevation. It thrives in logged areas and is regarded as a weed by foresters.

Uses. The leaves are occasionally used for thatching, and the fruits are edible.

GUIHAIA J. Dransf., S. K. Lee & F. N. Wei

This genus is closely related to both *Maxburretia* and *Rhapis*, and is somewhat intermediate in flower and fruit structure. It gets its name from the old Chinese word for the area in which one species grows, Guilin in Guangxi Province. Stems are short or subterranean, clustered, sometimes creeping, and form small clumps. Leaves are palmate, 6–14 in number, and form a rather open crown. Leaf sheaths are open and consist of coarse, black or brown fibers. These are either free and spinelike, or remain joined at their apices, forming a distinct point. Petioles have smooth, sharp margins. At the apex of the petiole there is a hastula. The blade is more or less silvery white on the lower surface, and is divided to three-quarters or more of its length into numerous leaflets. These leaflets are very unusual among coryphoid palms in that their folding is roof-shaped (reduplicate or Λ-shaped in cross section), rather than the more usual gutter-shaped (induplicate or V-shaped in cross section). Rarely the blade is undivided. The margins of the leaves have minute "thorns," almost like saw teeth, although these are not so pronounced as in *Rhapis*.

Inflorescences are branched to four orders, and are borne among the leaves. Inflorescences have only two bracts, again unusual among coryphoid palms. Individual plants bear either male or female flowers, and these are very small and arranged spirally along the flowering branches. Fruits are small, globose to almost ellipsoid, blue-black, and one-seeded. The endosperm is homogeneous (although penetrated by an irregular intrusion of the seed coat), germination is remote, and the seedling leaf is narrow and undivided.

Guihaia contains two species distributed in southern China and northern Vietnam (Dransfield et al. 1985; Dransfield & Zona 1997). However, variation in the genus is complex. A few specimens are intermediate, with leaf sheath fibers as in *G. grossifibrosa* and leaves as in *G. argyrata* (see also Dransfield & Zona 1997). Other specimens have undivided leaves or leaves with only two leaflets. The two species have overlapping distributions along the border between China and Vietnam.

Guihaia argyrata (S. K. Lee & F. N. Wei) S. K. Lee, F. N. Wei & J. Dransf.   PLATE 34
shishankui (Chi)

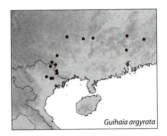

Guihaia argyrata

Field characters. Stems clustered, to 0.5 m tall and 5 cm diameter, erect or creeping, obscured by old leaf bases. Leaf sheath fibers stiff, erect, separating and becoming spinelike; leaf blades divided into 14–26 leaflets, these densely silvery white on the lower surface. Inflorescences to 0.8 m long; fruits almost globose, to 0.6 cm diameter, blue-black.

Range and habitat. China (Guangxi, Guangdong, Guizhou) and Vietnam (Northern); seasonal forest on steep slopes of karst limestone hills to 1000 m elevation.

Uses. None recorded.

Synonym. *Trachycarpus argyratus* S. K. Lee & F. N. Wei

Guihaia grossifibrosa (Gagnep.) J. Dransf., S. K. Lee & F. N. Wei   PLATE 34
lui (Vie)

Key to the Species of *Guihaia*

1a. Leaf sheath fibers stiff, erect, separating and becoming spinelike; leaf blades densely silvery white on the lower surface; stems to 0.5 m tall and 5 cm diameter . . . . *G. argyrata.*

1b. Leaf sheath fibers curved, remaining joined, not separating into stiff spines; leaf blades scarcely silvery white on the lower surface; stems to 2.5 m tall and 8 cm diameter . . . . . *G. grossifibrosa.*

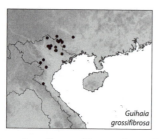

Guihaia
grossifibrosa

Field characters. Stems solitary or clustered, to 2.5 m tall and 8 cm diameter, erect or leaning, densely covered with persistent leaf bases. Leaf sheath fibers united at their apices, forming a distinct point; leaf blades sometimes undivided, usually divided into 2–21 leaflets, these scarcely silvery white on the lower surface. Inflorescences to 0.7 m long; fruits ellipsoid to ovoid, to 1 cm long and 1 cm diameter, blue-black.

Range and habitat. China (Guangxi, Guangdong) and Vietnam (Northern); seasonal forest on steep slopes of karst limestone hills at 500–1100 m elevation.

Uses. None recorded.

Notes. See Averyanov et al. (2005) for an account of this species in Vietnam.

Synonyms. *Rhapis filiformis* Burret, *Rhapis grossifibrosa* Gagnep.

HYPHAENE Gaertn.
(*Chamaeriphes* Dill., *Cucifera* Delile, *Doma* Lam., *Douma* Poir.)

Stems are remarkable in that those of some species are often branched several times by equal forking. Other species either have short and subterranean or swollen stems, and these can be either solitary or clustered. Stems of younger plants are often covered by the persistent remains of the leaf bases. Leaves are costapalmate, numerous, rather large, and form an open crown. Leaf sheaths are open and are split at the base to give a central triangular cleft. Sheaths and petioles are densely hairy. Petioles are elongate and the margins are covered with curved or straight, stout thorns. At the apex of the petiole there is a prominent hastula. The blade is divided into numerous leaflets, and these are briefly split at the apex. Leaflets are frequently waxy.

Inflorescences are borne among the leaves and are usually pendulous, and individual trees bear either male or female inflorescences. Male inflorescences are branched to two orders and are covered by several bracts. Flowering branches are borne in groups of 1–6(–13) and are rather thick. They are covered with small overlapping bracts, each covering a pit. Each pit contains three male flowers. Female inflorescences are rather similar to the males. Each pit of the flowering branch contains only one

female flower, and these are very large, with leathery sepals and petals. Fruits are large, irregularly shaped and often lobed, brownish, one-to three-seeded, and borne on a short stalk. The mesocarp is fibrous, and the name of the genus comes from a Greek word *hyphaino*, alluding to these fibers. The seeds are covered in a thick, bony endocarp. Endosperm is homogeneous, germination is remote, and the seedling leaf is undivided.

Hyphaene contains about eight species, most of them in Africa, but there are others in Arabia. One African species also occurs in Madagascar. They usually occur in arid areas. One species just reaches our area on the west coast of India.

Hyphaene dichotoma (White)   PLATE 34
Furtado
doum palm, ravan tad (Ind)

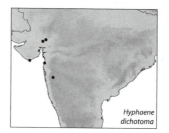

Hyphaene
dichotoma

Field characters. Stems branched at several places by equal forking, to 15 m tall and 30 cm diameter. Leaf blade divided into about 40 leaflets. Male inflorescences with about 6 flowering branches; fruits irregularly ovoid or oblong, to 7 cm long and 6 cm diameter, brownish.

Range and habitat. India (Guyjarat, Maharashtra); sand dunes or open, seasonally dry areas, at low elevations.

Uses. None recorded.

Notes. Possibly occurring farther south in India, perhaps to Goa. There are reports (e.g., Furtado 1970; Govaerts & Dransfield 2005) of its occurrence in Sri Lanka. It is possibly introduced from Africa.

Synonyms. *Borassus dichotomus* White, *Hyphaene indica* Becc., *Hyphaene taprobanica* Furtado

IGUANURA Blume
(*Slackia* Griff.)

Stems are clustered or less often solitary and seldom reach more than a few meters in height. They are ringed with prominent leaf scars, and stems of some species have stilt roots at the base. Rarely stems are short and subterranean. Leaves are pinnate or occasionally undivided and 5–12 in number. Leaf sheaths are closed and form crownshafts in some species, whereas in others sheaths persist and disintegrate on the stem and do not form crownshafts. In some

Key to the Species of *Iguanura*

1a. Leaflets linear to broad, with parallel margins and veins (if leaf undivided, then blade more than 1 m long); crownshaft absent . . . . 2.
1b. Leaflets broad, with diverging margins and veins (if leaf undivided, then blade less than 1 m long); crownshaft present or absent . . . . 3.

2a. Inflorescences with 1 or 2 (rarely to 7) flowering branches . . . . *I. geonomiformis.*
2b. Inflorescences with 3–15 flowering branches . . . . *I. wallichiana.*

3a. Leaf sheaths without earlike flaps at the apices; peduncles short, to 4 cm long; fruits with 2 lobes at the apices . . . . *I. bicornis.*
3b. Leaf sheaths with 2 short, earlike flaps at the apices; peduncles elongate, to 30 cm long; fruits rounded at the apices . . . . 4.

4a. Flowering branches 1–6 . . . . 5.
4b. Flowering branches 9–15 . . . . 6.

5a. Stems solitary; flowering branches 1 or 2 (rarely to 4), erect . . . . *I. thalangensis.*
5b. Stems clustered, rarely solitary; flowering branches 3–6, spreading . . . . *I. polymorpha.*

6a. Stems to 3 m tall and 3.5 cm diameter; leaf rachis to 1.3 m long; flowering branches spreading and intertwining . . . . *I. divergens.*
6b. Stems to 1.5 m tall and 2 cm diameter; leaf rachis to 0.5 m long; flowering branches wiry . . . . *I. tenuis.*

species, two short earlike flaps are present at the apices of the leaf sheaths, although these soon fall from older leaves. Leaflets are regularly arranged along the rachis. They are linear to broad, and the margins (and veins) can diverge giving an almost triangular shape to the leaflet. Leaflets are always jagged at the apices.

Inflorescences are spicate or branched to two orders and are borne below or among the leaves. The peduncle is often slender and elongate, and it and the slender flowering branches are covered with scales—hence the generic name, from the supposed resemblance of these to the tail of an iguana. Inflorescences are covered initially with two bracts. Flowers are unisexual and are borne in threes of a central female and two lateral males. These groups of flowers are usually sunken slightly into the flowering branches. Fruits are small, ovoid to ellipsoid and ridged or lobed, and one-seeded. Often fruits ripen through a series of colors, from green to white to pink or red. The endosperm is homogeneous or ruminate, germination is adjacent, and the seedling leaf is bifid or undivided.

Iguanura contains 32 species, occurring from Peninsular Thailand to Sumatra and Borneo. Seven species occur in our area (Hodel 1998; Kiew 1976, 1979; Lim 1996, 1998).

Iguanura bicornis Becc.

PLATE 34

mak faet (Tha)

Field characters. Stems clustered, to 3 m tall, rarely more, and 2.2 cm diameter. Crownshafts present, without earlike flaps at the apices; leaf rachis to 0.8 m long; leaflets broad, with diverging margins

and veins, 5–10 per side of rachis, rarely the blade undivided. Inflorescences borne below the leaves; peduncle to 4 cm long, with 4–8 spreading flowering branches; fruits oblong-ovoid, with 2 lobes at the apices, to 2 cm long and 1.8 cm diameter, reddish.

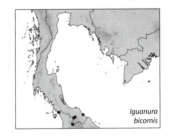

Iguanura
bicornis

Range and habitat. Thailand (Peninsular) (also in Peninsular Malaysia); lowland or montane rain forest to 1500 m elevation.
Uses. None recorded.

Iguanura divergens Hodel

mak tok (Tha)

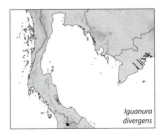

Iguanura
divergens

Field characters. Stems clustered, to 3 m tall and 3.5 cm diameter. Crownshafts absent, the old leaf sheaths persisting, with earlike flaps at the apices; leaf rachis to 1.3 m long; leaflets broad, with diverging margins and veins, 4 or 5 per side of rachis. Inflorescences borne below the leaves; peduncle to 25 cm long, with 9–13 spreading and intertwining flowering branches; fruits not known.

Range and habitat. Thailand (Peninsular); lowland rain forest to 800 m elevation.

Uses. None recorded.

Notes. Collected only once in Peninsular Thailand. Similar to some forms of the variable *I. polymorpha*. Hodel (1998) described the leaf sheaths as persistent; Lim (1998) described them as deciduous, perhaps based on cultivated plants.

Iguanura geonomiformis Mart.
mak pinae (Tha)

Field characters. Stems clustered or solitary, to 4 m tall and 2.5 cm diameter. Crownshafts absent, the old leaf sheaths persisting, with earlike flaps at the apices; leaf rachis to 1 m long; leaflets linear to broad, with parallel margins and veins, to 5 per side of rachis, or leaves undivided and briefly bifid. Inflorescences borne among the leaves; peduncles to 25 cm long, with 1 or 2 (rarely to 7) erect flowering branches; fruits ellipsoid, to 2 cm long and 1 cm diameter, maturing white to red.

Range and habitat. Thailand (Peninsular) (also in Peninsular Malaysia); lowland rain forest at low elevations.

Uses. None recorded.

Notes. Although included by Dransfield et al. (2004) in the checklist of Thai palms, no specimens from there have been seen and no map is provided. Similar to and formerly included in *I. wallichiana*.

Synonyms. *Iguanura malaccensis* Becc., *Iguanura geonomiformis* var. *malaccensis* (Becc.) Ridl., *Iguanura geonomiformis* var. *ramosa* Ridl., *Iguanura wallichiana* var. *elatior* Kiew, *Iguanura wallichiana* var. *malaccensis* (Becc.) Kiew, *Slackia geonomiformis* (Mart.) Griff.

Iguanura polymorpha Becc.
mark-jay (Tha)

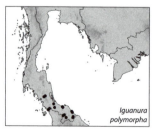

Iguanura polymorpha

Field characters. Stems clustered, rarely solitary, to 4 m tall and 2 cm diameter. Crownshafts present, with

earlike flaps at the apices; leaf rachis to 1 m long; leaflets broad, with diverging margins and veins, 4–11 per side of rachis, or leaf undivided and briefly bifid, with wavy margins. Inflorescences borne below, sometimes among the leaves; peduncles to 20 cm long, with 3–6 spreading flowering branches; fruits ellipsoid, to 2 cm long and 0.8 cm diameter, red.

Range and habitat. Thailand (Peninsular) and probably adjacent Myanmar (also in Peninsular Malaysia); lowland rain forest to 700 m elevation.

Uses. None recorded.

Synonyms. *Iguanura arakudensis* Furtado, *Iguanura brevipes* Hook. f., *Iguanura ferruginea* Ridl., *Iguanura polymorpha* var. *canina* Becc., *Iguanura polymorpha* var. *integra* C. K. Lim, *Iguanura speciosa* Hodel

Iguanura tenuis Hodel
maag lung saeng (Tha)

Iguanura tenuis

Field characters. Stems solitary or clustered, to 1.5 m tall and 2 cm diameter. Crownshafts absent, the old leaf sheaths persisting, with earlike flaps at the apices; leaf rachis to 0.5 m long; leaflets broad, with diverging margins and veins, 4 or 5 per side of rachis. Inflorescences borne below the leaves; peduncles to 30 cm long, with 9–15 spreading, wiry flowering branches; fruits narrowly ovoid, to 1.2 cm long and 0.6 cm diameter, pinkish.

Range and habitat. Thailand (Peninsular); lowland rain forest to 600 m elevation.

Uses. None recorded.

Notes. Endemic to the central part of Peninsular Thailand. Similar to some forms of the variable *I. polymorpha*. Two varieties are recognized: var. *tenuis*, with clustered stems; and var. *khaosokensis* C. K. Lim, with solitary stems.

Iguanura thalangensis C. K. Lim   PLATE 35

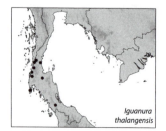

Iguanura thalangensis

Field characters. Stems solitary, to 2 m tall and 1.5 cm diameter. Crownshafts absent or occasionally present, with earlike flaps at the apices; leaf rachis to 0.6 m long; leaflets broad, with diverging margins and veins, 4 or 5 per side of rachis. Inflorescences borne among the leaves; peduncles to 20 cm long, with 1 or 2 (rarely to 4) erect flowering branches; fruits ovoid, to 1.5 cm long and 1 cm diameter, pinkish.
Range and habitat. Thailand (Peninsular); lowland rain forest to 200 m elevation.
Uses. None recorded.

Iguanura wallichiana (Mart.) Becc.   PLATE 35
mrang (Tha)

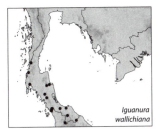

Iguanura wallichiana

Field characters. Stems clustered, to 3 m tall and 3.5 cm diameter. Crownshafts absent, the old leaf sheaths persisting, with earlike flaps at the apices; leaf rachis to 2 m long; leaflets linear to broad, with parallel margins and veins, 5–30 per side of rachis, occasionally leaf undivided and deeply bifid. Inflorescences borne among the leaves; peduncles to 75 cm long, with 3–15 spreading and intertwining flowering branches; fruits ovoid, to 2 cm long and 1 cm diameter, pink or red.
Range and habitat. Thailand (Peninsular) and probably adjacent Myanmar (also in Peninsular Malaysia and Sumatra); lowland rain forest to 800 m elevation.
Uses. None recorded.
Notes. Three varieties are recognized: var. *major* Becc., with large, undivided leaves, from Peninsular Malaysia; var. *rosea* C. K. Lim, with pinnate leaves and fruits ripening pink to red, from Peninsular Malaysia; and var. *wallichiana*, with pinnate leaves and fruits ripening pink, from Thailand, Peninsular Malaysia, and Sumatra.
Synonyms. *Areca wallichiana* Mart., *Geonoma pynaertiana* Sander, *Iguanura multifida* Hodel, *Iguanura spectabilis* Ridl., *Iguanura wallichiana* var. *minor* Becc., *Slackia insignis* Griff.

JOHANNESTEIJSMANNIA
H. E. Moore
(*Teysmannia* Reichb. f. & Zoll.)

The name of this genus comes from a Dutch horticulturalist who worked at Bogor Gardens in Java,

Johannes Teijsmann (1808–1882). Stems are solitary, short and stout, and sometimes creeping or subterranean. Leaves are costapalmate and 20–30 in number. Leaf sheaths are open and eventually disintegrate into a mass of fibers. Petioles are elongate and have small, sharp thorns along the margins. There is no hastula at the apices of the petiole. The leaf blades are the most distinctive feature of the genus—they are large, undivided, strongly folded, and diamond-shaped. The basal margins often have small thorns, similar to those of the petiole, and the apical margins are notched.

Inflorescences are branched to five orders, and are borne among the leaves and are often partially hidden by accumulated leaf litter. They are covered by several bracts. Flowers are small and are bisexual. Fruits are also distinctive. They are large, globose with warty protuberances, brownish, and one-seeded (sometimes two- or three-seeded). The endosperm is homogeneous (although penetrated by an irregular intrusion of the seed coat), germination is remote, and the seedling leaf is undivided.

Johannesteijsmannia contains four species, occurring in Peninsular Thailand, Peninsular Malaysia, Sumatra, and Borneo. One species occurs in our area (Dransfield 1972b; Hodel 1998).

Johannesteijsmannia altifrons   PLATE 35
(Reichb. f. & Zoll.) H. E. Moore
bang sun, lipe (Tha)

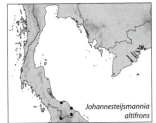

Johannesteijsmannia altifrons

Field characters. Stems solitary, short and subterranean. Leaf blades undivided, diamond-shaped, to 3.5 m long. Inflorescences borne at leaf bases, to 1 m long; fruits globose, to 5 cm diameter, warty, brownish.
Range and habitat. Thailand (Peninsular) (also in Borneo, Peninsular Malaysia, and Sumatra); lowland rain forest to 900 m elevation.
Uses. Much sought after as an ornamental plant.
Synonym. *Teysmannia altifrons* Reichb. f. & Zoll.

KERRIODOXA J. Dransf.

The name of this genus comes from an Irish botanist, Arthur Francis George Kerr (1877–1942), who collected over 20,000 plant specimens in Thailand between 1902 and 1932, including this palm. Stems are solitary, short and stout, sometimes subterranean, and are usually covered with persistent leaf bases. Leaves are palmate and 25–35 in number. Leaf sheaths are open and not fibrous. Petioles are elongate, black, and have very sharp margins. At the apices of the petiole there is a prominent hastula. The large leaf blades are circular in outline and are shortly split into numerous leaflets. The blade is grayish white on the lower surface.

Inflorescences are branched to five orders and are borne among the leaves. They are covered by several large, swollen, persistent bracts. Flowers are small and unisexual, and the plants are dioecious. Fruits are large, globose, yellowish brown, one-seeded, and are borne on short stalks. The endosperm is ruminate, germination is remote, and the seedling leaf is undivided and lobed at the apex.

Kerriodoxa contains one species, occurring in Peninsular Thailand (Dransfield 1983; Hodel 1998).

Kerriodoxa elegans J. Dransf.   PLATE 36
praya thalang (Tha)

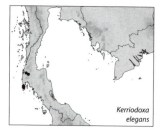

Kerriodoxa
elegans

Field characters. Stems solitary, to 7 m tall and 20 cm diameter, or sometimes short and subterranean. Leaf blades circular in outline, grayish white on the lower surface, split into as many as 100 leaflets. Inflorescences borne among the leaves, to 0.5 m long; fruits globose, to 5 cm diameter, yellowish brown.

Range and habitat. Thailand (Peninsular); lowland rain forest to 300 m elevation.

Uses. Used as an ornamental plant.

Notes. Known from only two localities in Peninsular Thailand—Phuket and Khao Sok National Park.

KORTHALSIA Blume
(*Calamosagus* Griff.)

This rattan genus was named after Pieter Willem Korthals (1807–1892), a Dutch botanist who explored Indonesia and collected specimens of these palms. The genus is distinctive in several respects. Stem branching commonly takes place not only at the base, but also high up on the stem, and a vast network of stems can build up in the forest canopy. Leaves are pinnate, numerous, and are spirally arranged. Leaf sheaths are closed, lack knees and flagella, but have conspicuous ocreas. These can take various forms—sheathing, netlike, or swollen and forming ant chambers. These chambers usually have a small hole made by the ants. Sheaths and other parts of the leaf are spiny. The leaf rachis, at least in adult leaves, terminates in a long cirrus, lacking leaflets but with grapnel-like spines, and this serves as a climbing organ. Leaflets are regularly arranged along the rachis, and are unmistakable in their jagged apices and narrowly to broadly rhomboidal shape. Leaflets are usually silvery gray on the lower surface, and some species have stalked leaflets.

Korthalsia is semelparous; all inflorescences, 1–12 at a time at the stem apex, are produced and flower together over a short period of time, and after fruiting the stem dies. Inflorescences are subtended by much reduced leaves, are usually branched to two orders, and are covered in overlapping bracts. The flowering branches are also distinctive in their thick, brown,

Key to the Species of *Korthalsia*

1a. Ocreas swollen and forming ant chambers . . . . 2.
1b. Ocreas not swollen, sheathing . . . . 3.

2a. Ocreas to 4 cm long, with to 0.2-cm-long spines . . . . *K. rostrata.*
2b. Ocreas to 20 cm long, with to 0.8-cm-long spines . . . . *K. scortechinii.*

3a. Leaflets 14–20 per side of rachis, narrowly rhomboidal, silvery brown on the
    lower surfaces . . . . *K. flagellaris.*
3b. Leaflets 4–11 per side of rachis, rhomboidal, gray or whitish on the lower
    surfaces . . . . 4.

4a. Stems 1 cm diameter; Andaman Islands . . . . *K. rogersii.*
4b. Stems to 7 cm diameter; all other areas, including Andaman and Nicobar
    islands . . . . 5.

5a. Ocreas to 20 cm long . . . . *K. laciniosa.*
5b. Ocreas to 5 cm long . . . . 6.

6a. Leaflets gray on lower surfaces; Thailand (Peninsular) . . . . *K. rigida.*
6b. Leaflets green on lower surfaces; Cambodia . . . . *K. bejaudii.*

densely hairy appearance. Flowers are bisexual, again unusual among the scaly-fruited palms, and are borne in dense spirals along the flowering branches. Fruits are globose, ellipsoid, or obovoid; brownish; usually one-seeded; and are covered with overlapping scales. The endosperm is homogeneous or ruminate, germination is adjacent, and the seedling leaf is undivided or bifid with jagged margins.

Korthalsia contains 27 species, widely distributed from the Andaman and Nicobar islands to New Guinea. Seven species occur in our area (Basu 1992; Dransfield 1979a, 1981; Evans et al. 2001, 2002; Hodel 1998; Renuka 1995).

Korthalsia species are not so important economically as species of *Calamus*. Even though the canes are strong and durable, they are covered at the nodes with persistent leaf bases, and removal of these disfigures the cane. Nevertheless, they are widely used at a local scale. In the following descriptions, stem diameter includes the leaf sheaths.

Korthalsia bejaudii Gagnep.
kompong-cham (Cbd)

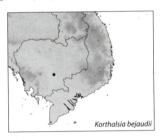

Korthalsia bejaudii

Field characters. Stems clustered, climbing, to 10 m long and 3 cm diameter. Leaf sheaths greenish brown with brown hairs, with scattered, brown, triangular, to 1-cm-long spines; ocreas open, to 4 cm long, spiny or without spines; leaf rachis to 1 m long with to 8 rhomboidal leaflets per side, these green on lower surfaces; cirrus to 0.5 m long. Inflorescences to 0.6 m long; fruits globose, to 1 cm diameter, brown.
Range and habitat. Cambodia; lowland rain forest at low elevations.
Uses. None recorded.
Notes. Very close to, and perhaps not distinct from, *K. laciniosa* (Evans et al. 2002)—see notes under that species.

Korthalsia flagellaris Miq.   PLATE 36
wai sasao nam (Tha)

Field characters. Stems clustered, branching in the canopy, climbing, to 40 m long and 5 cm diameter. Leaf sheaths green with brown scales, with scattered, brown, flattened, to 1-cm-long spines (often in a line below the petiole); ocreas sheathing, to 15 cm long; leaf rachis to 1.5 m long with 14–20 narrowly rhomboidal leaflets per side, these silvery brown on the

lower surfaces; cirri to 1.1 m long. Inflorescences to 0.8 m long; fruits obovoid, to 2 cm long and 1.1 cm diameter, yellowish brown.

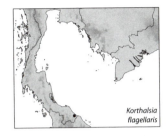

Korthalsia flagellaris

Range and habitat. Thailand (Peninsular) (also in Borneo, Peninsular Malaysia, and Sumatra); lowland rain forest in peat swamps at low elevations.
Uses. Provides a large-diameter cane used in furniture making and basketry.
Synonym. *Korthalsia rubiginosa* Becc.

Korthalsia laciniosa   PLATES 36 & 37
(Griff.) Mart.
bordah, lal bet (And, Ncb), wai taleuk (Lao), sakan kyein (Mya), wai sadao (Tha), may da, may tamvong (Vie)

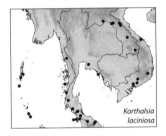

Korthalsia laciniosa

Field characters. Stems clustered, branching above ground level, climbing, to 75 m long and 7 cm diameter. Leaf sheaths green with brown hairs and brown scales, with scattered, black, triangular, to 1.9-cm-long spines; ocreas sheathing, becoming loose and netlike in older leaves, to 20 cm long; leaf rachis to 2 m long with 9–11 rhomboidal leaflets per side, these gray on the lower surfaces; cirri to 1.2 m long. Inflorescences to 0.8 m long; fruits globose to ellipsoid, to 2 cm long and 1.5 cm diameter, brown.
Range and habitat. Andaman and Nicobar islands, Cambodia, Laos (Southern), Myanmar (Tanintharyi), Thailand (Peninsular, Southeast), and Vietnam (Central, Southern) (also in Java, Peninsular Malaysia, the Philippines, Singapore, and Sumatra); lowland or montane rain forest or dryer forest, to 1100 m elevation.
Uses. Produces a cane used in furniture making and basketry.
Notes. A widespread and variable species. Specimens from central Laos, included here, may represent a new species characterized by a short, open ocrea (Evans et al. 2002). In this respect they approach *K. bejaudii*.

Synonyms. *Calamosagus harinifolius* Griff., *Calamosagus laciniosus* Griff., *Calamosagus wallichiifolius* Griff., *Korthalsia andamanensis* Becc., *Korthalsia grandis* Ridl., *Korthalsia scaphigera* Kurz, *Korthalsia teysmannii* Miq., *Korthalsia wallichiifolia* (Griff.) H. Wendl.

Korthalsia rigida Blume
wai-dao-nu (Tha)

Korthalsia rigida

Field characters. Stems clustered, branching in the canopy, climbing, to 75 m long and 2.5 cm diameter. Leaf sheaths green with gray hairs and brown scales, with scattered, dark brown, flattened, triangular, to 1-cm-long spines, often spines in vertical rows along the sheath opposite the petiole; ocreas sheathing, to 5 cm long; leaf rachis to 1.8 m long with 4–8 rhomboidal leaflets per side, these gray on the lower surfaces; cirri to 0.9 m long. Inflorescences to 0.8 m long; fruits globose, to 1 cm diameter, greenish brown.
Range and habitat. Thailand (Peninsular) (also in Borneo, Peninsular Malaysia, the Philippines, Singapore, and Sumatra); lowland or montane rain forest, to 1100 m elevation.
Uses. Provides a cane used in basketry.
Notes. A widespread and variable species.
Synonyms. *Calamosagus ochriger* Griff., *Calamosagus polystachys* (Mart.) H. Wendl., *Korthalsia ferox* Becc. var. *malayana* Becc., *Korhtalsia hallieriana* Becc., *Korthalsia paludosa* Furtado, *Korthalsia polystachya* Mart.

Korthalsia rogersii Becc.

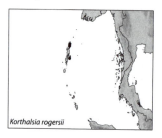

Korthalsia rogersii

Field characters. Stems clustered, climbing, to 45 m long and 1 cm diameter. Leaf sheaths green with brown hairs, with scattered, brown, triangular, to

0.5-cm-long spines; ocreas sheathing, to 10 cm long; leaf rachis to 0.7 m long with 5–8 rhomboidal leaflets per side, these whitish on the lower surfaces; cirri to 0.3 m long. Inflorescences to 0.5 m long; fruits obovoid, to 2 cm long and 1.8 cm diameter, yellowish.
Range and habitat. Andaman Islands (Diglipur, Havlock, Radhanger, South Andaman); lowland rain forest at low elevations.
Uses. None recorded.
Notes. Mathew et al. (2007) give a recent account of this species.

Korthalsia rostrata Blume

Field characters. Stems clustered, branching in the canopy, climbing, to 25 m long and 1.5 cm diameter. Leaf sheaths green with brown hairs, with scattered, black-tipped, to 0.2-cm-long spines; ocreas swollen and forming ant chambers, brown, to 4 cm long; leaf rachis to 0.5 m long with 3–7 narrowly rhomboidal leaflets per side, these gray on the lower surfaces; cirri to 0.6 m long. Inflorescences to 0.7 m long; fruits ellipsoid, to 2 cm long and 1.2 cm diameter, orange-brown.
Range and habitat. Thailand (Peninsular) (also in Borneo, Peninsular Malaysia, Singapore, and Sumatra); lowland rain forest to 800 m elevation.
Uses. Provides a cane used in basketry.
Notes. Reported to occur in Peninsular Thailand (Dransfield et al. 2004), but no specimens from there have been seen and no map is provided.
Synonyms. *Calamosagus scaphigera* (Mart.) Griff., *Ceratolobus rostratus* (Blume) Becc., *Korthalsia lobbiana* H. Wendl., *Korthalsia machadonis* Ridl., *Korthalsia scaphigera* Mart.

Korthalsia scortechinii Becc.
wai kung (Tha)

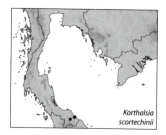

Korthalsia scortechinii

Field characters. Stems clustered, branching in the canopy, climbing, to 35 m long and 2.5 cm diameter. Leaf sheaths green with brown hairs, with scattered, dark brown, triangular, to 0.8-cm-long spines; ocreas swollen and forming ant chambers, brown, to 20 cm long; leaf rachis to 1.3 m long with to 11 narrowly rhomboidal leaflets per side, these gray on the lower surfaces; cirri to 1.25 m long. Inflorescences to 0.4 m long; fruits ellipsoid, to 2 cm long and 1.1 cm diameter, brown.

Range and habitat. Thailand (Peninsular) (also in Peninsular Malaysia and Singapore); lowland rain forest to 900 m elevation.

Uses. None recorded.

LICUALA Wurmb
(*Pericycla* Blume, *Dammera* K. Schum.)

The genus name is derived from a Latinized version of a local name for the palm in the Celebes, *leko wala*. Stems are solitary or clustered, usually rather small, and sometimes short and subterranean. Leaves are palmate and 5–28 in number. Leaf sheaths are open and often fibrous on the margins. An ocrea is present at the sheath apices, and sometimes this is elongate and conspicuous. Petioles are normally thorny along the margins, but sometimes the thorns are small, few, or absent. At the apices of the petioles there is a prominent hastula. Blades are usually strongly folded, circular in outline, and are undivided or more often divided into leaflets. Divided blades have leaflets that are split to their bases into several multifold leaflets, and these are often wedge-shaped. The apices of leaflets may be blunt or shallowly to deeply indented, and these indentations are more pronounced on lateral leaflets. Sometimes the central one, or central few leaflets, are borne on a short stalk. In a few species, the central leaflet may be split to the apex of the costa into two lobes, and then the costa has a gland on the lower surface.

Most species of *Licuala* are monoecious (produce bisexual flowers) but a few species from China and Vietnam are dioecious and have separate male and female plants. Inflorescences are borne among the leaves and are covered with numerous, sheathing bracts. There may be one to several partial inflorescences, and each of these may be unbranched or branched to one or two orders. Each partial inflorescence is subtended by a conspicuous bract, and this bract may be tubular or swollen, and may become tattered. Flowers are either solitary or borne in groups of two or more. Flowers are bisexual with six stamens and three carpels in the monoecious species. In the dioecious species, the male inflorescences may differ from the female ones. Fruits are usually quite small; globose, ellipsoid, or ovoid; variously colored; and one-seeded. Petals either remain erect during fruit development, or, in the dioecious species, become recurved. The endosperm is homogeneous (although penetrated by an irregular intrusion of the seed coat), germination is remote, and the seedling leaf is undivided and lanceolate.

Licuala contains about 145 species, occurring from Bhutan and northeastern India throughout Southern and Southeast Asia and into the western Pacific (Vanuatu). Thirty-five species occur in our area (Barfod & Saw 2002; Beccari 1933; Gagnepain & Conrard 1937; Henderson et al. 2007, 2008b; Hodel 1998; Magalon 1930; Saw 1997).

The species of *Licuala* are difficult to key using stem and leaf characters only, and therefore several characters from inflorescences, flowers, and fruits are included in the following key. In the key and species descriptions, where flowers are always solitary on the flowering branches they are referred to as solitary, but where flowers are both solitary and in groups on the flowering branches, they are referred as in groups.

Key to the Species of *Licuala*

(continued)

Key to the Species of *Licuala* (continued)

8a. Stems forming large clumps of equal-sized stems . . . . *L. spinosa.*
8b. Stems solitary, or clustered and then with basal shoots, but not forming large clumps of
    equal-sized stems . . . . 9.

9a. Ocreas conspicuous, to 80 cm long . . . . *L. distans.*
9b. Ocreas small and inconspicuous . . . . 10.

10a. Partial inflorescences unbranched; flowers more than 1 cm long; partial inflorescence
    bracts tubular . . . . *L. peltata.*
10b. Partial inflorescences branched; flowers less than 1 cm long; partial inflorescence
    bracts swollen . . . . *L. merguensis.*

11a. Cambodia . . . . *L. spinosa.*
11b. Thailand and Vietnam . . . . 12.

12a. Thailand . . . . 13.
12b. Vietnam . . . . 27.

13a. East, Southeast . . . . 14.
13b. Peninsular . . . . 16.

14a. Stems forming large clumps of equal-sized stems; inflorescences longer than the leaves;
    petiole thorns stout, to 1.2 cm long, borne all along the petioles . . . . *L. spinosa.*
14b. Stems solitary, or clustered and then with few stems, but not forming large clumps of equal-sized
    stems; inflorescences shorter than the leaves; petiole thorns less than 0.3 cm long, borne on
    the lower half of the petioles . . . . 15.

15a. Stems clustered; inflorescences with branched or unbranched partial inflorescences . . . . *L. pitta.*
15b. Stems solitary or with basal shoots; inflorescences with unbranched partial
    inflorescences . . . . *L. poonsakii.*

16a. Stems forming large clumps of equal-sized stems; inflorescences longer than
    the leaves . . . . 17.
16b. Stems solitary, or clustered and then with basal shoots, but not forming large
    clumps of equal-sized stems; inflorescences shorter than the leaves . . . . 18.

17a. Flowers hairy; petiole thorns stout, to 1.2 cm long, borne all along the petioles . . . . *L. spinosa.*
17b. Flowers not hairy; petiole thorns small, to 0.5 cm long, borne along the
    basal half of the petioles . . . . *L. paludosa.*

18a. Ocreas conspicuous, to 80 cm long . . . . *L. distans.*
18b. Ocreas small and inconspicuous . . . . 19.

19a. Partial inflorescences unbranched or with 2 branches . . . . 20.
19b. Partial inflorescences branched with more than 2 branches . . . . 23.

20a. Blades divided into 3–6 leaflets. . . . . 21.
20b. Blades divided into 9–30 leaflets . . . . 22.

21a. Stems short and subterranean on flowering plants; petioles to 0.9 m long; partial
    inflorescences to 3 . . . . *L. pusilla.*
21b. Stems to 1.5 m tall on flowering plants; petioles to 0.3 m long; partial
    inflorescences 1 or 2 . . . . *L. scortechinii.*

22a. Flowers more than 1 cm long, borne on long, pendulous flowering branches; partial
    inflorescence bracts tubular . . . . *L. peltata.*
22b. Flowers less than 1 cm long, borne on short, erect flowering branches; partial inflorescence
    bracts swollen . . . . *L. kunstleri.*

23a. Petioles to 0.9 m long; blades to 0.5 m wide; leaflets 3–11; inflorescences to 0.3 m long . . . . . *L. triphylla.*
23b. Petioles more than 1 m long; blades more than 0.6 m wide; leaflets 6–33; inflorescences more
    than 0.6 m long . . . . 24.

24a. Inflorescences more than 1.2 m long . . . . 25.
24b. Inflorescences less than 0.7 m long . . . . 26.

25a. Inflorescence bracts tubular; flowers in groups . . . . *L. glabra.*
25b. Inflorescence bracts swollen; flowers solitary . . . . *L. malajana.*

26a. Petioles to 3 m long; partial inflorescence bracts swollen and tattering . . . . *L. merguensis.*
26b. Petioles to 1.2 m long; partial inflorescence bracts tubular . . . . *L. modesta.*

27a. Dioecious; central leaflet not borne on a short stalk, split as far as the apex of the costa into 2
    lobes (rarely the central one not split but then rhomboidal); costas with a small but distinct
    gland on the lower surfaces (except on rhomboidal ones); fruits globose with the petals
    becoming recurved as the fruits develop . . . . 28.
27b. Monoecious; central leaflet not split into 2 lobes, or rarely split but then not to apex of costa;
    costas without a gland on the lower surfaces; fruits ellipsoid or globose, the petals remaining
    erect as the fruits develop . . . . 34.

28a. Inflorescences curved down below the leaves; flowering branches thick and fleshy. . . . . 29.
28b. Inflorescences erect or arching among the leaves; flowering branches thin and wiry . . . . 30.

29a. Leaflets 5–13, mottled light and dark green . . . . *L. dasyantha.*
29b. Leaflets 26–32, not mottled . . . . *L. acaulis.*

30a. Sheaths and petioles with dense, black scales . . . . *L. hexasepala.*
30b. Sheaths and petioles without dense, black scales . . . . 31.

31a. Leaflets 13–26; partial inflorescence bracts flattened . . . . *L. centralis.*
31b. Leaflets 3–11; partial inflorescence bracts tubular . . . . 32.

32a. Middle leaflet not split, rhomboidal . . . . *L. manglaensis.*
32b. Middle leaflet split, triangular . . . . 33.

33a. Male inflorescences with 2–5 branched partial inflorescences; female inflorescences with
    1 unbranched partial inflorescence . . . . *L. calciphila.*
33b. Male inflorescences with 1 branched partial inflorescence; female inflorescences with
    1 or 2 branched partial inflorescences . . . . *L. magalonii.*

34a. Flowering branches and flowers not hairy; bases of flowers forming short stalks . . . . 35.
34b. Flowering branches and flowers usually hairy; bases of flowers not forming short
    stalks . . . . 36.

35a. Inflorescences with 1 or 2 partial inflorescences . . . . *L. atroviridis.*
35b. Inflorescences with about 5 partial inflorescences . . . . *L. glaberrima.*

36a. Partial inflorescences unbranched . . . . 37.
36b. Partial inflorescences branched . . . . 38.

37a. Leaflets with curved sides; Central . . . . *L. radula.*
37b. Leaflets with straight sides; Southern . . . . *L. cattienensis.*

38a. Flowering branches angular, zigzag; flowers borne on prominent floral stalks; leaflets
    with curved sides . . . . *L. bracteata.*
38b. Flowering branches neither angular nor zigzag; flowers seldom borne on floral stalks; leaflets
    with straight sides, rarely curved . . . . 39.

39a. Flowers spaced far apart . . . . *L. taynguyensis.*
39b. Flowers spaced close together . . . . 40.

40a. Flowers solitary . . . . 41.
40b. Flowers in groups . . . . 43.

41b. Floral stalks prominent, to 2.5 mm long; flower buds 6.5–7.5 mm long . . . . *L. longiflora.*
41b. Floral stalks inconspicuous; flower buds 3.5–5 mm long . . . . 42.

(continued)

Key to the Species of *Licuala* (continued)

42a. Flowering branches 7–14 on each partial inflorescence, 12–14 cm long, sparsely covered with brown hairs . . . . *L. bidoupensis.*

42b. Flowering branches 2–5 on each partial inflorescence, 3.5–11 cm long, densely covered with short, golden brown hairs . . . . *L. averyanovii.*

43a. Middle few leaflets remaining joined at their apices; indentations at leaf apices 14–20 cm deep . . . . *L. bachmaensis.*

43b. Middle few leaflets not joined at their apices; indentations at leaf apices shallow . . . . 44.

44a. Middle leaflet not split; leaflets with curved sides . . . . *L. robinsoniana.*

44b. Middle leaflet split, although not to apex of costa; leaflets with straight sides . . . . 45.

45a. Leaflets 4; flowering branches 3.5–5 cm long; fruits 1.2–1.5 cm long and 0.6 cm diameter, ellipsoid . . . . *L. ellipsoidalis.*

45b. Leaflets 6–40; flowering branches 12–40 cm long; fruits 0.6–0.8 diameter, globose . . . . 46.

46a. Flowers hairy; petiole thorns stout, to 1.2 cm long, borne all along the petioles . . . . *L. spinosa.*

46b. Flowers not hairy; petiole thorns small, to 0.5 cm long, borne along the basal half of the petioles . . . . *L. paludosa.*

Licuala acaulis Henderson, N. K. Ban & N. Q. Dung
la non (Vie)

PLATE 37

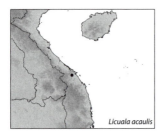

Licuala acaulis

Field characters. Stems solitary, to 0.4 m tall, often short and subterranean. Petioles to 1.5 m long; blades to 1 m wide, divided into 26–32 leaflets, the central one split almost to the base into 2 lobes. Dioecious; inflorescences shorter than the leaves, curved down, to 0.5 m long with 1 branched partial inflorescence; partial inflorescence bracts splitting; flowering branches thick and fleshy, not hairy; flowers solitary, not hairy; fruits not known.
Range and habitat. Vietnam (Central); lowland rain forest at 350–500 m elevation.
Uses. None recorded.

Licuala atroviridis Henderson, N. K. Ban & N. Q. Dung
la non (Vie)

PLATE 38

Field characters. Stems solitary, to 0.3 m tall and 14 cm diameter, often short and subterranean. Petioles to 1.4 m long; blades to 1.2 m wide, divided into 22–28 leaflets, the central one not split, borne on a short stalk. Monoecious; inflorescences shorter than

the leaves, erect, to 1 m long with 1 or 2 branched partial inflorescences; partial inflorescence bracts tubular; flowering branches straight, not hairy; flowers in groups, not hairy; bases of flowers forming stalks; fruits not known.

Licuala atroviridis

Range and habitat. Vietnam (Central); lowland rain forest at 350 m elevation.
Uses. None recorded.

Licuala averyanovii Henderson, N. K. Ban & N. Q. Dung
la non (Vie)

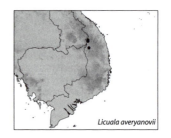

Licuala averyanovii

Field characters. Stems to 2 m tall, branching and diameter not known. Petioles to 3 m long; blades to

1.2 m wide, divided into 22–26 leaflets, the central one not split. Monoecious; inflorescences erect, with at least 6 branched partial inflorescences; partial inflorescence bracts tubular; flowering branches straight, hairy; flowers solitary, hairy; fruits ellipsoid, 0.9–1 cm long and 0.6–0.7 cm diameter, color not known, the petals remaining erect as the fruits develop.

Range and habitat. Vietnam (Central); lowland rain forest at 700–900 m elevation.

Uses. None recorded.

Licuala bachmaensis Henderson, N. K. Ban & N. Q. Dung
PLATE 38

la non (Vie)

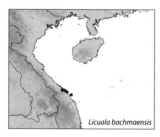
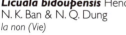
Licuala bachmaensis

Field characters. Stems solitary, to 1.5 m tall and 20 cm diameter, often short and subterranean. Petioles to 1.8 m long; blades to 1.3 m wide, divided into 12–18 leaflets, these deeply indented at the apices, the central one not split, borne on a short stalk, some leaflets joined at their apices. Monoecious; inflorescences much longer than the leaves, erect, to 3.4 m long with up to 11 branched partial inflorescences; partial inflorescence bracts tubular; flowering branches straight, densely hairy; flowers in groups, hairy; fruits ellipsoid, 1 cm long and 0.5 cm diameter, red, the petals remaining erect as the fruits develop.

Range and habitat. Vietnam (Central); lowland rain forest and persisting in disturbed areas to 1150 m elevation.

Uses. Planted as an ornamental, and the leaves are used to make raincoats.

Licuala bidoupensis Henderson, N. K. Ban & N. Q. Dung
PLATE 38

la non (Vie)

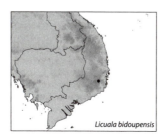
Licuala bidoupensis

Field characters. Stems clustered, to 2.5 m tall and 4.5 cm diameter. Petioles to 1.3 m long; blades to 0.9 m wide, divided into 21–25 leaflets, the central one not split, borne on a short stalk. Monoecious; inflorescences longer than the leaves, erect, to 1.8 m long with up to 8 branched partial inflorescences; partial inflorescence bracts tubular; flowering branches straight, densely hairy; flowers solitary, hairy; fruits ellipsoid, 1 cm long and 0.5 cm diameter, red, the petals remaining erect as the fruits develop.

Range and habitat. Vietnam (Southern); montane rain forest at 1200 m elevation.

Uses. None recorded.

Licuala bracteata Gagnep.

cay mac cac, cay moc coc, la non, sa rac (Vie)

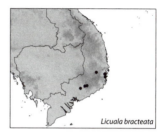
Licuala bracteata

Field characters. Stems clustered, to 4 m tall and 5 cm diameter. Petioles to 1.3 m long; blades to 0.9 m wide, divided into 19–28 leaflets, these with curved sides, the central one not split, borne on a short stalk. Monoecious; inflorescences shorter than the leaves, erect, to 1 m long with to 7 branched partial inflorescences; partial inflorescence bracts tubular; flowering branches zigzag, densely hairy; flowers borne on prominent stalks, in groups, hairy; fruits ellipsoid, to 0.8 cm long and 0.6 cm diameter, red, the petals remaining erect as the fruits develop.

Range and habitat. Vietnam (Southern); lowland rain forest at 400–900 m elevation.

Uses. The stems are used to make tool handles and the leaves to make hats.

Licuala calciphila Becc.
PLATE 38

la non, ra nui da voi (Vie)

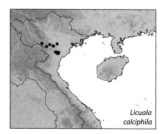
Licuala calciphila

Field characters. Stems clustered, to 2 m tall and 2 cm diameter. Petioles to 0.9 m long; blades to 0.6 m

wide, divided into 5–7 leaflets, the central one split for half or more its length into 2 broad lobes. Plants dioecious; male inflorescences shorter than the leaves, arching, to 1 m long with 1–5 branched partial inflorescences; female inflorescences shorter than the leaves, arching, to 1 m long, unbranched; partial inflorescence bracts tubular; flowering branches straight, hairy; flowers hairy, males in groups, females solitary; fruits globose, 1 cm diameter, red, the petals becoming recurved as the fruits develop.
Range and habitat. Vietnam (Northern); lowland or montane rain forest, often on limestone outcrops, at 200–1200 m elevation.
Uses. None recorded.
Synonyms. *Licuala fatua* Becc., *Licuala tomentosa* Burret, *Licuala tonkinensis* Becc.

Licuala cattienensis Henderson, N. K. Ban & N. Q. Dung
la toi (Vie)   PLATE 39

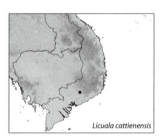

Licuala cattienensis

Field characters. Stems solitary, or with 1 main stem and basal shoots, to 2 m tall and 4 cm diameter. Petioles to 1.4 m long; blades to 0.8 m wide, divided into about 12 leaflets, the central one not split. Monoecious; inflorescences shorter than the leaves, erect, to 1.2 m long with 2–4 unbranched partial inflorescences; partial inflorescence bracts tubular; flowering branches angular, hairy; flowers in groups; fruits ellipsoid, to 0.8 cm long and 0.6 cm diameter, red, the petals remaining erect as the fruits develop.
Range and habitat. Vietnam (Southern); lowland rain forest at low elevations.
Uses. None recorded.

Licuala centralis Henderson, N. K. Ban & N. Q. Dung
la non (Vie)   PLATE 39

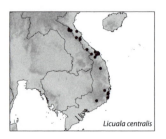

Licuala centralis

Field characters. Stems clustered, to 5 m tall and 4 cm diameter. Petioles to 1.3 m long; blades to 1 m wide, divided into 13–26 leaflets, the central one split to the base into 2 lobes. Dioecious; inflorescences shorter than the leaves, erect, to 0.7 m long with 2–4 branched partial inflorescences; partial inflorescence bracts flattened, densely brown hairy; flowering branches straight, hairy; flowers not hairy, males in groups, females solitary; fruits globose, 0.8 cm diameter, white, the petals becoming recurved as the fruits develop.
Range and habitat. Vietnam (Central); lowland rain forest or in disturbed areas, to 1000 m elevation.
Uses. The leaflets are commonly used in the manufacture of hats.

Licuala dasyantha Burret
cay lua khua, la non, lua khua (Vie)   PLATES 39 & 40

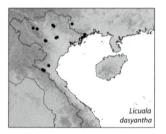

Licuala dasyantha

Field characters. Stems solitary or clustered, to 1.5 m tall and 6 cm diameter, often short and subterranean. Petioles to 2 m long; blades to 1 m wide, divided into 5–13 leaflets, mottled dark and light green on newly opened leaves, the central one split into 2 broad lobes. Dioecious; inflorescences shorter than the leaves, curved down, to 0.7 m long with 1 branched or unbranched partial inflorescence (male inflorescences with more flowering branches); partial inflorescence bracts tubular, tattering; flowering branches thick and fleshy, hairy; flowers hairy, males in groups, females solitary; fruits irregularly globose, to 0.8 cm diameter, red, the petals becoming recurved as the fruits develop.
Range and habitat. China (Guangxi) and Vietnam (Northern); lowland rain forest at 100–1000 m elevation.
Uses. None recorded.

Licuala distans Ridl.
paw si sip (Tha)   PLATE 40

Field characters. Stems solitary, to 5 m tall and 10 cm diameter. Petioles to 2.3 m long; ocreas conspicuous, brown, to 80 cm long; blades to 1.2 m wide, divided into 28–35 leaflets, these deeply indented at the apices, the central one not split, the central few leaflets sometimes borne on a short stalk. Monoecious; inflorescences shorter than the leaves, erect, to 2.8 m long with to 8 branched partial inflorescences; partial inflorescence bracts tubular; flowering branches straight, not hairy, with prominent floral stalks; flowers not hairy, solitary; fruits ovoid, to 1.7 cm long and 1.2 cm diameter, pink, the petals remaining erect as the fruits develop.

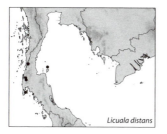

Licuala distans

Range and habitat. Thailand (Peninsular) and probably Myanmar (Tanintharyi); lowland rain forest to 850 m elevation.
Uses. None recorded.
Notes. Endemic to the west coast of central Peninsular Thailand.

Licuala ellipsoidalis Henderson, N. K. Ban & N. Q. Dung

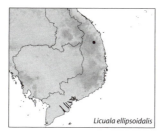

Licuala ellipsoidalis

Field characters. Stems to 1 m tall, branching and diameter not known. Petioles to 0.6 m long; blades to 0.3 m wide, divided into about 4 leaflets, the central one split into 2 broad lobes. Monoecious; inflorescences shorter than the leaves, erect, to at least 0.3 m long with at least 3 branched partial inflorescences; partial inflorescence bracts tubular; flowering branches straight, hairy, 3.5–5 cm long; flowers hairy, in groups; fruits ellipsoid, to 1.5 cm long and 0.6 cm diameter, the petals remaining erect as the fruits develop, color not known.
Range and habitat. Vietnam (Central); montane rain forest at 1100–1200 m elevation.
Uses. None recorded.

Licuala fordiana Becc.   PLATE 40
kai shue, sui hua zhou lu (Chi)

Field characters. Stems clustered, short and subterranean. Petioles to 1.5 m long; blades to 1 m wide, divided into 15–22 narrow leaflets, the central one not split. Monoecious; inflorescences shorter than the leaves, erect, to 1.5 m long with 3–7 unbranched

(or sometimes with 2 or 3 branches) partial inflorescences, these remaining parallel to the inflorescence axis; partial inflorescence bracts tubular; flowering branches straight, hairy; flowers hairy, in groups, borne on prominent floral stalks; fruits globose, to 0.8 cm diameter, red, the petals remaining erect as the fruits develop.

Licuala fordiana

Range and habitat. China (Guangdong, Hainan); lowland rain forest to 500 m elevation.
Uses. The leaves are used to make raincoats.
Notes. The inflorescences are short at flowering time and elongate during fruit development. The specimens from Guangdong differ slightly from those from Hainan and may represent a distinct species.

Licuala glaberrima Gagnep.

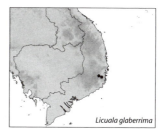

Licuala glaberrima

Field characters. Stems not known. Petioles to 1.1 m long; blades to 1 m wide, divided into 18–20 leaflets, the central one not split. Monoecious; inflorescences shorter than the leaves, erect, to 1 m long with to 5 branched partial inflorescences; partial inflorescence bracts tubular; flowering branches straight, not hairy; flowers not hairy, in groups; bases of flowers forming stalks; fruits not known.
Range and habitat. Vietnam (Southern); montane rain forest at 1000–1500 m elevation.
Uses. None recorded.

Licuala glabra Griff.
pba-la (Tha)

Field characters. Stems solitary or rarely with basal shoots, rarely short and subterranean, more often to 2 m tall and 7 cm diameter. Petioles to 2.2 m long; blades to 1.1 m wide, divided into 6–33 leaflets, the central one as wide or wider than the others, sometimes split into 2 or 3 lobes, sometimes borne on a short stalk. Monoecious; inflorescences shorter than the leaves, arching, to 2 m long with 4–11 branched partial inflorescences; partial inflorescence bracts tubular; flowering branches straight, not hairy, rarely with some hairs; flowers not hairy, in groups; fruits ellipsoid, to 1.5 cm long and 1 cm diameter, orange, the petals remaining erect as the fruits develop.

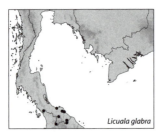

Range and habitat. Thailand (Peninsular) (also in Peninsular Malaysia); lowland or montane rain forest to 1300 m elevation.
Uses. None recorded.
Notes. A variable species, especially in stem and leaf morphology. Two varieties are recognized: var. *glabra*, with more than 14 leaflets, from Thailand (Peninsular) and Peninsular Malaysia; and var. *selangorensis* Becc., with fewer than 14 leaflets, from Peninsular Malaysia and possibly also Thailand (Peninsular).
Synonym. *Licuala longepedunculata* Ridl.

Licuala hainanensis Henderson, Guo & Barfod
PLATE 41
ci zhou lu, chun shue, dong fang zhou lu (Chi)

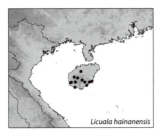

Field characters. Stems clustered, to 4 m tall and 3 cm diameter. Petioles to 1.6 m long; blades to 1.2 m wide, divided into 14–17 leaflets, the central one split almost to the base into 2 lobes. Dioecious; inflorescences shorter than the leaves, erect, to 1 m long with 3–5 branched partial inflorescences; partial inflorescence bracts tubular; flowering branches straight, hairy; flowers not hairy, males in groups, females solitary fruits globose, to 0.9 cm diameter, orange or red, the petals becoming recurved as the fruits develop.
Range and habitat. China (Hainan); lowland rain forest to 600 m elevation.
Uses. The leaves are used to make raincoats.

Notes. Previously misidentified as *L. spinosa* (Henderson et al. 2007).

Licuala hexasepala Gagnep.
PLATE 41
cay mac cac, sai (Vie)

Field characters. Stems clustered, to 1 m tall and 2 cm diameter. Sheaths and petioles covered with dense, black scales; petioles to 0.4 m long; blades to 0.3 m wide, divided into 8–11 leaflets, the central one split to the base into 2 lobes. Dioecious; inflorescences shorter than the leaves, arching, to 0.4 m long with 1 branched partial inflorescence; partial inflorescence bracts tubular; flowering branches straight, hairy; flowers hairy, males in groups, females solitary; fruits globose, to 0.7 cm diameter, red, the petals becoming recurved as the fruits develop.
Range and habitat. Vietnam (Southern); montane rain forest at 1300–2000 m elevation.
Uses. None recorded.

Licuala kunstleri Becc.
tan diao (Tha)

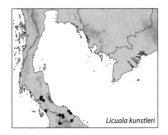

Field characters. Stems solitary, sometimes with basal shoots, short and subterranean or to 1.5 m tall and 8 cm diameter. Petioles to 2 m long; blades to 1 m wide, divided into 9–19 leaflets, the central one wider than the others, not split. Monoecious; inflorescences shorter than the leaves, erect, to 0.7 m long with to 5 unbranched partial inflorescences (rarely with 2 or 3 branches); partial inflorescence bracts swollen; flowering branches straight, hairy; flowers hairy, in groups, borne on prominent floral stalks; fruits globose, to 1.2 cm diameter, orange-red, the petals remaining erect as the fruits develop.

Range and habitat. Thailand (Peninsular) (also in Peninsular Malaysia); lowland rain forest to 800 m elevation.
Uses. None recorded.

Licuala longiflora Henderson, N. K. Ban & N. Q. Dung
la non duc (Vie)

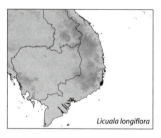

Licuala longiflora

Field characters. Stems solitary, to 3 m tall and 4 cm diameter. Petioles to 0.8 m long; blades to 0.8 m wide, divided into 19–29 leaflets, the central one not wider than the others, not split, sometimes borne on a short stalk. Monoecious; inflorescences much longer than the leaves, erect, to 2.5 m long with 7 or 8 branched partial inflorescences; partial inflorescence bracts tubular; flowering branches straight, densely hairy; flowers solitary, hairy, the buds 6.5–7.5 mm long, borne on prominent floral stalks; fruits not known.
Range and habitat. Vietnam (Southern); montane rain forest at 1000 m elevation.
Uses. None recorded.
Notes. Known only from Nui Chua National Park in Ninh Thuan Province.

Licuala magalonii Henderson, N. K. Ban & N. Q. Dung
cay la ma ca, la non, la non nham (Vie)   PLATE 41

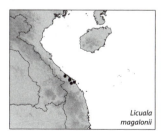

Licuala magalonii

Field characters. Stems solitary or clustered, sometimes short and subterranean, to 1.5 m tall and 2.5 cm diameter. Petioles to 0.6 m long; blades to 0.5 m wide, divided into 3 leaflets, the central one wider than the others and split into 2 broad lobes. Dioecious; inflorescences shorter than the leaves, arching, to 0.5 m long with 1 (rarely 2) branched partial inflorescences; partial inflorescence bracts tubular; flower-

ing branches straight, hairy; flowers not hairy, males in groups, females solitary; fruits globose, to 1 cm diameter, orange, the petals becoming recurved as the fruits develop.
Range and habitat. Vietnam (Central); montane rain forest at 1000–1500 m elevation.
Uses. None recorded.

Licuala malajana Becc.
ka pho khao (Tha)

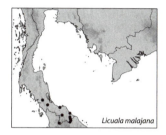

Licuala malajana

Field characters. Stems solitary or with basal shoots, short and subterranean or to 3 m tall and 7 cm diameter. Petioles to 2.5 m long; blades to 1.1 m wide, divided into 13–30 narrow leaflets, the central one not wider than the others, not split, sometimes borne on a short stalk. Monoecious; inflorescences shorter than the leaves, erect, to 1.3 m long with to 9 branched partial inflorescences; partial inflorescence bracts swollen; flowering branches straight, hairy; flowers hairy, solitary; fruits globose, to 1 cm diameter, orange, the petals remaining erect as the fruits develop.
Range and habitat. Thailand (Peninsular) (also in Peninsular Malaysia); lowland or montane rain forest, to 1500 m elevation.
Uses. None recorded.
Notes. Two varieties are recognized: var. *humilis* Saw, with solitary, subterranean stems, from Peninsular Malaysia; and var. *malajana*, with clustered, aerial stems, from Thailand and Peninsular Malaysia.

Licuala manglaensis Henderson, N. K. Ban & N. Q. Dung

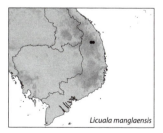

Licuala manglaensis

Field characters. Stems to 1 m tall, branching and diameter not known. Petioles to 0.4 m long; blades to 0.3 m wide, divided into about 5 leaflets, the central one wider than the others, not split, rhomboidal. Dioecious;

inflorescences shorter than the leaves, erect, to 0.8 m long with 1 branched partial inflorescence; partial inflorescence bracts tubular; flowering branches straight, hairy; flowers hairy, males in groups, females solitary; fruits globose, to 0.8 cm diameter, the petals becoming recurved as the fruits develop, color not known.

Range and habitat. Vietnam (Central); montane rain forest at 1100–1200 m elevation.

Uses. None recorded.

Notes. Unlike other dioecious species, the central leaflet is not split, but is rhomboidal in shape.

Licuala merguensis Becc.   PLATE 41
ka ching (Tha)

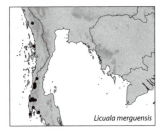

Licuala merguensis

Field characters. Stems solitary or with basal shoots, short and subterranean or to 3 m tall and 8 cm diameter. Petioles to 3 m long; blades to 1 m wide, divided into 9–17 leaflets, the central one wider than the others, not split, sometimes the central few leaflets borne on a short stalk. Monoecious; inflorescences shorter than the leaves, erect, to 0.7 m long, with to 7 branched partial inflorescences; partial inflorescence bracts swollen and tattering, giving the inflorescence a "messy" appearance; flowering branches straight, densely hairy; flowers hairy, in groups; fruits globose, to 1 cm diameter, red, the petals remaining erect as the fruits develop.

Range and habitat. Myanmar (Tanintharyi) and Thailand (Peninsular); lowland or montane rain forest, to 1200 m elevation.

Uses. None recorded.

Notes. Endemic to the west coast of Peninsular Thailand and adjacent Myanmar.

Synonym. *Licuala hirta* Hodel

Licuala modesta Becc.

Field characters. Stems solitary or with basal shoots, to 3 m tall and 3 cm diameter. Petioles to 1.2 m long; blades to 0.6 m wide, divided into 7–22 leaflets, the central one not wider than the others except when leaflets few, not split, not borne on a short stalk. Monoecious; inflorescences shorter than the leaves, erect or arching, to 0.6 m long with to 5 branched partial inflorescences; partial inflorescence bracts tubular; flowering branches straight, hairy; flowers hairy, in groups; fruits globose, to 1 cm

diameter, reddish, the petals remaining erect as the fruits develop.

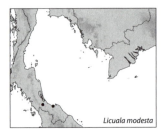

Licuala modesta

Range and habitat. Thailand (Peninsular) (also in Peninsular Malaysia); lowland rain forest at 250–500 m elevation.

Uses. None recorded.

Synonym. *Licuala wrayi* Becc.

Licuala paludosa Griff.
ga-por (Tha), cây mat cat, na lat nan (Vie)

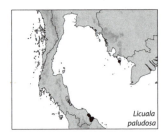

Licuala paludosa

Field characters. Stems clustered, forming large clumps of equal-sized stems, to 7 m tall and 7 cm diameter. Petioles to 3 m long; petiole thorns small, to 0.5 cm long, borne along the basal half of the petioles; blades to 1.5 m wide, divided into 7–40 leaflets, the central one not wider than the others, split into 2 lobes. Monoecious; inflorescences longer than the leaves, erect, to 2 m long with to 7 branched partial inflorescences; partial inflorescence bracts tubular; flowering branches straight, hairy, 12–20 cm long; flowers hairy, in groups; fruits globose to obovoid, to 1 cm diameter, orange-red or red, the petals remaining erect as the fruits develop.

Range and habitat. Thailand (Peninsular) and Vietnam (Southern) (also in Borneo, Peninsular Malaysia, and Sumatra); coastal swamp forest at low elevations.

Uses. The leaves are used to make raincoats and hats.

Synonyms. *Licuala aurantiaca* Hodel, *Licuala amplifrons* Miq., *Licuala oxleyi* H. Wendl., *Licuala paludosa* var. *winkleriana* Becc., *Licuala paniculata* Ridl., *Licuala spinosa* var. *brevidens* Becc.

Licuala peltata Roxb.   PLATE 42
gobol (And, Ncb), kurud, lepcha (Ind), kapadah, salu (Mya), ga-por, ka ching (Tha)

Field characters. Stems solitary, to 8 m tall and 10 cm diameter, often covered with spinelike leaf bases. Petioles to 4 m long; blades to 1.8 m wide, divided into 7–30 leaflets (rarely blades undivided), the central one sometimes wider than the others, not or rarely split. Monoecious; inflorescences longer than the leaves, erect, to 4 m long with to 7 unbranched, pendulous partial inflorescences; partial inflorescence bracts tubular; flowering branches straight, densely hairy; flowers hairy, solitary, more than 1 cm long; fruits globose to ellipsoid, to 2 cm long and 1 cm diameter, orange, the petals remaining erect as the fruits develop.

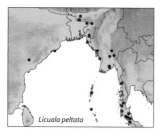

Licuala peltata

Range and habitat. Andaman and Nicobar islands, Bangladesh, northern and northeastern India (Assam, Jharkhand, Meghalaya, Orissa, Sikkim, Tripura), Myanmar (Bago, Rakhine, Tanintharyi, Yangon), Thailand (Peninsular), and possibly Bhutan (also in Peninsular Malaysia); lowland rain forest or drier forest, often on limestone soils, to 500 m elevation.
Uses. The leaves are used for thatching and for making hats and umbrellas.
Notes. Two varieties are recognized: var. *peltata*, with divided leaves, from throughout the range of the species; and var. *sumawongii* Saw, with undivided leaves, from Thailand and Peninsular Malaysia.

Licuala pitta Vatcharakorn ex Barfod & Pongsattayapipat

Licuala pitta

Field characters. Stems clustered, to 2.5 m tall and 3 cm diameter. Petioles to 1.5 m long; blades to 0.7 m wide, divided into 11–15 leaflets, the central one not wider than the others, not split. Monoecious; inflorescences shorter than the leaves, arching, to 0.9 m long with 4 or 5 branched or unbranched partial inflorescences, these remaining parallel to the inflorescence axis; partial inflorescence bracts swollen and split-

ting; flowering branches angular, hairy; flowers hairy, solitary; fruits not known.
Range and habitat. Thailand (East); lowland rain forest, to 450 m elevation.
Uses. None recorded.

Licuala poonsakii Hodel
ta pho dong (Tha)

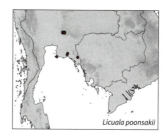

Licuala poonsakii

Field characters. Stems solitary or with basal shoots, to 3 m tall and 5 cm diameter. Petioles to 1.7 m long; blades to 0.9 m wide, divided into 9–12 leaflets, the central one usually wider than the others, not split. Monoecious; inflorescences shorter than the leaves, arching, to 1.5 m long with to 7 unbranched partial inflorescences, these remaining parallel to the inflorescence axis; partial inflorescence bracts swollen and splitting; flowering branches angular, hairy; flowers hairy, in groups; fruits globose to ellipsoid, to 1.3 cm diameter, red, the petals remaining erect as the fruits develop.
Range and habitat. Thailand (East, Southeast); lowland rain forest or seasonal forest, to 800 m elevation.
Uses. None recorded.

Licuala pusilla Becc.
ka pho nuu (Tha)

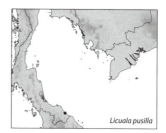

Licuala pusilla

Field characters. Stems solitary, short and subterranean. Petioles to 0.9 m long; blades to 0.4 m wide, divided into 3 or 4 or more leaflets, the central one much wider than the others, not split. Monoecious; inflorescences shorter than the leaves, erect, to 0.3 m long with to 3 unbranched partial inflorescences; partial inflorescence bracts swollen; flowering branches straight, hairy; flowers hairy, in groups;

fruits globose to ovoid, to 1 cm long and 0.8 cm diameter, red, the petals remaining erect as the fruits develop.
Range and habitat. Thailand (Peninsular) (also in Peninsular Malaysia); lowland rain forest to 500 m elevation.
Uses. None recorded.
Synonym. *Licuala tansachana* Hodel

Licuala radula Gagnep.
cay mat cat (Vie)

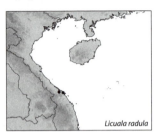

Licuala radula

Field characters. Stems to 0.7 m tall and 2.5 cm diameter, branching not known. Petioles to 0.8 m long; blades to 1 m wide, divided into 12 or 13 narrow leaflets, these with curved sides, the central one not wider than the others, not split. Monoecious; inflorescences longer than the leaves, erect, to 0.8 m long with 2 or 3 unbranched partial inflorescences; partial inflorescence bracts tubular; flowering branches angular, densely hairy; flowers hairy, in groups; fruits globose, to 1 cm diameter, red, the petals remaining erect as the fruits develop.
Range and habitat. Vietnam (Central); lowland rain forest to 900 m elevation.
Uses. The leaves are used to make hats.

Licuala robinsoniana Becc. PLATE 42
la non, mac cac (Vie)

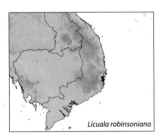

Licuala robinsoniana

Field characters. Stems clustered, to 1.5 m tall and 1.7 cm diameter. Petioles to 0.8 m long; blades to 0.4 m wide, divided into about 6 narrow leaflets, these with curved sides, the central one not split. Monoecious; inflorescences shorter than the leaves, to 0.5 m long, erect, with to 4 branched partial inflorescences; partial inflorescence bracts tubular; flowering branches straight, densely hairy; flowers

hairy, in groups; fruits globose, to 0.8 cm diameter, red, the petals remaining erect as the fruits develop.
Range and habitat. Vietnam (Southern); lowland rain forest at low elevations.
Uses. The leaves are used for making rain hats.

Licuala scortechinii Becc.

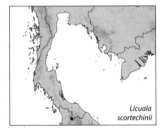

Licuala scortechinii

Field characters. Stems solitary, rarely with basal shoots, sometimes creeping, to 1.5 m tall and 2 cm diameter. Petioles to 0.3 m long; blades to 0.3 m wide, divided into 4–6 leaflets, the central one wider than the others, not split. Monoecious; inflorescences shorter than the leaves, arching, to 0.4 m long with 1 or 2 bifurcate partial inflorescences; partial inflorescence bracts swollen; flowering branches straight, hairy; flowers hairy, in groups; fruits globose, to 0.5 cm diameter, reddish, the petals remaining erect as the fruits develop.
Range and habitat. Thailand (Peninsular) (also in Peninsular Malaysia); lowland rain forest to 800 m elevation.
Uses. None recorded
Synonym. *Licuala delicata* Hodel

Licuala spinosa Thunb.
char (And), ba ao, phaav (Cbd), ga-por (Tha), cay la lip (Vie)

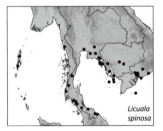

Licuala spinosa

Field characters. Stems clustered, forming large clumps of equal-sized stems, to 5 m tall and 5 cm diameter. Petioles to 2.5 m long; petiole thorns stout, to 1.2 cm long, borne all along the petioles; blades to 1.5 m wide, divided into 13–25 narrow leaflets, the central one not markedly wider than the others, not or sometimes split, sometimes borne on a short stalk. Monoecious; inflorescences longer than the leaves, erect, to 3 m long, with to 10 branched partial inflorescences; partial inflorescence bracts tubular; flowering branches straight, hairy, 20–40 cm long; flowers hairy, in groups; fruits globose to ellipsoid, to 0.8 cm diameter, red or yellowish, the petals remaining erect as the fruits develop.

Range and habitat. Andaman Islands, Cambodia, Myanmar (Tanintharyi), Thailand (Peninsular, Southeast), and Vietnam (Southern) (also in Borneo, Peninsular Malaysia, the Philippines, and Sumatra); lowland rain forest in low, wet places, or in savannas, scrub forest, or disturbed areas, to 600 m elevation.

Uses. The leaves are used to make raincoats.

Synonyms. *Corypha pilearia* Lour., *Licuala acutifida* Mart. var. *peninsularis* Becc., *Licuala horrida* Blume, *Licuala pilearia* (Lour.) Blume, *Licuala ramosa* Blume, *Licuala spinosa* var. *cochinchinensis* Becc., *Licuala spinosa* var. *eriantha* Becc.

Licuala taynguyensis Barfod & Borchs.
la non (Vie)

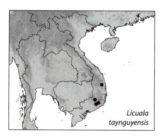

Licuala taynguyensis

Field characters. Stems solitary, to 2 m tall and 3 cm diameter. Petioles to 1 m long; blades to 1 m wide, divided into 19–21 leaflets, these lobed at the apices, the central one not split. Monoecious; inflorescences longer than the leaves, erect, to 2.5 m long with to 9 branched partial inflorescences; partial inflorescence bracts tubular; flowering branches zigzag, densely hairy; flowers hairy, in groups, spaced far apart; fruits ellipsoid, to 1 cm long and 0.6 cm diameter, red, the petals remaining erect as the fruits develop.

Range and habitat. Vietnam (Central); lowland rain forest to 1000 m elevation.

Uses. None recorded.

Licuala triphylla Griff.
ga-por-nu (Tha)

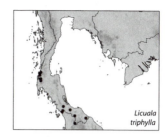

Licuala triphylla

Field characters. Stems solitary, short and subterranean. Petioles to 0.9 m long; blades to 0.5 m wide, divided into 3–11 leaflets, the central one wider than the others, not split, usually borne on a short stalk. Monoecious; inflorescences shorter than the leaves, erect, to 0.3 m long, with 3 or 4 branched partial inflorescences; partial inflorescence bracts tubular; flowering branches straight, hairy; flowers hairy, in groups; fruits ellipsoid, to 0.8 cm long and 0.6 cm diameter, red, the petals remaining erect as the fruits develop.

Range and habitat. Thailand (Peninsular) (also in Borneo and Peninsular Malaysia); lowland rain forest to 500 m elevation.

Uses. None recorded.

Synonyms. *Licuala filiformis* Hodel, *Licuala stenophylla* Hodel, *Licuala ternata* Griff., *Licuala triphylla* var. *integrifolia* Ridl.

LIVISTONA R. Br.
(Saribus Blume, *Wissmannia* Burret)

This genus was named after a Scottish horticulturist, Patrick Murray, Baron Livingstone (died 1671). Stems are solitary, often large and stout, and usually rough with persistent leaf bases. Leaves are palmate or costapalmate, 10–60 in number, and usually form a dense crown. Dead leaves often persist as a skirt below the crown. Leaf sheaths are open and often very fibrous, and old sheaths form a mass of reddish brown, interwoven fibers. Petioles are normally

Key to the Species of *Livistona*

1a. Inflorescences much longer than the leaves; Vietnam (Northern) . . . . *L. halongensis.*
1b. Inflorescences not longer than the leaves; all other areas, including Vietnam . . . . 2.

2a. Leaflets stiff at the apices . . . . *L. jenkinsiana.*
2b. Leaflets pendulous at the apices . . . . 3.

3a. Leaf blades irregularly divided into groups of leaflets . . . . *L. saribus.*
3b. Leaf blades regularly divided, the leaflets not in groups . . . . 4.

4a. Inflorescences to 2.2 m long; Japan (Bonin Islands) . . . . *L. boninensis.*
4b. Inflorescences to 1.2 m long; China (Guangdong, Hainan), Japan (Ryukyu Islands), and
Taiwan (Chishan Island) . . . . *L. chinensis.*

thorny on the margins, and younger plants tend to have more thorns than older ones. At the apex of the petiole there is a prominent hastula. Blades are costapalmate, markedly so in adult leaves. They are green or variously waxy or dull green and are divided either to about half their length or almost to the base into numerous leaflets. These leaflets are again split and sometimes pendulous at the apices.

Inflorescences are borne among the leaves and are branched up to five orders. Rarely, an inflorescence can consist of three separate but equal branches arising from the same leaf axil. Inflorescences are covered with numerous sheathing bracts. Flowers are bisexual with six stamens and three carpels; rarely plants produce either male flowers or female flowers. Often groups of flowers are borne together on short stalks. Fruits are globose to ellipsoid; purple-black, blue-black, blue, brown, to orange or red; one-seeded; and usually borne on short stalks. The endosperm is homogeneous (although penetrated by an irregular intrusion of the seed coat), germination is remote, and the seedling leaf is undivided and lanceolate.

Livistona is a relatively large genus of palms, widespread but scattered from Northeast Africa and India to Australia, New Guinea, the Solomon Islands, north to the Philippines, China, Japan, and the Bonin Islands. It contains approximately 36 species, half of them Australian. Five species occur in our area (Dowe 2001, 2003). Several species are commonly cultivated.

Livistona boninensis (Becc.) Nakai
cabbage palm (Jap)

Livistona boninensis

Field characters. Stems to 20 m tall and 30 cm diameter. Leaves palmate, grayish green; blades regularly divided to about half way into 50–85 leaflets, these deeply split and pendulous at the apices. Inflorescences to 2.2 m long; fruits globose to pear-shaped, to 3 cm long and 2.8 cm diameter, green.

Range and habitat. Japan (Bonin Islands, and apparently introduced into the nearby Volcano Islands); deciduous forest on steep, rocky slopes in coastal areas, at low elevations.

Uses. None recorded.

Synonyms. *Corypha japonica* Killitz, *Livistona chinensis* var. *boninensis* Becc.

Livistona chinensis (Jacq.) R. Br. ex Mart.
PLATE 43
biro, kuba (Jap)

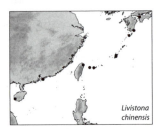

Livistona chinensis

Field characters. Stems to 15 m tall and 30 cm diameter. Leaves palmate, glossy to grayish green; blades regularly divided to approximately half way into 80–90 leaflets, these split and pendulous at the apices. Inflorescences to 1.2 m long; fruits globose to ellipsoid or pear-shaped, to 2.6 cm long and 1.8 cm diameter, green or blue-green.

Range and habitat. China (Guangdong, Hainan), Japan (Ryukyu Islands and southern Japanese islands of Aoshima, Kyushu, Shikoku, and Tsukishima), and Taiwan (Chishan Island); coastal forests, often on sandy soils, at low elevations.

Uses. Widely planted as an ornamental throughout tropical and subtropical areas of the world.

Synonyms. *Chamaerops biroo* Sieb., *Latania chinensis* Jacq., *Livistona chinensis* var. *subglobosa* (Hassk.) Becc., *Livistona dournowiana* Hort., *Livistona japonica* Nakai, *Livistona mauritiana* Wall., *Livistona okinawensis* Hort., *Livistona oliviformis* (Hassk.) Mart., *Livistona ovaliformis* Hort., *Livistona sinensis* Griff., *Livistona subglobosa* (Hassk.) Mart., *Saribus chinensis* (Jacq.) Blume, *Saribus oliviformis* Hassk., *Saribus subglobosus* Hassk.

Livistona halongensis T. H. Nguyen & Kiew
PLATE 43
co ha long (Vie)

Livistona halongensis

Field characters. Stems to 10 m tall and to 20 cm diameter, with conspicuous leaf scars. Leaves green on lower surface; blades regularly divided into 45–70 leaflets, these shortly split and slightly pendulous at the apices. Inflorescences to 3.4 m long, much longer than the leaves; fruits globose, to 1.2 cm diameter, dark green.

Range and habitat. Vietnam (Northern); Cat Ba and other islands in Ha Long Bay, on limestone cliffs and ridges, at low elevations.

Uses. None recorded.

Notes. Known only from Halong Bay, near Haiphong in Vietnam.

Livistona jenkinsiana Griff. PLATE 43

gao shan pu kui (Chi), tayik, toko pat (Ind), taw tan (Mya), kor (Tha)

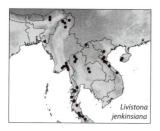

Livistona jenkinsiana

Field characters. Stems to 25 m tall and to 30 cm diameter. Leaves green or slightly grayish on lower surface; blades regularly divided into 70–100 leaflets, these shortly split and stiff at the apices. Inflorescences to 2 m long; fruits globose to ellipsoid or pear-shaped, to 3.5 cm long and 2.5 cm diameter, bluish.

Range and habitat. Bangladesh, Bhutan, China (Hainan, Yunnan), India (Arunachal Pradesh, Assam, Nagaland, Sikkim), Myanmar (Bago, Kachin, Mon, Sagaing, Tanintharyi), Thailand (East, North, Northeast, Peninsular, Southwest), Vietnam, and probably Laos (also in Peninsular Malaysia); forest and open areas, commonly planted in villages or other disturbed places, at 100–2500 m elevation.

Uses. The leaves are commonly used for thatching, and small plantations are maintained for leaf harvesting; the seeds are eaten as a substitute for betel nut; in Hainan the fruits are used medicinally.

Notes. Fruit size and shape are very variable.

Synonyms. *Latania jenkinsiana* (Griff.) Devansaye, *Livistona fengkaiensis* X. W. Wei & M. Y. Xiao, *Livistona jenkinsii* Griff., *Livistona moluccana* Hort., *Livistona speciosa* Kurz, *Saribus jenkensii* (Griff.) Kuntze, *Saribus speciosus* (Kurz) Kuntze

Livistona saribus (Lour.) Merr. ex Chev.

rok (Tha), cay (Vie)

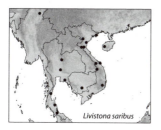

Livistona saribus

Field characters. Stems solitary, to 40 m tall and to 65 cm diameter, rough with old leaf bases. Leaves green on the lower surface; blades irregularly divided into groups of leaflets, with 80–90 leaflets in total, these deeply split and pendulous at the apices. Inflorescences to 2.3 m long; fruits globose to ellipsoid, to 2.5 cm long and 2 cm diameter, blue or blue-gray.

Range and habitat. Cambodia, China (Guangdong, Hainan), Laos, Myanmar (Kachin), Thailand (East, Peninsular, Southeast, Southwest), and Vietnam (throughout) (also in Borneo, Java, Peninsular Malaysia, the Philippines, and Sumatra); lowland rain forest or dry forest, often cultivated, usually in low-lying, wet places, at low elevations, sometimes to 600 m.

Uses. Often cultivated as an ornamental plant.

Synonyms. *Chamaerops cochinchinensis* Lour., *Corypha saribus* Lour., *Livistona cochinchinensis* (Lour.) Mart., *Livistona diepenhorstii* Hassk., *Livistona hasseltii* (Hassk.) Hassk., *Livistona hoogendorpii* Teijsm. & Binn., *Livistona inaequisecta* Becc., *Livistona spectabilis* Griff., *Livistona tonkinensis* Magalon, *Livistona vogamii* Becc., *Pholidocarpus diepenhorstii* (Hassk.) Burret, *Rhapis cochinchinensis* (Lour.) Mart., *Sabal hoogendorpii* (Teijsm. & Binn.) Kuntze, *Saribus cochinchinensis* (Lour.) Blume, *Saribus hasseltii* Hassk., *Saribus hoogendorpii* (Teijsm. & Binn.) Kuntze

LOXOCOCCUS H. Wendl.

Stems are moderate in size, solitary, ringed with prominent leaf scars, and are somewhat swollen at the base. Leaves are pinnate, 6–12 in number, and dead leaves fall cleanly from the stem. Leaf sheaths are closed and form a prominent, reddish brown crownshaft. Petioles are short. Leaflets are numerous, regularly arranged, lanceolate, and spread in the same plane. The apices of the leaflets, especially those near the ends of the leaves, are jagged.

Inflorescences are branched to two orders and are borne below the crownshaft. Two bracts are present on the inflorescence. The numerous flowering branches are red at flowering time and spread stiffly. Flowers are red, unisexual, and are arranged in threes of a central female and two lateral male flowers. Fruits are small, globose, reddish brown, and one-seeded. The beak of the fruit is slightly offset from center, hence the Greek name for the genus, from the words *loxos*, meaning slanting, and *kokkos*, meaning seed. The endosperm is ruminate, germination is adjacent, and the seedling leaf is bifid.

Loxococcus contains one species, occurring only in Sri Lanka. It grows in lowland or montane rain forest, often on steep, rocky slopes.

Loxococcus rupicola (Thwaites) PLATE 44
H. Wendl. & Drude
dothalu, dotalu gas (Srl)

Field characters. Stems solitary, to 12 m tall and 12 cm diameter. Leaf rachis to 2.5 m long with to 35 leaflets per side, these stiffly spreading, jagged at the apices. Inflorescences branched to 2 orders; fruits globose, to 2.5 cm diameter, reddish brown.

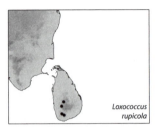

Loxococcus
rupicola

Range and habitat. Sri Lanka (Kandy, Kegalle, Ratnapura); lowland or montane rain forest, often on steep, rocky slopes, at 300–1500 m elevation.
Uses. The seeds are used as a substitute for betel nut.
Synonym. *Ptychosperma rupicola* Thwaites

MAXBURRETIA Furtado
(*Liberbaileya* Furtado, *Symphyogyne* Burret)

This genus is named for the eminent German botanist Max Burret (1883–1964), who studied palms for many years in the Berlin Herbarium. Stems are small, clustered, and are sometimes short and subterranean. They are almost always obscured by persistent leaf bases. Leaves are small, palmate, and about 20 in number. Leaf sheaths are open and fibrous, and these fibers can be spiny. Petioles are elongate, and at the apices there is a prominent hastula. Leaf blades are divided into numerous, single-fold leaflets, and are paler green on the lower surfaces.

Inflorescences are branched to three orders and are borne among the leaves. They are covered with persistent bracts. Inflorescences bear male and female flowers, or can be dioecious. Flowers are simple in structure, are borne singly, and male flowers have six stamens. Fruits are small, ellipsoid, yellowish brown, and one-seeded. They are hairy at first, although these hairs wear off with age. The endosperm is homogeneous (although penetrated by a thin, irregular intrusion of the seed coat), germination is remote, and the seedling leaf is undivided.

Maxburretia contains three species, occurring in Peninsular Thailand and Peninsular Malaysia. Two species occur in our area (Dransfield 1978; Hodel 1998).

Maxburretia furtadoana J. Dransf.   PLATE 44
mark-pra-ra-hu (Tha)

Field characters. Stems clustered, to 3 m tall and 5 cm diameter. Leaf sheath fibers disintegrating into a mass of spines around the stem; blades divided into 20–32 leaflets. Inflorescences to 0.5 m long; fruits globose to ovoid, to 1 cm long and 0.7 cm diameter, yellowish brown.

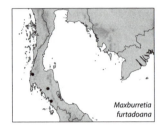

Maxburretia
furtadoana

Range and habitat. Thailand (Peninsular); lowland rain forest on rocky, limestone cliffs, to 800 m elevation.
Uses. None recorded.

Maxburretia gracilis (Burret) J. Dransf.
mark ku (Tha)

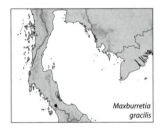

Maxburretia
gracilis

Field characters. Stems clustered, to 7 m tall and 8 cm diameter. Leaf sheath fibers remaining joined at their apices; blades divided into 25–30 leaflets. Inflorescences to 0.9 m long; fruits globose to ovoid, to 1 cm long and 0.5 cm diameter, brown.
Range and habitat. Thailand (Peninsular) (also in the Langkawi Islands of Peninsular Malaysia, near the Thai border); forest on rocky, limestone cliffs of the Langkawi Islands, to 500 m elevation.
Uses. None recorded.
Synonyms. *Liberbaileya gracilis* (Burret) Burret, *Liberbaileya lankawiensis* Furtado, *Symphyogyne gracilis* Burret

Key to the Species of *Maxburretia*

1a. Leaf sheath fibers disintegrating into a mass of spines around
   the stem . . . . *M. furtadoana.*
1b. Leaf sheath fibers remaining joined at their apices . . . . *M. gracilis.*

MYRIALEPIS Becc.
(*Bejaudia* Gagnep.)

This genus, along with *Plectocomia* and *Plectocomiopsis*, makes up a closely related group of high-climbing rattans. Stems are clustered and often form dense thickets. Leaves are pinnate, numerous, and are borne in a spiral pattern. Leaf sheaths are closed and, as in *Plectocomia* and *Plectocomiopsis*, lack knees and flagella. These characters help distinguish the group from other rattans. Sheaths are covered with oblique rows of spines, and the ocrea is scarcely developed. Petioles are short or absent. The leaf rachis terminates in a long cirrus, lacking leaflets but with grapnel-like spines on the lower surfaces. Leaflets are regularly or irregularly arranged along the rachis and spread in the same plane. Unlike *Plectocomia*, they are green on the lower surfaces and have minute dots.

Myrialepis is semelparous; all inflorescences of a stem, to 13 at a time, are produced together at the top of the stem. They flower over a short period of time, and after fruiting the stem dies. Plants are also dioecious. Inflorescences are branched to three orders and are covered in overlapping bracts. Male flowers are borne in small groups along the flowering branches; female flowers are also borne in small groups. Fruits are more or less globose, greenish, usually one-seeded, and covered with many, minute, overlapping scales. The name of the genus refers to these small scales, and comes from the Greek words *myrioi*, meaning very many, and *lepis*, meaning scale. The endosperm is homogeneous, germination is adjacent, but the form of the seedling leaf is not known.

Myrialepis contains one species, widely distributed throughout Indochina, the Malay Peninsula, and reaching Sumatra (Dransfield 1979a; Evans et al. 2001, 2002; Hodel 1998).

Myrialepis paradoxa (Kurz) J. Dransf.
PLATE 44

wai namsay (Lao), yamatha khyeing (Mya), wai chaang, wai-gung (Tha), song rup (Vie)

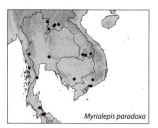
Myrialepis paradoxa

Field characters. Stems clustered, forming thickets, climbing, to 45 m long and 7 cm diameter. Leaf sheaths green with reddish brown hairs, with short or long, oblique rows of needlelike, yellowish brown, to 5-cm-long spines; leaf rachis to 3.5 m long with 15–40 lanceolate leaflets per side, these regularly or irregularly

arranged and then spreading in different planes; cirri to 1.5 m long. Inflorescences to 0.75 m long; fruits depressed globose, to 2.5 cm long and 3 cm diameter, greenish.

Range and habitat. Cambodia, Laos, Myanmar (Tanintharyi), Thailand, and Vietnam (Southern) (also in Peninsular Malaysia, Singapore, and Sumatra); lowland to montane rain forest, usually at forest margins or in disturbed places, to 1600 m elevation.

Uses. Provides a low-quality cane sometimes used in basketry.

Synonyms. *Bejaudia cambodiensis* Gagnep., *Calamus paradoxus* Kurz, *Myrialepis floribunda* (Becc.) Gagnep., *Myrialepis scortechinii* Becc., *Palmijuncus paradoxus* (Kurz) Kuntze, *Plectocomiopsis annulata* Ridl., *Plectocomiopsis floribunda* Becc., *Plectocomiopsis paradoxa* (Kurz) Becc., *Plectocomiopsis scortechinii* (Becc.) Ridl.

NANNORRHOPS H. Wendl.

Stems are short, often subterranean, clustered, and can branch dichotomously. In fact, the genus name alludes to these stems, and comes from the Greek words *nannos*, meaning short, and *rhops*, meaning a bush or shrub. Leaves are palmate and 15–30 in number. Leaf sheaths are open and disintegrate into woolly, brown fibers. Petioles are elongate and lack thorns on the margins. There is no hastula. Blades are divided into numerous leaflets, and these are somewhat waxy on both surfaces.

Nannorrhops is semelparous. One stem of a pair of dichotomous stems flowers, while the other stem continues to grow vegetatively. On the flowering stem, several inflorescences are produced at the same time, giving the appearance of one large inflorescence. The production of these inflorescences marks the end of the life of the stem bearing them. Inflorescences are branched to four orders and are borne among the leaves but project upwards above the leaves. Inflorescences are covered by several bracts. The simple flowers are borne in small groups. Fruits are globose to ellipsoid, brownish, and usually one-seeded. Endosperm is homogeneous, germination is remote, and the seedling leaf is undivided.

Nannorrhops contains one species, distributed in drier regions of the Arabian Peninsula (Yemen, Oman), Iran, Afghanistan, and Pakistan (Moore 1980; Mughal 1992).

Nannorrhops ritchiana (Griff.) Aitch.
PLATE 45

chatai, marzi, patha (Pak)

Field characters. Stems clustered, to 8 m tall and 60 cm diameter, sometimes short and subterranean, often forming large colonies. Leaf blades divided into about 40 leaflets. Inflorescences to 2.5 m long, emerging among and above the leaves; fruits globose, to 2 cm diameter, yellowish brown.

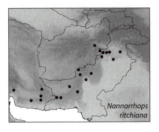

*Nannorrhops
ritchiana*

Range and habitat. Afghanistan and Pakistan (Bal-uchistan, Punjab) (also in Iran, Oman, and Yemen); arid, open areas, often on limestone soils, to 1500 m elevation.

Uses. The leaves are intensively used for weaving into ropes, mats, bags, sandals, and other items.

Notes. Leaf color is quite variable, and it is possible that more than one species is present.

Synonyms. *Chamaerops ritchiana* Griff., *Nannor-rhops arabica* Burret, *Nannorrhops naudiniana* Becc., *Nannorrhops stocksiana* Becc.

NENGA H.Wendl. & Drude

The name of this genus is derived from a local name for the plants in Java. Stems are solitary or clustered and range from moderate to short or even subterra-nean. Usually stems are green, and in some species there are prominent stilt roots at the base. Leaves are pinnate, 4–7 in number, and spread horizontally. Leaf sheaths are closed and usually form a prominent, green or yellowish crownshaft, although in one spe-cies this does not develop. Leaflets are regularly ar-ranged along the rachis and spread in the same plane. They are usually linear, one- to several-veined, and sometimes, especially at the leaf apices, the leaflets are joined with only a short split at the tip, giving com-pound leaflets with lobed apices.

Inflorescences are branched to one order (rarely to two orders or spicate) and are borne below the crownshaft, rarely among the leaves. In bud they are covered with just one bract. Flowers are unisexual and are borne in threes of a central female and two lateral males. These groups of flowers are spirally arranged along the flowering branches, for about three-quarters their length. On the apical part of the flowering branches, however, only male flowers are borne. This part withers after the male flowers fall, leaving a brown tip. Fruits are small, ovoid to ellip-soid, often red, and one-seeded. The endosperm is

ruminate, germination is adjacent, and the seedling leaf is bifid.

Nenga contains five species, naturally occurring from Peninsular Thailand and Vietnam to Peninsular Malaysia, Sumatra, Java, and Borneo. They are usu-ally small to moderate-sized, understory palms. There are three species in our area (Fernando 1983; Hodel 1998; Lim & Whitmore 2001b).

Nenga is closely related to both *Areca* and *Pinanga*. It differs from *Areca* in its thicker flowering branches and spirally arranged flowers. It is more difficult to distinguish from *Pinanga*. Usually in *Nenga* the female flowers and fruits are not borne throughout the flowering branches, as in *Pinanga*, and the apical part of the branches, with male flow-ers only, withers after the flowers have fallen. A more technical character is that the seeds are laterally attached to the fruits in *Nenga* and basally attached in *Pinanga* and *Areca*.

Nenga banaensis (Magalon) Burret   PLATE 45
cây cau rung (Vie)

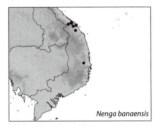

Nenga banaensis

Field characters. Stems solitary, or with basal shoots, to 6 m tall and 3.5 cm diameter. Leaf sheaths forming a yellowish crownshaft; blades to 1.5 m long with 13–20, glossy leaflets per side of rachis. Inflorescences with to 6 erect flowering branches; fruits ellipsoid, to 1.4 cm long and 1 cm diameter, color not known.

Range and habitat. Vietnam (Central); lowland rain forest, at low elevations.

Uses. The palm hearts are eaten and fruits are used as a substitute for betel nut.

Synonyms. *Areca banaensis* (Magalon) Burret, *Areca microspadix* Burret, *Pinanga banaensis* Magalon, *Pinanga nannospadix* Burret, *Nenga nannospadix* (Burret) Burret

Nenga macrocarpa Scort.
mak nag chang thon (Tha)

Key to the Species of *Nenga*

Plate 49. *Pholidocarpus macrocarpus*; habit; Thailand (top left). *Pinanga acuminata*; habit; Myanmar (top right). *Pinanga adangensis*; habit; Thailand (bottom left). *Pinanga adangensis*; fruits; Thailand (bottom right).

Plate 50. *Pinanga annamensis*; habit; Vietnam (top left). *Pinanga annamensis*; inflorescence; Vietnam (top right). *Pinanga auriculata* var. *merguensis*; habit; Thailand (bottom left). *Pinanga auriculata* var. *merguensis*; fruits; Thailand (bottom right).

Plate 51. *Pinanga baviensis*; habit; Vietnam (top left). *Pinanga baviensis*; infructescence; Vietnam (top right). *Pinanga cattienensis*; habit; Vietnam (bottom left). *Pinanga cattienensis*; infructescence; Vietnam (bottom right).

Plate 52. *Pinanga cupularis*; inflorescence; Vietnam (top left). *Pinanga declinata*; leaf sheaths; Vietnam (top right). *Pinanga disticha*; inflorescence and infructescences; Thailand (bottom left). *Pinanga gracilis*; habit; India (bottom right).

Plate 53. *Pinanga griffithii*; infructescence; Myanmar (top left). *Pinanga humilis*; habit; Vietnam (top right). *Pinanga humilis*; inflorescence and infructescences; Vietnam (bottom left). *Pinanga plicata*; habit; Myanmar (bottom right).

Plate 54. *Pinanga plicata*; infructescence; Myanmar (top left). *Pinanga quadrijuga*; habit; Vietnam (top right). *Pinanga quadrijuga*; infructescences; Vietnam (bottom left). *Pinanga riparia*; inflorescences; Thailand (bottom right).

Plate 55. *Pinanga sylvestris*; habit; Myanmar (top left). *Pinanga versicolor*; habit; Myanmar (top right). *Pinanga versicolor*; young leaf; Myanmar (bottom left). *Plectocomia assamica*; leaf sheath; Myanmar (bottom right).

Plate 56. *Plectocomia assamica*; fruits; Myanmar (top left). *Plectocomia elongata* var. *elongata*; leaf sheath; Vietnam (top right). *Plectocomia elongata* var. *elongata*; infructescence; Vietnam (bottom left). *Plectocomia himalayana*; leaf sheath; China (bottom right).

Plate 57. *Plectocomia microstachys*; leaf sheath; China (top left). *Plectocomia pierreana*; leaf sheath; Vietnam (top right). *Plectocomia pierreana*; fruits; Vietnam (bottom left). *Plectocomiopsis geminiflora*; fruits; Vietnam (bottom right).

Plate 58. *Rhapis excelsa*; habit; Vietnam (top left). *Rhapis excelsa*; leaf sheaths; Vietnam (top right). *Rhapis laosensis*; habit; Vietnam (bottom left). *Rhapis laosensis*; inflorescence; Vietnam (bottom right).

Plate 59. *Rhapis micrantha*; habit; Vietnam (top left). *Rhapis micrantha*; leaf sheaths; Vietnam (top right). *Rhapis puhuongensis*; habit; Vietnam (bottom left). *Rhapis puhuongensis*; fruits; Vietnam (bottom right).

Plate 60. *Rhapis vidalii*; habit; Vietnam (top left). *Rhopaloblaste augusta*; habit; cultivated, Florida (top right). *Salacca glabrescens*; leaf bases and inflorescences; Thailand (bottom left). *Salacca glabrescens*; fruits; Thailand (bottom right).

Plate 61. *Salacca griffithii*; habit; China (top left). *Salacca secunda*; fruits; Myanmar (top right). *Salacca secunda*; leaf bases and old male inflorescence; Myanmar (bottom left). *Salacca wallichiana*; male flowers; Myanmar (bottom right).

Plate 62. *Salacca wallichiana*; female flowers; Thailand (top left). *Salacca wallichiana*; fruits; Thailand (top right). *Satakentia liukiuensis*; habit; cultivated, Hawaii (bottom left). *Trachycarpus fortunei*; habit; China (bottom right).

Plate 63. *Trachycarpus fortunei*; inflorescence; China (top left). *Trachycarpus geminisectus*; habit; Vietnam (top right). *Trachycarpus oreophilus*; habit; Thailand (bottom left). *Wallichia caryotoides*; habit; Myanmar (bottom right).

Plate 64. *Wallichia disticha*; leaf sheaths; China (top left). *Wallichia marianneae*; female inflorescence; Thailand (top right). *Wallichia oblongifolia*; habit; Myanmar (bottom left). *Wallichia oblongifolia*; lower surface of leaflets; India (bottom right).

Field characters. Stems solitary, to 6 m tall and 7 cm diameter. Leaf sheaths forming a crownshaft; blades to 2 m long with to 30 leaflets per side of rachis. Inflorescences with to 5 spreading flowering branches; fruits ellipsoid, to 4 cm long and 2 cm diameter, purple-black.

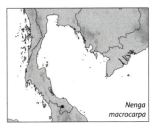

Nenga
macrocarpa

Range and habitat. Thailand (Peninsular) (also in Peninsular Malaysia); lowland rain forest, to 800 m elevation.
Uses. None recorded.

Nenga pumila (Blume)   PLATES 45 & 46
H. Wendl.
kache (Tha)

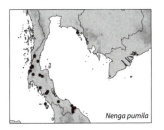

Nenga pumila

Field characters. Stems clustered, to 7 m tall and 3–7 cm diameter. Leaf sheaths forming a crownshaft; blades to 3 m long with 27–38 linear-lanceolate leaflets per side of rachis. Inflorescences with 2–7 pendulous flowering branches; fruits ellipsoid, to 3 cm long and 1.5 cm diameter, orange-red.
Range and habitat. Thailand (Peninsular, Southeast) and probably adjacent Myanmar (Tanintharyi) (also in Borneo, Java, Peninsular Malaysia, Singapore, and Sumatra); lowland to montane rain forest, often in swamps, to 1300 m elevation.
Uses. None recorded.
Notes. Two varieties are recognized: var. *pachystachya* (Blume) Fernando, from Borneo, Singapore, Sumatra, Thailand, and Peninsular Malaysia; and var. *pumila*, with smaller, orange-brown fruits, from Java.
Synonyms. *Areca nenga* Blume, *Areca pumila* Blume, *Areca wendlandiana* (Scheff.) H. Wendl., *Nenga intermedia* Becc., *Nenga schefferiana* Becc., *Nenga wendlandiana* Scheff., *Nenga wendlandiana* f. *hexapetala* Becc., *Nenga wendlandiana* var. *malaccensis* Becc., *Pinanga nenga* (Blume) Blume, *Pinanga nenga* var.

pachystachya Blume, *Pinanga pumila* (Blume) Blume, *Ptychosperma nenga* (Blume) Teijsm. & Binn.

NYPA Steck.
(*Nipa* Thunb.)

The name of this genus, frequently but incorrectly spelled *Nipa*, comes from a local name in Indonesia, where the palm is very common. Stems of *Nypa* are unusual for several reasons. They are creeping and seldom visible above the mud in which they grow, and they also branch dichotomously (i.e., a main branch splits into two equal branches). Roots grow from the lower surfaces of the stems. These creeping, branching stems form large colonies in suitable habitats. Leaves are pinnate, 3–15 in number, and arise stiffly from each stem apex. Leaf sheaths are open and relatively short, and petioles are elongate and stout. Leaflets are numerous and are regularly arranged and spread in the same plane. They have conspicuous, brown hairs on the lower surfaces, along the midveins.

Inflorescences are branched to five or six orders, and are borne on a stout stalk arising from among the leaves. The flowers are borne in a dense head at the top of this stalk. Male flowers are densely arranged along short flowering branches, and these are closely covered with light brown bracts. In the center of the inflorescence are the female flowers. These are also borne in a condensed head. Fruits are densely arranged in a cluster containing many fruits. As they develop the fruiting heads become pendulous. Fruits are large, irregularly globose, flattened and angled, dark brown, and usually one-seeded. The endosperm is homogeneous or ruminate and the seedling leaf is bifid. Seeds start germinating while still on the plant, and the germinating seedling falls from the plant and floats in water.

Nypa, with only one species, differs from all other palms in its unusual inflorescence morphology. It also has a long fossil history, and fossil fruits of *Nypa* are known from scattered sites from the late Cretaceous. Since that time it has changed little in morphology, at least the fruits. It is now widespread throughout Southern Asia, from Sri Lanka to Thailand, and from there through Indonesia to New Guinea and the Solomon and Ryukyu Islands and just reaching Australia. It has become naturalized in several other places (e.g., Cameroon, Nigeria, Panama, and French Guiana). It occurs in dense stands in muddy, low-lying, tidally flooded areas, mangrove swamps, or less often in other flooded places near the sea.

Nypa fruticans Wurmb   PLATE 46
goolga gucina, gubna (Ban, Ind), chak (Cbd), dani, htani (Mya), jark (Tha), cay dua nuoc (Vie)

Field characters. Stems creeping, not visible, dividing equally, forming large colonies, to 60 cm diameter.

Leaves stiffly erect; blades to 9 m long with 57–100 leaflets per side, these regularly arranged and spreading in the same plane. Inflorescences erect, to 2 m long; fruits densely packed in a rounded head, each obovoid, flattened, to 15 cm long and 10 cm diameter, brown.

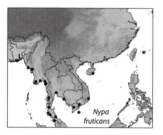

Nypa
fruticans

Range and habitat. Andaman and Nicobar islands, Bangladesh, Cambodia, China (Hainan), India (West Bengal), Myanmar (Mon, Tanintharyi, Yangon), Japan (Ryukyu Islands), Sri Lanka, Thailand (Peninsular, Southeast), and Vietnam (Central, Southern) (also in Australia, Indonesia, Malaysia, New Guinea, the Philippines, and the Solomon Islands); low-lying, estuarine, tidally flooded areas, mangrove swamps, or sometimes in wet areas near the sea, at low elevations.
Uses. An important palm, both for the leaves, which are commonly used as thatch, and the inflorescences, which are tapped for sugar and alcohol. There are many other minor uses.
Synonyms. *Cocos nypa* Lour., *Nipa arborescens* Wurmb, *Nipa litoralis* Blanco, *Nipa fruticans* (Wurmb) Thunb.

ONCOSPERMA Blume

Stems are tall, clustered or rarely solitary, usually prominently ringed, and are often spiny (sometimes impressively so!). The spines, however, tend to wear off with age. In one species the stems branch above ground level. Leaves are pinnate, 11–35 in number, and dead leaves fall cleanly from the stem. Leaf sheaths form a prominent crownshaft, and this is variously spiny. A long thread, from the margins of the leaf, often hangs down from the base of newly opened leaves. Leaflets are numerous, regularly or irregularly arranged (and then spreading in different planes), linear to lanceolate, and sometimes pendu-

lous. Leaflets are not spiny but often have prominent brown scales on one or both surfaces.

Inflorescences are branched to two orders and are borne below the crownshaft. The two bracts covering the inflorescence are often spiny, with wavy spines forming an attractive pattern. Both bracts fall early, before the flowers open. The short peduncle may be nonspiny or densely covered with spines. The numerous flowering branches are pendulous. Flowers are white, unisexual, and are arranged in threes of a central female and two lateral male flowers. Fruits are small, globose, purple-black or rarely red, often somewhat waxy, and one-seeded. The Latin name of the genus is derived from the Greek words *onkos*, meaning a tumor, and *sperma*, a seed, in apparent reference to the form of the seed. The endosperm is ruminate, germination is adjacent, and the seedling leaf is bifid.

Oncosperma contains five species, widely distributed from Sri Lanka to the Philippines. They occur in lowland or montane rain forest, from the landward side of mangrove swamps to steep slopes at higher elevations. Three species occur in our area.

Oncosperma fasciculatum Thwaites   PLATE 46
kata kitul (Srl)

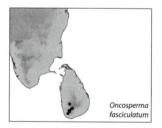

Oncosperma
fasciculatum

Field characters. Stems clustered, usually only one well developed, sometimes branching above ground level, to 20 m tall and 15 cm diameter, with rings of black, flattened spines. Leaf rachis to 3 m long with to 55 leaflets per side, these irregularly arranged and spreading in different planes. Inflorescence peduncles not spiny; flowering branches slender; fruits globose, to 1.2 cm diameter, purple-black.
Range and habitat. Sri Lanka; lowland to montane rain forest, often on steep, rocky slopes, to 1500 m elevation.
Uses. The palm hearts are eaten.

Key to the Species of *Oncosperma*

1a. Leaflets irregularly arranged and spreading in different planes; Sri Lanka . . . . *O. fasciculatum.*
1b. Leaflets regularly arranged and spreading in the same plane; Cambodia, Thailand, and Vietnam . . . . 2.

2a. Leaflets pendulous; flowering branches slender; low elevations near the sea; Cambodia,
Thailand (Peninsular), and Vietnam (Southern) . . . . *O. tigillarium.*
2b. Leaflets spreading; flowering branches stout; higher elevations away from the sea;
Thailand (Peninsular) . . . . *O. horridum.*

Oncosperma horridum (Griff.) Scheff.
lao-cha-own-khao, tung han (Tha)

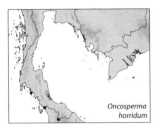

Oncosperma
horridum

Field characters. Stems clustered, rarely solitary, to 25 m tall and 25 cm diameter, spiny. Leaf rachis to 4 m long with 82–110 leaflets per side, these regularly arranged and spreading in a vertical plane because of the twisted rachis. Inflorescence peduncles densely spiny; flowering branches stout; fruits globose, to 1.7 cm diameter, black.
Range and habitat. Thailand (Peninsular) (also in Borneo, Peninsular Malaysia, the Philippines, and Sumatra); lowland rain forest to 1000 m elevation.
Uses. The stems, which are durable in seawater, are used in construction; and the palm heart is eaten.
Synonym. *Areca horrida* Griff.

Oncosperma tigillarium (Jack) Ridl.   PLATE 47
lao-cha-own, libong (Tha), cay nhum (Vie)

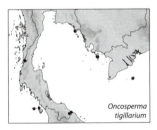

Oncosperma
tigillarium

Field characters. Stems clustered, to 25 m tall and 15 cm diameter, spiny, forming large clumps. Leaf rachis to 3.5 m long with 46–100 leaflets per side, these regularly arranged and pendulous. Inflorescence peduncles sparsely spiny; flowering branches slender; fruits globose, to 1 cm diameter, purple-black.
Range and habitat. Cambodia, Thailand (Peninsular), and Vietnam (Southern) (also in Borneo, Java, Sumatra, and Peninsular Malaysia); lowland rain forest in coastal areas, usually in wet, swampy places or at the edges of mangrove swamps, at low elevations.
Uses. The stems, which are durable in seawater, are used in construction.
Synonyms. *Areca nibung* Griff., *Areca spinosa* Hasselt & Kunth, *Areca tigillaria* Jack, *Euterpe filamentosa* Kunth, *Keppleria tigillaria* (Jack) Meisn., *Oncosperma cambodianum* Hance, *Oncosperma filamentosum* (Kunth) Blume

ORANIA Zipp.
(*Halmoorea* J. Dransf. & N. W. Uhl, *Macrocladus* Griff., *Sindroa* Jum.)

The name of this genus commemorates F.G.L. Willem van Nassau, Prince of Orange (*Oranje* in Dutch—hence *Orania*) (1792–1849). Stems are moderate to tall, solitary, and usually prominently ringed. Leaves are pinnate, about 20 in number, and are spirally arranged, although in some species they are arranged in one plane (distichously). Leaf sheaths are open and do not form a crownshaft. Leaflets are numerous, regularly or irregularly arranged (and then spreading in different planes), linear to lanceolate, and sometimes pendulous. The apices of the leaflets are jagged, and the undersides of the leaflets are silvery gray or silvery brown.

Inflorescences are branched to three orders and are borne among the leaves. Two unequal bracts cover the inflorescence. The second, larger one is often torpedo-shaped. The numerous flowering branches are spreading and rather thin. Flowers are white, unisexual, and are arranged in threes of a central female and two lateral male flowers. Fruits are relatively large, globose, yellowish or brownish, and one- to three-seeded. The endosperm is homogeneous, germination is remote, and the seedling leaf is bifid or pinnate.

Orania contains 18 species, occurring from Peninsular Thailand to New Guinea, with one species in Madagascar. One species occurs in our area.

Orania sylvicola (Griff.) H. E. Moore   PLATE 47
mak phon, pon (Tha)

Orania sylvicola

Field characters. Stems solitary, to 20 m tall and 25 cm diameter. Leaf sheaths split, not forming crownshafts; rachis to 3.5 m long with 63–75 regularly arranged leaflets per side, these silvery brown on the lower surfaces. Inflorescences borne among the leaves, becoming below the leaves in fruit; fruits globose, to 4 cm diameter, yellowish brown.
Range and habitat. Thailand (Peninsular) (also in Peninsular Malaysia and Sumatra); lowland rain forest, below 250 m elevation.
Uses. None recorded—the palm heart is reported to be poisonous.
Synonyms. *Macrocladus sylvicola* Griff., *Orania macrocladus* Mart.

PHOENIX L.

(Dachel Andans., *Elate* L., *Fulchironia* Lesch., *Palma* Mill., *Phoniphora* Neck., *Zelonops* Raf.)

The genus takes its name from its best-known species, the date palm, for which *Phoenix* is the Greek word. Stems range from solitary to clustered and from short and subterranean to large and aerial. They are usually somewhat rough with very close nodes and are often covered with persistent leaf bases. Leaves are pinnate and 8–50 in number. Leaf sheaths are open. The leaves are distinctive, and the genus can easily be recognized by the leaves alone. Leaflets are V-shaped (induplicate) in cross section instead of the more usual Λ-shaped (reduplicate). The leaflets at the base of the leaf are modified into short, stout, sharp spines. Any palm with pinnate leaves, V-shaped leaflets, and basal spines must be a *Phoenix*.

Inflorescences are branched to one order and are borne among the leaves. Individual plants produce either male or female inflorescences (i.e., the plants are dioecious). Flowering branches are often borne in groups or spirals along the inflorescence rachis. Flowers are small, simple, and unisexual. Fruits are obo-

void, oblong, or ellipsoid; various shades of black or brown; and usually one-seeded. The fleshy mesocarp is thick and sweet-tasting in the date palm but rather thin and bitter in other species. The endosperm is usually homogeneous, rarely ruminate, germination is remote, and the seedling leaf is undivided.

Phoenix contains 15 species, widely distributed from the Canary Islands across the Mediterranean, Africa, the Middle East, India, Southern Asia, and just reaching the Philippines. Species occur in a great variety of habitats, from desert oases to mangrove forests. The date palm, *P. dactylifera*, is widely cultivated. Nine species occur in our area (Barrow 1998; Dransfield 2005).

Phoenix acaulis Roxb.

khajuri, schap (Ind)

Field characters. Stems solitary, short and subterranean, bulblike, densely covered with old leaf bases. Leaves to 1.8 m long; leaflets 16–24 per side of rachis, irregularly arranged and spreading in different planes. Inflorescences short, borne at ground level; male inflorescences erect, with to 15 flowering branches; female inflorescences erect, with to 20 flowering branches;

Key to the Species of *Phoenix*

1a. Leaflets regularly arranged and spreading in the same plane; leaflets with persistent scales on lower surfaces of midrib . . . . 2.
1b. Leaflets irregularly arranged and spreading in different planes; leaflets without persistent scales . . . . . 4.

2a. Stems solitary or clustered, to 3 m tall and 10 cm diameter; rocky river banks or cliffs, sometimes with stems submerged; China, Laos, Myanmar, and Vietnam . . . . *P. roebelinii.*
2b. Stems solitary, to 5 m tall and 25 cm diameter; lowland or montane rain forest; Andaman Islands, Bhutan, and northeastern India . . . . 3.

3a. Endosperm homogeneous; Bhutan and northeastern India. *P. rupicola.*
3b. Endosperm ruminate; Andaman Islands . . . . *P. andamanensis.*

4a. Stems clustered, to 12 m tall, forming dense clumps; leaf scars visible on stems; leaf sheaths with distinct ocreas at the apices; coastal regions of Andaman and Nicobar islands, Bangladesh, Cambodia, India, Myanmar Thailand, and Vietnam . . . . *P. paludosa.*
4b. Stems solitary or clustered, short and subterranean or to 30 m tall, not forming dense clumps; leaf scars not visible on stems; leaf sheaths without distinct ocreas at the apices; inland regions in Bangladesh, Bhutan, Cambodia, China, India, Myanmar, Nepal, Sri Lanka, Taiwan, Thailand, and Vietnam . . . . 5.

5a. Stems short and subterranean or to 5 m tall . . . . 6.
5b. Stems tall and aerial, to 30 m tall . . . . 7.

6a. Female inflorescences short, with to 20 flowering branches; stems solitary; northern India and Nepal . . . . *P. acaulis.*
6b. Female inflorescences elongate, becoming arched, with to 40 flowering branches; stems solitary or clustered; Bangladesh, Bhutan, Cambodia, China, India, Myanmar Taiwan, Thailand, and Vietnam . . . . *P. loureiroi.*

7a. Leaflets 4-ranked; southern India and Sri Lanka . . . . *P. pusilla.*
7b. Leaflets not 4-ranked; widespread . . . . 8.

8a. Stems clustered or solitary; fruits oblong, to 7 cm long and 3 cm diameter . . . . *P. dactylifera.*
8b. Stems solitary; fruits obovoid, to 2.5 cm long and 1.2 cm diameter . . . . *P. sylvestris.*

fruits obovoid, to 1.8 cm long and 0.8 cm diameter, blue-black; endosperm homogeneous.

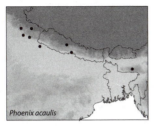

Phoenix acaulis

Range and habitat. India (Assam, Meghalaya, Bihar, Sikkim, Uttar Pradesh, and possibly Rajasthan, Punjab, and West Bengal), Nepal, and possibly Bhutan and Myanmar; open forest, scrub, savannas, and pine forest, 200–1500 m elevation.
Uses. Starch from the stems is eaten in times of famine.
Notes. Often confused with the more widespread *P. loureiroi*.
Synonym. *Phoenix acaulis* var. *melanocarpa* Griff.

Phoenix andamanensis S. Barrow

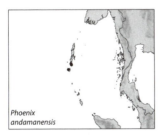

Phoenix andamanensis

Field characters. Stems solitary, to 5 m tall and 15 cm diameter. Leaves to 2.4 m long; leaflets numerous, regularly arranged and spreading in the same plane, with persistent scales on lower surfaces of midribs. Inflorescences not known; fruits oblong, to 1.9 cm long and 1 cm diameter, dark brown; endosperm ruminate.
Range and habitat. Andaman Islands (Cinque, Little Andaman, North Andaman, Rutland); lowland rain forest or scrub forest, to 700 m elevation.
Uses. None recorded.

Phoenix dactylifera L.
date palm

Field characters. Stems solitary or clustered, to 30 m tall and 50 cm diameter, with persistent, diamond-shaped leaf bases. Leaves to 5 m long; leaflets to 200 per side of rachis, regularly arranged and spreading in the same plane. Male inflorescences erect, with numerous flowering branches; female inflorescences erect, becoming pendulous, with numerous flowering branches; fruits variable in shape, usually oblong, to

7 cm long and 3 cm diameter, brown or black; endosperm homogeneous.
Range and habitat. Widely cultivated throughout North Africa, Near East, Middle East, and parts of Afghanistan, India, and Pakistan (no map provided).
Uses. The edible fruits—dates—are an important item in the diet of people throughout its range. Widely planted as an ornamental.
Synonyms. *Palma dactylifera* (L.) Mill., *Palma major* Garsault, *Phoenix atlantica* var. *maroccana* A. Chev., *Phoenix chevalieri* D. Rivera, *Phoenix dactylifera* var. *adunca* D. H. Christ, *Phoenix dactylifera* var. *costata* Becc., *Phoenix dactylifera* var. *cylindrocarpa* Mart., *Phoenix dactylifera* var. *gonocarpa* Mart., *Phoenix dactylifera* var. *oocarpa* Mart., *Phoenix dactylifera* var. *oxysperma* Mart., *Phoenix dactylifera* var. *sphaerocarpa* Mart., *Phoenix dactylifera* var. *sphaerosperma* Mart., *Phoenix dactylifera* var. *sylvestris* Mart., *Phoenix excelsior* Cav., *Phoenix iberica* D. Rivera, *Phoenix major* Garsault

Phoenix loureiroi Kunth   PLATE 47
khajuri (Ind), ku chuk, thinbaung (Mya), peng, pum peng (Tha), muong (Vie)

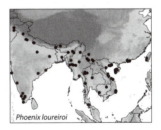

Phoenix loureiroi

Field characters. Stems solitary or clustered, to 5 m tall and 40 cm diameter, or sometimes short and subterranean, with persistent, diamond-shaped leaf bases. Leaves to 2 m long; leaflets to 130 per side of rachis, irregularly arranged and spreading in different planes. Male inflorescences erect, with to 30 flowering branches; female inflorescences elongate, erect, becoming arched, with to 40 flowering branches; fruits ovoid to obovoid, to 1.8 cm long and 0.9 cm diameter, black, blue-black, or dark purple; endosperm homogeneous.
Range and habitat. Bangladesh, Bhutan, Cambodia, China (Fujian, Guangdong, Guangxi, Hainan, Hong Kong, Yunnan), India (Andhra Pradesh, Assam, Bihar, Himachal Pradesh, Jammu and Kashmir, Karnataka, Kerala, Madhya Pradesh, Maharashtra, Orissa, Sikkim, Tamil Nadu, Uttar Pradesh, West Bengal), Myanmar (Chin, Kachin, Magway, Sagaing), Nepal, Pakistan, Taiwan, Thailand (Central, East, North, Southwest), and Vietnam (throughout); open forest, pine forest, open grassy areas, dunes, often on steep slopes, persisting in disturbed areas and in places subject to burning, to 1700 m elevation.
Uses. The leaves are woven into various domestic items, especially mats and brooms, or used for thatching.

Notes. A widespread species, especially variable in terms of stem development. Two varieties are recognized: var. *loureiroi*, with a thin brown line along the leaf margins, from Cambodia, China, Myanmar, Taiwan, Thailand, and Vietnam (and also in the Philippines); and var. *pedunculata* (Griff.) Govaerts, without a brown line along the leaf margins, from Bangladesh, Bhutan, India, and Nepal.

Synonyms. *Phoenix hanceana* Naudin, *Phoenix hanceana* var. *formosana* Becc., *Phoenix hanceana* var. *philippinensis* Becc., *Phoenix humilis* Royle, *Phoenix humilis* var. *hanceana* (Naudin) Becc., *Phoenix humilis* var. *loureiroi* (Kunth) Becc., *Phoenix humilis* var. *pedunculata* (Griff.) Becc., *Phoenix humilis* var. *robusta* Becc., *Phoenix humilis* var. *typica* Becc., *Phoenix loureiroi* var. *humilis* S. Barrow, *Phoenix ouseleyana* Griff., *Phoenix pedunculata* Griff., *Phoenix pusilla* Lour., *Phoenix pygmaea* Raeusch., *Phoenix robusta* Becc. & Hook. f.

Phoenix paludosa Roxb.   PLATE 47
peng (Cbd), hetal, hintala (Ind), thin-boung (Mya), peng-tha-le (Tha), cay cha la rieng (Vie)

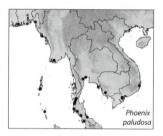
Phoenix paludosa

Field characters. Stems clustered, forming dense clumps, to 8 m tall and 16 cm diameter, with visible leaf scars. Leaves to 3 m long; leaf sheaths with distinct ocreas at the apices; leaflets 30–65 per side of rachis, irregularly arranged and spreading in different planes. Male inflorescences erect, broomlike, with to 50 flowering branches; female inflorescences erect, with to 37 flowering branches; fruits ovoid-ellipsoid, to 2 cm long and 1 cm diameter, blue-black; endosperm homogeneous.

Range and habitat. Andaman and Nicobar islands, Bangladesh, Cambodia, India (Orissa, West Bengal), Myanmar (Ayeyarwaddy, Rakhine), Thailand (Peninsular, Southwest), and Vietnam (Southern) (also in Peninsular Malaysia and Sumatra); coastal regions, often at edges of mangrove and coastal swamps, at low elevations.

Uses. Fibers from the leaves are woven into rope, and the stems are used in construction. There are many other local uses, including medicinal.

Synonyms. *Phoenix andamanensis* W. Mill., *Phoenix siamensis* Miq.

Phoenix pusilla Gaertn.   PLATE 48
eentha, eethie (Ind), inchu (Srl)

Field characters. Stems solitary or clustered, to 6 m tall and 30 cm diameter. Leaves to 3 m long; leaflets to 100 per side of rachis, irregularly arranged and spreading in 4 ranks. Male inflorescences erect, with to 70 flowering branches; female inflorescences erect, becoming arched, with to 120 flowering branches; fruits ovoid, to 1.5 cm long and 0.8 cm diameter, red, ripening black; endosperm homogeneous.

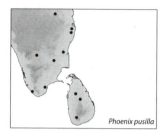
Phoenix pusilla

Range and habitat. Southern India (Andhra Pradesh, Kerala, Tamil Nadu) and Sri Lanka; lowland forest or open areas, often in disturbed places, and commonly near the sea, to 700 m elevation.

Uses. The leaves are used in weaving and the fruits are eaten.

Synonyms. *Phoenix farinifera* Roxb., *Phoenix zeylanica* Trimen

Phoenix roebelinii O'Brien   PLATE 48
jiangbian cikui (Chi), cha rang (Vie)

Phoenix roebelinii

Field characters. Stems solitary or clustered, to 3 m tall and 10 cm diameter, straight or twisted, rough with persistent leaf bases. Leaves to 2 m long; leaflets to 50 per side of rachis, regularly arranged and spreading in the same plane, with persistent scales on lower surfaces of midribs. Male inflorescences pendulous, with to 20 flowering branches; female inflorescences erect, with to 50 flowering branches; fruits obovoid, to 1.8 cm long and 0.7 cm diameter, orange-brown; endosperm homogeneous.

Range and habitat. China (Yunnan), Laos (Northern), Myanmar (Shan), and Vietnam (Northern); scattered localities on rocky river banks or cliffs, sometimes with stems submerged, especially along the Mekong, Nu Jiang (Salween), and Lancang Jiang rivers, at low elevations.

Uses. Widely planted as an ornamental.

Phoenix rupicola T. Anders.
ada, schap (Ind), tarika (Bhu)

PLATE 48

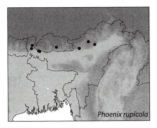

Phoenix rupicola

Field characters. Stems solitary, to 5 m tall and 25 cm diameter (sometimes flowering when still very short), smooth, with visible leaf scars. Leaves to 2.5 m long; leaflets to 70 per side of rachis, regularly arranged and spreading in the same plane, with persistent scales on lower surfaces of midribs. Male inflorescences erect, with numerous flowering branches; female inflorescences erect, becoming pendulous, with to 120 flowering branches; fruits obovoid, to 1.9 cm long and 0.8 cm diameter, reddish brown; endosperm homogeneous.

Range and habitat. Bhutan, northeastern India (Arunachal Pradesh, Assam, Sikkim, West Bengal), and possibly Nepal; lowland or montane rain forest, often on steep, rocky hillsides, to 1200 m elevation.

Uses. The fruits are eaten.

Phoenix sylvestris (L.) Roxb.
kubong (Bhu), eechcha, ita chettu, khajur (Ind), khaji (Pak)

PLATE 48

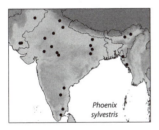

Phoenix sylvestris

Field characters. Stems solitary, to 20 m tall and 100 cm diameter, with persistent, diamond-shaped leaf bases. Leaves to 4 m long; leaflets to 90 per side of rachis, irregularly arranged and spreading in different planes. Male inflorescences erect, with numerous flowering branches; female inflorescences erect, becoming pendulous, with to 60 flowering branches; fruits obovoid, to 2.5 cm long and 1.2 cm diameter, orange-yellow; endosperm homogeneous.

Range and habitat. Bangladesh, Bhutan, India, Myanmar (Rakhine), Nepal, and Pakistan; open, grassy areas subject to seasonal flooding, persisting in disturbed areas and often cultivated, at low elevations.

Uses. The stems are tapped for their sweet sap, and the fruits are processed for jellies.

Synonyms. *Elate sylvestris* L., *Elate versicolor* Salisb.

PHOLIDOCARPUS Blume

Stems are tall, solitary, and covered with rough leaf scars. Leaves are costapalmate, 40–50 in number, and form a dense crown. Leaf sheaths are open and consist of closely woven, reddish brown fibers. Petioles are elongate and are usually covered with stout, bulbous-based thorns, and often have two yellow stripes on the lower surfaces. At the apex of the petiole there is a prominent hastula. The blade is deeply divided into broad, wedge-shaped segments, and these are again divided into numerous leaflets. This leaf division distinguishes *Pholidocarpus* from all species of *Livistona* except *L. saribus*.

Inflorescences are branched to four orders and are borne among the leaves. They are covered with overlapping, tubular bracts. Flowers are small, bisexual, and are borne singly along the flowering branches. Fruits are large, irregularly globose, brownish, one-seeded, and are either smooth or more often corky-warted. The name of the genus comes, inappropriately, from these fruits, from the Greek words *pholidos*, meaning scale, and *carpus*, meaning a fruit. Endosperm is homogeneous but is penetrated by the seed coat and appears ruminate, germination is remote, and the seedling leaf is undivided and lanceolate.

Pholidocarpus contains six species, distributed in Thailand, Malaysia, and Indonesia, and occurs in lowland rain forest. One species occurs in our area (Hodel 1998).

Pholidocarpus macrocarpus Becc.
ka pao (Tha)

PLATE 49

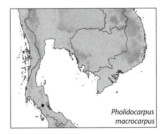

Pholidocarpus macrocarpus

Field characters. Stems to 20 m tall and 40 cm diameter. Petioles with stout, bulbous-based thorns to 7 cm long on the margins and with 2 yellow stripes on lower surfaces; leaf blades irregularly divided almost to the base into wide segments, these divided again into numerous leaflets. Inflorescences borne among the leaves; fruits globose to ovoid-oblong, to 12 cm diameter, dull or rusty brown with a warty surface.

Range and habitat. Thailand (Peninsular) (also in Peninsular Malaysia, Singapore, and Sumatra); lowland rain forest in swampy, seasonally flooded areas, at low elevations.

Uses. None recorded.

PINANGA Blume

(*Cladosperma* Griff., *Ophiria* Becc., *Pseudopinanga* Burret)

Stems are clustered or less often solitary, usually covered with reddish brown or gray scales and ringed with prominent leaf scars, and range from tall to short or subterranean. Most species have rather short stems, and the genus gets its name from the Malay work *pinang*, which refers to any small palm. Leaves are pinnate or occasionally undivided and 5–11 in number. Leaf sheaths are closed and form a prominent, green or yellowish crownshaft, and this is usually covered in variously colored scales. In a few species a crownshaft does not develop. Leaflets are regularly arranged along the rachis and spread in the same plane, and are linear to sigmoid and one- to several-veined. Leaflets vary in their width, even within the same species. At the leaf apex, the leaflets are joined with only a short split at the tip, giving the leaflets a lobed appearance. In some species with narrow leaflets, this lobed appearance of the apical leaflets is not easy to see.

Inflorescences are branched to one order with a few flowering branches, or sometimes with one flowering branch, and are borne below the crownshaft, rarely among the leaves. They are covered in bud with just one bract, the prophyll. After the prophyll falls away the flowering branches usually become pendulous but may remain erect or spreading. Flowering branches are usually smooth, but in a few species are hairy. Flowers are unisexual and are borne in threes of a central female and two lateral males. Flower groups are either arranged in two opposite rows along the flowering branches or, less often, spirally arranged in three to six rows, but in both cases they occur right to the end of the branch. Fruits are small; ellipsoid to globose or spindle-shaped; commonly beaked; red, orange, or black; and one-seeded. Fruits often ripen through a series of colors, commonly from green to pink to red to black. The endosperm is ruminate, rarely homogeneous, germination is adjacent, and the seedling leaf is bifid.

Pinanga contains about 130 species, occurring from India through Indochina and into Southeast Asia as far east as New Guinea. They usually occur in the understory of lowland rain forests. There are 34 species in our area (Gagnepain & Conrard 1937; Henderson 2007b; Henderson et al. 2008c; Hodel 1998; Hooker 1894; Lim 2001).

Pinanga is closely related to both *Nenga* and *Areca*. All three genera are distinguished by the absence of a peduncular bract, the inflorescence being covered only by the first bract, the prophyll. *Pinanga* is further distinguished by the flower groups, which are borne throughout the flowering branches; in *Nenga* and *Areca* the groups are borne near the base of the branches, and the apical parts have only male flowers. This is noticeable even when the plants are in fruit because both *Nenga* and *Areca* usually have dead, hanging "tails" below the fruits, representing the parts of the flowering branches with only male flowers. Another useful character is that *Pinanga* tend to have reddish brown or gray scaly stems, whereas these are green in *Areca* and *Nenga*.

Key to the Species of *Pinanga*

8a. Flowers and fruits spirally arranged along the flowering branches; rachis to 1 m long with
9–13 leaflets per side . . . . *P. cattienensis.*
8b. Flowers and fruits arranged in 2 opposite rows along the flowering branches; rachis to 0.4 m
long with 5–7 leaflets per side . . . . *P. humilis.*

9a. Inflorescences spicate; flowering branches 6–10 cm long; endosperm homogeneous . . . . 10.
9b. Inflorescences branched, rarely spicate; flowering branches 9.5–29 cm long; endosperm ruminate . . . 11.

10a. Inflorescences pendulous; female flowers with the sepals and petals joined into a cupule . . . *P. cupularis.*
10b. Inflorescences erect; female flowers with free, overlapping sepals and petals . . . . *P. kontumensis.*

11a. Stems forming large clumps; flowering branches rectangular in cross section; sheaths
and petioles green . . . . 12.
11b. Stems solitary or clustered but then with 1 or 2 main stems and basal shoots; flowering
branches triangular in cross section; sheaths and petioles yellowish . . . . 13.

12a. Stems with scattered, reddish brown scales; Central, Northern . . . . *P. baviensis.*
12b. Stems with a continuous covering of gray or brown scales; Southern . . . . *P. quadrijuga.*

13a. Leaflets linear, 20 or 21 per side of rachis, contracted at the bases; flowering
branches spreading . . . . *P. declinata.*
13b. Leaflets curved, 6–12 per side of rachis, not contracted at the bases; flowering
branches pendulous . . . . *P. annamensis.*

14a. China and Taiwan . . . . 15.
14b. Myanmar and Thailand . . . . 19.

15a. Taiwan . . . . *P. tashiroi.*
15b. China . . . . 16.

16a. Inflorescences with 1 flowering branch; flowers and fruits spirally arranged or borne in
3 rows along the flowering branch; Tibet, Yunnan . . . . 17.
16b. Inflorescences with more than 1 flowering branch, rarely with 1 flowering branch;
flowers and fruits arranged in 2 opposite rows along the flowering branches; Fujian, Guangxi,
Guangdong, Hainan, Yunnan . . . . 18.

17a. Flowers and fruits borne in 3 rows along the flowering branch; flowering branch angular;
Tibet . . . . *P. gracilis.*
17b. Flowers and fruits spirally arranged along the flowering branch; flowering branch rounded,
not angular; Yunnan . . . . *P. acuminata.*

18a. Leaflets 10–28 per side of rachis; flowering branches 3–8; Yunnan . . . . *P. sylvestris.*
18b. Leaflets 3–6 per side of rachis, or rarely leaf undivided; flowering branches 1–4; Fujian,
Guangdong, Guangxi, Hainan, eastern Yunnan . . . . *P. baviensis.*

19a. Myanmar . . . . 20.
19b. Thailand . . . . 29.

20a. Leaf sheaths not forming a distinct crownshaft; inflorescences pushing through the
persistent, disintegrating leaf sheaths; Tanintharyi . . . . *P. simplicifrons.*
20b. Leaf sheaths forming a distinct crownshaft; inflorescences borne below the leaves and
developing after the leaf has fallen; all areas, including Tanintharyi . . . . 21.

21a. Inflorescences with 1 flowering branch . . . . 22.
21b. Inflorescences with 2–8 flowering branches . . . . 25.

22a. Flowers and fruits spirally arranged along the flowering branches; Kachin . . . . *P. acuminata.*
22b. Flowers and fruits spirally arranged, or arranged in 2 opposite rows along the flowering branches;
Ayeyarwady, Bago, Tanintharyi . . . . 23.

23a. Leaflets 1-veined, narrow; flowers and fruits arranged in 2 opposite rows along the
flowering branches . . . . *P. hymenospatha.*
23b. Leaflets multiveined, broad; flowers and fruits spirally arranged along the flowering branches . . . . . 24.

(continued)

Key to the Species of *Pinanga* (continued)

24a. Stems to 1 m tall; Ayeyarwady . . . . *P. lacei.*
24b. Stems to 10 m tall; Bago . . . . *P. hexasticha.*

25a. Petioles very short, to 2 cm long; leaflets strongly folded . . . . *P. plicata.*
25b. Petioles well developed, 10–70 cm long; leaflets not strongly folded . . . . 26.

26a. Flowers and fruits spirally arranged along the flowering branches . . . . 27.
26b. Flowers and fruits arranged in 2 opposite rows along the flowering branches . . . . 28.

27a. Newly opened leaflets mottled light and dark green; flowering branches not hairy; Bago,
      Magway, Mon, Yangon . . . . *P. versicolor.*
27b. Newly opened leaflets green, not mottled; flowering branches hairy; Kachin, Sagaing . . . . . . *P. griffithii.*

28a. Leaflets linear, 10–28 per side of rachis; Kachin . . . . *P. sylvestris.*
28b. Leaflets sigmoid, 5–10 per side of rachis; Tanintharyi . . . . *P. auriculata.*

29a. Flowers and fruits spirally arranged along the flowering branches; inflorescences erect . . . . 30.
29b. Flowers and fruits arranged in 2 opposite rows along the flowering branches;
      inflorescences pendulous . . . . 31.

30a. Rachis to 2.5 m long with (2–)5–22 leaflets per side . . . . *P. scortechinii.*
30b. Rachis to 0.5 m long with 2 or 3 leaflets per side . . . . *P. polymorpha.*

31a. Stems solitary; leaflets sigmoid . . . . *P. auriculata.*
31b. Stems clustered, rarely solitary; leaflets linear or curved, not sigmoid, or leaves undivided . . . . 32.

32a. Leaflets mottled light and dark green; flowering branches hairy . . . . 33.
32b. Leaflets green, not mottled; flowering branches smooth, not hairy . . . . 34.

33a. Rachis with 8–13 linear leaflets per side; inflorescences with 2–6 flowering branches,
      5–20 cm long . . . . *P. watanaiana.*
33b. Rachis with 2–10 broad, curved leaflets per side, or leaf undivided; inflorescences with
      1 (rarely 2) flowering branches, 7–8 cm long . . . . *P. disticha.*

34a. Leaves with 10–28 leaflets per side of rachis; petioles 10–130 cm long . . . . 35.
34b. Leaves with 2–15 leaflets per side of rachis, or leaves undivided; petioles 2–30 cm long,
      rarely to 100 cm long . . . . 39.

35a. Flowering branches 5–8 cm long; leaflets light gray on the lower surfaces . . . . *P. perakensis.*
35b. Flowering branches 9–35 cm long; leaflets green on the lower surfaces . . . . 36.

36a. Flowering branches thick and stout, not triangular in cross section . . . . *P. malaiana.*
36b. Flowering branches slender, triangular in cross section . . . . 37.

37a. Sheaths and petioles yellowish . . . . *P. adangensis.*
37b. Sheaths and petioles green . . . . 38.

38a. Petioles 35–90 cm long; 2 or 3 flowering branches, 9–15 cm long; Peninsular . . . . *P. badia.*
38a. Petioles 10–25 cm long; 3–8 flowering branches, 9–26 cm long; East, North, Southeast . . . . *P. sylvestris.*

39a. Stems loosely clustered, spreading by long rhizomes . . . . 40.
39b. Stems tightly clustered . . . . 41.

40a. Flowering branch 1; stems to 1 m tall and 0.7 cm diameter . . . . *P. paradoxa.*
40b. Flowering branches 2–4; stems to 5 m tall and 3 cm diameter . . . . *P. riparia.*

41a. Flowering branches 4 or 5, zigzag; fruits brownish yellow . . . . *P. fractiflexa.*
41b. Flowering branches 1 or 2, not zigzag; fruits red . . . . 42.

42a. Leaflets to 9 per side of rachis; leaf sheaths forming a distinct crownshaft; inflorescences
      borne below the leaves and developing after the leaf has fallen . . . . *P. subintegra.*
42b. Leaflets 2 or 3 per side of rachis, or leaves undivided; leaf sheaths not forming a distinct
      crownshaft; inflorescences pushing through the persistent, disintegrating leaf sheaths . . . *P. simplicifrons.*

Pinanga acuminata Henderson   PLATE 49

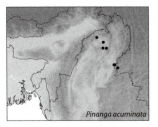

Pinanga acuminata

Field characters. Stems clustered, to 5 m tall and 2 cm diameter. Leaves pinnate; crownshafts present, yellowish green with reddish brown scales; petioles to 30 cm long; rachis to 0.7 m long with 6–9 narrow, curved leaflets per side. Inflorescences pendulous, rarely erect, with 1 smooth flowering branch, 11–19 cm long; flowers and fruits spirally arranged along the flowering branch; fruits ellipsoid, to 1.8 cm long and 1 cm diameter, red.
Range and habitat. China (Yunnan) and Myanmar (Kachin); lowland rain forest to 1000 m elevation.
Uses. None recorded.

Pinanga adangensis Ridl.   PLATE 49
maak aadang (Tha)

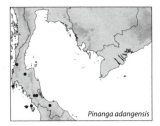

Pinanga adangensis

Field characters. Stems clustered, to 8 m tall and 5 cm diameter. Leaves pinnate; crownshafts present, yellowish with purplish scales; petioles 30–50 cm long; rachis to 2 m long with to 26 linear leaflets per side. Inflorescences spreading to pendulous, with 5–7 smooth flowering branches, 18–35 cm long, these triangular in cross section; flowers and fruits arranged in 2 opposite rows along the smooth flowering branches; fruits ovoid to obovoid, to 1.8 cm long and 1.2 cm diameter, purple-black.
Range and habitat. Thailand (Peninsular, Southeast) (also in Peninsular Malaysia); lowland rain forest, commonly near streams and rivers, and often on islands, to 200 m elevation.
Uses. None recorded.

Pinanga annamensis Magalon   PLATE 50
cay cau rung, cau nui, cau rung (Vie)

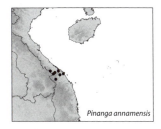

Pinanga annamensis

Field characters. Stems clustered, to 5 m tall and 3.5 cm diameter, forming small clumps with few stems. Leaves pinnate; crownshafts present, yellowish with reddish scales; petioles to 50 cm long, yellowish; rachis 0.8–1.2 m long with 8–12 broad, curved leaflets per side. Inflorescences pendulous, with 2–5 smooth flowering branches, 20–29 cm long, these triangular in cross section; flowers and fruits arranged in 2 opposite rows along the flowering branches; fruits ovoid, to 1.8 cm long and 1.2 cm diameter, pink or red.
Range and habitat. Vietnam (Central); lowland or montane rain forest at 100–1200 m elevation.
Uses. None recorded.

Pinanga auriculata Becc.   PLATE 50
mak bala, ka tao len (Tha)

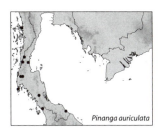

Pinanga auriculata

Field characters. Stems solitary, to 4 m tall and 3 cm diameter. Leaves pinnate; crownshafts present, whitish green, with whitish or brownish scales; petioles 15–30 cm long; rachis to 1 m long with 5–10 sigmoid leaflets per side. Inflorescences pendulous, with 2–6 smooth flowering branches, 8–15 cm long; flowers and fruits arranged in 2 opposite rows along the flowering branches; fruits ellipsoid to globose, to 2 cm long and 1 cm diameter, ripening from white to red to black.
Range and habitat. Myanmar (Tanintharyi) and Thailand (Peninsular) (also in Borneo and Peninsular Malaysia); lowland rain forest to 800 m elevation.
Uses. None recorded.
Notes. Three varieties are recognized: var. *auriculata* from Borneo; var. *leucocarpa* C. K. Lim, with fewer, more widely spaced leaflets, from the east coast of Thailand and Peninsular Malaysia; and var. *merguensis* (Becc.) C. K. Lim, with to 9 leaflets per side, from the west coast of Myanmar, Thailand, and Peninsular Malaysia.

Synomyms. *Pinanga bowiana* Hodel, *Pinanga patula* var. *merguensis* Becc.

Pinanga badia Hodel
mak khao (Tha)

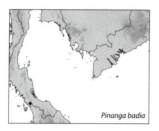

Pinanga badia

Field characters. Stems clustered, to 3 m tall and 2.5 cm diameter. Leaves pinnate; crownshafts present, green with brownish scales; petioles 35–90 cm long; rachis to 1.8 m long with 17–23 linear leaflets per side. Inflorescences pendulous, with 2 or 3 smooth flowering branches, 9–15 cm long, these triangular in cross section; flowers and fruits arranged in 2 opposite rows along the flowering branches; fruits ovoid, to 1.7 cm long and 0.8 cm diameter, red or pink.
Range and habitat. Thailand (Peninsular) (also in Peninsular Malaysia); lowland rain forest to 500 m elevation.
Uses. None recorded.

Pinanga baviensis Becc.   PLATE 51
ka shaan chuk, shan pan long (Chi), cau chuot (Vie)

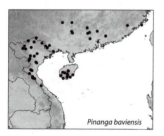

Pinanga baviensis

Field characters. Stems clustered or solitary, to 5 m tall and 2.5 cm diameter, forming large clumps. Leaves pinnate; crownshafts present, green with reddish scales; petioles to 33 cm long; rachis to 1 m long with 3–12 broad to narrow, curved leaflets per side, rarely leaves undivided. Inflorescences pendulous, with 2–5 (rarely 1) smooth flowering branches, 10–15 cm long; flowers and fruits arranged in 2 opposite rows along the flowering branches; fruits ellipsoid, to 2.5 cm long and 1 cm diameter, red.
Range and habitat. China (Fujian, Guangdong, Guangxi, Hainan, eastern Yunnan) and Vietnam

(Central, Northern); lowland rain forest, to 1000 m elevation.
Uses. None recorded.
Synonyms. *Pinanga discolor* Burret, *Pinanga sinii* Burret, *Pinanga viridis* Burret

Pinanga cattienensis Henderson,   PLATE 51
N. K. Ban & N. Q. Dung

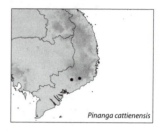

Pinanga cattienensis

Field characters. Stems clustered, forming dense clumps, to 1.5 m tall and 2 cm diameter. Leaves pinnate; crownshafts absent, the sheaths open; petioles to 116 cm long; rachis to 1 m long with 9–13 broad to narrow, curved leaflets per side. Inflorescences horizontal, pushing through the disintegrating leaf sheaths, with 3 or 4 smooth flowering branches, 9–13 cm long; flowers and fruits spirally arranged along the flowering branches; fruits ellipsoid, to 2 cm long and 0.6 cm diameter, red-pink.
Range and habitat. Vietnam (Southern); lowland rain forest in seasonally flooded areas, at low elevations.
Uses. None recorded.

Pinanga cupularis Henderson,   PLATE 52
N. K. Ban & N. Q. Dung
cay cau rung se, ca nui (Vie)

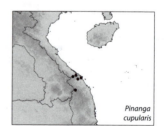

Pinanga cupularis

Field characters. Stems clustered, rarely solitary, to 2 m tall and 0.8 cm diameter. Leaves pinnate or undivided; crownshafts present, covered with reddish brown scales; petioles to 6 cm long; rachis to 0.4 m long with 2–4 broad, curved leaflets per side, rarely leaf undivided. Inflorescences pendulous, with 1 smooth flowering branch, 3–7 cm long; flowers and fruits arranged in 2 rows along the flowering branch; fruits narrowly ellipsoid, to 2 cm long and 0.4 cm diameter.

Range and habitat. Vietnam (Central) and possibly Laos; lowland or montane rain forest, at 200–1400 m elevation.

Uses. None recorded.

Notes. Futher distinguished by its male flowers with only four stamens and female flowers that have the sepals joined into a cupule and fruits with homogeneous endosperm.

Pinanga declinata Henderson, N. K. Ban & N. Q. Dung
PLATE 52

cau chuot, cao cuo chuoc, cau rung (Vie)

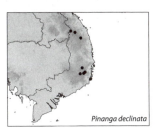

Pinanga declinata

Field characters. Stems clustered, to 5 m tall and 5.5 cm diameter, forming small clumps. Leaves pinnate; crownshafts present, yellowish with reddish brown scales; petioles to 52 cm long, yellowish; rachis to 1.1 m long with 20 or 21 linear leaflets per side, these contracted at the bases. Inflorescences spreading, with 4–8 smooth flowering branches, 15–22 cm long, these triangular in cross section; flowers and fruits arranged in 2 rows along the flowering branches; fruits narrowly ellipsoid, to 2 cm long and 0.7 cm diameter, color not known.

Range and habitat. Vietnam (Central, Southern); montane rain forest or pine forest, at 1100–1900 m elevation.

Uses. None recorded.

Pinanga dicksonii (Roxb.) Blume

kattu kamuku (Ind)

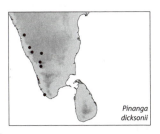

Pinanga dicksonii

Field characters. Stems forming loose clusters, to 8 m tall and 12 cm diameter. Leaves pinnate; crownshafts present, green or yellowish with reddish scales; petioles 7–8 cm long; rachis to 1.5 m long with 20–25 linear leaflets per side. Inflorescences pendulous, sometimes erect, with 4–8 smooth flowering

branches, 13–26 cm long; flowers and fruits arranged in 2 opposite rows along the flowering branches; fruits oblong to ellipsoid, to 1.5 cm long and 1.0 cm diameter, reddish.

Range and habitat. Southern India (Karnataka, Kerala, Maharashtra, Tamil Nadu); lowland rain forest at 350–1000 m elevation.

Uses. The seeds are chewed as a substitute for betel nut.

Synomyms. *Areca dicksonii* Roxb., *Ptychosperma dicksonii* (Roxb.) Mart., *Seaforthia dicksonii* (Roxb.) Mart.

Pinanga disticha (Roxb.) H. Wendl.
PLATE 52

mark-wing (Tha)

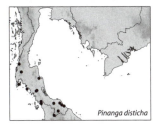

Pinanga disticha

Field characters. Stems forming loose clusters, to 1.4 m tall and 1 cm diameter. Leaves undivided or pinnate; crownshafts present, green; petioles 2–15 cm long; rachis to 0.6 m long; leaves undivided or with 2–10 broad, curved leaflets per side, mottled light and dark green. Inflorescences pendulous, with 1 (rarely 2) hairy flowering branch, 7–8 cm long; flowers and fruits arranged in 2 opposite rows along the flowering branch; fruits ovoid, to 1.5 cm long and 1 cm diameter, red.

Range and habitat. Thailand (Peninsular) (also in Peninsular Malaysia, Singapore, and Sumatra); lowland rain forest to 800 m elevation.

Uses. None recorded.

Synonyms. *Areca disticha* Roxb., *Areca humilis* Roxb., *Pinanga bifida* Blume, *Ptychosperma distichum* (Roxb.) Miq., *Seaforthia disticha* (Roxb.) Mart.

Pinanga fractiflexa Hodel

Pinanga fractiflexa

Field characters. Stems clustered, to 4 m tall and 5 cm diameter. Leaves pinnate; crownshafts present, green with reddish brown scales; petioles 70–100 cm long; rachis to 2 m long with to 8 linear, curved leaflets per side. Inflorescences pendulous, with 4 or 5 smooth, zigzag flowering branches, to 17 cm long; flowers and fruits arranged in 2 opposite rows along the flowering branches; fruits ovoid, to 3 cm long and 1.5 cm diameter, brownish yellow.

Range and habitat. Thailand (Peninsular); lowland rain forest to 600 m elevation.

Uses. None recorded.

Pinanga gracilis Blume   PLATE 52
gooa soopari (Ban), khur (Bhu), ram gua, tartiang (Ind)

Pinanga gracilis

Field characters. Stems clustered, sometimes solitary, to 4 m tall and 1.5 cm diameter. Leaves pinnate; crownshafts present, green with reddish brown scales; petioles 9–13 cm long; rachis to 0.6 m long with 3–8 broad or narrow, curved leaflets per side. Inflorescences pendulous, with 1 angular, smooth flowering branch, 12–20 cm long; flowers and fruits borne in 3 rows along the flowering branch; fruits ellipsoid, to 1.8 cm long and 1 cm diameter, red.

Range and habitat. Bangladesh, Bhutan, China (Tibet), India (Arunachal Pradesh, Assam, Manipur, Nagaland, Sikkim, Tripura), and Nepal; lowland or montane rain forest, to 1200 m elevation.

Uses. The inflorescence buds are eaten.

Synonyms. *Areca gracilis* Buch.-Ham., *Nenga gracilis* (Blume) Becc., *Seaforthia gracilis* (Blume) Mart.

Pinanga griffithii Becc.   PLATE 53

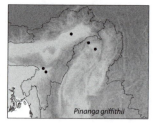
Pinanga griffithii

Field characters. Stems clustered, to 3 m tall and 2 cm diameter. Leaves pinnate; crownshafts present, green with reddish brown scales; petioles to 25 cm long; rachis to 1 m long with 3–10 broad or narrow, curved leaflets per side. Inflorescences pendulous, with 2 or 3 densely hairy flowering branches, 15–21 cm long; flowers and fruits spirally arranged along the

flowering branches; fruits ellipsoid, to 1.5 cm long and 0.7 cm diameter, purple-black.

Range and habitat. India (Assam) and Myanmar (Kachin, Sagaing); lowland rain forest, at low elevations.

Uses. None recorded.

Synonym. *Pinanga tomentosa* Henderson

Pinanga hexasticha (Kurz) Scheff.
tawkun (Mya)

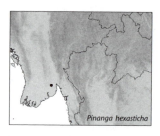
Pinanga hexasticha

Field characters. Stems solitary, to 10 m tall and 10 cm diameter. Leaves pinnate; crownshafts present, green; petioles 7–10 cm long; rachis to 1.5 m long with numerous linear leaflets per side. Inflorescences pendulous, with 1 smooth flowering branch, to 30 cm long; flowers and fruits spirally arranged along the flowering branch; fruits not known.

Range and habitat. Myanmar (Bago); lowland rain forest, often in marshy places in southern parts of Pegu Yomah, at low elevations.

Uses. None recorded.

Notes. Not recently collected and poorly known. Judging by the dimensions in the original description, it must be a spectacular palm.

Synonym. *Areca hexasticha* Kurz

Pinanga humilis Henderson,   PLATE 53
N. K. Ban & N. Q. Dung
cau nui (Vie)

Pinanga humilis

Field characters. Stems clustered, to 1 m tall and 1 cm diameter. Leaves pinnate; crownshafts absent, the sheaths open; petioles to 78 cm long; rachis to 0.4 m long with 5–7 broad to narrow, curved leaflets per side. Inflorescences horizontal, pushing through the disintegrating leaf sheaths, with 1–3 smooth flowering branches, 4–4.5 cm long; flowers and fruits arranged in 2 opposite rows along the flowering

branches; fruits ellipsoid, to 1.7 cm long and 0.5 cm diameter, color not known.
Range and habitat. Vietnam (Central); lowland rain forest at low elevations.
Uses. None recorded.

Pinanga hymenospatha Hook. f.

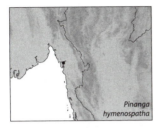

Field characters. Stem branching not known, to approximately 1 m tall and 0.5 cm diameter. Leaves pinnate; crownshafts present, green, with reddish scales; petioles to 8 cm long; rachis to 0.2 m long with 15 or 16 narrow, linear leaflets per side. Inflorescences with 1 smooth flowering branch, 3 cm long; flowers and fruits spirally arranged along the flowering branch; fruits not known.
Range and habitat. Myanmar (Tanintharyi); lowland rain forest, at low elevations.
Uses. None recorded.
Notes. It is remarkable that this distinctive species, first collected in the late 1840s, has never been re-collected. A second collection from the same locality, that of *P. simplicifrons*, has also not been re-collected in Myanmar, and all other collections are from southern Thailand.

Pinanga kontumensis Henderson, N. K. Ban & N. Q. Dung

Field characters. Stem branching not known, to 2 m tall and 1 cm diameter. Leaves pinnate; crownshafts present, green with reddish brown scales; petioles to 3.5 cm long; rachis to 0.25 m long with 3 curved leaflets per side. Inflorescences erect, with 1 smooth flowering branch, 9–11 cm long; flowers and fruits arranged in 2 opposite rows along the flowering branch; fruits ellipsoid, to 1.5 cm long and 0.4 cm diameter, color not known.

Range and habitat. Vietnam (Central); montane rain forest at 1000–1200 m elevation.
Uses. None recorded.
Notes. Futher distinguished by its fruits with homogeneous endosperm.

Pinanga lacei Henderson

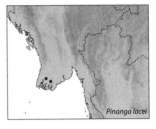

Field characters. Stem branching not known, to 1 m tall and 1 cm diameter. Leaves pinnate; crownshafts present, green with reddish scales; petioles 2–3 cm long; rachis to 0.3 m long with 5–7 linear, curved leaflets per side. Inflorescences with 1 smooth flowering branch, 9–11 cm long; flowers and fruits spirally arranged along the flowering branch; fruits ellipsoid, to 1.5 cm long and 0.7 cm diameter.
Range and habitat. Myanmar (Ayeyarwady); lowland rain forest at low elevations.
Uses. None recorded.

Pinanga malaiana (Mart.) Scheff.
mak nga chang yak (Tha)

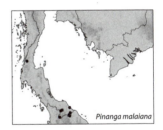

Field characters. Stems clustered, rarely solitary, to 7 m tall and 7 cm diameter. Leaves pinnate; crownshafts present, green with yellowish or purplish scales; petioles 40–130 cm long; rachis to 2 m long with 24–28 linear leaflets per side, these grayish on the lower surfaces. Inflorescences pendulous, with 3–6 smooth, thick flowering branches, 20–29 cm long; flowers and fruits arranged in 2 opposite rows along the flowering branches; fruits oblong to ovoid, to 2.5 cm long and 1.5 cm diameter, ripening green to yellowish red to purple-black.
Range and habitat. Thailand (Peninsular) (also in Peninsular Malaysia and Sumatra); lowland rain forest to 800 m elevation.
Uses. None recorded.

Synonyms. *Areca haematocarpon Griff.*, *Areca malaiana* (Mart.) Griff., *Seaforthia malaiana* Mart., *Ptychosperma malaianum* (Mart.) Miq.

Pinanga manii Becc.
apara, okshuak (And, Ncb)

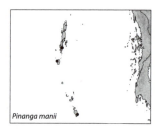
Pinanga manii

Field characters. Stems solitary, to 16 m tall and 15 cm diameter. Leaves pinnate; crownshafts present, green, with reddish scales; petioles 44–61 cm long; rachis to 2 m long with 14–30 linear leaflets per side. Inflorescences pendulous, with 17–50 smooth, spirally arranged flowering branches, 10–23 cm long; flowers and fruits arranged in 2 opposite rows along the flowering branches; fruits ellipsoid, to 2 cm long and 1 cm diameter, red, turning black.
Range and habitat. Andaman (South Andaman) and Nicobar Islands (Great Nicobar Island); lowland rain forest at low elevations.
Uses. The palm hearts are eaten, the leaves are used for thatching, and the stems are used for construction.
Notes. Reports of *P. coronata* (Blume) Blume from the Andaman Islands are probably based on *P. manii*.
Synonyms. *Pinanga andamanensis* Becc., *Pinanga manii* var. *kurziana* Becc.

Pinanga paradoxa (Griff.) Scheff.
mark-jay-dang (Tha)

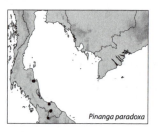
Pinanga paradoxa

Field characters. Stems loosely clustered, spreading by long rhizomes, sometimes new shoots developing at leaf scars, to 1.5 m tall and 0.7 cm diameter. Leaves pinnate; crownshafts present, green, with reddish brown scales; petioles 2–5 cm long; rachis to 0.4 m long with 3–20 narrow, curved leaflets per side. Inflorescences pendulous, with 1 (rarely to 4) smooth flowering branch, 2–6 cm long; flowers and fruits arranged in 2 opposite rows along the flowering branch; fruits ovoid, to 1.8 cm long and 1 cm diameter, ripening red to black.
Range and habitat. Thailand (Peninsular) (also in Peninsular Malaysia); lowland or montane rain forest, to 1300 m elevation.
Uses. None recorded.
Notes. Two varieties are recognized: var. *paradoxa*, with 3–8 multiveined leaflets per side of rachis, from Thailand and Peninsular Malaysia; and var. *unicostata* C. K. Lim, with to 20 one-veined leaflets per side of rachis, from Peninsular Malaysia.
Synonyms. *Areca curvata* Griff., *Areca paradoxa* Griff., *Kentia paradoxa* (Griff.) Mart., *Nengella paradoxa* (Griff.) Becc., *Ophiria paradoxa* (Griff.) Becc., *Pinanga curvata* (Griff.) Becc.

Pinanga perakensis Becc.
che lueang (Tha)

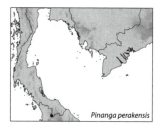
Pinanga perakensis

Field characters. Stems clustered, to 2.5 m tall and 4 cm diameter. Leaves pinnate; crownshafts present, yellowish with reddish brown or purplish scales; petioles 25–60 cm long; rachis to 2 m long with 15–23 linear leaflets per side, these light gray on the lower surfaces. Inflorescences pendulous, with 3–7 smooth flowering branches, 5–8 cm long; flowers and fruits arranged in 2 opposite rows along the flowering branches; fruits oblong to ellipsoid, to 2 cm long and 1 cm diameter, ripening pink to black.
Range and habitat. Thailand (Peninsular) (also in Peninsular Malaysia); lowland or montane rain forest, to 1250 m elevation.
Uses. None recorded.
Synonym. *Pinanga densifolia* Ridl.

Pinanga plicata Henderson   PLATES 53 & 54

Field characters. Stems clustered, to 2 m tall and 1.7 cm diameter. Leaves pinnate; crownshafts present, green with reddish brown scales; petioles very short, to 2 cm long; rachis to 0.4 m long with 3 broad, strongly folded leaflets per side. Inflorescences pendulous, with 3 smooth flowering branches, to 15 cm long; flowers and fruits spirally arranged along the flowering branches; fruits (immature) ellipsoid, 1.5 cm long and 0.7 cm diameter, color not known.

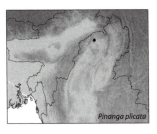

Range and habitat. Myanmar (Kachin); lowland rain forest at low elevations.
Uses. None recorded.

Pinanga polymorpha Ridl.
mak chae (Tha)

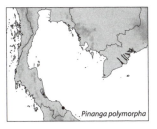

Field characters. Stems clustered, rarely solitary, to 3 m tall and 2.5 cm diameter. Leaves pinnate; crownshafts present, yellowish with brown scales; petioles to 30 cm long; rachis to 0.5 m long with 2 or 3 broad, curved leaflets per side, often mottled light and dark green, often gray on the lower surfaces. Inflorescences usually erect, with 1–4 smooth flowering branches, to 10 cm long; flowers and fruits spirally arranged along the flowering branches; fruits ovoid, to 1.4 cm long and 1.2 cm diameter, purple-black.
Range and habitat. Thailand (Peninsular) (also in Peninsular Malaysia); lowland rain forest to 800 m elevation.
Uses. None recorded
Synonyms. *Pinanga brewsteriana* Ridl., *Pinanga glaucescens* Ridl., *Pinanga robusta* Becc., *Pinanga wrayi* Furtado

Pinanga quadrijuga Gagnep.   PLATE 54
cau rung, lang, r'nan (Vie)

Field characters. Stems clustered, forming large clumps, to 3 m tall and 2 cm diameter, with a continuous covering of gray or brown scales. Leaves pinnate; crownshafts present, green with reddish scales; petioles to 20 cm long; rachis to 0.9 m long with 5 or 6 broad, curved leaflets per side. Inflorescences pendulous, with 2–4 smooth flowering branches, 9.5–12 cm long; flowers and fruits arranged in 2 opposite rows

along the flowering branches; fruits ovoid, to 1.3 cm long and 0.7 cm diameter, pink or red.

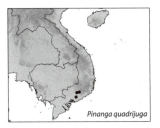

Range and habitat. Vietnam (Southern); lowland rain forest at low elevations.
Uses. None recorded.

Pinanga riparia Ridl.   PLATE 54
mak-j-pru (Tha)

Field characters. Stems loosely clustered, spreading by long rhizomes, to 5 m tall and 3 cm diameter. Leaves pinnate; crownshafts present, green with grayish scales; petioles to 15 cm long; rachis to 0.8 m long with 3–9 narrow, curved leaflets per side. Inflorescences pendulous, with 2–4 smooth flowering branches, 12–20 cm long; flowers and fruits arranged in 2 opposite rows along the flowering branches; fruits oblong to ellipsoid, to 1.3 cm long and 0.7 cm diameter, ripening red to black.
Range and habitat. Thailand (Peninsular) (also in Peninsular Malaysia, Singapore, and Sumatra); lowland rain forest, usually along river banks or other wet places, to 300 m elevation.
Uses. None recorded.
Synonym. *Pinanga patula* var. *riparia* (Ridl.) Becc.

Pinanga scortechinii Becc.
du kong, mark (Tha)

Field characters. Stems clustered, forming loose clusters, to 4 m tall and 5 cm diameter. Leaves pinnate; crownshafts present, green or yellowish; petioles 35–100 cm long; rachis to 2.5 m long with 5–22 (rarely 2) linear leaflets per side, sometimes mottled light and dark green. Inflorescences erect, with 3–9 smooth flowering branches, 5–8 cm long; flowers and fruits arranged spirally along the flowering branches; fruits ovoid to ellipsoid, to 1.5 cm long and 1 cm diameter, black.

Pinanga scortechinii

Range and habitat. Thailand (Peninsular); lowland rain forest to 1000 m elevation.
Uses. None recorded.
Notes. Also in Peninsular Malaysia.
Synonym. *Pinanga fruticans* Ridl.

Pinanga simplicifrons (Miq.) Becc.
mak che bala (Tha)

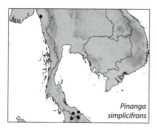

Pinanga simplicifrons

Field characters. Stems clustered, to 1.5 m tall and 1.5 cm diameter. Leaves pinnate or undivided; crownshafts absent, the sheaths open; petioles 7–30 cm long; rachis to 0.3 m long with 2 or 3 broad, curved leaflets per side, or leaves undivided. Inflorescences pendulous, pushing through the disintegrating leaf sheaths, with 1 or 2 smooth flowering branches, 2–3 cm long; flowers and fruits arranged in 2 opposite rows along the flowering branches; fruits ovoid, often curved, to 2 cm long and 1 cm diameter, red.
Range and habitat. Myanmar (Tanintharyi) and Thailand (Peninsular) (also in Borneo, Peninsular Malaysia, and Sumatra); lowland rain forest to 600 m elevation.
Uses. None recorded.
Notes. Two varieties are recognized: var. *simplicifrons*, with undivided or few pinnate leaves, from Borneo, Sumatra, Myanmar, Thailand (Peninsular), and Peninsular Malaysia; and var. *pinnata* C. K. Lim, with pinnate leaves, from Peninsular Malaysia.
Synonym. *Ptychosperma simplicifrons* Miq.

Pinanga subintegra Ridl.

Field characters. Stems clustered, to 1.5 m tall and 0.5 cm diameter. Leaves undivided or pinnate; crown-

shafts present, green; petioles to 17 cm long; rachis to 1 m long with 2–15 linear, curved leaflets per side, or leaves undivided. Inflorescences pendulous, with 1 smooth flowering branch, 4–5 cm long; flowers and fruits arranged in 2 opposite rows along the flowering branch; fruits ellipsoid, to 1.7 cm long and 0.5 cm diameter, red.
Range and habitat. Thailand (Peninsular) (also in Peninsular Malaysia and Sumatra); lowland rain forest at low elevations.
Uses. None recorded.
Notes. Four varieties are recognized: var. *subintegra*, usually with undivided leaves, from Peninsular Malaysia; var. *multifida* (Becc.) C. K. Lim, with more-divided leaves, from Peninsular Malaysia; var. *intermedia* Furtado, with the leaflets more widely spaced, from Thailand and Peninsular Malaysia; and var. *beccariana* (Furtado) C. K. Lim, with one-veined leaflets, from Sumatra and Peninsular Malaysia. Variety *intermedia* was reported by Lim (2001) to occur in Thailand, but no specimens from there have been seen and no map is provided.
Synonyms. *Pinanga beccariana* Furtado, *Pinanga paradoxa* var. *multifida* Becc., *Pinanga paradoxa* var. *subintegra* (Ridl.) Becc.

Pinanga sylvestris (Lour.) Hodel   PLATE 55
sla condor (Cbd), mak ling (Tha), cao cuo chuoc (Vie)

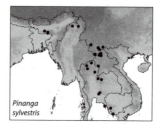

Pinanga sylvestris

Field characters. Stems clustered, to 6 m tall and 3.5 cm diameter. Leaves pinnate; crownshafts present, green or yellowish with reddish scales; petioles 10–25 cm long; rachis to 1.3 m long with 10–28 linear leaflets per side. Inflorescences pendulous, occasionally erect, with 3–8 smooth flowering branches, 9–26 cm long, these triangular in cross section; flowers and fruits arranged in 2 opposite rows along the flowering branches; fruits ellipsoid, to 2.3 cm long and 1 cm diameter, red.
Range and habitat. Cambodia, China (Yunnan), India (Meghalaya), Myanmar (Kachin), Laos, and Thailand (East, North, Southeast); lowland or montane rain forest, 100–1750 m elevation.
Uses. None recorded.
Synonyms. *Areca sylvestris* Lour., *Seaforthia sylvestris* (Lour.) Blume, *Pinanga chinensis* Becc., *Pinanga cochinchinensis* Blume, *Pinanga duperreana* Pierre, *Pinanga hookeriana* Becc., *Pinanga macroclada* Burret, *Ptychosperma cochinchinensis* (Blume) Miq., *Ptychosperma sylvestris* (Lour.) Miq.

Pinanga tashiroi Hayata

Pinanga tashiroi

Field characters. Stems clustered, to 5 m tall and 5 cm diameter. Leaves pinnate; crownshafts present, green; petioles to 60 cm long; rachis to 1.5 m long with numerous linear leaflets per side. Inflorescences pendulous, with about 30 smooth flowering branches, to 21 cm long; flowers and fruits arranged in 2 opposite rows along the flowering branches; fruits ovoid to globose, to 1.8 cm long and 1.2 cm diameter, red.
Range and habitat. Taiwan (Lanyu Island); lowland rain forest to 450 m elevation.
Uses. The seeds are chewed as a substitute for betel nut.
Notes. Close to, and perhaps not distinct from, *P. maculata* Porte of the Philippines.
Synonym. *Pseudopinanga tashiroi* (Hayata) Burret

Pinanga versicolor Henderson   PLATE 55

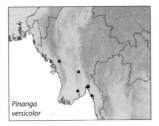

Pinanga versicolor

Field characters. Stems clustered, to 5 m tall and 3.5 cm diameter. Leaves pinnate; crownshafts present, whitish to yellowish with brown scales; petioles 30–70 cm long; rachis to 1 m long with 5–19 broad to narrow, curved leaflets per side, mottled light and dark green especially when newly opened. Inflorescences pendulous, with 3–5 nonhairy flowering branches, 10–15 cm long; flowers and fruits spirally arranged along the flowering branches; fruits ellipsoid, to 1.5 cm long and 0.7 cm diameter, color not known.
Range and habitat. Myanmar (Bago, Magway, Mon, Yangon); lowland or montane rain forest at 100–1400 m elevation.
Uses. None recorded.

Pinanga watanaiana C. K. Lim

Field characters. Stems clustered, to 2.5 m tall and 3.5 cm diameter. Leaves pinnate; crownshafts present, yellowish to brownish with purple-brown scales; petioles 10–45 cm long; rachis 0.7–1 m long with 8–14 linear leaflets per side, mottled light and dark green. Inflorescences pendulous, sometimes erect, with 2–6 hairy flowering branches, 5–20 cm long; flowers and fruits arranged in 2 opposite rows along the flowering branches; fruits ovoid, to 1.5 cm long and 1 cm diameter, ripening red to black.

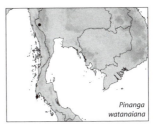

Pinanga watanaiana

Range and habitat. Thailand (Peninsular, Southwest); lowland rain forest, to 500 m elevation.
Uses. None recorded.
Notes. *Pinanga watanaiana*, from Phuket Island, was illustrated by Hodel (1998; plate 71, D, E), although it was given the name *P. fruticans* (that name is now regarded as a synonym of *P. scortechinii*). A second illustration (plate 72, A) is of a plant from much farther north, in Kanchanaburi Province. *Pinanga watanaiana* is thus known only from two distant localities. It bears a close resemblance to *P. versicolor*, but differs in its hairy flowering branches with flowers and fruits arranged in 2 opposite rows.

PLECTOCOMIA Mart. & Blume

This rattan genus contains some of the largest climbing palms in terms of stem diameter. Although stems usually appear solitary, in some species basal shoots can develop into new plants after the main stem dies, and in other species branches appear on stems above ground level. Leaves are pinnate and to 20 or more in number. Leaf sheaths, as in the related *Plectocomiopsis* and *Myrialepis*, lack knees and flagella, and *Plectocomia* also lacks an ocrea. Sheaths are usually covered in distinctive spines and brownish or whitish hairs. The spines are often arranged in oblique rows consisting of closely spaced spines joined to one another at their bases, resembling combs. The leaf rachis terminates in a long cirrus, lacking leaflets but with grapnel-like spines. Leaflets are irregularly (rarely regularly) arranged along the rachis and usually spread in different planes, giving the leaf a plumose appearance. Leaflets are sometimes green but more often grayish on the lower surfaces, but this gray covering may wear off as the leaf ages.

Plectocomia is semelparous; all inflorescences, 2–20 at a time at the stem apex, are produced and flower together over a short period of time, and after fruiting the stem dies. Plants are also dioecious.

Key to the Species of *Plectocomia*

1a. Leaflets green on the lower surfaces, minutely spiny on the margins, with elongate
   threadlike apices, without prominent submarginal veins . . . . *P. himalayana.*
1b. Leaflets grayish on the lower surfaces, not or rarely spiny along the margins, without
   elongate, threadlike apices, with prominent submarginal veins . . . . 2.

2a. Leaflets regularly arranged and spreading in the same plane; northeastern India (Arunachal
   Pradesh, Assam, Meghalaya) and northern Myanmar (Kachin, Sagaing) . . . . *P. assamica.*
2b. Leaflets clustered and spreading in different planes, rarely almost regularly arranged;
   Cambodia, China (Hainan, Yunnan), Laos, Myanmar (Tanintharyi), Thailand (Central,
   East, North, Peninsular), and Vietnam . . . . 3.

3a. Leaf sheath spines borne on ridges in distinct, long, oblique rows; fruit scales with reddish
   brown, woolly, lacerate, erect apices; Cambodia, Myanmar (Tanintharyi), Thailand
   (Peninsular), and Vietnam (Central) . . . . *P. elongata.*
3b. Leaf sheath spines solitary or usually borne in short rows; fruit scales fringed only; China
   (Hainan, Yunnan), Cambodia, Laos, Thailand (Central, East, North), and Vietnam . . . . 4.

4a. China (Hainan) . . . . *P. microstachys.*
4b. Cambodia, China (Yunnan), Laos, Thailand (Central, East, North), and Vietnam . . . . *P. pierreana.*

Inflorescences are usually branched to two orders, and are borne among reduced-size leaves. Inflorescences are covered in distinctive, overlapping bracts that obscure the flowers. In fact, the name of the genus is derived from these bracts, from the Greek words *plectos*, meaning plaited, and *come*, meaning hair, in reference to the supposed similarity of the flowering branches to plaited hair. Male flowers are very fragrant and are borne in pairs, and these are densely crowded along the short flowering branches. Female flowers are solitary and fewer per flowering branch. Fruits are globose, brownish, usually one-seeded, and are covered with overlapping scales. The apices of these scales are sometimes woolly with lacerate, erect apices, giving the fruit a spiny or fuzzy appearance. The endosperm is homogeneous, germination is adjacent, and the seedling leaf is undivided.

Plectocomia contains 16 species, widely distributed from northwestern India to China, and reaching south into the Philippines, Borneo, Sumatra, and Java. Five species occur in our area (Evans et al. 2001, 2002; Hodel 1998; Madulid 1981).

Plectocomia assamica Griff.   PLATES 55 & 56
runool (Ind), sin kyein (Mya)

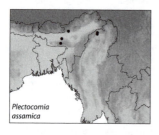

Plectocomia
assamica

Field characters. Stems solitary, climbing, to 15 m long and 15 cm diameter. Leaf sheaths grayish green

with reddish brown hairs, with scattered or short rows of yellowish brown, stout, to 6-cm-long spines; leaf rachis to 5 m long with 18–44 lanceolate leaflets per side, these regularly arranged and spreading in the same plane, silvery gray on the lower surfaces, with prominent submarginal veins and nonspiny margins; cirri to 2.5 m long. Inflorescences to 1 m long; flowering branch bracts to 5 cm long, felty on outer surfaces; fruits globose, to 2.5 cm diameter; fruit scales reddish brown with woolly, lacerate, erect apices.

Range and habitat. India (Arunachal Pradesh, Assam, Meghalaya) and northern Myanmar (Kachin, Sagaing); lowland rain forest on steep slopes at 220–850 m elevation.

Uses. The stems are sometimes used in furniture making.

Notes. The very thick stems are not flexible as in other rattans, and remain stiff and erect.

Synonyms. *Plectocomia bractealis* Becc., *Plectocomia khasyana* Griff.

Plectocomia elongata Mart. &   PLATE 56
Blume
kyein-ban (Mya), wai-tong-plong, wai-pongg-rad (Tha), cây mây tuong (Vie)

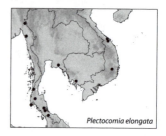

Plectocomia elongata

Field characters. Stems solitary or with basal shoots, to 50 m long and 15 cm diameter. Leaf sheaths dark green with whitish or brownish hairs, with oblique rows of brown, needlelike, to 4-cm-long spines; leaf rachis to 6 m long with 40–70 lanceolate leaflets per side, these clustered and spreading in different planes, grayish on the lower surfaces, with prominent submarginal veins and nonspiny margins; cirri to 3 m long. Inflorescences to 1 m long; flowering branch bracts to 7 cm long, with few feltlike hairs on outer surfaces; fruits globose, to 3 cm diameter; fruit scales reddish brown with woolly, lacerate, erect apices.

Range and habitat. Cambodia, Myanmar (Kayin, Mon, Tanintharyi), Thailand (Peninsular, Southeast), and Vietnam (Central) (also in Borneo, Java, Peninsular Malaysia, the Philippines, Singapore, and Sumatra); lowland or montane rain forest or seasonal forest, often in disturbed places, to 2000 m elevation.

Uses. The stems are used in basketry. As with other species of *Plectocomia*, the stems split too easily to be of much use.

Notes. Two varieties are recognized: var. *elongata*, with solitary stems, from Borneo, Java, Singapore, Sumatra, Thailand, Myanmar, Vietnam, and Peninsular Malaysia; and var. *philippinensis* Madulid, with clustered stems, from the Philippines.

Synonyms. *Calamus maximus* Reinw., *Plectocomia crinita* Gentil, *Plectocomia elongata* var. *bangkana* Becc., *Plectocomia griffithii* Becc., *Plectocomia hystrix* Linden, *Plectocomia ichythospinus* auct., *Plectocomia macrostachya* Kurz, *Plectocomia sumatrana* Miq., *Rotang maximus* Baill.

Plectocomia himalayana Griff.   PLATE 56
gowri bet (Bhu), gao-di-gou-ye-teng (Chi), runool, tehri bet (Ind), wai hok (Tha)

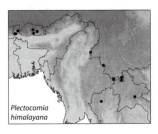

Plectocomia himalayana

Field characters. Stems clustered or sometimes solitary, flexuose, climbing, to 20 m long and 10 cm diameter. Leaf sheaths brown with brownish hairs, with rows of brown, needlelike, to 2.5-cm-long spines encircling the sheath; leaf rachis to 1.5 m long with 25–30 lanceolate leaflets per side, these clustered and spreading in different planes, green on the lower surfaces, usually attached by short stalks, with elongate, threadlike apices, without prominent submarginal veins and minutely spiny on the margins; cirri to 1 m long. Inflorescences to 0.8 m long; flowering branch bracts densely hairy on outer surfaces; fruits globose, to 1.5 cm diameter; fruit scales yellowish brown, fringed, without bristly, erect apices.

Range and habitat. Bhutan, China (Yunnan), India (Sikkim, West Bengal), Laos (Northern), Nepal, and Thailand (North); montane rain forest at 1500–2500 m elevation.

Uses. The stems are too soft to be of much use, but the pith from the stem is occasionally eaten.

Synonym. *Plectocomia montana* Griff.

Plectocomia microstachys Burret   PLATE 57
hsiao-gou-ye-teng, xiao gou ye teng (Chi)

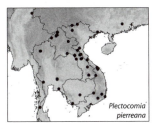

Plectocomia microstachys

Field characters. Stems solitary, climbing, to 15 m long and 6 cm diameter. Leaf sheaths green with whitish hairs, with short rows of yellowish, needlelike, to 1-cm-long spines; leaf rachis to 1.5 m long with 25–30 lanceolate leaflets per side, these clustered and spreading in different planes, grayish on the lower surfaces, with prominent submarginal veins and nonspiny margins; cirri to 1.5 m long. Inflorescences to 0.7 m long; flowering branch bracts to 2.5 cm long, not hairy on outer surfaces; fruits globose to ellipsoid, to 2 cm diameter; fruit scales brownish, fringed only, without bristly, erect apices.

Range and habitat. China (Hainan); lowland rain forest at 300–950 m elevation.

Uses. None recorded.

Notes. Very similar to, and perhaps not distinct from *P. pierreana*.

Plectocomia pierreana Becc.   PLATE 57
phdau tres (Cbd), gou-ye-teng (Chi), wai chawang, wai lao (Lao), geh pah deh, wai sadao (Tha), gol sieng (Vie)

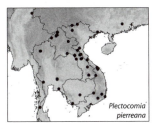

Plectocomia pierreana

Field characters. Stems solitary or clustered, sometimes branching above ground, climbing, to 50 m long and 10 cm diameter. Leaf sheaths green with reddish brown hairs, with stout, yellowish brown, to

2-cm-long spines, these usually borne in short rows; leaf rachis to 4 m long with 18–40 linear-lanceolate to broadly lanceolate leaflets per side, these clustered and spreading in different planes, sometimes almost regularly arranged, grayish on the lower surfaces, with prominent submarginal veins and nonspiny margins; cirri to 1.5 m long. Inflorescences to 1.1 m long; flowering branch bracts to 5 cm long, not or scarcely hairy on outer surfaces; fruits globose to ellipsoid, to 2.3 cm diameter; fruit scales yellowish brown, fringed only, without bristly, erect apices.
Range and habitat. Cambodia, China (Guangdong, Guangxi, Yunnan), Laos (Central), Thailand (Central, East, North), and Vietnam (throughout); lowland or montane rain forest to 1200 m elevation.
Uses. Provides a poor-quality cane used in handicrafts; the shoot is eaten.
Notes. *Plectocomia kerriana* was recognized as a distinct species by Evans et al. (2002), but is included here in *P. pierreana*. The only two known specimens of *P. kerriana* have leaflets with minutely spiny margins—unusual in *P. pierreana*—and are from the same locality as the only specimen of *P. himalayana* from Thailand.
Synonyms. *Plectocomia barthiana* Hodel, *Plectocomia cambodiana* Gagnep., *Plectocomia kerriana* Becc.

PLECTOCOMIOPSIS Becc.

This genus is very similar to the preceding, hence the name, meaning *Plectocomia*-like. Stems are clustered and climb high into the canopy. One unusual feature of some species is that the naked stems are triangular in cross section. Leaves are pinnate, to 22 in number, and are borne in a spiral pattern. Leaf sheaths, as in the related *Plectocomia* and *Myrialepis*, lack knees and flagella, but an ocrea is usually present. Sheaths are covered with short, scattered spines, although sometimes these are absent. The leaf rachis terminates in a long cirrus, lacking leaflets but with grapnel-like spines. Leaflets are regularly arranged along the rachis, and spread in the same plane. They have long, narrow apices, and are green with conspicuous, yellow spines on the upper surfaces.

Plectocomiopsis is semelparous; all inflorescences, 5–15 at a time at the stem apex, are produced and flower together over a short period of time, and after fruiting the stem dies. Plants are also dioecious. Inflorescences are branched to two or three orders and are borne among the leaves. Inflorescences are covered in overlapping bracts. Male flowers are borne in dense clusters along the short flowering branches, and female flowers are also borne in small

groups. Fruits are more or less globose, brownish, usually one-seeded, and are covered with overlapping scales. The endosperm is homogeneous, germination is adjacent, and the seedling leaf is bifid.

Plectocomiopsis contains five species, two of which occur in our area (Dransfield 1979a; Evans et al. 2001, 2002; Hodel 1998).

Plectocomiopsis geminiflora (Griff.)   PLATE 57
Becc.
phdau chno (Cbd), wai deng (Lao), wai-gung-nam-pry, wai kung (Tha), may dot dang (Vie)

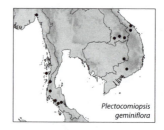

Plectocomiopsis geminiflora

Field characters. Stems clustered, forming thickets, climbing, to 50 m long and 6 cm diameter. Leaf sheaths green with grayish hairs and scattered, yellow, needlelike, to 6-cm-long spines; ocrea dry, becoming tattered; leaf rachis to 3 m long with 20–45 lanceolate leaflets per side, these regularly arranged; cirri to 2 m long. Inflorescences to 0.4 m long; fruits depressed globose, to 3 cm long and 3.5 cm diameter, brown.
Range and habitat. Cambodia, Laos (Southern), Myanmar (Tanintharyi), Thailand (Peninsular), and Vietnam (also in Borneo, Peninsular Malaysia, and Sumatra); lowland or montane rain forest, usually in disturbed places, to 800 m elevation.
Uses. Provides a poor-quality cane used in basketry; the palm heart is eaten.
Synonyms. *Calamus geminiflorus* Griff., *Calamus turbinatus* Ridl., *Plectocomia geminiflora* (Griff.) H. Wendl., *Plectocomiopsis geminiflora* var. *billitonensis* Becc., *Plectocomiopsis geminiflora* var. *borneensis* Becc.

Plectocomiopsis wrayi Becc.
wai daeng (Tha)

Field characters. Stems clustered, forming thickets, climbing, to 30 m long and 4 cm diameter, naked stems triangular in cross section. Leaf sheaths green with reddish brown hairs and scattered, yellow, needlelike, to 0.3-cm-long spines; ocrea very short,

Key to the Species of *Plectocomiopsis*

1a. Leaf sheath spines to 6 cm long; ocrea becoming tattered; Cambodia, Laos (Southern),
    Myanmar (Tanintharyi), Thailand (Peninsular), and Vietnam . . . . *P. geminiflora.*
1b. Leaf sheath spines to 0.3 cm long; ocrea not becoming tattered; Thailand (Peninsular) . . . . . . *P. wrayi.*

yellowish brown; leaf rachis to 1.5 m long with 15–22 lanceolate leaflets per side, these regularly arranged; cirri to 1 m long. Inflorescences to 0.5 m long; fruits depressed globose, to 2.7 cm long and 3 cm diameter, brown.

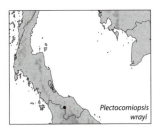

Plectocomiopsis wrayi

Range and habitat. Thailand (Peninsular) (also in Peninsular Malaysia); lowland rain forest, usually in swamps, to 250 m elevation.
Uses. None recorded.
Synonym. *Plectocomiopsis dubia* Becc.

RHAPIS L. f.

Stems are slender, clustered, and spread by rhizomes to form small to large clumps. The name *Rhapis* is based on these stems and comes from the same Greek word, meaning a rod. Stems are covered, especially in the upper part, with fibrous, persistent leaf bases—otherwise they are green. *Rhapis* is one of the very few coryphoid palms that have elongate internodes, usually visible near the base of the stem. Leaves are small, palmate, and 12–22 in number. Leaf sheaths are fibrous and consist of two layers of fibers, sometimes of different thicknesses, and these form a square or diagonal mesh. At the apices of the sheaths are fibrous ocreas, which either persist or disintegrate. At the apices of the petioles there are small hastulas. Leaflets are few to numerous, and the number of leaflets per leaf is a useful identification character, as is the degree of splitting between the leaflets. The folding of the leaves is interesting. In most coryphoid palms, the leaflets are V-shaped in cross section, a condition known as induplicate. In *Rhapis*,

Key to the Species of *Rhapis*

1a. Leaflets with more or less straight sides and jagged apices; China (Fujian, Guangdong, Hainan, Hong Kong, Yunnan, and possibly Guizhou) and Vietnam (Central, Northern) . . . . *R. excelsa*.
1b. Leaflets with curved sides and more or less pointed apices; China, Laos, Thailand, and Vietnam . . . . 2.

2a. Blades split to the base, or at least some leaflets split to the base . . . . 3.
2b. Blades not split to the base . . . . 6.

3a. Leaflets linear; Vietnam (Northern) . . . . *R. vidalii*.
3b. Leaflets lanceolate; China (Guangdong, Guangxi, Hainan), Laos (Central), Thailand (Central, East, Northeast, Southeast, Southwest), and Vietnam (Central, Northern) . . . . 4.

4a. Fruits not borne on short stalks; Laos (Central), Thailand (Central, East, Northeast, Southeast, Southwest), and Vietnam (Central) . . . . *R. subtilis*.
4b. Fruits borne on short stalks; China (Guangdong, Guangxi, Hainan) and Vietnam (Northern) . . . . . . 5.

5a. Leaflets 2–4; China (Guangdong, Guangxi, Hainan) . . . . *R. gracilis*.
5b. Leaflets 5–10; Vietnam (Northern) . . . . *R. micrantha*.

6a. Blades split for about half their length; Vietnam (Central) . . . . *R. puhuongensis*.
6b. Blades split for more than half their length; China (Guangxi, Guizhou, eastern Yunnan), Thailand (Peninsular), and Vietnam (Central, Northern) . . . . 7.

7a. First inflorescence bract swollen, splitting laterally, with the inflorescence emerging laterally from the bract; Laos (Central, Northern), Thailand (Northeast), and Vietnam (Central, Northern) . . . . *R. laosensis*.
7b. First inflorescence bract tubular, splitting apically, with the inflorescence emerging apically from the bract; China, Laos, Thailand, and Vietnam . . . . 8.

8a. Blades divided into 3–6 leaflets; China (Guangxi) and Vietnam (Northern) . . . . *R. robusta*.
8b. Blades divided into 5–23 leaflets; China (Guangxi, Guizhou, eastern Yunnan), Thailand (Peninsular), and Vietnam (Central, Northern) . . . . 9.

9a. Fruits borne on short stalks; China (Guangxi, eastern Yunnan) and probably Vietnam (Northern) . . . . *R. multifida*.
9b. Fruits not borne on short stalks; China (Guizhou and possibly Guangxi) and Thailand (Peninsular) . . . 10.

10a. Flowering branches hairy; China (Guizhou and possibly Guangxi) . . . . *R. humilis*.
10b. Flowering branches not hairy; Thailand (Peninsular) . . . . *R. siamensis*.

the splits take place between the upper and lower folds, rather than along the upper fold. Another distinctive feature of *Rhapis* leaves is the minute "thorns," almost like saw teeth, that occur along the leaflet margins and on the veins. You can feel them even if you can't see them!

Inflorescences are branched to three orders and are borne among the leaves. They are covered with persistent bracts. These closely sheath the inflorescence in most species, but in one they are swollen and nonsheathing. Inflorescences usually bear either all male or all female flowers (i.e., dioecious). However, occasionally bisexual flowers are produced. Flowers are simple in structure, borne singly, and male flowers have six stamens. Fruits are small, globose to ellipsoid or ovoid, variously colored, usually one-seeded, and sometimes borne on short stalks. The endosperm is homogeneous (although penetrated by an irregular intrusion of the seed coat), germination is remote, and the seedling leaf is undivided.

Rhapis contains 11 species, widely distributed from southern China to Thailand, Laos, and Vietnam, with an outlying occurrence in Sumatra. All species occur in our area (Averyanov et al. 2006; Beccari 1933; Hastings 2003; Hodel 1998; Trudgen et al., 2008). Plants are commonly grown as ornamentals, and have been introduced into many areas, including southern Japan where they have become naturalized.

Stem diameter measurements given here do not include the leaf sheaths.

Rhapis excelsa (Thunb.) A. Henry   PLATE 58
tsung, tsung-chu (Chi), cau lui (Vie)

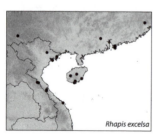

Rhapis excelsa

Field characters. Stems clustered, to 3 m tall and 2 cm diameter. Ocreas not persistent; blades not split to the base, divided into 2–15 leaflets, these with more or less straight sides and jagged apices. Inflorescences borne among the leaves, branched to 2 or 3 orders; first inflorescence bract tubular, splitting apically, with the inflorescence emerging apically from the bract; flowering branches not hairy; fruits globose to ellipsoid, to 1 cm long and 0.8 cm diameter, yellow.
Range and habitat. China (Fujian, Guangdong, Hainan, Hong Kong, Yunnan, possibly Guizhou) and Vietnam (Central, Northern); scattered localities in lowland forest or dry forest, to 1000 m elevation.

Uses. The stems are used for chopsticks and walking sticks; widely planted as an ornamental, and introduced into Japan.
Synonyms. *Chamaerops excelsa* Thunb., *Chamaerops kwanwortsik* Siebold, *Rhapis aspera* W. Baxter, *Rhapis cordata* W. Baxter, *Rhapis divaricata* Gagnep., *Rhapis flabelliformis* L'Hér., *Rhapis kwamwonzick* Siebold, *Rhapis major* Blume, *Trachycarpus excelsus* (Thunb.) H. Wendl.

Rhapis gracilis Burret
tsung (Chi)

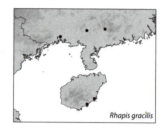

Rhapis gracilis

Field characters. Stems clustered, to 2 m tall and 0.5 cm diameter. Ocreas not persistent; blades split to the base, divided into 2–4 leaflets, these with curved sides and more or less pointed apices. Inflorescences borne among the leaves, branched to 2 orders; first inflorescence bract tubular, splitting apically, with the inflorescence emerging apically from the bract; flowering branches usually not hairy; fruits globose, to 0.8 cm diameter, blue-green, borne on short stalks.
Range and habitat. China (Guangdong, Guangxi, Hainan); lowland forest on limestone slopes, to 900 m elevation.
Uses. None recorded.
Notes. Hastings (2003) included Laos (Central) in the range of this species, but no specimens from there have been seen.

Rhapis humilis Blume
tsung (Chi)

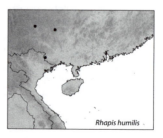

Rhapis humilis

Field characters. Stems clustered, to 6 m tall and 3 cm diameter. Ocreas persistent; blades not split to the base, divided into 7–20 leaflets, these with curved sides and more or less pointed apices. Inflorescences borne among the leaves, branched to 3 orders; first inflorescence bract tubular, splitting apically, with the inflorescence emerging apically from the bract; flowering branches hairy; fruits not known.

Range and habitat. China (Guizhou, possibly Guangxi); lowland dry forest on slopes, to 1000 m elevation.

Uses. Planted as an ornamental.

Notes. Naturalized in Japan (Kyushu Island). A doubtful species, known mostly from cultivated plants of unknown origin.

Synonyms. *Chamaerops excelsa* var. *humilior* Thunb., *Chamaerops sirotsik* H. Wendl., *Licuala waraguh* Blume, *Licuala wixu* Blume, *Rhapis javanica* Blume, *Rhapis sirotsik* H. Wendl.

Rhapis laosensis Becc. PLATE 58
may khaing, thao shan (Lao), jung (Tha), cay lui (Vie)

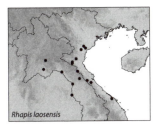

Rhapis laosensis

Field characters. Stems clustered, to 3 m tall and 2 cm diameter. Ocreas usually not persistent; blades not split to the base, divided into 3–15 leaflets, these with curved sides and pointed, hooded apices. Inflorescences borne among the leaves, branched to 2 orders; first inflorescence bract swollen, splitting laterally, with the inflorescence emerging laterally from the bract and curving down; flowering branches short, not hairy; fruits ovoid-ellipsoid, to 1 cm long and 0.8 cm diameter, color not known.

Range and habitat. Laos (Central, Northern), Thailand (Northeast), and Vietnam (Central, Northern); lowland, dry forest, often on limestone soils on rocky slopes, to 600 m elevation.

Uses. Planted as an ornamental.

Synonym. *Rhapis macrantha* Gagnep.

Rhapis micrantha Becc. PLATE 59
cay lui (Vie)

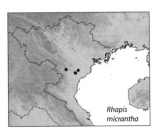

Rhapis micrantha

Field characters. Stems clustered, to 2 m tall and 1 cm diameter. Ocreas not persistent; blades split to the base, divided into 5–10 leaflets, these with curved sides and more or less pointed apices. Inflorescences borne among the leaves, branched to 3 orders; first inflorescence bract tubular, splitting apically, with the inflorescence emerging apically from the bract; flowering branches not hairy or with few hairs; fruits globose to ellipsoid, to 0.8 cm diameter, white, borne on short stalks.

Range and habitat. Vietnam (Northern); lowland forest on slopes of limestone mountains, to 1000 m elevation.

Uses. Widely planted as an ornamental.

Notes. Hastings (2003) included Laos (Central) in the range of this species, but no specimens from there have been seen.

Rhapis multifida Burret
tzung-chu (Chi)

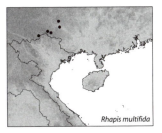

Rhapis multifida

Field characters. Stems clustered, to 2.5 m tall and 2.5 cm diameter. Ocreas persistent; blades not split to the base, divided into 14–23 linear leaflets, these with curved sides and more or less pointed apices. Inflorescences borne among the leaves, branched to 3 orders; first inflorescence bract tubular, splitting apically, with the inflorescence emerging apically from the bract; flowering branches hairy; fruits globose, to 0.8 cm diameter, yellow, borne on short stalks.

Range and habitat. China (Guangxi, eastern Yunnan) and probably Vietnam (Northern); lowland and montane forest on rocky slopes, to 1500 m elevation.

Uses. Planted as an ornamental.

Rhapis puhuongensis M. S. Trudgen, PLATE 59
T. P. Anh & Henderson
lui (Vie)

Field characters. Stems clustered, to 1 m tall and 0.5 cm diameter. Ocreas persistent; blades split to about half their length, divided into 14–16 leaflets, these with curved sides and pointed apices. Inflorescences borne among the leaves, branched to 2 orders; first inflorescence bract tubular, splitting laterally, with the inflorescence emerging laterally from the bract; bracts scarcely overlapping; flowering branches hairy; fruits ellipsoid, to 0.5 cm diameter, color not known, borne on long, swollen stalks.

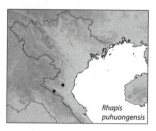

Rhapis
puhuongensis

Range and habitat. Vietnam (Central); lowland forest on slopes on limestone mountains, at low elevations.
Uses. None recorded.

Rhapis robusta Burret
zhongzhu (Chi)

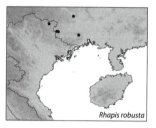

Rhapis robusta

Field characters. Stems clustered, to 1.5 m tall and 0.6 cm diameter. Ocreas persistent; blades not split to the base, divided into 3–6 leaflets, these with curved sides and more or less pointed apices. Inflorescences borne among the leaves, branched to 2 orders; first inflorescence bract tubular, splitting apically, with the inflorescence emerging apically from the bract; bracts not or scarcely overlapping; flowering branches usually not hairy; fruits ellipsoid, to 0.5 cm diameter, color not known, borne on short stalks.
Range and habitat. China (Guangxi) and Vietnam (Northern); lowland forest on slopes on limestone mountains, 300–1000 m elevation.
Uses. None recorded.

Rhapis siamensis Hodel
jung (Tha)

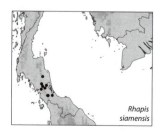

Rhapis
siamensis

Field characters. Stems clustered, to 5 m tall and 2.5 cm diameter. Ocreas not persistent; blades not split to the base, divided into 5–12 leaflets, these with curved sides and more or less pointed apices. Inflorescences borne among the leaves, branched to 1 or 2 orders; first inflorescence bract tubular, splitting apically, with the inflorescence emerging apically from the bract; flowering branches not hairy; fruits globose to ovoid, to 1 cm diameter, whitish.
Range and habitat. Thailand (Peninsular); lowland forest on limestone outcrops, to 200 m elevation.
Uses. Widely cultivated as an ornamental plant.
Notes. Although Hastings (2003) included *R. siamensis* within *R. subtilis*, there appear to be consistent differences between the two, and here *R. siamensis* is recognized as a distinct species.

Rhapis subtilis Becc.
cay lui (Lao), jung (Tha), mat cat lao (Vie)

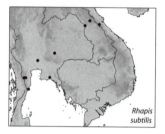

Rhapis
subtilis

Field characters. Stems clustered, to 2.5 m tall and 2 cm diameter. Ocreas not persistent; blades split to the base, at least in some leaflets, divided into 2–13 leaflets, these with curved sides and more or less pointed apices. Inflorescences borne among the leaves, branched to 1 or 2 orders; first inflorescence bract tubular, splitting apically, with the inflorescence emerging apically from the bract; flowering branches not hairy; fruits globose to ovoid, to 0.5 cm diameter, whitish.
Range and habitat. Laos (Central), Thailand (Central, East, Northeast, Southeast, Southwest), and Vietnam (Central) (also in Sumatra); deciduous forest or scrub forest on sandstone soils, at low elevations.
Uses. Widely cultivated as an ornamental plant.
Notes. Very variable in size.

Rhapis vidalii Aver., H. T. Nguyen   PLATE 60
& L. K. Phan
lui, tanh san (Vie)

Field characters. Stems clustered, to 2 m tall and 0.5 cm diameter. Ocreas not persistent; blades split to the base, divided into 6–10 narrow leaflets, these with curved sides and pointed apices. Inflorescences borne among the leaves, branched to 3 orders; first inflorescence bract tubular, splitting laterally, with the inflorescence emerging laterally from the bract;

flowering branches not hairy; fruits globose, to 0.9 cm diameter, white, borne on long stalks.

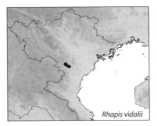

Rhapis vidalii

Range and habitat. Vietnam (Northern); lowland seasonal forest on limestone soils, at 300–800 m elevation.
Uses. None recorded.

RHOPALOBLASTE L. f.
(Ptychoraphis Becc.)

Stems are small to large, solitary or rarely clustered, and are ringed with prominent leaf scars. Leaves are pinnate and 5–17 in number. Leaf sheaths are closed and form a prominent, green crownshaft, although this is sometimes obscured by persistent, old leaves. Petioles are short to elongate. Leaflets are regularly arranged along the rachis and spread in the same plane. They are linear and one-veined, and sometimes pendulous.

Inflorescences are branched to four orders and are borne below the crownshaft. They are covered initially with two bracts, and these fall before flowering time. Inflorescences bear numerous, slender flowering branches. One distinctive feature of all but one species is that the two basal branches of the inflorescence are strongly recurved. Flowers are unisexual and are borne in threes of a central female and two lateral males. Fruits are small; globose, ovoid, or ellipsoid; orange, red, or yellow; and one-seeded. The endosperm is ruminate and the embryo is large. The derivation of the name is from the Greek words *rhopalon*, meaning a club, and *blaste*, meaning a bud, in reference to the large, club-shaped embryo. Germination is adjacent and seedling leaves are pinnate.

Rhopaloblaste contains six species, occurring in the Nicobar Islands, Western Malaysia, the Moluccas, New Guinea, New Ireland, and the Solomon Islands. One species occurs in our area (Banka & Baker 2004).

Rhopaloblaste augusta (Kurz) PLATE 60
H. E. Moore

Field characters. Stems solitary, to 25 m tall and 30 cm diameter. Leaves pinnate; petiole very short; leaflets regularly arranged, spreading in the same plane, pendulous, to 100 per side of rachis. Inflores-

cences borne below the leaves; fruits ellipsoid, to 2.6 cm long and 1.5 cm diameter, orange-red.

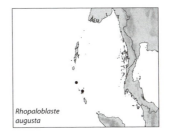

Rhopaloblaste augusta

Range and habitat. Nicobar Islands (Camorta, Car Nicobar, possibly other islands); scrub or mixed forest at low elevations.
Uses. None recorded.
Synonyms. *Areca augusta* Kurz, *Ptychoraphis augusta* (Kurz) Becc.

SALACCA Reinw.
(Lophospatha Burret, Salakka Reinw., Zalacca Rumph.)

The name of this genus comes from the local Malay name, *salak*. Stems are clustered, short and subterranean, and are mostly obscured by the persistent leaf bases. Leaves are pinnate, sometimes undivided (not ours), spiny, and 6–20 per stem in number. Leaf sheaths are open and do not form crownshafts. Sheaths and petioles are elongate and covered in flattened spines. These spines are often in short rows or sometimes arranged in whorls that completely encircle the sheaths and petioles. Leaflets of pinnate leaves are usually sigmoid, less often linear, and are regularly arranged and spread in the same plane or, more often, are irregularly arranged and spread in different planes. In some species the leaflets (or leaves, if undivided) are silvery gray on the lower surfaces (not ours). The leaflets at the apex of pinnate-leafed plants are usually joined, giving a compound terminal leaflet, sometimes called a flabellum. A few species do not have this compound terminal leaflet.

There are two kinds of flowering in *Salacca*. A few species are semelparous, and the inflorescences are borne simultaneously in the axils of reduced leaves on a short stem. After flowering, the stem dies. Most species are iteroparous, and the inflorescences are borne sequentially, emerging from a groove on the outer side of the subtending leaf sheath. Unlike the leaves, inflorescences are not spiny. They are branched to two orders or sometimes spicate and are covered in numerous, persistent, sheathing bracts. Plants are dioecious, and male and female inflorescences of the same species can be quite different from one another in general appearance. They can be very short and spicate, short and branched, or very long, branched, and rooting at the apex and forming new plants. In male inflorescences the flowers are borne

Key to the Species of *Salacca*

1a. Leaflets linear, those at apex of leaf split, or the apical pair sometimes not split or only partially so; plants semelparous, the inflorescences borne simultaneously in the axils of reduced leaves on a short stem; China, northeastern India, Myanmar (Kachin, Sagaing), and Thailand (North) . . . . 2.
1b. Leaflets sigmoid, those at apex of leaf not split, or only briefly split, forming a broad, compound, terminal leaflet; plants iteroparous, the inflorescences borne sequentially, emerging from a groove on the outer side of the subtending sheath; Myanmar (Bago, Karen, Mon, Tanintharyi, Yangon) and Thailand (Peninsular, Southeast) . . . . 3.

2a. Leaflets regularly arranged and spreading in the same plane . . . . *S. griffithii.*
2b. Leaflets irregularly arranged and spreading in different planes . . . . *S. secunda.*

3a. Sheath and petiole spines in whorls surrounding the sheath and petiole; leaf rachis to 7 m long, with 40–60 leaflets per side . . . . *S. wallichiana.*
3b. Sheath and petiole spines solitary or in short rows; leaf rachis to 4 m long, with 23–30 leaflets per side . 4.

4a. Stems loosely clustered; male inflorescences to 4 m long, rooting at the apex and forming new plants; male flowering branches 3, hairy . . . . *S. stolonifera.*
4b. Stems densely clustered; male inflorescences to 0.6 m long, erect and not rooting at the apex; male flowering branches to 25, not hairy . . . . *S. glabrescens.*

in densely arranged pairs on short, thick flowering branches. In female inflorescences the flowers are either solitary or borne in pairs, and are also densely arranged on the flowering branches. Fruits are ovoid, obovoid, or pear-shaped; reddish brown; usually 3-seeded; and are covered in numerous overlapping scales. In all species the tips of the scales are turned up and give the fruit a spiny appearance. The endosperm is homogeneous, germination is adjacent, and the seedling leaf is bifid.

Salacca contains about 20 species, widespread from northeastern India and Myanmar through southern China, Thailand, and western Malaysia to Sumatra, Java, Borneo, and the Philippines. *Salacca* is not easily distinguished from *Eleiodoxa*, and the two genera need reassessing (Henderson 2008). Five species occur in our area (Henderson 2008; Hodel 1998). Another species from outside of our area, *S. zalacca* (Gaertn.) Voss, is commonly cultivated for its edible fruits, and is seen in southern Peninsular Thailand.

Salacca glabrescens Griff.   PLATE 60
sala, sala thai (Tha)

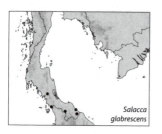

Field characters. Stems short and subterranean, densely clustered. Sheaths and petioles with short

rows of spines; leaf rachis 2–4 m long with 23–30 sigmoid leaflets per side, these irregularly arranged in clusters and spreading in slightly different planes, apical leaflets not split, forming a broad, compound, terminal leaflet. Male inflorescences to 0.6 m long, with to 25 nonhairy flowering branches; female inflorescences to 0.25 m long; fruits pear-shaped, to 5 cm long and 4 cm diameter, reddish, densely covered in flattened, spinelike scales.

Range and habitat. Thailand (Peninsular) (also in Peninsular Malaysia); lowland rain forest at low elevations.

Uses. None recorded.

Salacca griffithii Henderson   PLATE 61
yone (Mya), kaan haan, kaa haan (Tha)

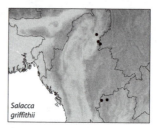

Field characters. Stems short and subterranean, clustered. Sheaths and petioles with short rows of spines; leaf rachis to 4.5 m long with 35–42 lanceolate leaflets per side, these regularly arranged and spreading in the same plane, apical leaflets split, not forming a broad, compound, terminal leaflet. Male inflorescences elongate, females congested among leaf bases; fruits obovoid, 6–8 cm long and 6–8 cm diameter, brown, densely covered in flattened, spinelike scales.

Range and habitat. China (Yunnan), Myanmar (Kachin), and Thailand (North); lowland rain forest or more often in disturbed areas, at low elevations.
Uses. The leaves are commonly used for thatching.

Salacca secunda Griff.   PLATE 61
jenk (Ind), yone (Mya)

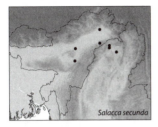

Salacca secunda

Field characters. Stems short and subterranean, clustered. Sheaths and petioles with short rows of spines; leaf rachis to 2 m long with 39–44 lanceolate leaflets per side, these irregularly arranged and spreading in different planes, apical leaflets split, not forming a broad, compound, terminal leaflet. Male inflorescences elongate, females congested among leaf bases; fruits obovoid, to 6 cm long and 6.5 cm diameter, brown, densely covered in flattened, spinelike scales.
Range and habitat. India (Arunachal Pradesh, Assam, Nagaland) and Myanmar (Kachin, Sagaing); lowland rain forest or often in disturbed areas, usually in low-lying, wet places, to 800 m elevation.
Uses. The leaves are commonly used for thatching.

Salacca stolonifera Hodel
la kam khao (Tha)

Salacca stolonifera

Field characters. Stems short and subterranean, loosely clustered. Sheaths and petioles with short rows of spines; leaf rachis to 2.5 m long with to 17 sigmoid leaflets per side, these irregularly arranged in clusters and spreading in different planes, apical leaflets not split, forming a broad, compound, terminal leaflet. Male inflorescences to 4 m long, rooting at the apex and forming new plants, with 3 hairy flowering branches; female inflorescences not known; fruits ellipsoid to obovoid, brown, densely covered in spinelike scales.

Range and habitat. Thailand (Peninsular); lowland rain forest in swamps, at low elevations.
Uses. None recorded.

Salacca wallichiana Mart.   PLATES 61 & 62
rakam (Tha), yeinga, yenaung (Mya)

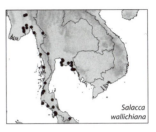

Salacca wallichiana

Field characters. Stems subterranean, creeping, to 5 m long and 20 cm diameter, clustered. Sheaths and petioles surrounded by whorls of spines; leaf rachis to 7 m long with 40–60 sigmoid leaflets per side, these irregularly arranged in clusters and spreading in different planes, apical leaflets not split, forming a broad, compound, terminal leaflet. Male inflorescences to 3 m long, with 10 densely hairy flowering branches; female inflorescences to 0.7 m long; fruits obovoid, to 8 cm long and 4 cm diameter, reddish brown, densely covered in flattened, spinelike scales.
Range and habitat. Myanmar (Bago, Karen, Mon, Tanintharyi, Yangon) and Thailand (Peninsular, Southeast) (also in Peninsular Malaysia and Sumatra); lowland rain forest or dry forest, often in wet areas, or commonly planted, usually below 200 m elevation.
Notes. This species is commonly planted for its edible fruits and may be introduced to other areas, for example Laos and Vietnam. Specimens from southeastern Thailand are reported to occur in drier forest and are somewhat different morphologically from specimens from Peninsular Thailand. They may represent a distinct species.
Uses. The fruits are commonly eaten, although the Indonesian *S. zalacca* (Gaertn.) Voss is more important for its edible fruits.
Synonyms. *Calamus zalacca* Roxb., *Salacca beccarii* Hook. f., *Salacca macrostachya* Griff.

SATAKENTIA H. E. Moore

This genus was named for Toshihiko Satake (1910–1998), a student of palms and correspondent of Harold Moore, who first described the genus. Stems are tall and solitary, ringed with prominent leaf scars, and usually have a mass of adventitious roots at the base. Leaves are pinnate, 10–14 in number, and dead leaves fall cleanly from the stem. Leaf sheaths are closed and form a prominent, green or reddish green crownshaft. Petioles are usually very short. Leaflets are numerous, regularly arranged, one-veined, lanceolate, and spread horizontally in the same plane.

Inflorescences are branched to two orders, and are borne below the crownshaft. They are covered initially by deciduous bracts—a prophyll and two peduncular bracts. Flowering branches are densely hairy. Flowers are unisexual and are arranged in threes of a central female and two lateral male flowers. Fruits are small, ovoid or ellipsoid, black, and one-seeded. The endosperm is homogeneous, germination is adjacent, and the seedling leaf is bifid.

Satakentia contains one species from Japan, in the Ryukyu Islands (Moore 1969; Pintaud & Setoguchi 1999).

Satakentia liukiuensis (Hatus.)   PLATE 62
H. E. Moore
no-yashi (Jap)

Satakentia
liukiuensis

Field characters. Stems solitary, to 20 m long and 30 cm diameter. Leaf rachis to 3 m long, with to 100 leaflets per side, these regularly arranged and spreading in the same plane. Inflorescences borne below the leaves; fruits ovoid-ellipsoid, to 1.3 cm long and 0.7 cm diameter, black.
Range and habitat. Japan, Ryukyu Islands (Ishigaki, Iriomote); lowland forest at low elevations.
Notes. Often occurring in large, even-sized populations.
Uses. The fruits are eaten.
Synonym. *Gulubia liukiuensis* Hatus.

TRACHYCARPUS H. Wendl.

Stems are solitary, tall and aerial or rarely short and subterranean. They are usually covered with persistent, fibrous leaf sheaths, although stems of older plants may lose this covering, leaving a bare, ringed trunk. Leaves are palmate, 6–25 in number, and usually form a dense crown. Dead leaves often persist as a skirt below the crown. Leaf sheaths are open and very fibrous, and old sheaths form a mass of interwoven fibers. The fibers at the apex of the sheath on younger leaves form a prominent appendage, the ocrea. Petioles are elongate and often bear small, blunt teeth along the margins. At the apex of the petiole there is a small or prominent hastula. Blades are green, gray-green, or bright white waxy on the lower surfaces, and are divided into numerous, stiff leaflets. These leaflets are again shortly split at their apices. In one species, two or three leaflets are not completely split and are joined together in groups.

Inflorescences are branched to four orders, and are borne among the leaves. They are covered with

Key to the Species of *Trachycarpus*

1a. Leaflets more than 65 per leaf; transverse veinlets of the leaflets clearly visible; fruits oblong or oblong-ellipsoid . . . . 2.
1b. Leaflets fewer than 70 per leaf; transverse veinlets of the leaflets barely visible; fruits kidney-shaped, wider than long . . . . 3.

2a. Petioles 2.5 cm wide, the margins nearly smooth; hastulas small; India (Sikkim, West Bengal) . . . . *T. latisectus.*
2b. Petioles less than 2.5 cm wide, the margins toothed; hastulas prominent; India (Meghalaya, Nagaland, possibly Manipur), Myanmar (Chin), and Nepal . . . . *T. martianus.*

3a. Stems short and subterranean; leaflets 20–30 per leaf; China (Yunnan) . . . . *T. nanus.*
3b. Stems tall and aerial; leaflets 40–70 per leaf; widespread including China (Yunnan) . . . . 4.

4a. Blades bright white-waxy on the lower surfaces . . . . 5.
4b. Blades green or gray-green on the lower surfaces . . . . 6.

5a. Leaflets less than 45 per leaf, joined in groups of 2 or 3; Vietnam (Northern). . . . . *T. geminisectus.*
5b. Leaflets more than 45 per leaf, not joined in groups; China (Yunnan) . . . . *T. princeps.*

6a. Leaf sheath fibers short, brittle, deciduous, not forming an ocrea; hastulas prominent; India (Manipur) and Thailand (North) . . . . *T. oreophilus.*
6b. Leaf sheath fibers long, hairy, persistent, forming an ocrea; hastulas short; Bhutan, China, India, Myanmar, Nepal, and Vietnam . . . . 7.

7a. Ocreas less than 20 cm long; India (Uttarakhand) . . . . *T. takil.*
7b. Ocreas more than 25 cm long; Bhutan, China, India, Myanmar, Nepal, and Vietnam . . . . *T. fortunei.*

numerous sheathing bracts and are usually yellow-ish at flowering time. Inflorescences produce uni-sexual flowers and the plants are dioecious. Fruits are kidney-shaped or oblong, grooved, yellowish brown to purple-black, often with a whitish "bloom," and one-seeded. The genus gets its name from the Greek words *trachys*, meaning rough, and *carpos*, a fruit, although the derivation of this name is not ap-parent. The endosperm is homogeneous or scarcely ruminate (although penetrated by an irregular intru-sion of the seed coat), germination is remote, and the seedling leaf is undivided and lanceolate.

Trachycarpus contains eight species, widely distrib-uted in northern India, Nepal, Bhutan, and China, and reaching southwards into northern Thailand and Vietnam. They usually grow in steep, rocky places at higher elevations. Most species have restricted distri-butions, and many have suffered from overexploita-tion. All species occur in our area (Beccari 1933; Gib-bons 1996; Kimnach 1977). The stem diameters given here are for the stems without the leaf sheath fibers.

Trachycarpus fortunei (Hook.)   PLATES 62 & 63
H. Wendl.
co canh (Vie)

Field characters. Stems solitary, to 12 m tall and 15 cm diameter. Leaf sheath fibers long, hairy, persis-tent, forming an ocrea more than 25 cm long; petiole margins finely toothed; hastulas short; blades to 1.2 m wide, green on lower surfaces, divided to about three-quarters their length into 40–50 leaflets, the transverse veinlets barely visible. Inflorescences 0.7–0.9 m long; fruits kidney-shaped, to 0.9 cm long and 1.4 cm diameter, black with a waxy bloom.
Range and habitat. Bhutan, China, India, Myanmar, Nepal, and Vietnam; always cultivated, at 100–2400 m elevation (no map provided).
Uses. Fibers are collected from the leaf bases and made into coats and other items (brooms, brushes, and doormats), wax is collected from the fruits, and a hemostatic drug is extracted from the seeds. Widely cultivated as an ornamental, especially in cooler climates.
Notes. Always planted or naturalized and appar-ently not known in the wild.
Synonyms. *Chamaerops fortunei* Hook., *Chamaerops excelsa* Thunb., *Trachycarpus caespitosus* Becc., *Tra-chycarpus excelsa* H. Wendl., *Trachycarpus wagneri-anus* Becc.

Trachycarpus geminisectus Spanner,   PLATE 63
M. Gibbons, Nguyen & Anh
co la sinh doi (Vie)

Field characters. Stems solitary, to 2 m tall and 25 cm diameter. Leaf sheath fibers stiff and wiry, forming an ocrea; petioles to 1.4 cm wide, the margins with minute teeth; hastulas small; blades about 1.3 m wide, bright white-waxy on the lower surfaces, divided to about

three-quarters their length into about 40 leaflets, these joined in groups of 2 or 3, the transverse veinlets barely visible. Inflorescences to 0.5 m long; fruits kidney-shaped, to 1 cm long and 1.3 cm diameter, black.

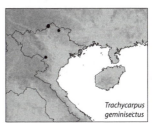

Trachycarpus geminisectus

Range and habitat. Vietnam (Northern) and pos-sibly adjacent China; montane forest on steep, lime-stone cliffs, at 1100–1600 m elevation.
Uses. None recorded.
Notes. Occurs very close to villages where *T. fortu-nei* is cultivated.

Trachycarpus latisectus Spanner, H. J. Noltie &
M. Gibbons
kasru (Ind)

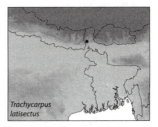

Trachycarpus latisectus

Field characters. Stems solitary, to 12 m tall and 17 cm diameter. Leaf sheath fibers coarse, forming an ocrea; petioles 2.5 cm wide, the margins without teeth; hastulas small; blades to 1.35 m wide, grayish white on the lower surfaces, divided to about half their length into 65–75 broad leaflets, the transverse veinlets clearly visible. Inflorescences to 1.5 m long; fruits oblong-ellipsoid, to 1.8 cm long and 1.3 cm diameter, yellowish brown.
Range and habitat. India (Sikkim, West Bengal); montane forest on steep, rocky slopes, to 2000 m elevation.
Uses. Planted locally as an ornamental.
Notes. A very rare palm in the wild.

Trachycarpus martianus (Wall.) H. Wendl.
deing-kleu, u kleu (Ind)

Field characters. Stems solitary, to 15 m tall and 15 cm diameter. Leaf sheaths not known; petiole margins with minute teeth; hastulas prominent; blades grayish white on the lower surfaces, divided to about half their length into 65–75 leaflets, the transverse veinlets clearly visible. Inflorescences to 1.5 m long; fruits oblong, to 1.2 cm long and 0.8 cm diameter, yellowish, becoming black.

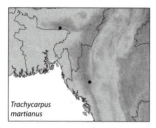

Range and habitat. India (Meghalaya, Nagaland, possibly Manipur), Myanmar (Chin), and Nepal; montane forest, on steep, rocky slopes or cliffs, at 1000–2000 m elevation.
Uses. None recorded.
Synonyms. *Chamaerops griffithii* Lodd., *Chamaerops khasyana* Griff., *Chamaerops martiana* Wall., *Chamaerops nepalensis* Lodd., *Chamaerops tomentosa* C. Morren, *Trachycarpus griffithii* (Lodd.) auct., *Trachycarpus khasyanus* (Griff.) H. Wendl.

Trachycarpus nanus Becc.

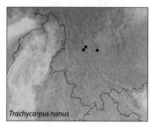

Field characters. Stems solitary, short and subterranean, to 5 cm diameter. Leaf sheaths not known; petioles to 1.5 cm wide, the margins with very small teeth; hastulas small; blades green or grayish on the lower surfaces, divided to more than two-thirds their length into 20–30 leaflets, the transverse veinlets barely visible. Inflorescences to 0.5 m long; fruits kidney-shaped, to 0.9 cm long and 1.3 cm diameter, yellowish to brown, with a thin waxy bloom.
Range and habitat. China (Yunnan); dry forest or open areas, at 1800–2300 m elevation.
Uses. Brushes are made from bundles of leaves.
Synonyms. *Chamaerops nana* (Becc.) Chabaud, *Trachycarpus dracocephalus* Ching & Y. C. Hsu

Trachycarpus oreophilus   PLATE 63
M. Gibbons & Spanner
kho doi, kho chiang dao (Tha)

Field characters. Stems solitary, to 12 m tall and 30 cm diameter. Leaf sheath fibers short, brittle, de-

ciduous, not forming an ocrea; petioles to 5 cm wide, the margins with very small teeth; hastulas prominent; blades to 1 m wide, gray-green on the lower surfaces, divided for more than half their length into 60–70 leaflets, the transverse veinlets barely visible. Inflorescences to 1 m long; fruits kidney-shaped, to 0.7 cm long and 1.2 cm diameter, yellow or yellowish brown.

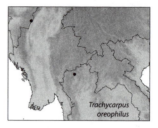

Range and habitat. India (Manipur) and Thailand (North); limestone cliffs, steep, rocky slopes, or grassland or deciduous forest on slopes, at 1500–2175 m elevation.
Uses. The stems are used in construction.
Notes. In Thailand, the only known population is at Doi Chiang Dao, near Chiang Mai, where most accessible trees have been felled. Probably also in Nagaland in India and adjacent Myanmar (Sagaing, Chin), and one unconfirmed occurrence in Vietnam.
Synonym. *Trachycarpus ukhrulensis* Lorek & Pradhan

Trachycarpus princeps M . Gibbons, Spanner & S.Y. Chen

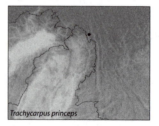

Field characters. Stems solitary, to 8 m tall and 16 cm diameter. Leaf sheath fibers coarse, forming an ocrea to 10 cm long; petioles about 1.3 cm wide, the margins with very small teeth; hastulas present; blades 0.9–1.15 m wide, bright white-waxy on the lower surfaces, divided to about half their length into 45–48 leaflets, the transverse veinlets barely visible. Inflorescences to 0.8 m long; fruits kidney-shaped, to 0.8 cm long and 1 cm diameter, black with a waxy bloom.
Range and habitat. China (Yunnan); steep limestone cliffs, at 1550–1850 m elevation.
Uses. None recorded.

Notes. Known from one locality on steep cliffs along the River Nujiang, where it is under threat from hydro-electric development. A couple of other localities have been discovered recently in the same area.

Trachycarpus takil Becc.
jamar, jherg thakal (Ind)

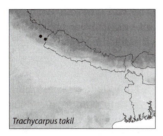

Trachycarpus takil

Field characters. Stems solitary, to 12 m tall and 15–18 cm diameter. Leaf sheath fibers long, hairy, persistent, forming an ocrea less than 20 cm long; petiole margins with very small teeth; hastulas short; blades to 1.2 m wide, gray-green on lower surfaces, divided to about half their length into 45–60 leaflets, the transverse veins barely visible. Inflorescences to 1 m long; fruits kidney-shaped, to 0.8 cm long and 1.2 cm diameter, black with a waxy bloom.
Range and habitat. India (Uttarakhand) and probably adjacent Nepal; montane forest to 2400 m elevation.

Uses. The sheath fibers are used to make rope.
Notes. The cutting of the trunks to obtain the sheath fibers has greatly reduced wild populations.

WALLICHIA Roxb.
(*Asraoa* J. Joseph, *Harina* Buch.-Ham., *Wrightea* Roxb.)

This small genus was named after Nathaniel Wallich (1786–1854), onetime Superintendent of the Botanic Gardens in Calcutta, India. Stems are small to moderate, solitary or clustered, and are usually covered in persistent, fibrous leaf bases. Leaves are pinnate, 3–18 in number, and are arranged spirally or, in one species, in one or a few planes. Leaf sheaths are fibrous, with reticulate fibers, and are closed but do not form a crownshaft. Petioles are well developed, rounded in cross section, and often covered in brown hairs. Leaflets are regularly or irregularly arranged, although even in the species with regularly arranged leaflets, the basal few leaflets are clustered and spread in different planes. Leaflets are linear to broadly lanceolate or oblong, and have uneven or lobed margins and jagged apices. The leaflet margins of some species are characteristically wavy. The apical leaflet is broadly triangular. Leaflets are usually silvery gray on the lower surfaces and often have broad bands of brown hairs parallel to the veins, especially near the apices. Leaflets are V-shaped (induplicate) in cross section,

Key to the Species of *Wallichia*

1a. Stems solitary; leaves arranged in 1 or a few planes; leaflets from middle of the leaf clustered and spreading in different planes . . . . *W. disticha.*
1b. Stems clustered; leaves spirally arranged; leaflets from middle of the leaf regularly arranged and spreading in the same plane . . . . 2.

2a. Stems short and subterranean, sometimes to 1 m tall and 40 cm diameter; leaflets oblong . . . . *W. oblongifolia.*
2b. Stems aerial, to 4 m tall and 10 cm diameter; leaflets lanceolate or broadly lanceolate . . . . 3.

3a. Stems to 0.6 m tall and 2 cm diameter; leaflets 2–4 per side of rachis; flowering branches 1–4. . . *W. nana.*
3b. Stems to 4 m tall and 10 cm diameter; leaflets 5–19 per side of rachis; flowering branches numerous, more than 10 . . . . 4.

4a. Stems bearing male inflorescences to 4 m tall, female stems much shorter, to 0.5 m tall; Myanmar (Bago) . . . . *W. lidiae.*
4b. Stems bearing male and female inflorescences about equal in length; Bangladesh, China, India, Myanmar (Kachin, Mon, Rakhine, Sagaing), Thailand, and Vietnam. . . . . 5.

5a. Stamens 3; China (Tibet) and India (Arunachal Pradesh) . . . . *W. triandra.*
5b. Stamens 6–19; Bangladesh, China (Guangxi, Yunnan), Myanmar, Thailand, and Vietnam . . . . 6.

6a. Leaflets scarcely lobed; Thailand (Peninsular) . . . . *W. marianneae.*
6b. Leaflets with pronounced lobes; Bangladesh, China, Myanmar, Thailand (North, Southwest), and Vietnam . . . . 7.

7a. Flowering branches short and congested, to 6 cm long; China (Guangxi, Yunnan) and Vietnam (Central, Northern) . . . . *W. gracilis.*
7b. Flowering branches longer and not congested, to 20 cm long; Bangladesh, China (Yunnan), Myanmar, and Thailand . . . . *W. caryotoides.*

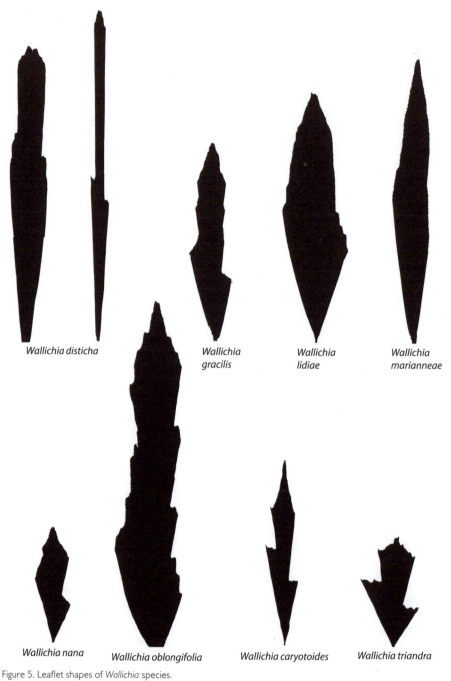

Wallichia disticha

Wallichia gracilis

Wallichia lidiae

Wallichia marianneae

Wallichia nana

Wallichia oblongifolia

Wallichia caryotoides

Wallichia triandra

Figure 5. Leaflet shapes of *Wallichia* species.

although this is not easy to see, except at the very base of the leaflets. The leaves subtending the apical inflorescences are usually much smaller than the others.

All species of *Wallichia* are semelparous. After a period of vegetative growth, several unisexual inflorescences are produced. The first one, at the top of the stem, is usually female, followed down the stem by males. Some stems, however, produce either male or female inflorescences. These are sometimes quite dissimilar in size and flowering branch thickness. Inflorescences are branched to one order, rarely spicate, and are borne among the leaves. They are covered with several, persistent, overlapping bracts. Male flowers have 3–19 stamens. Fruits are small to medium-sized; ellipsoid to ovoid; brownish, greenish, or reddish; and one- to three-seeded. The mesocarp contains irritating crystals. The endosperm is homogeneous, germination is remote, and the seedling leaf is undivided with jagged margins.

Wallichia contains eight species, all occurring in our area (Henderson 2007a). It is closely related to both *Caryota* and *Arenga* and is distinguished with difficulty from the latter. *Wallichia* has the sepals of the male flowers joined into a cupule, and *Arenga* has free, overlapping male sepals (Uhl & Dransfield 1987). This is not a practical character, because male flowers are seldom present. In the field, *Wallichia* may be distinguished by its strongly asymmetrical leaflets, which are usually deeply lobed (Fig. 5). *Arenga* leaflets are usually linear and only briefly lobed. There are exceptions to this—*Arenga caudata, A. hastata,* and *A. longicarpa*—but the leaflets of these have long, pointed apices (see Fig. 3), a shape not found in *Wallichia* species.

In the following key and descriptions, stem diameter includes the persistent leaf bases. The names *Didymosperma gracilis* Hook. f. and *Harina wallichia* Steud. are doubtful ones and are not included below as synonyms of other species.

Wallichia caryotoides Roxb.   PLATE 63
chilputta (Ban), walizong (Chi), saingpa, zanong (Mya), taou-rung-nu (Tha)

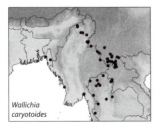

Wallichia caryotoides

Field characters. Stems clustered, to 3 m tall and 10 cm diameter. Leaves to 1.5 m long, spirally arranged; leaflets 8–12 per side of rachis, regularly arranged and spreading in the same plane, lanceolate, deeply lobed, silvery gray on the lower surfaces.

Inflorescences to 0.5 m long with 21–30 male flowering branches and 7–17 female branches; fruits ellipsoid to ovoid, to 1.7 cm long and 0.8 cm diameter, reddish.
Range and habitat. Bangladesh, China (Yunnan), Myanmar (Kachin, Mon, Rakhine, Sagaing), and Thailand (North, Southwest); lowland to montane rain forest, especially in rocky places on steep slopes, to 1800 m elevation.
Uses. None recorded.
Synonyms. *Wallichia mooreana* S. K. Basu, *Wallichia siamensis* Becc.

Wallichia disticha T. Anderson   PLATE 64
thakal (Bhu), katong (Ind), tao pha (Lao), minbaw, trung, zanong (Mya), mak na re suan (Tha)

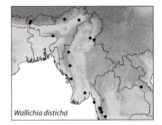

Wallichia disticha

Field characters. Stems solitary, to 9 m tall and 25 cm diameter. Leaves to 3.5 m long, arranged in 1 or a few planes; leaflets 45–73 per side of rachis, irregularly arranged and spreading in several planes, linear or lanceolate, shallowly lobed, silvery gray on the lower surfaces. Inflorescences to 1.2 m long with to 1000 male flowering branches and to 50 female branches; fruits ellipsoid, to 2.2 cm long and 1.5 cm diameter, reddish brown.
Range and habitat. Bangladesh, Bhutan, China (Yunnan), India (Arunachal Pradesh, Assam, Meghalaya, Sikkim, West Bengal), Laos (Central), Myanmar (Bago, Chin, Kachin, Kayin, Rakhine), Thailand (North, Southwest), and probably Nepal; lowland to montane rain forest, especially in rocky areas on steep slopes, often in disturbed places, to 1200 m elevation.
Uses. The pith from the stems is eaten in times of famine.
Notes. Known from scattered localities throughout its range. In historical times it may also have occurred farther to the west, in Jharkhand in India. Leaflets vary considerably in shape, from linear to lanceolate (Fig. 5).
Synonmyms. *Wallichia yomae* Kurz, *Didymosperma distichum* (T. Anderson) Hook. f.

Wallichia gracilis Becc.
hsian-tung-lan (Chi), hoa ly (Vie)

Field characters. Stems clustered, to 2.5 m tall and 3 cm diameter. Leaves to 2.5 m long, spirally arranged; leaflets 5–9 per side or rachis, regularly arranged and spreading in the same plane, lanceolate, deeply lobed, silvery gray on the lower surfaces. Inflorescences to 0.4 m long with numerous flowering branches; fruits ellipsoid to ovoid, to 1.5 cm long and 1 cm diameter, red.

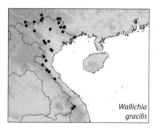

Range and habitat. China (Guangxi, Yunnan) and Vietnam (Central, Northern); lowland rain forest at 200–1000 m elevation.
Uses. None recorded.
Synonym. *Wallichia chinensis* Burret

Wallichia lidiae Henderson

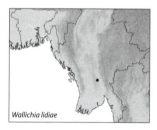

Field characters. Stems clustered, to 4 m tall and 4 cm diameter, stems with male inflorescences to 4 m tall, those with female inflorescences to 1 m tall. Leaves to 1 m long, spirally arranged; leaflets about 7 per side or rachis, regularly arranged and spreading in the same plane, broadly lanceolate, scarcely lobed, silvery gray on the lower surfaces. Inflorescences to 0.7 m long with numerous flowering branches; fruits not known.
Range and habitat. Myanmar (Bago); lowland rain forest at low elevations.
Uses. None recorded.
Notes. Known only from the Pegu Yoma in Myanmar.

Wallichia marianneae Hodel   PLATE 64
kuong (Tha)

Field characters. Stems clustered, to 1.6 m tall and 10 cm diameter. Leaves to 1.3 m long, spirally arranged; leaflets 5–10 per side of rachis, regularly arranged and spreading in the same plane, lanceolate, scarcely lobed, silvery gray on the lower surfaces. Inflores-

cences to 0.6 m long with about 10 male flowering branches; fruits ovoid to ellipsoid, to 1.1 cm long and 0.8 cm diameter, reddish purple.

Range and habitat. Thailand (Peninsular); lowland or montane rain forest at 600–1100 m elevation.
Uses. None recorded.

Wallichia nana Griff.
ipathi (Ind)

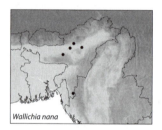

Field characters. Stems clustered, to 0.6 m tall and 2 cm diameter. Leaves to 0.5 m long, spirally arranged; leaflets 2–4 per side of rachis, regularly arranged and spreading in the same plane, lanceolate, deeply lobed, silvery gray on the lower surfaces. Inflorescences to 0.3 m long with 1–4 male flowering branches and 1–3 female branches; fruits ellipsoid, to 1.2 cm long and 1 cm diameter, whitish.
Range and habitat. India (Arunachal Pradesh, Assam, Meghalaya); lowland rain forest at low elevations.
Uses. None recorded.
Notes. Previously included in *Arenga*, but placed here because of its male flowers with the sepals joined into a cupule (Henderson 2007a).
Synomyms. *Arenga nana* (Griff.) H. E. Moore, *Blancoa nana* (Griff.) Kuntze, *Didymosperma nanum* (Griff.) H. Wendl. & Drude, *Harina nana* (Griff.) Griff.

Wallichia oblongifolia Griff.   PLATE 64
mihua walizong (Chi), takoru (Bhu, Nep), chilputta (Ind), zanong (Mya), khareto (Nep)

Field characters. Stems clustered, short and subterranean, sometimes to 1 m tall, to 40 cm diameter.

Leaves to 2.5 m long, spirally arranged; leaflets 16 or 17 per side of rachis, regularly arranged and spreading in the same plane, oblong, shallowly lobed, silvery gray on the lower surfaces. Inflorescences to 1 m long with numerous male flowering branches and 16–32 female branches; fruits ellipsoid to ovoid, to 1.5 cm long and 0.8 cm diameter, greenish brown to reddish.

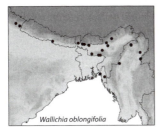
Wallichia oblongifolia

Range and habitat. Bangladesh, Bhutan, China (Yunnan), India (Arunachal Pradesh, Assam, Manipur, Meghalaya, Mizoram, Nagaland, Sikkim, Tripura, Uttarakhand), Myanmar (Kachin, Sagaing), and Nepal; lowland or montane rain forest, especially in rocky places on steep slopes, at 200–1200 m elevation.
Uses. The leaves are used for thatching and making brooms.
Notes. One of the commonest and most abundant palms of the Himalayan foothills, often mistakenly known as *W. densiflora*.

Synomyms. *Harina densiflora* (Mart.) Walp., *Harina oblongifolia* (Griff.) Griff., *Wallichia densiflora* Mart.

Wallichia triandra (J. Joseph) S. K. Basu

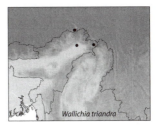
Wallichia triandra

Field characters. Stems clustered, to 3 m tall and 5 cm diameter. Leaves to 2 m long, spirally arranged; leaflets 11–19 per side of rachis, regularly arranged and spreading in the same plane, broadly lanceolate, deeply lobed, silvery gray on the lower surfaces. Inflorescences to 0.4 m long with numerous flowering branches; fruits ellipsoid, to 1.3 cm long and 0.7 cm diameter, reddish.
Range and habitat. China (Tibet) and India (Arunachal Pradesh); montane rain forest on steep slopes at 900–2000 m elevation.
Uses. None recorded.
Synonym. *Asraoa triandra* J. Joseph

Appendix
Checklist of Species by Country or Region

This list includes only definite occurrences and not possible or probable ones. Widely cultivated species (*Areca catechu*, *Cocos nucifera*, and *Phoenix dactylifera*) are also omitted.

Afaghanistan (1 species)
Nannorrhops ritchiana

Andaman and Nicobar Islands (29 species)
Areca triandra
Bentinckia nicobarica
Calamus andamanicus
Calamus baratangensis
Calamus basui
Calamus dilaceratus
Calamus longisetus
Calamus nicobaricus
Calamus palustris
Calamus pseudorivalis
Calamus semierectus
Calamus unifarius
Calamus viminalis
Caryota mitis
Corypha utan
Daemonorops aurea
Daemonorops kurziana
Daemonorops manii
Daemonorops rarispinosa
Daemonorops wrightmyoensis
Korthalsia laciniosa
Korthalsia rogersii
Licuala peltata
Licuala spinosa
Nypa fruticans
Phoenix andamanensis
Phoenix paludosa
Pinanga manii
Rhopaloblaste augusta

Bangladesh (24 species)
Areca triandra
Borassus flabellifer
Calamus erectus
Calamus flagellum
Calamus floribundus
Calamus gracilis
Calamus guruba
Calamus leptospadix
Calamus longisetus

Calamus nambariensis
Calamus tenuis
Calamus viminalis
Corypha taliera
Daemonorops jenkinsiana
Licuala peltata
Livistona jenkinsiana
Nypa fruticans
Phoenix loureiroi
Phoenix paludosa
Phoenix sylvestris
Pinanga gracilis
Wallichia caryotoides
Wallichia disticha
Wallichia oblongifolia

Bhutan (19 species)
Arenga micrantha
Calamus acanthospathus
Calamus erectus
Calamus flagellum
Calamus guruba
Calamus leptospadix
Calamus nambariensis
Calamus tenuis
Caryota maxima
Daemonorops jenkinsiana
Livistona jenkinsiana
Phoenix loureiroi
Phoenix rupicola
Phoenix sylvestris
Pinanga gracilis
Plectocomia himalayana
Trachycarpus fortunei
Wallichia disticha
Wallichia oblongifolia

Bonin Islands (2 species)
Clinostigma savoryanum
Livistona boninensis

Cambodia (32 species)
Areca triandra
Arenga caudata

Arenga westerhoutii
Borassus flabellifer
Calamus acanthophyllus
Calamus bousigonii
Calamus erinaceus
Calamus godefroyi
Calamus guruba
Calamus lateralis
Calamus palustris
Calamus rudentum
Calamus salicifolius
Calamus siamensis
Calamus tetradactylus
Calamus viminalis
Caryota mitis
Corypha lecomtei
Daemonorops jenkinsiana
Korthalsia bejaudii
Korthalsia laciniosa
Licuala spinosa
Livistona saribus
Myrialepis paradoxa
Nypa fruticans
Oncosperma tigillarium
Phoenix loureiroi
Phoenix paludosa
Pinanga sylvestris
Plectocomia elongata
Plectocomia pierreana
Plectocomiopsis geminiflora

China (69 species)
Arenga caudata
Arenga longicarpa
Arenga micrantha
Arenga westerhoutii
Calamus acanthospathus
Calamus albidus
Calamus austroguangxiensis
Calamus compsostachys
Calamus dianbaiensis
Calamus egregius
Calamus erectus
Calamus flagellum
Calamus gracilis
Calamus guruba
Calamus hainanensis
Calamus henryanus
Calamus macrorhynchus
Calamus melanochrous
Calamus multispicatus

Calamus nambariensis
Calamus oxycarpus
Calamus pulchellus
Calamus rhabdocladus
Calamus simplicifolius
Calamus tetradactyloides
Calamus tetradactylus
Calamus thysanolepis
Calamus viminalis
Calamus walkeri
Calamus wuliangshanensis
Caryota maxima
Caryota mitis
Caryota monostachya
Caryota obtusa
Chuniophoenix hainanensis
Chuniophoenix humilis
Daemonorops jenkinsiana
Guihaia argyrata
Guihaia grossifibrosa
Licuala dasyantha
Licuala fordiana
Licuala hainanensis
Livistona chinensis
Livistona jenkinsiana
Livistona saribus
Nypa fruticans
Phoenix loureiroi
Phoenix roebelinii
Pinanga acuminata
Pinanga baviensis
Pinanga gracilis
Pinanga sylvestris
Plectocomia himalayana
Plectocomia microstachys
Plectocomia pierreana
Rhapis excelsa
Rhapis gracilis
Rhapis humilis
Rhapis multifida
Rhapis robusta
Salacca griffithii
Trachycarpus fortunei
Trachycarpus nanus
Trachycarpus princeps
Wallichia caryotoides
Wallichia disticha
Wallichia gracilis
Wallichia oblongifolia
Wallichia triandra

India (71 species)
Areca triandra
Arenga micrantha
Arenga wightii
Bentinckia condapanna
Borassus flabellifer
Calamus acanthospathus
Calamus brandisii
Calamus delessertianus
Calamus dransfieldii
Calamus erectus
Calamus flagellum
Calamus floribundus
Calamus gamblei
Calamus gracilis
Calamus guruba
Calamus hookerianus
Calamus karnatakensis
Calamus kingianus
Calamus lacciferus
Calamus lakshmanae
Calamus leptospadix
Calamus meghalayensis
Calamus metzianus
Calamus nagbettai
Calamus nambariensis
Calamus neelagiricus
Calamus prasinus
Calamus pseudofeanus
Calamus pseudotenuis
Calamus rheedei
Calamus rotang
Calamus shendurunii
Calamus stoloniferus
Calamus tenuis
Calamus thwaitesii
Calamus travancoricus
Calamus vattayila
Calamus viminalis
Calamus wightii
Caryota maxima
Caryota obtusa
Caryota urens
Corypha taliera
Corypha umbraculifera
Daemonorops jenkinsiana
Hyphaene dichotoma
Licuala peltata
Livistona jenkinsiana
Nypa fruticans

Phoenix acaulis
Phoenix loureiroi
Phoenix paludosa
Phoenix pusilla
Phoenix rupicola
Phoenix sylvestris
Pinanga dicksonii
Pinanga gracilis
Pinanga griffithii
Pinanga sylvestris
Plectocomia assamica
Plectocomia himalayana
Salacca secunda
Trachycarpus fortunei
Trachycarpus latisectus
Trachycarpus martianus
Trachycarpus oreophilus
Trachycarpus takil
Wallichia disticha
Wallichia nana
Wallichia oblongifolia
Wallichia triandra

Japan (1 species)
Livistona chinensis

Laos (45 species)
Areca laosensis
Areca triandra
Arenga caudata
Arenga westerhoutii
Borassus flabellifer
Calamus acanthophyllus
Calamus acanthospathus
Calamus bimaniferus
Calamus erectus
Calamus evansii
Calamus flagellum
Calamus godefroyi
Calamus gracilis
Calamus guruba
Calamus harmandii
Calamus henryanus
Calamus laoensis
Calamus minor
Calamus nambariensis
Calamus oligostachys
Calamus palustris
Calamus poilanei
Calamus rhabdocladus
Calamus rudentum

Calamus siamensis
Calamus solitarius
Calamus tenuis
Calamus tetradactylus
Calamus viminalis
Caryota maxima
Caryota obtusa
Caryota sympetala
Corypha lecomtei
Daemonorops jenkinsiana
Korthalsia laciniosa
Livistona saribus
Myrialepis paradoxa
Phoenix roebelinii
Pinanga sylvestris
Plectocomia himalayana
Plectocomia pierreana
Plectocomiopsis geminiflora
Rhapis laosensis
Rhapis subtilis
Wallichia disticha

Myanmar (69 species)
Areca triandra
Arenga caudata
Arenga westerhoutii
Borassus flabellifer
Calamus acanthospathus
Calamus arborescens
Calamus concinnus
Calamus erectus
Calamus flagellum
Calamus floribundus
Calamus gracilis
Calamus guruba
Calamus henryanus
Calamus hukaungensis
Calamus hypoleucus
Calamus javensis
Calamus leptospadix
Calamus longisetus
Calamus luridus
Calamus melanacanthus
Calamus nambariensis
Calamus oxleyanus
Calamus palustris
Calamus peregrinus
Calamus platyspathus
Calamus rudentum
Calamus spicatus
Calamus tenuis

Calamus viminalis
Caryota maxima
Caryota mitis
Caryota obtusa
Corypha utan
Daemonorops jenkinsiana
Daemonorops kurziana
Korthalsia laciniosa
Licuala merguensis
Licuala peltata
Licuala spinosa
Livistona jenkinsiana
Livistona saribus
Myrialepis paradoxa
Nypa fruticans
Phoenix loureiroi
Phoenix paludosa
Phoenix roebelinii
Phoenix sylvestris
Pinanga acuminata
Pinanga auriculata
Pinanga griffithii
Pinanga hexasticha
Pinanga hymenospatha
Pinanga lacei
Pinanga plicata
Pinanga simplicifrons
Pinanga sylvestris
Pinanga versicolor
Plectocomia assamica
Plectocomia elongata
Plectocomiopsis geminiflora
Salacca griffithii
Salacca secunda
Salacca wallichiana
Trachycarpus fortunei
Trachycarpus martianus
Wallichia caryotoides
Wallichia disticha
Wallichia lidiae
Wallichia oblongifolia

Nepal (15 species)
Calamus acanthospathus
Calamus erectus
Calamus flagellum
Calamus leptospadix
Calamus nambariensis
Calamus tenuis
Daemonorops jenkinsiana
Phoenix acaulis

Phoenix loureiroi
Phoenix sylvestris
Pinanga gracilis
Plectocomia himalayana
Trachycarpus fortunei
Trachycarpus martianus
Wallichia oblongifolia

Pakistan (3 species)
Nannorrhops ritchiana
Phoenix loureiroi
Phoenix sylvestris

Ryukyu Islands (4 species)
Arenga ryukyuensis
Livistona chinensis
Nypa fruticans
Satakentia liukiuensis

Sri Lanka (18 species)
Areca concinna
Borassus flabellifer
Calamus deliculatus
Calamus digitatus
Calamus metzianus
Calamus ovoideus
Calamus pachystemonus
Calamus pseudotenuis
Calamus radiatus
Calamus rotang
Calamus thwaitesii
Calamus zeylanicus
Caryota urens
Corypha umbraculifera
Loxococcus rupicola
Nypa fruticans
Oncosperma fasciculatum
Phoenix pusilla

Taiwan (7 species)
Arenga engleri
Calamus beccarii
Calamus formosanus
Calamus siphonospathus
Livistona chinensis
Phoenix loureiroi
Pinanga tashiroi

Thailand (157 species)
Areca triandra
Areca tunku
Arenga caudata

Arenga hastata
Arenga obtusifolia
Arenga pinnata
Arenga westerhoutii
Borassodendron machadonis
Borassus flabellifer
Calamus acanthophyllus
Calamus acanthospathus
Calamus arborescens
Calamus axillaris
Calamus balingensis
Calamus blumei
Calamus bousigonii
Calamus burkillianus
Calamus caesius
Calamus castaneus
Calamus concinnus
Calamus densiflorus
Calamus diepenhorstii
Calamus erectus
Calamus erinaceus
Calamus exilis
Calamus flagellum
Calamus godefroyi
Calamus griseus
Calamus guruba
Calamus henryanus
Calamus insignis
Calamus javensis
Calamus laevigatus
Calamus longisetus
Calamus luridus
Calamus manan
Calamus nambariensis
Calamus oligostachys
Calamus ornatus
Calamus oxleyanus
Calamus palustris
Calamus pandanosmus
Calamus peregrinus
Calamus platyspathus
Calamus poilanei
Calamus rudentum
Calamus scipionum
Calamus sedens
Calamus setulosus
Calamus siamensis
Calamus solitarius
Calamus speciosissimus
Calamus spectatissimus

Calamus temii
Calamus tenuis
Calamus tetradactylus
Calamus tomentosus
Calamus viminalis
Calamus viridispinus
Caryota kiriwongensis
Caryota maxima
Caryota mitis
Caryota obtusa
Ceratolobus subangulatus
Corypha lecomtei
Corypha utan
Cyrtostachys renda
Daemonorops angustifolia
Daemonorops didymophylla
Daemonorops geniculata
Daemonorops grandis
Daemonorops jenkinsiana
Daemonorops kunstleri
Daemonorops leptopus
Daemonorops lewisiana
Daemonorops macrophylla
Daemonorops melanochaetes
Daemonorops monticola
Daemonorops propinqua
Daemonorops sabut
Daemonorops sepal
Daemonorops verticillaris
Eleiodoxa conferta
Eugeissona tristis
Iguanura bicornis
Iguanura divergens
Iguanura geonomiformis
Iguanura polymorpha
Iguanura tenuis
Iguanura thalangensis
Iguanura wallichiana
Johannesteijsmannia altifrons
Kerriodoxa elegans
Korthalsia flagellaris
Korthalsia laciniosa
Korthalsia rigida
Korthalsia rostrata
Korthalsia scortechinii
Licuala distans
Licuala glabra
Licuala kunstleri
Licuala malajana
Licuala merguensis
Licuala modesta

Licuala paludosa
Licuala peltata
Licuala pitta
Licuala poonsakii
Licuala pusilla
Licuala scortechinii
Licuala spinosa
Licuala triphylla
Livistona jenkinsiana
Livistona saribus
Maxburretia furtadoana
Maxburretia gracilis
Myrialepis paradoxa
Nenga macrocarpa
Nenga pumila
Nypa fruticans
Oncosperma horridum
Oncosperma tigillarium
Orania sylvicola
Phoenix loureiroi
Phoenix paludosa
Pholidocarpus macrocarpus
Pinanga adangensis
Pinanga auriculata
Pinanga badia
Pinanga disticha
Pinanga fractiflexa
Pinanga malaiana
Pinanga paradoxa
Pinanga perakensis
Pinanga polymorpha
Pinanga riparia
Pinanga scortechinii
Pinanga simplicifrons
Pinanga subintegra
Pinanga sylvestris
Pinanga watanaiana
Plectocomia elongata
Plectocomia himalayana
Plectocomia pierreana
Plectocomiopsis geminiflora
Plectocomiopsis wrayi
Rhapis laosensis
Rhapis siamensis
Rhapis subtilis
Salacca glabrescens
Salacca griffithii
Salacca stolonifera
Salacca wallichiana
Trachycarpus oreophilus
Wallichia caryotoides

Wallichia disticha
Wallichia marianneae

Vietnam (97 species)
Areca laosensis
Areca triandra
Arenga caudata
Arenga westerhoutii
Borassus flabellifer
Calamus acanthospathus
Calamus acaulis
Calamus bachmaensis
Calamus bousigonii
Calamus centralis
Calamus ceratophorus
Calamus crispus
Calamus dioicus
Calamus dongnaiensis
Calamus fissilis
Calamus flagellum
Calamus henryanus
Calamus kontumensis
Calamus lateralis
Calamus modestus
Calamus nambariensis
Calamus nuichuaensis
Calamus palustris
Calamus poilanei
Calamus rhabdocladus
Calamus rudentum
Calamus salicifolius
Calamus spiralis
Calamus tenuis
Calamus tetradactylus
Calamus thysanolepis
Calamus viminalis
Calamus walkeri
Caryota mitis
Caryota monostachya
Caryota obtusa
Caryota sympetala
Chuniophoenix nana
Corypha lecomtei
Daemonorops jenkinsiana
Daemonorops mollispina
Daemonorops poilanei
Guihaia argyrata
Guihaia grossifibrosa
Korthalsia laciniosa
Licuala acaulis
Licuala atroviridis

Licuala averyanovii
Licuala bachmaensis
Licuala bidoupensis
Licuala bracteata
Licuala calciphila
Licuala cattienensis
Licuala centralis
Licuala dasyantha
Licuala ellipsoidalis
Licuala glaberrima
Licuala hexasepala
Licuala longiflora
Licuala magalonii
Licuala manglaensis
Licuala paludosa
Licuala radula
Licuala robinsoniana
Licuala spinosa
Licuala taynguyensis
Livistona halongensis
Livistona jenkinsiana
Livistona saribus
Myrialepis paradoxa
Nenga banaensis
Nypa fruticans
Oncosperma tigillarium
Phoenix loureiroi
Phoenix paludosa
Phoenix roebelinii
Pinanga annamensis
Pinanga baviensis
Pinanga cattienensis
Pinanga cupularis
Pinanga declinata
Pinanga humilis
Pinanga kontumensis
Pinanga quadrijuga
Plectocomia elongata
Plectocomia pierreana
Plectocomiopsis geminiflora
Rhapis excelsa
Rhapis laosensis
Rhapis micrantha
Rhapis puhuongensis
Rhapis robusta
Rhapis subtilis
Rhapis vidalii
Trachycarpus fortunei
Trachycarpus geminisectus
Wallichia gracilis

References

Alam, M. 1990. Rattans of Bangladesh. Bangladesh Forest Research Institute, Chittagong, Bangladesh.

Amatya, S. 1997. The Rattans of Nepal. IUCN—The World Conservation Union, Gland, Switzerland.

Averyanov, L., Nguyen Tien Hiep & Phan Ke Loc. 2005. *Guihaia grossifibrosa* the dragon scale palm—an endangered species from limestone mountains in northern Vietnam and China. Palms 49: 131–142.

Averyanov, L., Nguyen Tien Hiep & Phan Ke Loc. 2006. *Rhapis vidalii* a new papyrus-like palm from Vietnam. Palms 50: 11–22.

Banka, R. & W. Baker. 2004. A monograph of the genus *Rhopaloblaste* (Arecaceae). Kew Bulletin 59: 47–60.

Barfod, A. & L. Saw. 2002. The genus *Licuala* (Arecaceae Coryphoideae) in Thailand. Kew Bulletin 57: 827–852.

Barrow, S. 1998. A monograph of *Phoenix* L. (Palmae: Coryphoideae). Kew Bulletin 53: 513–575.

Basu, S. 1987. *Corypha* palms in India. Journal of Economic and Taxonomic Botany 11: 477–486.

Basu, S. 1992. Rattans (Canes) in India. A monographic revision. Rattan Information Center, Kuala Lumpur, Malaysia.

Bayton, R. 2007. A revision of *Borassus* L. (Arecaceae). Kew Bulletin 62: 561–586.

Beccari, O. 1908. Asiatic palms—Lepidocaryeae. Part I. The species of *Calamus*. Annals of the Royal Botanic Garden Calcutta 11: 1–518, plates i–ii, 1–238.

Beccari, O. 1911. Asiatic palms—Lepidocaryeae. Part II. The species of *Daemonorops*. Annals of the Royal Botanic Garden Calcutta 12: 1–237, plates i–ii, 1–109.

Beccari, O. 1913. Asiatic palms—Lepidocaryeae. The species of *Calamus*. Supplement to Part 1. Annals of the Royal Botanic Garden Calcutta 11 (Appendix): 1–142, plates 1–83.

Beccari, O. 1933. Asiatic palms—Corypheae (ed. U. Martelli). Annals of the Royal Botanic Garden Calcutta 13: 1–356, plates i–xxxii, 1–70.

Brummitt, R. 2001. World Geographical Scheme for Recording Plant Distributions. Hunt Institute for Botanical Documentation, Pittsburgh, Pennsylvania.

Chen, S.-Y., K.-L. Wang, S.-J. Pei & Y.-D. Pu. 2002. New materials of rattan from Yunnan. Acta Botanica Yunnanica 24: 199–204.

de Zoysa, N. 2000. Arecaceae. Pages 33–93. In: M. Dassanayake (ed.), A Revised Handbook to the Flora of Ceylon. Volume XIV. A. A. Balkema, Rotterdam, Netherlands.

de Zoysa, N. & V. Vivekanandan. 1994. Rattans of Sri Lanka. An illustrated field guide. Sri Lanka Forest Department, Battaramulla, Sri Lanka.

Dhar, S. 1998. *Phoenix acaulis*. Principes 42: 11–12.

Dowe, J. 2001. Studies in the genus *Livistona* (Coryphoideae: Arecaceae). Ph.D. thesis, James Cook University, Townsville, Australia.

Dowe, J. 2003. The non-Australian species of *Livistona*. Palms and Cycads 79–80: 1–61.

Dransfield, J. 1970. Studies in the Malayan palms *Eugeissona* and *Johannesteijsmannia*. Ph.D. thesis, University of Cambridge, Cambridge, England.

Dransfield, J. 1972a. The genus *Borassodendron* (Palmae) in Malesia. Reinwardtia 8: 351–363.

Dransfield, J. 1972b. The genus *Johannesteijsmannia* H. E. Moore Jr. Gardens Bulletin of the Straits Settlement 26: 63–83.

Dransfield, J. 1978. The genus *Maxburretia*. Gentes Herbarum 11: 187–199.

Dransfield, J. 1979a. A Manual of the Rattans of the Malay Peninsula. Forest Department West Malaysia, Kuala Lumpur, Malaysia.

Dransfield, J. 1979b. A monograph of *Ceratolobus* (Palmae). Kew Bulletin 34: 1–33.

Dransfield, J. 1981. A synopsis of *Korthalsia* (Palmae—Lepidocaryoideae). Kew Bulletin 36: 163–194.

Dransfield, J. 1983. *Kerriodoxa*, a new coryphoid palm genus from Thailand. Principes 27: 3–11.

Dransfield, J. 2001. Two new species of *Daemonorops* (Arecaceae) from Vietnam. Kew Bulletin 56: 661–667.

Dransfield, J. 2005. The current state of *Phoenix* taxonomy. The Palm Journal 181: 4–8.

Dransfield, J. & S. Zona. 1997. *Guihaia* in cultivation: a case of mistaken identity. Principes 41: 70–73.

Dransfield, J., A. Barfod & R. Pongsattayapipat. 2004. A preliminary checklist to Thai palms. Thai Forest Bulletin (Botany) 32: 32–72.

Dransfield, J., Shu-Kang Lee & Fa-Nan Wei. 1985. *Guihaia* a new coryphoid genus from China and Vietnam. Principes 29: 3–12.

Dransfield, J., N. Uhl, C. Asumssen, W. Baker, M. Harley & C. Lewis. 2005. A new phylogenetic classification of the palm family Arecaceae. Kew Bulletin 60: 559–569.

Evans, T. 2000. The rediscovery of *Calamus harmandii*, a rattan endemic to southern Laos. Palms 44: 29–33.

Evans, T. & K. Sengdala. 2001. The Indochinese rattan *Calamus acanthophyllus*—a fire-loving palm. Palms 45: 25–28.

Evans, T. & K. Sengdala. 2002. The adoption of rattan cultivation for edible shoot production in Lao PDR and Thailand—from non timber forest product to cash crop. Economic Botany 56: 147–153.

Evans, T., K. Sengdala, O. Viengkham & B. Thammavong. 2001. A Field Guide to the Rattans of Lao PDR. Royal Botanic Gardens, Kew, United Kingdom.

Evans, T., K. Sengdala, B. Thammavong, O. Viengkham & J. Dransfield. 2002. A synopsis of the rattans (Arecaceae: Calamoideae) of Laos and neighbouring parts of Indochina. Kew Bulletin 57: 1–84.

Fernando, E. 1983. A revision of the genus *Nenga*. Principes 27: 55–70.

Furtado, C. 1956. Palmae Malesicae—XIX. The genus *Calamus* in the Malayan Peninsula. Gardens Bulletin of the Straits Settlement 15: 32–265.

Furtado, C. 1970. Asian species of *Hyphaene*. Gardens' Bulletin Singapore 25: 299–309.

Gagnepain, F. & L. Conrard. 1937. Palmiers. Pages 946–1056. In: H. Lecomte (ed.), Flore Générale de l'Indo-China. Volume 6. Masson, Paris, France.

Gibbons, M. 1996. *Trachycarpus* on parade. Chamaerops 24: 16–18.

Gibbons, M. & T. Spanner. 1993. In search of *Trachycarpus nanus*. Principes 37: 64–72.

Gibbons, M. & T. Spanner. 1994. *Trachycarpus martianus*. Principes 38: 89–94.

Gibbons, M. & T. Spanner. 1995a. *Nannorrhops ritchiana*, the mazari palm in Pakistan. Principes 39: 177–182.

Gibbons, M. & T. Spanner. 1995b. *Trachycarpus princeps*, the Stone Gate palm, an exciting new species from China. Principes 39: 65–74.

Govaerts, R. & J. Dransfield. 2005. World Checklist of Palms. Royal Botanic Gardens, Kew, United Kingdom.

Guo Lixiu & A. Henderson. 2007. Notes on *Calamus* (Palmae) in China—*C. macrorhynchus, C. oxycarpus* and *C. albidus*. Brittonia 59: 350–353.

Hahn, W. 1993. Biosystematics and evolution of the genus *Caryota* (Palmae: Arecoideae). Ph.D. thesis, University of Wisconsin, Madison, Wisconsin.

Hahn, W. 1999. Molecular systematics and biogeography of the Southeast Asian genus *Caryota* (Palmae). Systematic Botany 24: 558–580.

Hastings, L. 2003. A revision of *Rhapis*, the lady palms. Palms 47: 62–78.

Henderson, A. 2005. A new species of *Calamus* (Palmae) from Taiwan. Taiwania 50: 222–226.

Henderson, A. 2006. A new species of *Arenga* (Palmae). Taiwania 51: 298–301.

Henderson, A. 2007a. A revision of *Wallichia* (Palmae). Taiwania 52: 1–11.

Henderson, A. 2007b. *Pinanga* (Palmae) in Myanmar. Makinoa N. S. 6: 1–14.

Henderson, A. 2008. A new species of *Salacca* (Palmae) from Southern Asia. Makinoa N. S. 7: 87–92.

Henderson, A. & Guo Lixiu. 2008. The palms of Hainan. Palms 52: 41–45.

Henderson, A. & F. Henderson. 2007. New species of *Calamus* (Palmae) from Lao and Myanmar. Taiwania 52: 152–158.

Henderson, A., G. Galeano & R. Bernal. 1995. A Field Guide to the Palms of the Americas. Princeton University Press, Princeton, New Jersey.

Henderson, A., Guo Lixiu & A. Barfod. 2007. A new, dioecious, dimorphic species of *Licuala* (Palmae) from Hainan, China. Systematic Botany 32: 718–721.

Henderson, A., Ninh Khac Ban & Nguyen Quoc Dung. 2008a. New species of *Calamus* (Palmae) from Vietnam. Palms 52: 187–197.

Henderson, A., Ninh Khac Ban & Nguyen Quoc Dung. 2008b. New species of *Licuala* (Palmae) from Vietnam. Palms 52: 141–154.

Henderson, A., Ninh Khac Ban & Nguyen Quoc Dung. 2008c. New species of *Pinanga* (Palmae) from Vietnam. Palms 52: 63–69.

Henderson, A., C. Peters, U Myint Maung, U Saw Lwin, U Tin Maung Ohn, U Kyaw Lwin & U Tun Shaung. 2005. Palms of the Ledo Road, Myanmar. Palms 49: 115–121.

Hodel, D. 1998. The Palms and Cycads of Thailand. Allen Press, Lawrence, Kansas.

Hodel D. 2004. Night train to Mandalay. Part 1. Palms 48: 57–69.

Hooker, J. 1894. The Flora of British India. Volume 6. L. Reeve and Co., London, United Kingdom.

Kiew, R. 1976. The genus *Iguanura* Bl. (Palmae). Gardens Bulletin of the Straits Settlement 28: 191–226.

Kiew, R. 1979. New species and records of *Iguanura* (Palmae) from Sarawak and Thailand. Kew Bulletin 34: 143–145.

Kimnach, M. 1977. The species of *Trachycarpus*. Principes 21: 155–160.

Lakshmana, C. 1993. Rattans of South India. Evergreen Publishers, Bangalore, India.

Lim, C. K. 1996. Unravelling *Iguanura* Bl. (Palmae) in Peninsular Malaysia. Gardens' Bulletin Singapore 48: 1–64.

Lim, C. K. 1998. Notes on recent palm species and records from Peninsular Thailand. Principes 42: 110–119.

Lim, C. K. 2001. Unravelling *Pinanga* in Peninsular Malaysia. Folia Malaysiana 2: 219–276.

Lim, C. K. & T. Whitmore. 2001a. The endangered *Areca* palms of Peninsular Malaysia. Folia Malaysiana 2: 12–24.

Lim, C. K. & T. Whitmore. 2001b. A review of *Nenga* (Palmae) in Malaysia. Folia Malaysiana 2: 190–202.

Madulid, D. 1981. A monograph of *Plectocomia* (Palmae: Lepidocaryoideae). Kalikasan 10: 1–94.

Magalon, M. 1930. Contribution a l'Étude des Palmiers de l'Indochine Française. Les Presses Modernes, Paris, France.

Mathew, S. & S. Abraham. 1994. The vanishing palms of the Andaman and Nicobar islands, India. Principes 38: 100–104.

Mathew, S., M. Krishnaraj, A. Mohandas & P. Lakshminarasimhan. 2007. *Korthalsia rogersii*—a vanishing endemic palm of the Andaman Islands. Palms 51: 43–47.

Mogea, J. 1991. Revisi marga *Arenga* (Palmae). Ph.D. thesis, Pada Universitas Indonesia, Depak, Indonesia.

Moore, H. 1969. *Satakentia*—a new genus of Palmae—Arecoideae. Principes 13: 3–12.

Moore, H. 1980. Palmae. Pages 1–6. In: K. Rechinger (ed.), Flora Iranica. Akademische Druck und Verlagsanstalt, Graz, Austria.

Moore, H. & F. Fosberg. 1956. The palms of Micronesia and the Bonin Islands. Gentes Herbarum 8: 423–478.

Mughal, M. 1992. Spotlight on species: *Nannorrhops ritchieana*. Pakistan Journal of Forestry 42: 162–166.

Noltie, H. 1994. Flora of Bhutan. Volume 3 part 1. Royal Botanic Garden, Edinburgh, Scotland, United Kingdom.

Noltie, H. 2000. *Arenga micrantha*: a little known eastern Himalayan palm. Palms 44: 14–18.

Pei, S. J., S. Y. Chen & S. Q. Tong. 1991. Palmae. Flora Reipublicae Popularis Sinicae 13(1). Science Press, Beijing, China.

Pintaud, J.-C. & H. Setoguchi. 1999. *Satakentia* revisited. Palms 43: 194–199.

Pongsattayapipat R. & A. Barfod. 2005. On the identities of Thai sugar palms. Palms 49: 5–14.

Renuka, C. 1992. Rattans of the Western Ghats. A taxonomic manual. Kerala Forest Research Institute, Peechi, India.

Renuka, C. 1995. A Manual of the Rattans of Andaman and Nicobar Islands. Kerala Forest Research Institute, Peechi, India.

Renuka, C. 1999a. Palms of Kerala. Kerala Forest Research Institute, Peechi, India.

Renuka, C. 1999b. Notes on the identity of *Calamus delessertianus* Becc. Rheedea 9: 81–84.

Renuka, C. 2000. Field Identification Key for Rattans of Kerala. Kerala Forest Research Institute, Peechi, India.

Saw, L. 1997. A revision of *Licuala* (Palmae) in the Malay Peninsula. Sandakania 10: 1–95.

Trudgen, M., Tran Thi Phuong Anh & A. Henderson. 2008. *Rhapis puhuongensis*, a new species from Vietnam. Palms 53: 181–186.

Uhl, N. & J. Dransfield. 1987. Genera Palmarum. Allen Press, Lawrence, Kansas.

Vatcharakorn, P. 2005. Palms and Cycads of Thailand (in Thai). Amarin Printing and Publishing Company, Bangkok, Thailand.

Wei, C. 1986. A study of the genus *Calamus* in China. Guihaia 6: 17–40.

Zona, S. 1998. *Chuniophoenix* in cultivation. Principes 42: 198–200.

Index of Common Names

Index of Scientific Names

Accepted genera are capitalized and boldface; accepted species are lowercase and boldface.